For Stacy —
With thanks to an exceptional
friend of long standing. Good
things be to you.

THE MODOC WAR

A Story *of* Genocide *at the*
Dawn *of* America's Gilded Age

ROBERT AQUINAS McNALLY

[signature]

University of Nebraska Press
Lincoln & London

Publication of this volume was assisted by the Virginia
Faulkner Fund, established in memory of Virginia Faulkner,
editor in chief of the University of Nebraska Press.

Library of Congress Cataloging-in-Publication Data
Names: McNally, Robert Aquinas, author.
Title: The Modoc War: a story of genocide at the dawn of
America's Gilded Age / Robert Aquinas McNally.
Description: Lincoln: University of Nebraska Press, [2017] |
Includes bibliographical references and index.
Identifiers: LCCN 2017011122 (print)
LCCN 2017034893 (ebook)
ISBN 9781496201799 (cloth: alk. paper)
ISBN 9781496204226 (epub)
ISBN 9781496204233 (mobi)
ISBN 9781496204240 (pdf)
Subjects: LCSH: Modoc War, 1872–1873.
Classification: LCC E83.87 (ebook)
LCC E83.87 .M37 2017 (print)
DDC 973.8/2—dc23
LC record available at https://lccn.loc.gov/2017011122

Set in Garamond Premiere by John Klopping.

For my remarkable family:
Gayle Eleanor, Darren McNally and
Sara Pollock, Brian McNally and Renee Lucas
McNally, Ali Smookler, Aimée Smookler
and Arnaud Schneider.

And for the Modoc Nation, a people who,
though once slated for destruction, exhibits
still the bravery of resilient survival.
May we all continue.

CONTENTS

Part 4. Things Fall Apart

ILLUSTRATIONS

Maps

Figures

Following page 260

ACKNOWLEDGMENTS

You have heard it before: no writer ever fashions a book wholly on his or her own. It takes a village, from library denizens who find obscure materials to manuscript readers who ask, with more editorial savvy than you have, "Sure you want to tell it like this?"

Cheewa James, whom I met some twenty years before the idea for this book germinated, was always gracious and helpful in answering my questions about her Modoc ancestral line, which leads to Shacknasty Jim in the Lava Beds. Taylor Tupper, public relations manager for the Klamath Tribes, informed me, wisely, that "murder" applied to the Good Friday killings is a dirty word since it turns an act of war into a crime.

Daniel Woodhead III was kind enough to provide his self-published collection of contemporary newspaper accounts. Carol Chomsky of the University of Minnesota and Maeve Herbert Glass of Princeton University each dug out their monographs on the United States–Dakota military trials of 1862 and reviewed my draft chapter on the Fort Klamath trial with the trained eyes of lawyer and historian. Benjamin Madley of the University of California at Los Angeles gave me a proof of his groundbreaking paper on genocide and Modoc resistance and later read the entire manuscript. Greg Sarris also read my nearly last draft, generously taking time from the demands of his academic, writing, and tribal leadership positions.

Several fellow Golden Bears from the University of California at Berkeley proved invaluable. Claire Holmes, then associate vice chancellor for Public Affairs at the university and a former professional colleague, directed me to Robert David, a Klamath Tribes member who did his doctoral research at Cal on the archaeology of Klamath Basin rock art. Robert filled in various bits of missing information, shared his dissertation and monographs, and read my entire revised manuscript, catching numerous niggling errors and giving me a welcome thumbs-up. Mark Juergensmeyer, with whom I attended graduate school at Cal in the late 1960s and who is now a distinguished professor at the University of California at Santa Barbara, deepened my understanding of cosmic war and reviewed my chapter on that subject. Boyd Cothran, a historian now on the faculty of York University in Toronto, met me for coffee in Berkeley to share his analysis of the Modoc War and later reviewed portions of the manuscript with an historian's eye for detail and a writer's instinct for story. His enthusiasm for the project helped me through some of the doldrums of self-doubt that beset all writers.

Boyd also went out of his way to introduce me to Matthew Bokovoy of the University of Nebraska Press, who became first the book's champion and then its editor. Several other superb professionals at the press helped turn the manuscript into this book: Heather Stauffer, Sabrina Stellrecht, Rachel Gould, Roger Buchholz, John Klopping, and Rosemary Vestal. And freelancer Jonathan Lawrence did a great job of copyediting. I owe them all.

The late Carole Fisher brought me into the circle of the Shaw Historical Library at the Oregon Institute of Technology and introduced me to Lee Juillerat of the Klamath Falls *Herald and News*, Ryan Bartholomew of the Klamath County Historical Society, and Jim Compton, a retired journalist who was working on his own Modoc War book at the time of his sudden death. Stephen Most pointed me to his play on the war and answered my questions about the Klamath Basin from his expertise as the author of *River of Renewal*.

The people of the National Park Service gave new meaning to the title "public servant." Mike Reynolds, then superintendent for Lava Beds National Monument and the Tule Lake Unit of the Pacific National Monument, opened the doors to his facilities and staff. Beth Sanders, an intern at the time, located the archival materials I was looking for. Mary Merryman, curator of the Museum & Archives Collections, generously came down from her usual haunt at Crater Lake to allow me to spend two rainy, winter days in the library and archives of Lava Beds National Monument. And Park Ranger Angela Sutton had an

Acknowledgments

unerring eye for pulling books off the library's shelves that I had no idea existed and that proved helpful indeed.

Research on this book would have been impossible without the repeated help of the staff of the Bancroft Library at the University of California, Berkeley, an unrivaled archival source on California's history. Debra Kaufman of the California Historical Society, Marilyn Van Winkle of the Autry Museum of the American West, Coi Drummond-Gehrig of the Denver Public Library, and Scott Rook of the Oregon Historical Society unearthed and scanned photographs of the Modoc War's principals.

Finally, yet most importantly, my partner, Gayle Eleanor, demonstrated again that she is the world's best first reader. And she listened to my stories when, more than once, I showed up at the dinner table shaking my head over some newly excavated outrage. At such moments I realized yet again how blessed I am to share my life with her.

Prologue

Duel at Lost River

Second Lieutenant Frazier A. Boutelle kept a close eye on the two Indians stripped to the waist, loaded rifles in hand, faces set, eyes glaring. The pair were shouting in the Modoc tongue, words whose meaning the lieutenant failed to grasp but whose hostile tone he could never mistake. Boutelle was a career cavalryman, come up twice through the ranks, an experienced campaigner who had fought Confederates from Second Bull Run to Cold Harbor, and Indians from Texas to Oregon. In every twitching fiber of his body, Boutelle felt a fight coming on.[1]

His commander, Captain James Jackson, Troop B, First Cavalry, shared the same opinion. And he was ready to be done with this, feeling sicker by the moment, a growing weakness that the overnight ride through twenty straight hours of cold rain and sleet had only worsened.

"Mr. Boutelle, what do you think of the situation?" Jackson asked, his voice weak.

"There is going to be a fight," Boutelle answered, "and the sooner you open it, the better, before there are any more complete preparations."

Jackson agreed by ordering Boutelle and four enlisted men to disarm and arrest the two Modocs. A mixed-race lieutenant who kept secret the African American portion of his heritage in order to command white troopers, Boutelle knew more than a little about playing a role.[2] He unholstered his revolver and locked eyes with the Indian whose heavily scarred right cheek pulled an otherwise strong and handsome face into a perpetual sneer. His Modoc name was Chick-chack-am Lul-al-kuel-atko,[3] something local settlers wouldn't even try to wrap their mouths around, so they dubbed him Scarface Charley. Boutelle saw something of himself in Charley. They were much alike: lean and quick, as threatening as pumas on the prod.

In the same split second, each made the move both knew was coming. Charley raised his rifle and Boutelle snapped his revolver up. The two weapons erupted as one, spewing black-powder smoke and heavy-caliber lead at a range of only a few yards.[4] In that instant the Modoc War—violent climax to a start-and-stop genocide that had spanned the better part of three decades—began.

The day was Friday, November 29, 1872, the time a soaked and gloomy 8 a.m. It was a day that so far had gone badly for both Scarface Charley and Frazier Boutelle. Things were about to get even worse.

PART 1

Holy Lands Here and There

We did not think of the great open plains, the beautiful rolling hills, and winding streams with tangled growth as "wild." Only to the white man was nature a "wilderness" and only to him was the land "infested" with "wild" animals and "savage" people. To us it was tame. Earth was bountiful and we were surrounded with the blessings of the Great Mystery.

—Luther Standing Bear, *Land of the Spotted Eagle*

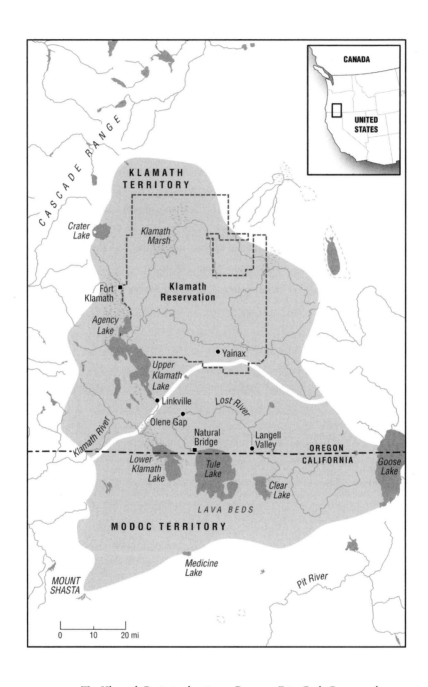

MAP 1. The Klamath Basin in the 1870s. Courtesy Erin Greb Cartography.

1

Bad to Worse

The enterprising white man, having seen and appreciated this
land of green meadows, silvery lakes and crystal streams,
determined to possess it.

—Ivan D. Applegate, "The Initial Shot"

For much of the next year, the Modoc War occupied center stage
in the American public mind. Fought on a remote, volcanic
steppe against an Indian nation few whites had ever heard of before,
this unlikely war rattled the administration of President Ulysses S.
Grant to its core, especially when it claimed the life of the only general officer to fall in a western Indian conflict. The Modoc War was
also the sole Indian fight in the West that drew an on-the-ground international correspondent. And it was the only Indian war in which a
reporter from a leading East Coast newspaper interviewed the leaders of a Native resistance in the middle of the conflict. Because of this
unrelenting media attention, the Modoc War prompted a powerful
debate over the fate of the fast-disappearing Native nations, the future
of the West, and the soul of the United States.

The day before his duel with Frazier Boutelle, however, Scarface
Charley had no idea that he was about to become historical. Although
he and the Lost River Modocs had been the target of military sur-
veillance, heated negotiations with the Bureau of Indian Affairs, and
growing hostility from their white neighbors, they had no reason to
believe that matters were coming to an armed head. Instead, Charley
and other Modoc leaders were sitting down with Henry Miller, the one
settler the Indians trusted, a man who lived alongside the Indians and

attested to his complete lack of trouble with them.[1] On that Thursday afternoon, about fourteen hours before the cavalry stormed into Lost River, Miller told the Modocs truthfully that he had no knowledge of military plans to roust the Indians. He vowed, too, that, should he learn of such a raid, he would warn the Indians.[2] That promise would soon prove fatal.

The Modocs felt so secure that, as dark fell, they posted no sentries. The men in the village on the east bank of Lost River organized the gambling game they loved for whiling away nights like this one: cold, windy, rainy with sleet. Scarface Charley left his house in the larger village on the west bank and canoed across the stream. He was feeling lucky.

Like Charley, Boutelle saw no momentous encounter headed his way a day earlier, even when Ivan Applegate galloped into Fort Klamath, Oregon, bearing orders from Thomas B. Odeneal, state superintendent for the Indian Bureau. A little over a year and a half earlier, a large band of Modocs had decided they were done with abusive Indian agents and the scanty food and clothing allotments that left them cold and hungry. Under the headman Kientpoos,[3] whom whites nicknamed Captain Jack, many of the Modocs left the Klamath Reservation. Most settled into traditional village sites on Lost River about a mile from its mouth on Tule Lake and rebuilt their substantial winter houses. The Lost River Modocs hoped to resume something of the nomadic and communal life they had known for unnumbered centuries.[4]

Most of the settlers flooding into the Lost River valley were less than enamored with living alongside Natives. In their eyes, there was nothing noble about these "savages." The settlers blamed the Modocs for every fence that fell and steer that disappeared. Responding to the rising hostility of his fellow Oregonians, Odeneal won approval from F. A. Walker, the commissioner of Indian Affairs in Washington, DC, to move the Modocs back to the reservation: "peaceably if you possibly can, but forcibly, if you must."[5]

Odeneal left his office in Salem and arrived at the Klamath Reservation on November 25, determined to bring this Modoc business to a head. He dispatched Ivan Applegate, an Indian Bureau employee, to Lost River. Applegate was to invite Kientpoos to meet with Odeneal in

Linkville—the closest Oregon settlement, which would change its name some twenty years later to Klamath Falls—or lead his people directly to the reservation. Kientpoos refused the invitation. It was, he knew, a ruse to arrest or kill him away from Lost River. Nor was he about to submit himself and his people to the reservation's cold and hunger once again. Applegate rode back to Linkville with Kientpoos's refusal.

Odeneal turned it into a pretext. He drafted a letter to Major John Green, the Fort Klamath commander, ordering him to dispatch a patrol to Lost River, arrest the Modoc leaders, and force the Indians onto the reservation.[6] Applegate gathered up Odeneal's letter, leapt back into the saddle, and galloped through the night to Fort Klamath, nearly forty miles north. He arrived about 5 a.m.

Awakened by the sergeant of the guard, Boutelle told Applegate to make himself comfortable until Major Green was up. Applegate let Boutelle know why he had come and asked the lieutenant whether he thought the major would send a force south. No way, Boutelle said. Green had clear instructions from up the chain of command that he was to confront the Modocs only with an overwhelming force, not Fort Klamath's single cavalry troop. The needed reinforcements could come only from frontier outposts two hundred miles to the east, and they would take a good two weeks to arrive.[7]

So it was one surprised Boutelle who at 8 a.m. received orders from Major Green, an officer who often confounded impetuosity with bravery, to prepare to ride to Lost River immediately. Boutelle reminded Green about the need for overwhelming force and said he was certain the Lost River Modocs would resist rather than surrender. The troop, Boutelle went on, was so small that it was sure to provoke a fight, not prevent one. The major refused the lieutenant's sound advice, concerned more about the army's reputation among the settlers of the Klamath Basin. "If I don't send the troops," he said, "they will think we are all afraid." Troop B was to proceed to Lost River—almost sixty miles away—and arrest Kientpoos and the other Modoc leaders first thing the next morning.[8]

By noon, Captain Jackson, Lieutenant Boutelle, and thirty-six enlisted men, along with Fort Klamath's assistant surgeon, headed out. Ivan Applegate came along as guide and interpreter. A couple of hours behind the troop, a pack train with four enlisted men carried food, ammunition, and medical and surgical supplies. The ride promised to be an ordeal. The weather deteriorated into a sleet and rain storm that soaked men and mounts and mired the roads.[9]

Rain was falling hard and wind whipping cold when Jackson's troop reached the outskirts of Linkville. The settlement, only five years old, was small and primitive: forty permanent residents, hotel, store, saloon, blacksmith's and carpenter's shops, and livery stable.[10] In minutes, the little town was buzzing with the news that soldiers in full fighting fettle were riding hard toward Lost River.

Oliver Applegate, Ivan's brother and a sub-agent on the Klamath Reservation, happened to be in town, as was Odeneal. Both rode out to meet the cavalry. Applegate claimed he wanted to rescue two of his reservation Indians from any fight, enlisted two helpers, and headed out in advance of the cavalry.[11]

Meanwhile, Odeneal took Jackson aside for a pep talk. The superintendent assured the captain there would be no fight; surely the feckless Modocs would cave before the least show of military force. And, he insisted, "If there is any fighting, let the Indians be the aggressors; fire not a gun except in self-defence, after they have first fired upon you or your men."[12] Odeneal planned to wrap feigned innocence around the aggressive act of showing up uninvited on the Modocs' doorstep at dawn.

Odeneal also told Dennis Crawley, the settler whose homestead lay closest to the Modocs' Lost River villages, and James "One-Arm" Brown, an Indian Bureau employee, to alert the settlers along Tule Lake in case the Modocs decided upon revenge. Crawley and Brown left Linkville behind Jackson's cavalry troop, joined by four other civilians eager to help run the Modocs out of the neighborhood.[13]

After riding through the freezing night, soldiers and civilians rendezvoused in the 4 a.m. darkness at the last ford across sluggish, deep, and steep-banked Lost River, some four miles upstream from the sleeping Modocs. Jackson dispatched Oliver Applegate and the civilians down the east bank. He told them to move into the village on that side of the river if they heard firing from the village on the west. Boutelle was happy to see the civilians go. He knew them for what they were: volunteer vigilantes "without order or authority," hot to kill Indians.[14] Even as this pick-up posse splashed across Lost River, Jackson led his cavalrymen and Ivan Applegate down the west bank.[15]

With the leading edge of dawn lightening the gloom, the cavalry halted a mile from the large Modoc village. The mounts, breathing hard, milled in the cold mud and filled the air with steam, fatigued muscles twitching beneath soaked hides. Lieutenant Boutelle, the seasoned fighter, announced that he wanted to strip the decks in case of action. He took off his overcoat and strapped it to his saddle, leaving him more exposed to the weather but freer to move fast. Something about Boutelle's combative eagerness enlivened the yellowlegs. The soaked, sleep-deprived, saddle-sore soldiers all stripped off their overcoats and cinched them to their saddles. Jackson took his troop at a trot to the edge of the sleeping village.[16]

On the east side of Lost River, civilians numbering nine or ten men, some with their families, gathered at Crawley's homestead.[17] They left the few women and children in the cabin and headed across sagebrush and bunchgrass to a gully some four hundred yards from the smaller Modoc village; all were armed. In the rising tide of adrenaline, Crawley and Brown forgot Odeneal's instructions to alert the unknowing settlers along the eastern shore of Tule Lake. That omission would prove disastrous.

At the western village's edge, Captain Jackson called halt and dismount, then designated a handful of troopers to hold the horses. The remaining soldiers formed into a skirmish line, loaded carbines at the ready, and moved forward.[18]

• • •

Snug in their winter houses, the unsuspecting Modocs slept. On the east side of the river, men who had spent the night gambling were just breaking up their game. As the sleety sky lightened and Scarface Charley canoed back across Lost River, he spotted blue-shirted soldiers advancing in a line toward the winter houses of the western village. Startled, he tied his canoe and climbed the steep bank, tripping on the way up. His rifle's blast cracked the stillness. The advancing cavalrymen tensed and double-timed while the Modocs on the west stirred from sleep and peered out into the gloom, rain, and sleet.

Already the soldiers had made it inside the village. Captain Jackson shouted commands in English, and Ivan Applegate echoed the orders in Chinook Jargon, the trade tongue of the Pacific Northwest. Jackson demanded to talk with Kientpoos. The chief, sleeping naked, rummaged about for something to pull on. He sent Bogus Charley out to talk in his unclothed stead.

Women and children knew to lie flat on the floor in their houses, which, partly dug down into the soil and subsoil, afforded protection against rifle fire. Some of the Modoc men emerged and milled about in the rainy open, waiting to see what the unexpected soldiers would do next. Scarface Charley, Bogus Charley, and several other men disappeared into their houses, then emerged stripped to the waist, each brandishing several loaded single-shot rifles. Sporting a red bandana tied into a headband, Scarface Charley handed a weapon to Black Jim, laid two at his feet, held another ready at his waist.

Seconds later Scarface and Boutelle fired at each other at a distance of but a few yards. Boutelle's pistol shot clipped Charley's bandana, skimming the side of the Modoc's head without breaking the skin. Charley's rifle slug traveled up the sleeve of Boutelle's left arm, his gun side, slicing blouse and cardigan yet missing flesh. Both men remained standing for the next instant, staring at one another, aware that death had passed them by.[19]

In the next fraction of a second every armed Indian and every armed white man was shooting and reloading and shooting again. The Modoc called Watchman went down dead in the first volley, as did a Sergeant Harris. Indians took cover behind the houses to shoot. Soldiers stood in the open and returned fire. Two or three Modocs were hit, none fatally, and seven more troopers fell, one wounded mortally. With all the racket, the soldiers holding the cavalry mounts dropped the reins, and the panicked horses stampeded.[20] One of the frightened mounts took a slug and went down, whinnying pitifully as it bled out.

Boutelle did what came naturally to his temperament: he ordered a charge. The Modocs fell back before the soldiers, less to retreat than to lure them into the open. Boutelle refused the bait. He had his troop-

Holy Lands Here and There

ers collect the women, old people, and children in the village and send them off toward their men. The lieutenant figured that the Modoc men would cease fighting if they got their families back. Indeed, the gun-fight fizzled out after only a few minutes.[21]

The soldiers raged through the empty Modoc village, shattered every abandoned weapon and threw the pieces into Lost River, then torched the houses.[22] With Lieutenant Boutelle covering the rear, Captain Jackson and his troopers fell back toward Crawley's homestead, bearing dead and wounded. Half the fight was over.[23]

•••

Scarface Charley's accidental warning shot had roused the Modocs on Lost River's east side as well. Men grabbed their weapons, came outside to see what the ruckus was about. Oliver Applegate ordered the white settlers to mount up and ride into the village, where he jumped off his horse and shook hands, no doubt awkwardly, with a surprised Curley Headed Doctor, the shaman. Applegate announced his bona fides in the stilted English whites affected with Natives: "I have come to save you, & befriend you. You know I am chief at Yainax [on the Klamath Reservation], and that I use your relatives well that are there. Come to me and lay down your arms, and I will see that the troops do not trouble you."[24]

The Modocs were unconvinced. Hooker Jim, who was Curley Headed Doctor's son-in-law and leader of the eastern village, broke, ran, and pushed a canoe into the river. A civilian pursued, drew a derringer, and demanded that Hooker return to the circle of whites and give up his rifle. Then a wrestling match broke out between a Modoc and one of Applegate's men over Hooker Jim's weapon.

At the very moment when Scarface Charley and Frazier Boutelle blasted at each other in Kientpoos's village, the gunfight on the east side of the river erupted as well. A white man fell dead in the first exchange, and one Modoc was wounded. George Small, one of the vigilantes, shot down a six-year-old child, then turned his shotgun on a mother with an infant. Most of the blast missed the mother yet cut her child in half.[25] Outnumbered and exposed, the civilians fell back toward Crawley's cabin. The Modocs gave chase, then stopped to launch distant potshots into the little structure, more for .50-caliber terror than lethal effect.[26]

Two neighboring settlers, who wondered what all the shooting was about, rode over for a look and stumbled into Modocs who were in no mood for white visitors. Wendolin Nus, the first full-time settler in the Klamath Basin, died in the volley. His companion, Joe Pennig, was maimed for life.[27]

· · ·

The Modocs chased out of the now-burning western village gathered at the mouth of Lost River, where the stream fanned out into Tule Lake. Hooker Jim sent his old, women, and young to join them. All the assembled Indians—Kientpoos and his men, including an unscathed Scarface Charley, plus the women, old people, and children from both sides of Lost River—piled into small canoes and pole-driven rafts. They faced a miserable all-day and all-night passage: wind-whipped and cold, soaked by rain and sleet. The fleeing Indians paddled and poled around the lake, holding to the shallows along shore, navigating toward the southwestern corner of Tule Lake and the Lava Beds, their traditional refuge in times of peril.[28]

Hooker Jim intended to go there, too, but first he had business to take care of: retribution for the shooting of women and children in his village. He and eight other men—Long Jim, Schonchin John and his son Peter Schonchin, Weium, Dave, Slolux, Billy, and Curley-Headed Doctor—made their way toward the Lava Beds the long way around, riding down the eastern shoreline. They were hunting settlers.[29]

The first to be shot down were the men of the Boddy family, immigrants from Australia who had settled on Tule Lake only three months earlier: William Boddy, his son-in-law Nicholas Schira, and Boddy's stepsons William and Richard Cravigan. The Indians surrounded yet spared Louisa Boddy and her daughter, Katherine Schira, then rode away. Whites killed women, Hooker Jim made clear; Modocs did not.[30]

Then it was the Brothertons, father William and sons W. K. and Rufus, who were cutting wood. Next the Indians set upon Henry Miller, the friend who had promised to warn them of impending military action. He died still ignorant of what had happened, of why the

Modocs thought him a traitor. From Miller's place the Indians rode on to shoot down more men whose names vary from one account to another. William Shearer or maybe Adam Shillingbow. A Collins or a Follins with no given name. John Tober, or was it Saper? And possibly Robert Alexander as well as C. Erasmus.[31]

Attacked by settlers, Hooker Jim and his men killed other settlers in response, somewhere between eleven and thirteen. The logic of retribution came out clear, cold, and deadly.

Yet when Hooker Jim and his riders arrived at the Lava Beds and told their friends and relations about the havoc they had wreaked, Scarface Charley and Kientpoos felt their stomachs turn over. The issue was not that the revenge was unjustified. It was rather that the whites would see the killings as atrocities demanding the extermination of every Modoc.

• • •

November 29, 1872, along the border of northeastern California and south-central Oregon delivered a major setback for the United States' effort to people the continent from sea to shining sea with white homesteaders. The settler dead numbered between thirteen and fifteen. In addition, the army suffered two killed and six wounded, two of them hurt too badly to return to duty. The Modocs suffered one fighter dead and three wounded yet able to recover and fight again.[32]

The body count favored the Modocs, so the Natives might appear the victors. Yet that day they lost their last villages and became a refugee band targeted for destruction, a people gone to ground in the sacred center of an ancient world.

2

Stone and Story

That dark mysterious plain . . . compelled attention. Here you trace
yawning fissures, there clusters of somber pits. Now you mark where
the lava is bent and corrugated in swelling ridges and domes, again
where it breaks into a rough mass of loose blocks. . . . [T]he Modoc
Lava Beds have for me an uncanny look. As I gazed the purple
deepened over all the landscape. Then fell the gloaming, making
everything still more forbidding and mysterious.
Then, darkness like death.

—John Muir, "Shasta Rambles and Modoc Memories"

In the days following the cavalry's raid on the Lost River villages,
the Modocs took stock. They had the clothes on their backs, the
outdated weapons in their hands, edible roots and dried beef cached
in nearby caves. And they had the land.

Americans detested and feared the convoluted, deceptive landscape
of the Lava Beds. They classified the place as badland, malpaís, unin-
habitable pedregal. Even John Muir, who sought out the loneliest wilderness and celebrated its glory, found the Lava Beds disturbing. Jesse
Applegate, uncle to Oliver and Ivan and among the area's earliest American explorers, likewise described the Lava Beds as violent and infernal.
"Imagine a smooth, solid sheet of granite, ten miles square, and 500
feet thick, covering resistless mines of gunpowder, scattered at irregular intervals under it," he wrote. "These mines are exploded simulta-
neously, rending the whole field into rectangular masses, from the size
of a match-box to that of a church, heaping these masses high in some
places, and leaving deep chasms in others. Following the explosion, the
whole thing is placed in one of Vulcan's crucibles, and heated up to a

point when the whole begins to fuse and run together, and then suffered to cool. The roughness of the upper surface remains as the explosion left it, while all below is honey-combed by the cracks and crevices caused by the cooling of the melted rock."[1]

Applegate was right about the upheaval and heat of the Lava Beds' creation. They arose in a series of lava flows dating back approximately thirty thousand years and continuing into the most recent few centuries. Much of the lava came from eruptions of Mammoth Crater, about ten miles to the south and one of the many vents of the Medicine Lake shield volcano. Rising to but 7,921 feet, this forested volcano is far less majestic in appearance than snow-capped, 14,179-foot Mount Shasta to the west. The Medicine Lake volcano, though, is bigger, some 150 miles around at its base. Its volume of 140 cubic miles—more than one and a half times that of Mount Shasta—makes it the largest volcano in the Cascade Range.[2]

Lava flowed from Medicine Lake's many vents in eruptions that averaged one or two every hundred years. Melted rock coursed through underground tubes and then onto the surface. Some flowed all the way to Tule Lake, where it turned into pillow basalts that made the southern shoreline look more sudden than shelved. Other flows moved across the surface, sometimes collapsing downward as tubes formed, then gave way, often before the prior layer had cooled and solidified. The net effect was to create a plateau raised somewhat above the level of Tule Lake and surrounded on three sides by huge cracked and tilted blocks of lava.

The northeast corner of the plateau, an area about 165 yards in diameter known as the Stronghold, offered a number of cave-like hollows where people could shelter against rain, snow, and strong wind. Deep cracks served as defense trenches, and beyond them fissures in the lava blocks provided outposts for scout-snipers. An enemy could approach the Stronghold only on foot and very slowly, always under the guns of the outposts and the trenches. The lava block closest to the lake gave defenders a path down to water, and snipers hidden there could prevent anyone from infiltrating along the lakeshore. The Stronghold even boasted a corral, a small, deep basin naturally enclosed on all sides but for one easy approach through which cattle could be herded. It offered something else as well: a hidden escape route in case the Stronghold had to be abandoned.[3]

This landscape was more than strategic to the Modocs, however. It offered shelter and food, for one thing. The Lava Beds lay in Mount Shasta's shadow and escaped the heaviest snows of winter. In summer the caves served up shelter against heat and cold storage for food. Plants offering food and fiber were abundant. Game, from waterfowl and rabbits to the wintering herd of big mule deer, was plentiful. Even in times of peace, the Modocs maintained villages and camps in the Lava Beds.[4]

And it was right here, according to Modoc mythology, that the Earth began. It happened in the dream time when only the creator, Gmukamps, and Tule Lake existed. The god dredged mud up from the lake bottom and pressed it between his great hands into an immense flat disk. Since the Earth demanded shape, he banked the disk's edges into hills and mountains. With his fingernail he cut channels for rivers, and he scooped out basins that filled to form other lakes. Fatigued from this masterwork, Gmukamps made a bed under the lake, crawled into it, and covered himself over with a last handful of mud. That mound over the bulge of his divine, sleeping body dried into the prominence now called Petroglyph Point.[5]

When the Modocs taking stock in early December 1872 looked across the wintry waters of Tule Lake toward that point on the far shore, they were looking at the place where the Earth began, where the god of creation slept still. This Stronghold was more than strong. It was sacred.

• • •

The foundational story of the Hebrew scriptures is the migration of the Chosen People from Egypt to the Promised Land of Israel. The Navahos tell of their arrival from the far north into the Four Corners country. Many modern Americans claim at least half their identity from somewhere else—African American, Polish American, Italian American, Mexican American, Chinese American, and so on. Many Americans, too, have family, clan, or nationality stories that place their genesis outside the United States. Thanks to the genealogical research of a cousin, I can tell you that the McNally from whom I am descended left County Antrim in 1820s Ireland and settled in Somerset, Ohio, to run a small sawmill and work as a carpenter.

The Modocs taking refuge in the Lava Beds were different. They were the descendants of an Indigenous people who had lived in this landscape since before time was time. The Modocs had no founding myths like the Hebrews, the Navahos, or the McNallys that were set in a landscape other than the one they lived in. In this place, they commenced and they continued.

Unlike Catholics heading to Rome, Muslims to Mecca, or Jews to Jerusalem, Modocs had no need for far pilgrimages to distant places believed to be holier than their home country. Right here was where it all began. And that cliff-rimmed mound you see over there, where prairie falcons wheel and scream and swallows dart for mosquitoes over the lake? That is the sleeping place of the creator. He slumbers where we are, in a place we can see, in the very same world we live in.

•••

The Modocs knew, too, that the land itself awoke now and again and demonstrated its power. The region they inhabited had been the site of one of North America's biggest bangs.

It occurred 7,700 years ago, in the prehistorical neighborhood of 5700 BCE, and left an impression that remains to this day. You can see the evidence some ninety miles north of Lost River and Tule Lake in a great rim of rock shaped like a broken bowl.

Once this was the body of a mountain, one modern geologists call Mount Mazama. Even as mountains go, Mazama was awesome, on the order of Mount Rainier or Mount Shasta, a volcanic cone of such girth and bulk that clouds crowded its peak and made their own weather. Mazama took shape over hundreds of thousands of years. Lava flowed up, out, and over, then cooled as it swamped what had been, laid new rock on top of old, and added altitude.

As the volcano grew, a pool within filled with melted rock, or magma. The pool overfilled and became a bottle too small for its swelling contents. Under the pressure, a vent in the northeast slope blew out. This explosion of pumice and ash was dozens of times the size of the 1980 Mount Saint Helens eruption. It reached thirty miles up into the atmosphere, where it caught the highest winds and crossed the continent all the way to the Greenland icecap. The dust was so copious that it cooled the atmosphere in the middle and northern latitudes by 0.6 to 0.7 degrees Celsius for one to three years, making it one of the Northern Hemisphere's most telling atmospheric events in recent geological history.[6]

One blast followed upon another, and with each explosion the mountain cracked, crumbled, and spewed. Hot rock and smoking magma plus fine dust and gritty pumice in pyroclastic clouds rolled down Mazama's flanks, trapping, suffocating, and cooking anything that lived there. In quick order the upper half of the mountain disappeared, blasted into rubble and dust that was blown into the air or swept into the surrounding valleys to depths of as much as three hundred feet.

When rains and snows came, a lake began to form in the broken bowl that had been the bottom of Mazama's magma chamber. This caldera, one mile deep and five miles across, caught runoff and melt. Over hundreds and thousands of years, as the pace of explosions slowed and then ceased, the caldera filled, its sediments settled, and the water took on an unearthly blue. This place Americans know now as Crater Lake.[7]

Archaeological evidence—volcanic dust burying sagebrush-fiber sandals in caves to the northeast—indicates that Indigenous people were living there when Mazama blew its top.[8] The evidence of their presence in the Klamath and Tule Lake Basins to the south of Mazama is mythic. These ancient people created a story to explain what must have seemed a cosmic catastrophe.

They knew Mazama as La-o Yaina, the throne of the god Llao, who ruled all beings, living and nonliving, of the realm below and used its terrible monsters to dominate the world above. The smoke and fire rising from La-o Yaina signified Llao's ongoing curse on the world aboveground. Not that Llao was immune to the charms of what lived topside, particularly the lovely young daughter of a local chief. One difficulty, though: Skell, the god of all beings, living and nonliving, of the world above, had his eye on the same gorgeous young thing. Light and dark, above and below, both drawn to the same exquisite damsel: such dualities must collide. The clash between Llao and Skell swelled into a titanic struggle. Wanting to tip the battle to Skell, three sha-

Holy Lands Here and There

mans threw themselves into the volcano's fire as a sacrifice. With the battle going his way, Skell summoned Snaith—the deity of storm, rain, and cold—to fill the chamber left by the bursting of Llao's mountain throne. Thus formed the lake.[9]

Even with its mythic elements, this story comes close to describing the Mazama explosion as a modern geologist would. In addition to the veracity of eyewitness reporting, it offers the cosmic awe that makes a place sacred. These days, anyone with a car and a credit card can head to Crater Lake National Park, drive the rim, and gaze upon the exquisite blue water. In the old times, though, this was a special place reserved only for certain chiefs, shamans of high spiritual accomplishment, and those brave enough to aspire to mystic heights. They knew what had happened here, how it had transformed the world, how it offered the potential for visions and wisdom. Natives came as seekers and supplicants, not tourists.[10]

For the Modocs, the Medicine Lake highlands and Medicine Lake itself played much the same role as Crater Lake did for their northern cousins, the Klamaths. The mountain and the lake were the high point, the place where one could seek the most important vision of one's spiritual life and gain supernatural power. A series of ascending ridges punctuated by cinder cone buttes that the Modocs called the "stair steps of the creator" connected the villages around Tule Lake to the Medicine Lake highlands and the lake itself. After ascending the smaller buttes to gain the strength of increasingly powerful visions delivered by the spirits of the place, one could take a ritual bath as Gmukamps had taught his son Isis in these very waters. To the Modocs this was the place of highest spiritual ascent.[11]

• • •

When Mazama blew apart around 5700 BCE, Indigenous people were already longtime occupants of this corner of the West. In fact, the ancestors of the Klamaths and the Modocs had been in the vicinity for at least four thousand and possibly almost seven thousand years.[12]

When the first people arrived somewhere between 12,500 and 10,000 BCE, Pluvial Lake Modoc filled much of what is now the Klamath Basin. The lake was one of several extensive bodies of water that dotted western North America and the Great Basin in this period of wet climate. Pluvial Lake Modoc eventually reached the 4,200-foot line, about 125 feet higher than the current level of Tule Lake.[13]

These first people likely arrived from deeper inside the West, probably from the country where the upper Columbia and Snake Rivers flow. They were pursuing the hairy elephants, shaggy llama-like camels, and enormous bison of this Ice Age time. These hunters traveled fast in small bands that tracked the movable feasts of hoofed prey and used big-bladed spears cast with atlatls to kill them.[14]

All the while, the ice shelves to the north were thinning and shrinking, the climate drying and warming, the great lake retreating. The elephants, bison, and camels grew scarcer, then vanished. Hunters turned to smaller game—deer, elk, pronghorns, bighorn sheep. And they sought ducks, geese, swans, and fish along the lakes, rivers, and sloughs. The Natives moved in smaller circles of migration and set up seasonal camps in places of abundance for hunting and gathering.

Around the time a rebellious preacher named Jesus was stirring crowds two continents away, the Lost River people made the bow and arrow their weapon of choice. Hunters also used bolas of cordage and stones flung out over the water to wrap up fleeing ducks and geese as they were lifting off the water. Plucked, gutted, dried, pounded into meal, the birds thickened stews and soups. And their skins, pulled off with the down attached, then cut into strips and twisted, were woven into blankets and shawls against winter.

As the men hunted, the women gathered and winnowed, dug and dried tubers, bulbs, roots, seeds, and the rare leafy vegetable. They devised digging sticks of mountain mahogany, turned up whole fields along streams and lakes, roasted their gathering in fires, dried seeds in the sun and sacked them. Nettles were dried and pounded to make cloth something like linen, and tules—the ever-present, ever-useful giant sedge that grows in the shallows of lakes and swamps—were woven into shoes, mats, hats, baskets, ropes.[15]

• • •

The name *Modoc* derives from the tribal name for Tule Lake, *móatak* or *móatak é-ush*, meaning "lake of the extreme south." The people to the north were the Klamaths, who spoke a dialect of the same language, passed on the same mythic stories, and sprang from the same original group of migrating hunters. The Modocs and the Klamaths separated in the late eighteenth century and remained distantly familial. The Klamaths occupied the shores and marshes of Upper Klamath Lake and the rivers feeding it. The home country of the Modocs lay to the south, roughly from Mount Shasta on the west to Goose Lake on the east and Medicine Lake on the south. The Modocs, likely never numbering more than two thousand people, occupied nearly twenty winter villages and a half-dozen or so summer fishing camps on Clear, Tule, and Lower Klamath Lakes and along Lost River. The river was the beating heart of this country. Lost River offered fast water and slow, forests and grasslands, upland and swamp, juniper and sage, suckers and pintails, antelope and marmot, tules and bunchgrass along its semicircular sixty-mile course from Clear Lake to Tule Lake. The name came from American settlers who marveled at how the flow disappeared into a multitude of tiny, easy-to-lose threads in Langell Valley and gathered again in the narrow defile known as Olene Gap and continued its loop toward Tule Lake. Nowhere were Modoc villages more tightly packed than along the last few miles of Lost River above Tule Lake.[16]

In winter, the Modoc bands crowded inside substantial houses. Rising from a pit four feet deep, framed with timbers and long poles, then roofed over with tule mats, bark, grass, and the earth dug out during excavation, the winter house with its fire pit kept the season at bay. When cold lessened and snow retreated, usually in March, the Modocs dismantled their winter houses. Timbers were cleaned and piled beside the poles, the roofing materials stacked in a sheltered place, and the pit left open to wind and sun. Only the four framing timbers remained upright for rebuilding in late fall.[17]

With spring came sucker fish running up the streams feeding Clear and Tule Lakes. Except for the old and sick, who stayed behind and were brought food, the men, women, and children moved out to sites along Lost River and Willow Creek, east of Clear Lake. There they built dome shelters covered with mats. Men and women alike cut pine saplings in the hills, stripped off sprouts and twigs, planted the trunks in the ground, then hung the gutted, split, beheaded suckers from the branches to dry. As the sucker run crescendoed, the camp resembled houses set among trees leafed out with split, drying fish.

When the suckers no longer thrashed upstream in spawning hordes, the band moved to the digging grounds for epos, a milky-white root the women dried for eating raw later. Epos was a starchy staple to Modocs, as bread or potato was to Americans. The men fished for trout and scoured the wetlands for duck and goose eggs. Then, when camas root ripened into a prized yet scarce food, the band decamped to its scattered gathering grounds. In late summer, too, suckers seeking better aerated waters again left Tule and Clear Lakes to swim up Lost River and Willow Creek, leading to a scaled-down repeat of the spring's fishing season. As summer cooled into fall, the men hunted pronghorn and bighorn on the Lava Beds and the women gathered edible roots and seeds, all the while following practices that protected the traditional sites and ensured easy and abundant harvests in the following years. The Modocs were not agriculturalists, yet they did cultivate the plants they needed through burning, pruning, and weeding.[18]

Then the people headed back toward the winter villages to rebuild their houses, and the men took off for the highlands of the Modoc Plateau to hunt deer, antelope, and elk. There were trout, too, in the lakes and streams, and incoming ducks and geese clotting the sky and its low sun in untold millions. The bola was long gone. Now Modoc hunters used nets and a special wood-tipped arrow that skipped over the surface like a flat, flung stone to impale sitting birds. As winter descended, the Modocs retreated to the substantial houses of their winter villages.[19]

This season of cold and dark was a time of quiet, when Natives held to their houses and made no war. It was in this time of restful peace when Captain James Jackson, Lieutenant Boutelle, and Troop B, First Cavalry, showed up at Lost River to deliver a forceful message. The Modocs—whose chain of ancestry in the Lost River country stretched back over ten millennia—had no right to their land or, for that matter, to their lives.

Holy Lands Here and There

3

Running the Pagans Out of the Promised Land

Ask of me, and I shall give thee the heathen for thine inheritance,
and the uttermost parts of the Earth for thy possession.

—Psalm 2:8

In describing why he ordered his cavalry troop to charge into the midst of the Modocs at Lost River, Frazier Boutelle saw the tactic as obvious. "We were white and they were red," wrote Boutelle, the secretly mixed-race second lieutenant, without the least irony. "There was the almost invariable result. The dark skin gave way."[1]

Boutelle's reasoning was less rational and logical than mythic and religious. Convinced of his success by an unquestioned narrative about the strategic, technological, and moral supremacy of Americans over Indians, Boutelle charged. The lieutenant had such faith in this belief that he was willing to stake his life on it.

Boutelle was hardly alone in trusting his fate to American supremacy. His commanding officer, James Jackson, had a clear picture of his opponent in battle. "The Modoc Indians," he wrote, "belong generally to the race known as 'Digger Indians'—from living largely on esculent roots which the squaws dig, dry and cache for winter subsistence,—but they are much superior to the average Digger Indian, and more nearly allied in character—and by intermarriage—to the 'Rogue Rivers,' a warlike tribe, now about extinct, inhabiting at one time the western slope of the Cascade Mountains in Oregon."[2]

Jackson only sounded as if he knew what he was talking about. The language the Modocs and their cousins the Klamaths speak belongs to the Plateau Penutian family, which includes Nez Perce. The southwestern Oregon tribes lumped together as Rogue River Indians use

Na-Dené tongues from the same language family as Navaho, Apache, and Tlingit. The two linguistic groups are as unrelated as Teutonic and Semitic.

More to the point, Digger Indians existed only in the minds of American settlers. The term arose in California and the Great Basin as a loose, pejorative moniker for largely unrelated Native communities. Once the Digger gloss entered the frontier vocabulary, it took on metaphoric life. "Digger" served as a convenient slur, one that characterized Indians as treacherous, bloodthirsty, dirty, squalid, lice-ridden, and lazy. The rhyme with the slur for African Americans added nastiness. The word transformed Indians into irredeemable savages worthy to be exterminated.[3]

Jackson's use of "Digger" constituted less a racist demerit against his character than one more piece of evidence for the touchstone frontier myth about Americans and Indians: in every way—strategically, technologically, culturally, and morally—civilized people demonstrated superiority over purported savages, who needed to be swept aside to free the land of its Native burden and allow civilization to be sown.

Boutelle and Jackson had on their side not only the thirty-six enlisted men from Fort Klamath. They were backed, too, by a pair of Catholic popes as well as the Supreme Court of the United States—and, ultimately, by God Himself.

• • •

After securing his throne against various rivals, fifteenth-century Portuguese monarch Alfonso V (aka Afonso and Affonso) cast covetous eyes on the Moroccan realms in northwest Africa ruled by Saracen Turks. Because the invasion he contemplated pitted Christian against Muslim, Alfonso sought the blessing of the papacy. The pope at the time was Nicholas V, a small and sickly yet vastly educated man. With the church in need of armed champions to carry the faith forward, Nicholas felt no hesitation in endorsing Alfonso's invasion in the 1452 papal document *Dum Diversas*.

The pope's argument drew on the Old Testament story of Hebrew conquest. The god Yahweh selected Abraham's descendants as his people and established a covenant that promised them the rich land of

Holy Lands Here and There

Canaan. It mattered not that Canaan was already occupied by an array of nations. Since Yahweh had promised the land to the Hebrews, the invaders had the right—indeed, a divine obligation—to conquer it, dispossess the inhabitants, and either expel or exterminate them.

The scriptures put unforgivingly bloodthirsty language in Yahweh's mouth: "By little and little I will drive them out from before thee, until thou be increased, and inherit the land. And I will set thy bounds from the Red Sea even unto the sea of the Philistines, and from the desert unto the river: for I will deliver the inhabitants of the land into your hand; and thou shalt drive them out before thee. . . . They shall not dwell in thy land" (Exodus 23:30–33). The God of Exodus was commanding genocide.

Pope Nicholas depicted the Christian struggle against Muslim Saracens as a spiritual battle following the Old Testament precedent: "the enemies of the name of Christ, always aggressive in contempt of the orthodox faith, could be restrained by the faithful of Christ and be subjugated to the Christian religion." To encourage the Morocco invasion, Nicholas granted Alfonso and all his fighting men forgiveness for their sins. And, to add secular incentive to this holy war, Nicholas gave the conquering Portuguese the right to enslave vanquished Saracens and confiscate conquered lands: "we grant to you full and free power . . . to invade, conquer, fight, subjugate the Saracens and pagans, and other infidels and other enemies of Christ . . . and to lead their persons in perpetual servitude."[4]

Three years later—and two years after Christian Constantinople fell to the Turks and became Muslim Istanbul, sending a shiver of fear through Europe—Pope Nicholas extended the logic of *Dum Diversas* to a world grown even more perilous for Catholicism. This new document, *Romanus Pontifex*, granted the right of dominion by conquest over all pagans and all lands that Christian Europeans might encounter anywhere on the face of the Earth. The entire planet had now become the Promised Land for Christians. Its conquest, accompanied by expulsion or extermination of the Native inhabitants, was divinely mandated.[5]

When Christopher Columbus sailed to the New World almost forty years later, he came ashore under this Christian banner. And, as the world expanded, so did the doctrine of conquest. In the year following Columbus's voyage, Pope Alexander VI promulgated four documents, called the Alexandrine Bulls, or Bulls of Donation, that divided the newly discovered West between the Spanish and Portuguese monarchs and granted them divine right of possession. By the time the Protestant Reformation displaced the Catholic Church in parts of Europe, the doctrine of conquest had worked its way into civil law into Spain, and from there into the legal codes of France and Great Britain. British policy and law injected the doctrine of conquest into American thinking and belief.[6]

The founders of the United States were eager to portray their new republic as a contemporary version of the Promised Land and to cast the republic's founding documents as a covenant similar to the one Yahweh made with Israel. Benjamin Franklin proposed to the Continental Congress in 1776 that the Great Seal of the United States depict Moses leading the Israelites through the miraculously divided Red Sea. Thomas Jefferson had a similarly biblical idea. He wanted the seal to show the Israelites being guided through the desert toward their new home by clouds and fire. Prominent clergyman Abiel Abbott preached in his 1799 Thanksgiving sermon that "the people of the United States come nearer to a parallel with Ancient Israel, than any other nation upon the globe."[7]

Like the many peoples of Canaan whose subjugation Yahweh dictated, Indians were the pagans Americans must subdue, dispossess, and remove or exterminate. Even worse, these Indigenous heathens posed a temptation to the settlers' faith. "People are ready to run wild in the woods again and to be as Heathenish as ever, if you do not prevent it," warned Puritan minister Increase Mather almost a hundred years before the founding of the republic.[8] Whenever and wherever Indians blocked the expansionist ambitions of European settlers, that struggle pitted Satan's minions in red skin against God's people in white. Righteousness demanded conquest, and conquest allowed enslavement, dispossession, and removal or extermination. Indians could knuckle under and admit the rights of whites to rule their lands, die in battle, or move west and take up with their own kind beyond the frontier. Such were their only choices.

The best, and holiest, use of this new Promised Land required no less. Indians hunted and gathered, whereas American settlers tilled and farmed. Leaving the land in pagan hands consigned it to an idleness that mocked the divine plan for the subjugation of the Earth. In 1802 John Quincy Adams, later president of the United States, wrote, "What is the right of a huntsman to the forest of a thousand miles over which he has accidentally ranged in quest of prey? . . . Shall the fields and valleys, which a beneficent God has formed to teem with the life of innumerable multitudes, be condemned to lasting barrenness?"[9] Fittingly, a young signal officer bearing the name John Quincy Adams would serve in the Modoc War and help deliver a resounding no to his namesake's rhetorical question.

• • •

The various threads of policy, law, and religious belief were woven into a unanimous 1823 decision by the United States Supreme Court that set the legal basis for the Indian wars of the nineteenth century and poured the foundation of American Indian law to this day. That decision is *Johnson v. M'Intosh*. Remarkably, the case involved no Natives as either plaintiffs or defendants. Although their lands and their futures were at stake, Indians had nothing to say in the matter.

The roots of *Johnson v. M'Intosh* reached back before the Revolutionary War. In 1763, King George III prohibited colonial settlers from moving west of the Allegheny Mountains and authorized only the British Crown to acquire Indian lands. A black market in land emerged for white men who skirted British law.[10] One such group of speculators, known as the Illinois Land Company, purchased large tracts from Indian nations. After the war, the land company hoped to validate the legality of its purchases with the new United States government.

That chance came in 1818 with the U.S. government's sale of Illinois acreage to William M'Intosh. Claiming that the sale fell within the boundaries of the Illinois Land Company's holdings and was its land to sell, not the United States', the company sued M'Intosh under the name of Joshua Johnson, son and heir of an original investor. The case did not go the way the speculators hoped, however. The Supreme Court found against them and for M'Intosh, establishing the rule that only the federal government could buy and sell Indian land.[11]

The majority opinion, written by Chief Justice John Marshall, opened by distinguishing possession of land from title to it, then extended the papal doctrine of pagan conquest into a doctrine of discovery. Marshall asserted that "discovery gave title to the government by whose subjects, or by whose authority, it was made" and that the United States inherited this title from the colonial powers. Native rights to land were "impaired," and although the Indians rightfully occupied the land and used it, "their power to dispose of the soil at their own will, to whomsoever they pleased, was denied by the original fundamental principle, that discovery gave exclusive title to those [Europeans] who made it [the discovery]." Legally, Indian land differed in no way from unpopulated land: "no distinction was taken between vacant lands and lands occupied by the Indians."[12]

In Old World conquests, the conqueror was expected to assimilate the conquered or govern them as a separate entity. The depraved and heathen nature of the Native Americans undercut this expectation, according to Marshall, leaving no option but conquest and dispossession. "The tribes of Indians inhabiting this country were fierce savages," he wrote, and "to leave them in possession of their country, was to leave the country a wilderness; to govern them as a distinct people, was impossible." Indeed, the very presence of Indians exposed settlers "and their families to the perpetual hazard of being massacred."[13]

• • •

Massacres were atrocities that soldiers like James Jackson and Frazier Boutelle understood. It is doubtful that they had ever read *Johnson v. M'Intosh*, much less *Dum Diversas*, *Pontifex Romanus*, or the Bulls of Donation. Still they knew as sure as they drew American breath that Indians held no title to the land they roamed. Jackson and Boutelle knew, too, that the Natives' savagery, cruelty, and treachery made it impossible to deal with them as one would with civilized, Christian people. They knew well the stories Oregon settlers told of the bad old days of the 1840s and 1850s, tales that curdled American blood and made the Lost River raid the righteous removal of Natives so pagan from a land so promising.

4

Death Squads, Sex Slaves, and Knights of the Frontier

The two races . . . must ever remain at enmity. That a war of
extermination will continue to be waged between the races until the
Indian race becomes extinct must be expected. While we cannot
anticipate this result with but painful regret, the inevitable destiny of
the race is beyond the wisdom or power of man to avert.

—California Governor Peter Burnett, State of
the State Address, January 1851

When reports of the battle at Lost River traveled to the state
capitol in Salem, Governor LaFayette Grover knew full well
that responsibility for the outbreak lay entirely with the Modocs, a people considered "a band of robbers and murderers." He called them "the
most treacherous and blood-thirsty savages west of the Rocky Mountains," bad actors who attacked and butchered "unoffending emigrants,
with their wives and families, passing through the Modoc country
along the old southern overland road to Oregon" and left their bodies for the wolves. These Indians loved torture, and, to make matters
worse, "girls have been kept among them as captives for months to suffer more than torture, and in the end to meet their miserable death."[1]

Yet, even as Grover cited a death of toll of more than three hundred Americans, he ignored a salient fact: matters between whites and
Modocs had started off on a much better foot.

• • •

Except for a few freelance Canadian trappers who poked around the
Klamath Basin in the early 1820s—and were themselves mostly Native
and mixed-blood Métis—the Modocs first encountered European

Americans in the expansive personage of Peter Skene Ogden during the winter of 1826–27. Ogden, a Hudson's Bay Company man, had traveled south from Fort Vancouver on the Columbia River, leading thirty-five trappers and their wives and children on orders from Sir George Simpson, governor-in-chief of the Hudson's Bay Company. Simpson was keeping a wary eye on American trappers working the Rockies and venturing westward. If the beaver of the Northwest had already been trapped out by Hudson's Bay Company men, Simpson reasoned, the Yankees would not come.[2] It was Ogden's job to bring home all the fur to be had and keep the mountain men to the east.

Ogden did well by his charge, reporting at the end of his several expeditions that he had practically exterminated the beaver in the Great Basin. Yet, in one of those ironies history has a way of serving up, Ogden changed that landscape into something more attractive to Americans with a mind to stay and settle. Beaver dams deteriorated and the wetlands behind them drained away, leaving grassy meadows ideal for grazing cattle.[3] Ogden's fur desert dissuaded trappers yet would attract farmers and ranchers.

Beaver seeker that he was, Ogden was unimpressed with the Klamath country. On Christmas Day of 1826 he wrote in his journal: "this certainly is a country of Lakes but not of Rivers or Beaver and the more I see of it the less opinion I have of it."[4] Hunting was as fruitless as the trapping. If it had not been for the local Indians, Ogden and his expedition would have starved. The Natives brought roots, fattened dogs, and suckers to the hungry newcomers. Ogden was most fond of the fish, misnaming it a "fine large Carp—this is certainly a new Fish to me and nearly as good as White fish."[5]

Ogden and his party wound their way to Lost River, "a fine looking stream well lin'd with Willows and had some difficulty in discovering a fording place." Modocs on the far bank pointed out a crossing, known now as Olene Gap, that gave the trappers a way over the water "without wetting any thing."[6] Ogden dispatched two of his men to follow Lost River upstream while he bivouacked. The two worked all the way up to the river's source at Clear Lake marsh and returned in three days with but two beaver pelts and the sighting of just one lodge. To a trapper's eyes, Lost River was a lost cause.

Holy Lands Here and There

Plagued by cold, Ogden pillaged a vacant Modoc village for fuel. "We took the liberty of demolishing their Huts for fire wood at least the men I have warn'd them if the Natives should complain of this burgalary rather than it should be a cause of quarrel that they should pay for the theft."[7] The Modocs, who were likely off hunting, sought neither payment nor revenge for having their winter houses turned into firewood.

Ogden headed south to the Pit River ("a *fine* looking River for Beaver well wooded deep") in the spring.[8] He and his trappers, plus the women, children, and horses accompanying them, passed quickly through the Lost River country on their way back north to Fort Vancouver. With their exit the first round of white-Modoc contact ended, no shot fired nor arrow nocked.[9]

Ogden's expedition opened the Klamath Basin to influence from Canada and later the United States. A few Klamath traders went north with the Hudson's Bay expedition and learned how much they could make in horses and guns by selling slaves at The Dalles on the Columbia River. Seizing the opportunity, Klamath-Modoc raiding parties captured women and children from neighboring tribes and sold them north, connecting the region into the larger circle of the Pacific Northwest and shifting the political structure of the Klamath and Modoc nations to give the new traders greater power.[10]

Not for another twenty years would European Americans appear in the basin in any number, however. Then they would bring a change far greater than seasonal slaving.

• • •

Peer under the rocks, inside the shadows, and down the darkest paths of the Modoc War, and an Applegate always pops up. Somehow that fits. After all, it was the Applegates who brought the United States to the Klamath country.

Brothers Lindsay, Charles, and Jesse Applegate and their families emigrated from Missouri to Oregon in 1843. They settled in the Willamette Valley and soon plowed, planted, and harvested themselves into substantial net worth. At the time some six to seven thousand Americans had taken up residence in Oregon, where they lived in international limbo. Almost twenty years earlier, Great Britain and the United States had concluded a joint occupancy agreement that left the ultimate possession of the Pacific Northwest as a question to be settled in the future. If the two nations could not come to an agreement, war was possible. The American communities in the Willamette saw a southern route to Oregon as key to their survival. The new route would avoid the Columbia River and its dangerous rapids. It would bypass, too, the Hudson's Bay Company forts along the river and give Americans an easier, more secure way of getting to Oregon. And if worse came to worse and war broke out, a southern route could also serve as an American escape hatch.

The poor fortunes of the next two waves of summer emigrants further demonstrated the need for a new and improved route into Oregon. The year after the Applegates crossed the continent, muddy prairies so slowed the wagons' progress that they were caught by heavy snow in Oregon's Blue Mountains and had to winter over in the Walla Walla Valley. The next summer, mountain man Stephen Meek led a train of 150 to 200 wagons over a cutoff route across the Oregon desert to the central Cascades. Meek lost his bearings and took his charges into impossibly hard country. By the time they reached the Deschutes River, the wagon train had disintegrated into a frenzied starvation that cost some seventy-five lives.[11]

As the snows melted in the spring of 1846, a group led by Levi Scott set out from Polk County, Oregon, to find a southern route. Fear of Indians turned them back after only a few days. In Scott's failure, Lindsay and Jesse Applegate saw an opportunity. Lining up thirteen companions, including seasoned mountain man Moses "Black" Harris, they resolved to find a direct route from the Willamette to Fort Hall, an emigrant way station in what is now Idaho. To find out what they were getting themselves into, the Applegates paid a visit to Peter Skene Ogden at Fort Vancouver.[12]

Now fifty-six years old, Ogden had grown obese, yet he remained as wily as ever. He warned the Applegates that the Indians of the Klamath Basin were "fierce and war-like savages, who would attack every party entering their country, steal their traps, waylay and murder the men." Lindsay Applegate was skeptical. He suspected that Ogden was gin-

Holy Lands Here and There

ning up the story to protect Hudson's Bay Company interests along the Columbia River, discourage the Yankees, and keep them home.[13]

Undaunted by Ogden and apparently ignorant that the United States and Great Britain had just concluded an agreement that made Oregon an American possession,[14] the Applegate party set out from the Willamette Valley on June 20. Heading southeast, the fifteen men and their riding mounts and packhorses followed and crossed the Umpqua and Rogue Rivers to the Siskiyou Mountains, then bore east. Close to Lower Klamath Lake they discovered that someone else white had passed through just before them.

That someone, the Applegates would later learn, was John C. Frémont. Guided by the legendary Kit Carson, Frémont and a force of some sixty men had come north from California to map the very route the Applegates were proposing. When Indians attacked the American camp on the northwestern shore of Upper Klamath Lake and killed three men, Carson orchestrated revenge raids on local Indian villages. Whatever they did not kill, Carson's men burned.[15] Then Frémont and his force left for California, about six weeks before the Applegates came across their trail heading south.

With word of Carson's attacks circulating on the Indigenous telegraph, the Modocs kept their distance from the Oregonians and set signal fires on the hills. The explorers skirted Lower Klamath Lake, then cut across the rough lava country on the north side of Tule Lake, following a trail in the network of paths that linked camps and villages through Modoc territory.[16] David Goff, one of the party, spotted a band of mountain sheep and, longing for fresh meat on the fire, took after them. Soon Goff was lost, with a group of armed Modoc men tracking him at a distance. When the rest of the Applegate party appeared, the Indians quickly retreated to canoes and fled across the lake.

Still following long-used Modoc trails, the Applegates came to Lost River, close by the then-unoccupied winter village where Frazier Boutelle and Scarface Charley would try to kill each other twenty-seven years later. Sluggish but deep and some eighty feet wide, steep-banked Lost River posed a significant obstacle. A Modoc man showed the explorers Natural Bridge, a rock ledge that crossed the river only a foot or two under the surface. Men and horses sloshed across.[17]

The Applegate party climbed out of the Tule Lake Basin, followed the trail through the juniper-dotted hills to the east, and crossed Lost River yet again, a few miles north of where, in those days, it poured out of an extensive marsh at the north end of Clear Lake. Now the Applegates were on the Modoc Plateau, a great lava-cap tableland that extends eastward to Goose Lake. They rounded the lake and climbed the mountain ridge on its eastern shore. It was, they thought in the mistaken geography of the time, the Sierra Nevada. The peaks actually belonged to a separate range, an outlier of the Cascades now known as the Warners. At the top of the pass, the Applegates looked east into the sere expanse of the Great Basin.

After a thirsty crossing of the Black Rock Desert, the Oregonians came to the Humboldt River, a milky stream that offered gut-scouring alkali water, firewood, and pasture for the horses. The course of the Humboldt, they knew, led toward Fort Hall. Jesse Applegate and four others left the rest of the party and headed for the fort. They reached it on August 8, some six weeks after setting out from Oregon.

There Jesse and his companions persuaded about a hundred wagonloads of emigrants to follow them back to the Willamette Valley. A new way into Oregon—called the Applegate Trail or the South Emigrant Road—had been blazed.[18]

• • •

As the Applegate Trail became better marked with the passage of each wagon train, more and more emigrants followed it, particularly after the discovery of gold in southern Oregon and northern California. Between 1850 and 1855 some thirty-five thousand people entered Oregon, most of them along the Applegate Trail.[19]

All these people and wagons, plus their herds of oxen, horses, cattle, pigs, and sheep, tromped through the heart of the Modocs' realm. Their route, following trails the Modocs had used for millennia and the Applegates had expropriated, became a highway of destruction: grass grazed to the roots, firewood burned, game shot, watercourses fouled. To make matters worse, the diseases Americans carried, including typhoid, smallpox, measles, whooping cough, and cholera, crossed into the Indigenous populations. Among the Plains tribes, the most lethal of these maladies

Holy Lands Here and There

was cholera, which followed wagon trains from 1849 through 1854 in a dark bacterial cloud. Smallpox and measles both became epidemic at midcentury as well. These diseases fell heavily on Native peoples, killing young and old disproportionately and shattering their societies. The Modocs lost their share, in an 1847 epidemic, most likely of measles, that claimed some 150 lives. That was a horrific toll among a people already depleted by a winter starvation that had killed off as much as half the nation's population less than twenty years earlier.[20]

Americans, however, had little incentive to clean up their bad biological act. Since primitive Indians simply had to give way before civilization's superiority, settlers saw cholera, smallpox, and measles as instruments to speed the inevitable progression from pagan world to Christian. Of Oregon's fast-declining Indians, the missionary Gustavus Hines said that "the hand of Providence is removing them to give place to a people more worthy of this beautiful and fertile country."[21]

Hines was admitting a reality Americans rarely recognize: the settler colonialism that drove emigrants into the West was premised on destroying Indigenous inhabitants and occupying their land. However extermination occurred—by gunshot, starvation, disease, or cultural destruction—eliminating Native nations to make room for incoming Americans became both noble and inevitable.[22] And it amounted to genocide.

• • •

In purely lexical terms, genocide did not exist before 1944, the year Polish lawyer Raphaël Lemkin coined the term by combining the Greek root *genos*, meaning "race" or "tribe," with the Latin *cide*, meaning "killing." "Generally speaking, genocide does not necessarily mean the immediate destruction of a nation," Lemkin wrote. "It is intended rather to signify a coordinated plan of different actions aiming at the destruction of essential foundations of life of national groups, with the aim of annihilating the groups themselves."[23] Lemkin went on to lay the international legal foundation that led the United Nations General Assembly to define the crime in 1948 and make its prosecution an essential component of international law enforcement.

Given the timing of Lemkin's scholarship, it is hardly surprising that

Nazi Germany's extermination campaign against Jews, Gypsies, and others came to define the way we think of genocide: a centrally planned, highly coordinated campaign using an industrial-engineering model to achieve the highest possible efficiency in slaughter. Yet Lemkin himself pointed out the fallacy of thinking that genocide began only with World War II. The Nazi genocide was but "an old practice in modern development," he wrote, citing Rome's destruction of Carthage in 146 BCE and the obliteration of the city of Magdeburg in Europe's Thirty Years' War as but two examples.[24] Indeed, when death overtook him, Lemkin was working on a book about historical genocides, including that of the Native peoples of North America.[25]

The fate befalling the Modocs lacked a Wannsee Conference, with its outline for the Nazis' destruction of Europe's Jews, or an Auschwitz, where the extermination of peoples became a finely tuned industrial operation. Yet, even as the Reverend Hines was smacking his lips at the destruction of Oregon's Indians as inevitable and godly, the situation in Modoc country was about to rise toward the legal definition of genocide set by the United Nations: "any of the following acts committed with intent to destroy, in whole or in part, a national, ethnical, racial or religious group, as such: a) Killing members of the group; b) Causing serious bodily or mental harm to members of the group; c) Deliberately inflicting on the group conditions of life calculated to bring about its physical destruction; d) Imposing measures intended to prevent births within the group."[26]

· · ·

Reeling from the measles epidemic, the Modocs had little energy to resist the first flood of emigrants. Throughout 1847 and 1848 newcomers passed through Modoc country with little incident except occasional thievery. As far as the emigrants were concerned, Indians were pests on the same order as wolves. Should these wild things make off with an unguarded heifer or ox, the emigrants laced the remains with strychnine in the hope that Indians or wolves would come back for poisonous seconds.[27]

In 1849 the Modocs began to fight back by attacking wagon trains at a place called Wa-ga-kanna, or Little Canyon, and later known to

Holy Lands Here and There

Americans as Bloody Point. The route from Clear Lake crossed high, dry, rocky country, then angled down toward Tule Lake below a steep volcanic prominence. Grass grew thick and green in the narrow meadow between the tule-fringed water's edge and the cliff, and the lake glistened cool and refreshing under the high, hot sun. Exhausted emigrants failed to notice how this seemingly perfect campsite squeezed them between lake and cliff with no escape route. The many boulders and tall tules provided camouflage for a Modoc war party to creep close at night and attack at first light.[28]

Tales of atrocities spread across southern Oregon and northern California and grew with each telling. In 1850, the story went, Modocs butchered at least eighty would-be settlers. The sole survivor stumbled all the way to Jacksonville, Oregon, bearing his tale of slaughter. John Ross, a colonel in the state militia, rode out with a posse and found the charred remains of looted wagons amid rotting, fly-ridden, wolf-torn corpses. Posse members maintained that parents had been forced to watch the killing of their children, then they themselves were dismembered. The Indians, they continued, smashed babies and small children against rocks, shattering skulls and scattering brains, and the Modocs pursued one young woman for a mile and a half, then cut her throat and sliced off her breasts.[29]

The next summer, a Modoc war party slaughtered some one hundred emigrants south of Lower Klamath Lake and threw the hacked bodies into a stream. The only survivors, according to a later account, were two teenage sisters whom Modoc men kept for fun and games. Soon the girls became objects of contention among men and of jealousy among women. A quarrel over sexual rights to one girl led to her killing. The fate of the second girl remained unknown. Likely she met a similar fate, since yet another version of the same story had it that jealous Modoc women did the killing this time.[30]

Against such provocations, something had to be done. The Modocs needed to be taught a lesson from which they could never recover.

• • •

The posses that ride out in classic Western movies like John Ford's *The Searchers* are cast as groups of neighbors set to right a wrong, protect women and children, and nestle back into their cozy homesteads once justice is done. The Modocs, though, told a different version of what was happening along the emigrant road and of the death squads preparing to descend upon their country.

It comes from Jeff Riddle, a half-Modoc, half-white man who was the only child of an interracial couple who served as interpreters and go-betweens during the Modoc War. Riddle learned of the bad old days from aged Modocs who had survived them.

When the Natives spotted the first wagon trains, they fled to the hills in fear. People on horseback, like Ogden and his trappers and the Applegate explorers, they understood, but creaking wagons, lowing oxen, and grunting pigs in noisy, dust-raising mobs were something altogether too alien. At first the Modocs took the emigrants to be spirits sent to punish them. Then they realized that these strange beings were human, and they approached. In return the emigrants offered coffee, bread, and bacon, to which Natives took a great liking.

All remained harmonious until the Pit River Indians waylaid a wagon train near modern-day Alturas, California, in the shadow of the Warner Mountains. The survivors made their way to the mining town of Yreka, well to the west, and sounded the alarm. John D. Cosby raised a militia of sixty-five men and headed for the ambush site. Along the way the posse passed small bands of Modocs, and peace prevailed. After all, the militia was hunting the Pit Rivers, who proved utterly elusive.

On the way back to Yreka, the empty-handed militiamen camped on the eastern side of Tule Lake. Cosby and his men did not know that a Pit River war party had followed them and was waiting for night to attack. The surprise assault was over quickly, with several white men wounded, one seriously, by the time the Pit Rivers slipped away. That fight soured the mood in Cosby's posse.

When the militiamen broke camp in the morning and rode on, they came across fourteen Modocs in a summer village cooking their breakfast. Cosby ordered them shot down: men, women, and children. Three survivors then ran from one village to the next along Lost River, spreading the news of the unprovoked attack and sending the Indians into the hills to hide.

Meanwhile, Cosby's posse-turned-death-squad crossed Lost River at Natural Bridge and turned toward Hot Creek, east of Lower Klamath Lake, where the Natives had not yet heard what Cosby was up to. When they approached the militiamen to ask for bread, bacon, and coffee, they were met with rifle fire. Posse members scalped the dead and hung the dripping trophies from saddle pommels.

Back in Yreka, Cosby boasted that he and his men had fought two pitched battles against Modocs. The vigilantes kept to themselves the truth that the scalps they displayed were lifted from Natives who meant them no harm.

Cosby's raid was both typical of the time and sanctioned by state policy. Exacted one village at a time, supported by white public opinion, and funded by tax dollars, genocide was the point and purpose of California's midcentury posses and militias. In January 1851, when Peter Burnett, the first civilian governor of the new state, declared in his annual message to the legislature that a war of extermination was inevitable, he portrayed himself and his state not as committing wholesale murder but yielding to the inevitable.[31] The argument worked; the California legislature appropriated a half-million dollars to fund militia campaigns against Natives. Cosby was doing a job of murder, the one the movies never told us about, and getting paid for it out of the state's coffers.[32] And should the Indigenous people fight back, those acts of resistance became new atrocities that justified even greater destruction, a smokescreen of apparent conflict shifting the rhetoric from genocide to war and obscuring the crime.[33]

• • •

After riding with Cosby's death squad and glorying in the vigilantes' triumphant return to Yreka, Ben Wright decided the year remained young enough to slaughter more Indians before winter closed the backcountry. He formed a follow-up militia on the ostensible mission of retrieving horses and mules rustled from a packer in Butte Valley. Leading twenty men, Wright rode back into Modoc country.

A man cut from the same rawhide as Wild Bill Hickok and Wyatt Earp, Wright was one of those shadowy characters who flocked to the western frontier's moral anarchy. He lived on the literal and figurative edge where light and dark, fact and fiction, bravery and brutality meld.

Raised in Indiana in a Quaker household, Wright moved away from his home country and religion, drifting west to Kansas after his mother's death and a fight with the blacksmith to whom he was apprenticed. The twenty-year-old Wright joined a wagon train headed for Oregon in the summer of 1847. The party included Joel Palmer, who was moving his family to Oregon after spending the prior year in the new territory.[34] The connection to Palmer would prove central to the last act of Wright's drama.

On the way west Wright became enamored of a comely seventeen-year-old who, the story goes, was killed in the only Indian raid to befall the wagon train. Unrequited and embittered, Wright swore himself the vengeance-seeking enemy of all things Native. Only months after reaching Oregon, he joined the territorial militia fighting the Cayuse Indians around what is now Walla Walla, Washington. Service with the Indian-hunting volunteers sharpened Wright's guiding and skirmishing skills and focused his hatred. After discharge in 1848, Wright crossed the state line and settled in the gold-mining camps along Cottonwood Creek, a tributary of the Klamath River some twenty miles north of the rough-and-ready California mining town of Yreka. Uninterested in work as backbreaking as mining, Wright made his living by killing Indians for the bounties paid out by various mining towns. Over time he came to affect the fashion of the very people he hunted: wearing buckskins, growing his hair long and flowing, and, unlike most American men of the time, shaving his face clean but for a soul patch under the lower lip. Wright looked so much like an Indian that, in one nighttime skirmish with Native fighters, another vigilante grabbed him by the hair, dragged him to the ground, and was on the verge of driving a knife into his chest before recognizing him as a white man. Despite that near-death experience, Wright refused to part with his gone-Native style.[35]

Samuel A. Clarke, a contemporary newspaperman, wrote: "Ben Wright was an Indian killer. That was what he thought Indians were made for. He generally kept an Indian woman, too, for convenience, but he was hostile to the men whenever he had an excuse." Wright liked to take trophies, lifting scalps, fingers, ears, and noses from his victims, often while they were still alive.[36] And when he was drinking, this mean man turned meaner still.

Wright was likely sober when the vigilantes seeking the rustled horses and mules rode past the village at Natural Bridge under the eyes of the Modocs. The Indians displayed no hostility despite Cosby's earlier raid, and the posse made a show of camping well downstream. Under cover of darkness Wright's men crept close to the village and, as the sun rose, opened fire. The Indians, armed only with bows and arrows, could only flee. More than a dozen were killed.

Next Wright and his men fell upon an island village where Lost River flowed into Tule Lake, chased the inhabitants into the marsh, hunted down and slaughtered fifteen Modocs hiding in the tules, and took others prisoner. When one of the captives broke away and ran, Wright pursued the man, sliced-and-diced him with a knife, and dragged the bled-out corpse back to camp to warn the other Indians against escape.

Meanwhile, survivors from the two attacks took shelter in the Lava Beds and hid in a large cave that just over twenty years later would figure prominently in the Modoc War. Out of food and beset by the cold and rain of early November, Wright had his posse pile brush and logs at the cave's mouth and set a fire. The blaze was still burning twenty-four hours later, and Wright decided the Indians inside had to be cooked or smothered. He and his men saddled up and rode back to Yreka, drawn more by dreams of warm beds, hot meals, and willing women than the slow spectacle of roasted, suffocated Indians. The vigilantes did not know that the Indians survived, emerged from the cave, and spread word among their kin of the terror that had befallen them.[37]

The Cosby and Wright raids changed everything for the Modocs, who now understood the whites' violence as an extermination campaign. The headman who was Kientpoos's father called the various Modoc bands into a council.

"Now, my people, I see we cannot get along with the white people," he said. "They come along and kill my people for nothing. Not only my men, but they kill our wives and children. I did not give the white man any cause to commit these murders. Now, what shall I do? Shall I run every time I see white people? If I do, they will chase us from valley to mountain, and from mountain to valley, and kill us all."

He saw no choice but to declare war on these now-unwelcome interlopers, to resist an invader bent on the Natives' destruction. "Shall we defend our wives and our children and our country?" asked Kient-poos's father. "I am not afraid to die. If I die in war against the white people, I will die for a good cause."

Backed by the headman of another band, this self-defense plan carried the day. From that time on, the Modocs saw emigrants as invaders who would pass through their country no longer.[38]

∙ ∙ ∙

With the Indians fighting back and the rumored toll of emigrants killed at Bloody Point rising during the summer following Cosby's and Wright's raids, an alarm went up across far northern California and southern Oregon. Charles McDermitt, the sheriff of California's Siskiyou County, raised a company of some thirty volunteers—later dubbed "brave, resolute, unselfish border knights"—to protect emigrant trains against the Modocs west of Goose Lake. After riding shotgun for three wagon, McDermitt came upon a starving white man near Lost River who claimed to be the sole survivor of a group of nine set upon by the Indians. McDermitt and his men took the man back to Yreka, where a public meeting determined to raise another militia to address the Modoc menace. Ben Wright was tapped as captain, and the volunteers under his command set out for Tule Lake.[39]

They arrived just in the nick of time, coming across a train of sixteen wagons and forty to sixty emigrants besieged by Modocs. The militiamen charged, and the Modocs fell back to the water, where the fight continued. According to W. T. Kershaw, one of the volunteers, not a member of their company was lost while thirty or thirty-five Indians were killed.[40]

Over the next two days, Kershaw reported, the volunteers found and buried twenty-one white dead. Militiamen from Jacksonville, Oregon, led again by John Ross, appeared as well. They pitched in and buried fourteen east of Natural Bridge on Lost River.[41]

Although the battlefield was littered with women's and children's clothing, only one of the cadavers was female, and none was a child. An abandoned Indian camp yielded a long hank of women's hair and various nursery items. As the militiamen saw it, the Modocs had captured the females and kids to enslave them. An abundance of wom-

Holy Lands Here and There

en's clothes appeared among the Natives of the Umpqua Valley soon thereafter, said to have been passed along in trade from Indians in the Klamath Basin.[42] That was the story, anyway.

The Oregonians returned to Jacksonville, while Wright and his Yreka volunteers spent the next three months escorting wagon trains from Clear Lake to Lower Klamath Lake. This duty gave Wright an occasional chance to kill. When he and some of his men spotted two Indian women running toward the Lava Beds for shelter, the mounted whites rode the pair down and fired. The older woman, a seventy-year-old, died outright. The younger suffered only an arm wound unlikely to kill her. Claiming mercy in putting the woman out of her misery, Wright drove a knife into her chest. She bled out at the former Quaker's feet.[43]

For Wright, that intimate kill was but an appetizer. To bring the wary Indians in close and in number, he ran up a white flag of truce and told the Modocs he wanted to talk peace and negotiate the return of prisoners. Falsely assured that Wright preferred parley over combat, a group of Modocs camped near him and his men at Natural Bridge, ate their beef and flour, and talked. At dawn on the sixth day, after sending his men to encircle the camp, Wright strapped on two revolvers, donned a serape to conceal them, and strode in among the sleeping Modocs. When he came to the Indian leader, Wright drew his weapons and killed the man, then zigzagged through the stunned Indians, shooting as he ran, while his men poured in rifle fire. Caught flat-footed and armed only with bows and arrows, Modoc men went down one after another. The whites gave the women no quarter as well. The few Indians who escaped into Lost River were prodded back to the surface with poles and blasted at close range.

Not a single white died in what became known as the Ben Wright Massacre. The number of Indian dead is variously given as between thirty and ninety.[44]

Wright and his men lifted scalps from the Modoc dead and then waved the grisly trophies in triumph on their return to the cheering townspeople of Yreka. They even made major money from the massacre thanks to the California legislature. Privates received four dollars a day for three months' service, more than eight times the per diem of a Regular Army private at the Lost River raid twenty years later. Wright himself drew $744—approximately $23,000 in today's currency—generous compensation for ninety days of taking his pleasure in the hunting and butchering of Indians.[45]

Nor did the murder raids stop following Wright's massacre. Two years after, a company of Oregon militia men raided Modoc villages along Tule and Goose Lakes and killed some two dozen Natives. Another two years after that, J. D. Cosby and more than two hundred California militiamen made a sweep through Modoc and Klamath country, even hauling boats over the mountains from Yreka to attack Indians in lake and marsh camps. The vigilantes fought a few small skirmishes that killed three of them—one from friendly fire—yet bagged but one Modoc, and that a woman. Still, Cosby and his officers sent glowing reports of narrow escapes and stunning victories back home, flat-out lies that the *Yreka Union* published, without confirmation, under triumphal headlines.

In the next legislative term, Cosby, a California state senator as well as a militia general, introduced a bill to pay himself and his militiamen for their horses, guns, and time, claiming that the campaign had put 185 Natives in the ground. The legislature bought the lie as readily as the hometown newspaper had and disbursed $188,000 in state funds. Several years later, the federal government sweetened the pot for Cosby and his vigilantes by kicking in another $80,000.[46] Indian killing paid well, even when the killers made up the death toll.

•••

By the close of the genocidal 1850s, the resistance of the shattered Modocs to the American invasion had ended, but for the rustling of an occasional steer or horse. Yet there would be blowback to this campaign of extermination, most notably to Ben Wright's murderous deception. The Modocs had learned that a white flag of truce was but a ruse to lure them into ambush. And two of the survivors of the massacre carried a lifelong enmity against white settlers that manifested itself fiercely in the long, bloody months after the Lost River raid. One was the shaman Curley Headed Doctor; the other, Schonchin John, was a would-be chief who wanted Kientpoos's position.

As for Wright, his career after the massacre moved steadily ahead.

His ways with Native people won him such admiration among American settlers that Joel Palmer, the Oregon Indian Affairs superintendent who knew Wright from their journey across the prairie together, appointed him Indian agent along the state's southern coast. There the Indian killer met his comeuppance in a manner that satisfies the usually unattainable standard of poetic justice.

The story opens in the muddy main street of rough, rain-soaked Port Orford. A drunken Wright assaulted Chetcoe Jennie, a $500-a-year government interpreter who was his Indian comfort woman of the moment, forcing her to strip naked before whipping her through the town. Set on avenging this ignominy, Jennie threw in with a group of Rogue River Indians who planned to stem the fast-rising flood of Americans by killing as many as they could in a single, coordinated attack. The rebels were led by a Shoshone named Enos who had once served as a guide with explorer John C. Frémont and as a scout for Wright himself on his Modoc campaigns. Enos, for reasons that remain hidden, was as motivated by revenge as was Chetcoe Jennie. Close to the mouth of the Rogue River, the vengeful pair and their co-conspirators set upon Wright, either after a dance that turned into a brawl or in a dawn ambush that also took down a militia captain named Poland and several of Poland's volunteers. Enos dispatched Wright with an axe, carved the dead man's chest open, and ate his heart raw, a vengeful meal he shared with Chetcoe Jennie.

Less than two months later, Enos died dangling and strangling from a lynch party's noose. Chetcoe Jennie, her revenge complete, vanished into the forest like smoke from a campfire, never to be seen again.[47]

• • •

Heartless as he was, Ben Wright had the last laugh. For all the blood that clung to his hands, Wright was highly, even heroically, regarded by his American neighbors and chroniclers. Historian and novelist Frances Fuller Victor wrote an 1881 apologia titled "A Knight of the Frontier," a man "who, so far as we know always labored in the cause of humanity."[48] Humanity, for both Wright and Victor, excluded Indians.

Victor's contemporary David Fagan offered a similar assessment of Wright. "He fought Indians after the manner of their own warfare, even to the scalping and mutilating of the dead, and to the use of strategy and treachery to get the foe within his grasp; but to his own race he was ever true and honorable," Fagan argued. "Taking all things together he was just the man for the emergency." William Brown, a twentieth-century writer, continued the tradition by asserting that Ben Wright was "a leader . . . a man of high moral principles."[49]

More is happening in these judgments than a simple misreading of the nature of a man, with or without heart. By the evidence, Wright was a sexual predator and a killer. Elevating his pitfalls of character into the realm of heroism requires standing the observed world on its head and turning vice into virtue. Such a transformation can occur only when an underlying and deep-seated myth creates facts as they need to be rather than what they are.

One such factoid is Governor Grover's claim of three hundred killings by the Modocs in the years leading up to the war. It likely came from a February 1863 report to the Bureau of Indian Affairs about Indian depredations written by Major C. S. Drew. The major had an agenda: he wanted to convince the powers in Washington, DC, that a fort needed to be built in the Klamath country to guard emigrant trains against Indians. As evidence for this new garrison, Drew totaled 151 murders. This was, he argued, too few, since Indians liked to wipe out whole emigrant parties and leave not a trace. "Two for every one [reported] killed is probably a fair estimate," Drew wrote. "This would give three hundred at least, and a total of killed and wounded of four hundred and fifty-one."[50]

Drew was hardly the only Indian fighter of the time who cooked the books. When Wright's men and Ross's men were burying the dead at Bloody Point in the late summer of 1852, the former reported twenty-one dead, the latter fourteen, which seems to be thirty-five. Yet the two groups were working together at least part of the time, and their reports counted some burials twice.

Often, too, a given attack was set in different places at different times by dueling versions of the same hearsay. Alfred Benjamin Meacham, the onetime Oregon Indian superintendent who would play a major role in the Modoc War, told about the slaughter of sixty-five emigrants and the capture of two girls at Bloody Point in 1852. Militia captain and unreliable newspaperman William Thompson described the killing of a hundred emigrants and the capture of two girls south of Lower Klamath Lake, on the other side of Tule Lake, two years earlier.[51] This is one incident counted twice by writers with a proclivity to the grandiose and florid.

Other details added ghoulish spice to the Modoc attacks. According to the rescue party of Oregon militiamen led by John Ross, the positions of bodies indicated that parents had been forced to watch the killing of their children before they themselves were butchered. Such a deduction would require a knowledge of crime-scene forensics far beyond anything Jacksonville's illiterate miners had on tap. Rather, they fantasized the explanation to justify their own vengeful butchery.

And then there are the lurid bits—the young woman at Bloody Point run down by Modoc attackers, her throat slit and breasts sliced off, and the two girls captured at Bloody Point or Lower Klamath Lake then held in sexual slavery until their jaded captors killed them.

Such tales are hardly unique to the Modocs. Stories of female captives held in sexual slavery by Indians were a dime a dozen along the frontier. Indeed, the captivity narrative is one of the most common tropes from America's settlement and expansion, reaching back into the late eighteenth century and tantalizing readers and listeners with tales of torture, hunger, and depravity.[52] No matter where emigrants ventured, these oft-repeated tales made clear, Indian men carried off white women to sexual violation so horrible that only death offered redemption.

Innocence was the operative theme of these tales. Americans moving west saw themselves as blameless, their motives pure, even as they, the new Chosen People, coveted the timber, gold, and arable meadows of the Indian-occupied Promised Land. This imagined innocence painted every action by emigrants in a bright and positive light and made the horrors of Indian resistance both more vicious and more symbolic. The emigrants had come in innocence, holding to faith in their God and trusting a nature that betrayed their pure designs. And, in the same way that the women were kidnapped by satanic Natives, the land was held captive and required liberation. Stories of capture and sexual slavery created the deep-seated outrage that allowed settlers to wrap themselves in the righteous vestments of injured innocence, destroy the Indians they held responsible, and rescue both violated white women and ill-used virgin land.[53] This was a righteous cleansing, a noble crusade, a holy genocide.

The mythic tales of sexual slavery served another function: they reversed reality. In the early days of the western frontier, American men far outnumbered American women. Saturday-night miners turned into rapists who thought little of forcing Indian women into sexual servitude and killing Indian men who objected. Invariably, Native women's bodies became the stage where violent men expressed their anxieties and uncertainties, from sexual fear to deep-down piss-off at failing to find the fortune that had lured them west.[54]

Which brings us back to Ben Wright. He was the prototype of this sort of frontiersman, predator and killer. Yet the upended moral and mythic world of the frontier raised such a criminal up as a heroic man of action. Wright sought to free captives and land from pagan occupiers and preserve the Christian newcomers' innocence of intention. Wright's purity of motivation justified his stratagem of treachery under a flag of truce and his mass murder of Indians just for being Indians. A treacherous slaughter became a bloody battle, and a psychopath assumed the mantle of heroic warrior. His sexual rapacity and love of homicide became instruments of empire demonstrating to Indians that their bodies, lives, and land belonged to the American invaders.[55]

• • •

For all the inflated claims of innocent Americans massacred by devilish Modocs, the Natives suffered far more. As the 1850s opened, the tribe numbered between one thousand and two thousand people. By the end of that genocidal decade, only some three hundred Modocs remained.[56] Armed resistance to the flood of emigrants, who were now not only passing through Modoc country but also settling its most fertile corners, became impossible. The Modoc leader Old Schonchin put it this way: "I thought that, if we killed all the white men, no more would come. We killed all we could; but they came more and more, like new grass in the spring. I looked around, and saw that many of our young men were dead, and could not come back to fight. My heart was sick. My people were few."[57]

The time had come for the Modocs to take a different tack.

5

The Peace That Wasn't, the Treaty That Was, Kind Of

The wishes and instructions of the government were very carefully
and fully explained to the Indians, and they exhibited a complete
willingness to become subjected to the United States, and cease
depredations upon the citizens thereof, in accordance with the
treaty. . . . Its provisions are . . . similar to those of other treaties . . .
with tribes in this State, but they differ from them in calling for the
expenditure of smaller amounts of money, and in subjecting the
Indians to a somewhat stricter control of the government.

—J. W. Perit Huntington, December 10, 1864

Returning from a trip to San Francisco on Valentine's Day in
1864, Elijah Steele discovered several hundred Indians filling
the yard of his Yreka home. His wife had been lecturing them, ami-
cably, on the best way for the Indigenous peoples to live with one
another and with Americans. They were listening. This was why they
had come: to talk peace.

A New York–born lawyer, Steele had emigrated to California during
the gold rush, hoping to make his fortune in the flumes. When he
panned more gravel than glitter, Steele returned to lawyering. Gaunt,
bony-faced, and fringe-bearded, Steele looked something like President Abraham Lincoln, who in September 1863 had appointed him
Indian Bureau superintendent across the northernmost tier of California counties. Politically Steele was what we would now call a progressive; he opposed slavery and named one of his sons after Charles
Darwin. Although he lacked any Romantic notion of savage nobility,
Steele worked on the Indians' behalf from an advocate's deep-down
sense of fairness and equity.

When Steele took the Indian Bureau job, Native affairs were in a sad state. Some Natives were fighting other Natives, and Indigenous bands across Mendocino and Humboldt Counties were killing Americans, who responded in death-squad kind. Poverty, disease, and malnutrition beset every Indian community. Steele addressed this dire situation by negotiating an end to the fighting and working to increase food supplies to Natives.

That success brought the Indigenous nations to Steele's front door. There were Klamaths, Modocs, and Shastas as well as communities from the Klamath, Sacramento, and Scott River valleys. The headmen included Lileks of the Klamaths, Old Schonchin of the Modocs, Josh and Jack of the Shastas, John of the Scott Valley Indians, and Jim of the Hamburg tribe. Old Schonchin was accompanied by Kientpoos, a young and rising political star. He was a solidly built man with a handsome face that appeared calm and collected. His Modoc name, though, meant "having heartburn," a reflection of the anxiety Kientpoos buried within his seemingly implacable exterior. The story goes that it was Steele who gave Kientpoos his Captain Jack nickname, since the Indian reminded the lawyer of a miner named Jack he knew from his gold rush days.[1]

The Indians recognized that things as they were could not continue. Despite Steele's efforts over the past months, starvation remained so widespread that one military commander acting on his own provided five tons of government beef and five and a half tons of flour to the Indians of the Klamath Basin. To bring in money, Natives sold children as slaves and women as prostitutes to Americans, a human commerce that destroyed families and cut the Indigenous birth rate because of venereal disease. The Klamaths and the Modocs were preparing for war after some of their men were killed by Shastas, a traditional enemy, inside American settlements. Sure that the settlers were protecting the Shastas, the Klamaths and the Modocs retaliated by stealing cattle and robbing travelers. The Fort Klamath commander executed a Klamath chief who hoped to exploit the Civil War as an opportunity for all Natives to rebel. With their world unwinding, the Indians wanted to arrive at a settlement that both recognized the new order and guaranteed them a secure place within it.

Although Steele lacked congressional authorization to conclude a treaty with Indians, he saw this unexpected opportunity as golden. "I deemed it my duty to call the council," he explained to Indian Affairs commissioner W. P. Dole, "believing that if I could arrange a settlement among the Indians . . . , I could arrange a permanent treaty with all for our benefit."[2]

In but two days, Steele and the five Native nations came to a straightforward agreement. Indians promised to live peacefully with one another, as well as whites, blacks, and Chinese, and to forgo war on other Native nations. Violators were to be surrendered to the Fort Klamath military for punishment. Travelers could cross Indian land without toll, except that Indians could charge for ferrying emigrants across rivers or guiding them through unknown country. Indians could enter American towns and other settled areas during the day as long as they carried a pass signed by a Fort Klamath officer. They agreed that when they were in town they would refrain from drunkenness and theft, carry bows and arrows only if hunting, and possess no firearms except weapons headed to the gunsmith for repair. The selling of children was to cease. In the case of women, the treaty allowed money to change hands only if the American married the Native woman legally.

At the end of the negotiation, the Indian leaders signed their names and made their marks on the treaty's pages. Steele fed them, provided forage for their mounts, and offered each leader two blankets to mark the conclusion of the agreement, the first of its kind with any of the nations. Everyone white and red left the gathering at Steele's house with some small glow of the love Valentine's Day stands for, the feeling that a binding agreement with the Great Father in Washington had quelled the ever-present threat of communal violence.

The Bureau of Indian Affairs reacted differently to the treaty Steele forwarded to them, however. Rather than submit it to the Senate for ratification, they simply stuck the document in a drawer and let it gather dust. And, to further indicate displeasure, Steele was fired.

As sensible as the treaty Steele made with the five Native nations was, it lacked the most crucial element: pushing Indians off their traditional land and onto a reservation. The Bureau of Indian Affairs wanted only treaties that ended Indian land rights.[3]

•••

Just such a treaty was struck later that same year at Council Grove, on the northeastern shore of Upper Klamath Lake. Acting Indian Affairs commissioner Charles E. Mix charged Oregon's superintendent, J. W. Perit Huntington, with the task of negotiating "an agreement on the part of the Indians to live on a proper reservation. . . . [W]ithin its limits there should be such natural resources as will enable the Indians, with but little assistance from the government, and for a time but little departure from their ordinary pursuits, to obtain a livelihood; and which shall also be as far removed as possible from white settlements, and least liable to be intruded upon by white settlers."[4] In other words, confine the Indians well away from Americans on land no settlers would want. And, oh yes, keep the cost low.

On October 9, 1864, Huntington met with more than a thousand Indian men, women, and children: 710 Klamaths, 339 Modocs, and 22 Yahooskin Paiutes (aka Snakes). The Klamaths were led by Lileks, Chiloquin, and twenty lesser chiefs; the Modocs by Old Schonchin and three others, including Kientpoos and Schonchin John, Old Schonchin's younger brother, a survivor of the Ben Wright Massacre; and the Yahooskins by Kiletoak and one other headman. Since the negotiators shared no first language, they used Chinook Jargon, a trade tongue that lacked the nuance complex agreements require. Despite the language difficulty—or perhaps because of it—a treaty that met the stipulation of ceding Native land and creating a reservation was settled by October 15.

The Klamath leaders made their marks with no hesitation. After all, the treaty turned much of their traditional territory into the reservation, so they simply stayed where they were. The Modoc and Yahooskin chiefs, Kientpoos among them, had to move their peoples off land they had long occupied. Still, they signed on. And Old Schonchin added an impressive show of agreement, facing south, laying one hand across his heart, and with the other indicating the passage of the sun from left to right. "Once my people were like sand along the shore," he said. "Now I call to them and only the wind answers. Four hundred strong young men went to war with the whites; only eighty are left. We will be good if the white man will let us, and be friends forever."[5]

A proud Huntington claimed he had had no trouble in getting the Indians to give up war on settlers: "The wishes and instructions of the government were very carefully and fully explained to the Indians, and they exhibited a complete willingness to become subjected to the United States, and cease depredations." Once the Senate ratified the treaty, the United States would acquire fifteen to twenty thousand square miles. Huntington's estimate of the purchase's extent embodied a certain fuzziness, since the treaty's boundaries were less than precise. This newly acquired land was in part severe, harsh, and high, but it also offered mineral wealth, natural pasture, and fertile soil awaiting miner, rancher, and farmer. Huntington was confident the Indians could support themselves even though the reservation lay well off any major avenue of travel and had too little arable land to attract interest from settlers. He felt certain of Senate ratification.[6]

In part, Huntington proved right. The Senate did approve the Council Grove Treaty, a full five years later and only with amendments that infuriated Kientpoos when he learned of them. Other chiefs who had signed the original treaty pressured him into agreeing to the new version, but he remained disgruntled at the United States' high-handedness in changing the terms unilaterally.[7] Only in February 1870, five and a half years after it was signed, was the treaty promulgated as law. More than another year passed before an executive order by President Ulysses S. Grant reserved a tract for the three Indigenous nations based on a survey of the treaty's fuzzy boundaries. The tract was plotted by surveyors who held financial interests in the Oregon Military Road Company. They drew the lines to work for the company and their pocketbooks against the Indians, lopping more than a half-million acres off what should have been a 1.4-million-acre reservation.[8] Fuzziness had yielded to larceny.

Huntington, indeed, struck an astounding deal. The treaty specified an initial allocation of $35,000 to settle the Indians on the reservation, followed by $8,000 a year for five years, $5,000 for the next five years, then $3,000 for a final five years—a total of $115,000 for food, clothing, farm tools, sawmill, foundry, school buildings, and the like. The federal government was paying a mere $6 to $8 per square mile for the land it acquired, or between $90 and $125 in today's money. This bargain-basement price made the Council Grove Treaty a land deal to wow the most wild-eyed speculator.

Yet the Senate's slowness to ratify this bargain meant that the Congress was even slower to allocate the promised funds. The Natives living on the reservation, mostly Klamaths, had to make do with very little. The winter of 1866 was so severe that Upper Klamath Lake froze solid and kept the Natives from fishing. There was far too little flour to meet the demand for food, and a short supply of blankets added cold to the Natives' miseries. As soon as thaw came, the Indians bolted for their favorite fishing spots and the prospect of their first decent meal in months.[9]

Conditions improved little from that low point. Although the Council Grove Treaty promised a sawmill, hospital, and schools, none of these structures were built. As for the small crop the Indians managed to raise in this land of long winters and early frosts, it was too little to feed all the Native mouths on the reservation.[10]

Once the treaty was signed and the land ceded, the United States government felt little or no further obligation to the dispossessed Natives. To make matters worse, the reservation occupied what had been the Klamaths' land. The surrender of their territory made the shortage of food on the reservation even more galling to the Modocs, who were reduced to killing their beloved horses for food.

The widespread feeling that they had been duped into signing a fool's agreement at Council Grove split the Modocs, radical democrats who expected their leaders to follow the will of the community. They chose sides between Old Schonchin, who remained true to his promise to the treaty, and Kientpoos, who argued that the Americans' failure to deliver on their part of the bargain negated the agreement. Kientpoos and everyone who supported his stand settled in on Lost River and refused the reservation.[11]

Yet the old homeland was changing around the Modocs. Although the Council Grove Treaty had yet to be promulgated and the land legally remained the Modocs', settlers were staking out homesteads as if they

Holy Lands Here and There

already had a right to the Lost River country. Cattle and sheep grazed the grass that had supported the mule deer and antelope Modoc men hunted, and snorting pigs plowed the marshes for the roots and seeds Modoc women once gathered.[12] The Christian agricultural civilization that was the bedrock of America's move west had reached Lost River, begun its transformation into farms and fields, and driven its Native people into a shrinking and hungry corner.

• • •

Kientpoos and the Lost River Modocs were still off the Klamath Reservation when A. B. Meacham succeeded Huntington as Oregon superintendent for the Indian Bureau in May 1869. Although Meacham got the job as payback for serving as a Republican organizer in Ulysses S. Grant's presidential campaign, he did know something of America's Natives.

Meacham's experience dated back to adolescence in Iowa. In the spring of 1845 a band of Sauk Indians under the chieftain Pow-e-shiek was removed from the Iowa River and exiled to the Skunk River, a hundred miles to the west. As for the land the Indians were leaving, "'The white man wanted it,' tells the story," Meacham wrote.[13] His father furnished a team for the removal, and young Alfred served as captain of the oxen.

What Meacham saw on that trip set a pattern for his later professional and political life. Whites, he noticed, dismissed Native Americans as "Injins" yet were more than willing to make money off them. The trip west took longer than it needed to, allowing the white drovers to boost their per diem, and they were compensated for the same number of days on the return trip even though they had no wagons to handle. Greedy Americans were padding the bill.

Although aghast at this corruption, the young Meacham found himself dazzled by Indian ways. Near the journey's end, when the Sauk band on the march neared another band that lived at the destination, "the younger people of both bands had adorned themselves with paint, beads, and feathers, and were each of them doing their utmost to fascinate the other. The scene presented was not only fantastic, but as civilized people would exclaim, 'most gay and gorgeous,' and exhilarating."[14] Meacham depicted Indians as the blushing maidens and shepherd swains that were a mainstay of Romantic poetry.

As settlers poured into the vacated Iowa River valley, the gray woodsmoke of Indian lodges gave way to black clouds belched from foundries and factories, the clear free-flowing river of old was clogged with dams and channeled into canals, and the flowering prairie was plowed under for corn. Meacham saw this change as inevitable and divine: "And now, . . . this lovely valley rings out a chant of praise to God, for his beneficence, instead of the weird song of Pow-e-shiek and his people at their return from crusades against their enemies."[15]

Meacham's sadness in regard to Indians was not that they had lost their world but that they were given no path to enter American life: "[Pow-e-shiek] and his people could not enjoy what other races always have, the privilege of a higher civilization; . . . while our gates are thrown wide open and over them is written in almost every tongue known among nations, 'Come share our country and our government with us,' it was closed behind him and his race, and over those words painted, in characters which he understood, 'Begone!'"[16]

Meacham wanted to turn these "noble savages" into Americans by means of the reservation, to transform red-skinned people into yeoman farmers and professing Christians by training them in civilization's skills and insulating them from its evils—saloon keepers, pimps, and Roman Catholics. Once the transformation occurred, the reservation could disappear and Indians take up their new roles. At a time when many Americans saw extermination as the best approach, this assimilationist strategy appeared humane and progressive.

In his new role as state Indian Affairs superintendent, Meacham toured the Oregon reservations. He eliminated the widespread prostitution of Indian women and illicit whiskey trading and assessed how Indians were faring in their transition to civilization. He decided as well to address the still-unsolved problem of the off-reservation Modocs. He sent a courier to Kientpoos to request a meeting at a neutral point along the Klamath River. The chief refused. If Meacham wanted to see him, Kientpoos stipulated, the superintendent could come to Lost River. Meacham decided to do just that, although he knew the undertaking dangerous. He requested the Fort Klamath commander to dispatch a cavalry detachment and have it wait for further instructions at Linkville, about twenty-five miles from Lost River, just in case. Every man in Meacham's entourage of a dozen or so was equipped with a Colt Navy six-shot revolver and a lever-action Henry repeating rifle, whose 28-rounds-per-minute rate of fire made it the assault rifle of its day. Meacham knew the Modocs would have him outnumbered, so he made sure to have them outgunned.

Heading toward Lost River, Meacham and his party blew past four Modocs sent to tell them to turn back, then rode boldly into the village. The place looked deserted; the people had taken refuge in their winter houses, waiting to see what Meacham had in mind. The Indian superintendent made a bold move. Though a portly man and no athlete, Meacham clambered down the rawhide ladder into the largest lodge under the watching eyes of the fifty armed men inside. There he encountered Kientpoos for the first time. The Indian "looked in my face with a sullen glitter in his eye, that no white man could imitate. He refused to shake hands, to speak, or smoke, and in fact it was evident that I was not only an unwelcome visitor, but was looked upon as an enemy." Coolly, Meacham lit his own pipe and proceeded "to make the best of a bad job."

The white man's boldness prompted an angry outburst from Scarface Charley that broke the ice. A conversation of sorts opened. Toby Riddle, an English-speaking cousin of Kientpoos whom he trusted, translated along with her husband, Frank, an American emigrant from Kentucky. Meacham demanded that the Modocs head to the Klamath Reservation. Kientpoos answered by calling all whites liars and swindlers. With nothing resolved and night falling, the Modocs made a temporary camp nearby for Meacham's entourage and prepared a just-caught fish for their dinner. Worried that treachery might be afoot, Meacham dispatched a courier to Linkville to tell the cavalry detachment to ride south and wait just outside the village.

Those orders forgotten in a blur of saloon whiskey, the troopers galloped into the center of the village well after midnight, sabers rattling over the snap and crack of sagebrush crushed under the horses' hooves. A lifelong teetotaler, Meacham was appalled. The Indians, gathered in council to listen to Curley Headed Doctor's shamanic incantations, scattered every which way. Only then did the yellowlegs encircle the village and capture the hundred and fifty or so women, children, and old people left behind. In what had to be a miracle, no shot was fired and no one, neither Modoc nor American, was harmed.

The next day, Meacham had the captive Modocs prepare to leave for the reservation. And he listened to Princess Mary, Kientpoos's sister, who spoke on the chief's behalf. Mary was a striking young woman who spoke good English and knew American ways well enough to be an effective go-between. Her brother was no coward, Mary persuaded Meacham, and she could induce him to come in once he learned that he would be forgiven and that no harm had befallen the people in his absence. Meacham agreed, and Mary set off for her brother's hideout in the Lava Beds. Kientpoos and the other men appeared a few days later, while Meacham and his party, the now-sober cavalrymen, and the captured Modocs were camped along the Klamath River on their way north. Just before the new year, Meacham conveyed the entire Lost River band onto the Klamath Reservation without a single casualty.

Kientpoos's sadness at the uprooting was terrible. "The white chief brought me here," he said on arriving at the reservation. "I feel ashamed of my people, because they are poor. I feel like a man in a strange country without a father." Yet Kientpoos wanted peace, and he was willing to take responsibility for it as the leader bound to hear and do the will of his community. "We will not throw away the white chief's [Meacham's] words. We will not hide them in the grass. I have planted a strong stake in the ground. I have tied myself with a strong rope. I will not dig up the stake. I will not break the rope. My heart is the heart of my people. I am their words. I am not speaking for myself. I speak their hearts."[17]

Despite Kientpoos's and the Modocs' good intentions, the new dispensation hardly lasted past Meacham's return to his office in Salem. Supplied with too little food and clothing, and both insulted and threatened by O. C. Knapp, a former military officer turned Indian agent, the Modocs as a group voted to abandon the reservation in the spring. Over time, some of them did go back to live under Old Schonchin on the Klamath Reservation near Yainax Butte. Those who accepted Kientpoos as leader stayed in their old haunts around Lost River.

Holy Lands Here and There

The whole bad experience of moving onto the reservation and having to leave it when the promise of a safe and secure life was broken soured the Modocs on Meacham. He himself passed responsibility for the Modoc exit on to Knapp: "I cannot blame the Indians for leaving, under such management."[18] Meacham fired Knapp, replaced him with his own brother, then proposed to the Indian Bureau a new six-square-mile Modoc reservation along Lost River and the northern shore of Tule Lake. Until the bureau made up its mind, Meacham agreed that the Natives could remain unmolested in their old country.[19]

The idea of a Lost River reservation for the Modocs would be a hard sell, Meacham knew: "This proposition will be strenuously opposed by persons who are endeavoring to obtain a large land interest in this part of the State."[20]

Meacham had that much right; returning ceded land to Natives was too much for the Bureau of Indian Affairs to swallow, and his failure with the Modocs made him a marked man. Backroom dealings soon separated him from the Oregon superintendency and passed it on to a man more in tune with the acquisitive spirit of the times: T. B. Odeneal.

Jesse Applegate, one of the earliest American pioneers in Oregon and a member of the group that opened the emigrant route that bore his family name, could not have been more pleased at the change. Meacham kept getting in the way of Applegate's big plan, the fulfillment of his goal in coming to Oregon in the first place. Odeneal looked more likely to do things the way Applegate wanted them done.

6

The Bacon of Three Hundred Hogs

Eastward I go only by force; but westward I go free. . . . I must
walk toward Oregon, and not toward Europe.

—Henry David Thoreau, "Walking"

Jesse Applegate's ambition climaxed a two-generation westward
migration that began with Daniel Applegate, a New Jersey native
who served as a fifer for George Washington's army during the Revolutionary War. By 1788 Daniel had moved west, to Kentucky, where
he married Rachel Lindsay. In 1821 he picked up his family and moved
yet again, to just outside St. Louis, Missouri. There Jesse and his brothers Lindsay and Charles grew up.[1]

Of the three sons, only Jesse received a formal education. He attended
Rock Spring Seminary across the Mississippi in Illinois, distinguished
himself in mathematics and surveying, and came home to teach school
and begin a surveying practice. Working for the state surveyor general
in St. Louis introduced him to the world of law and politics and made
him aware of the lands opening to settlement in Missouri and beyond.
Jesse learned about Oregon through mountain men like Jedediah Smith
and William Sublette of the Rocky Mountain Fur Company, whose
accounts he handled and with whom he sampled St. Louis's night life.

In time, Jesse tired of city living, perhaps because he missed a promotion. In 1832 he moved his family, along with his two brothers and
their mates and broods, to St. Clair County, in Missouri's Osage Valley. For Americans this was new country; the Native people, who gave
their name to the valley, had been moved off by treaty. The Applegate
brothers set to farming in this newly acquired region, and soon succeeded. An acquaintance estimated that Jesse came to be worth $10,000
in his time in the Osage, more than $300,000 in today's dollars.

A serpent, however, had penetrated the Applegates' Eden. Jesse and his brothers were anti-slavery Whigs in a staunchly Democratic and pro-slavery county. With free labor not to be found, the Applegates were reduced to renting slaves to work their farms, an experience that ran against their abolitionist grain. It hardly helped that the economy crashed in a depression that began in 1839 and lasted into 1843. In 1842 Jesse wrote to a friend that "twelve months ago I labored to advance—now I struggle harder to retain my position."[2]

By the next year Jesse had caught Oregon fever through correspondence with a friend living there and loving the new territory. Soon Jesse infected Charles and Lindsay, and the clan resolved to move their sizable households west yet again. In Jesse's case, this meant packing his wife, six children, and all their domestic goods, including the family Bible and a complete Shakespeare, into four wagons. Livestock came too, some one hundred head of cattle, horses, and oxen. Unable to find a buyer for his farm, Applegate simply walked away from the place he had built from the Indian-cleansed wilderness. Feed filled the abandoned barns, and from their rafters hung the newly cured bacon of three hundred hogs.[3] So great was the lure of greater riches to the west that a man like Jesse Applegate might leave behind such abundance and think himself moving up in the world.

• • •

Crossing the western wilds in 1843 remained a work in uncertain progress. The wagon train the Applegates joined was, at some one thousand people, the largest to attempt the route. Wagons, each drawn by a six-oxen team, totaled approximately 120, and the cattle and horses numbered in the thousands. The loose livestock hampered progress and became a source of contention among the emigrants. At the Blue River in northwest Missouri, the train divided. Families with only a few animals formed a lighter, faster-moving caravan, while those with substantial herds banded together to move their animals westward. Jesse Applegate took on a leadership role in this group, which called itself the cow column.[4]

Two thousand miles lay between the migration's beginning point in Independence, Missouri, and its destination in the Willamette Valley of Oregon. The route, charted by mountain men and one advance company of Protestant missionaries, angled across northeast Kansas and southeast Nebraska till it met the Platte River valley, with its water, rich pasture, and ready firewood. Following the Platte all the way into Wyoming, the people, wagons, and livestock crossed the Continental Divide. Beyond the upper reaches of the Green River they entered into modern Idaho to make for Fort Hall and then the Snake River. That watercourse led to Fort Boise and on into Oregon through the Blue Mountains toward the mighty Columbia River. It was here, near the conclusion of this grueling journey, that Jesse Applegate faced his greatest crisis.

Since no wagon road led around the slopes of Mount Hood, emigrants had to unload and float their goods and themselves down the Columbia in boats they built on the spot. The livestock and emptied wagons were left behind in the care of the Hudson's Bay Company at Fort Walla Walla, to be retrieved the following summer. Above The Dalles, named by French Canadian trappers for its rapids, the great river turned turbulent. Separating temporarily from brother Charles, Lindsay and Jesse divided their families into two boats: the two brothers, their wives, and most of their children, including two infants, in one; Lindsay's sons Warren and Elisha and Jesse's son Edward, along with an old man and two younger fellows, in the second. Lindsay and Jesse hired an Indian pilot to guide them through and added him to their boat.

Things went very wrong in the first rapid. The second boat failed to follow the piloted boat on the safest line through the roil and was pulled across the river by a strong current. Near the far shore a whirlpool seized the homemade vessel and sucked it under, dumping the occupants. The boat popped free of the vortex, and all the men and boys except Warren climbed back aboard. The current pushed the unsteered boat into a second, more violent whirlpool, which swallowed it. Elisha Applegate, who had disobeyed his mother and learned to swim back in Missouri, leapt free and stroked across the current to an island, where the two younger men joined him. The old man tried to rescue nonswimmer Edward, but the river swept the pair past the island and under the cliffs along the shore. There they disappeared.

Lindsay and Jesse Applegate, frantic with grief and fear, attempted to dive from their boat and swim to their sons, but their wives held them back, pleading that everyone would be lost to empty heroism. The men returned to the oars just in time to avoid colliding with a midstream boulder. Enduring the anguish of not knowing the ultimate fate of their children, they were swept along the rocky shoreline. As soon as the two Applegates landed on the first beach, Lindsay pulled out his rifle and stomped ashore, vowing vengeance on the Indian pilot. The Native had already disappeared.

The bodies of Warren and Elisha Applegate and the brave old man were never recovered. The boat itself was lost, as well as most of the gear. Some broken furniture, bedding, and clothing washed ashore, where local Indians scavenged what they could. The emigrants pushed on with their children unburied and their diminished possessions picked over.[5]

That loss, blamed on the mean-hearted Columbia and Native perfidy, marked both Lindsay and Jesse Applegate. It was one of the reasons why, three years later, they opened the South Emigrant Road from Fort Hall to the Willamette Valley. Even the Black Rock Desert was preferable to the Columbia's chamber of child-drowning horrors.

• • •

Settled in Oregon, Jesse Applegate attended to the pressing business of this emerging American outpost and his own fortunes within it. He played a leadership role in Oregon's Provisional Government legislature, where he had a hand in developing what became the state constitution. When Cayuse Indians rebelled during a smallpox epidemic and wiped out the Whitman mission in the eastern Oregon Territory, Applegate became one of three loan commissioners who helped fund the campaign to punish the Indians and rescue American hostages.

Three years after opening the South Emigrant Road, a still-restless Applegate sold his Willamette Valley farm and moved to the Umpqua Valley, in the shadow of a mountain he dubbed Yoncalla. Brothers Lindsay and Charles soon followed suit. There Jesse invested his expanding fortune into building one of Oregon's grandest houses. It boasted two stories, with nine rooms on the first floor and a parlor, complete with melodeon, and a library on the second. As suited a man with intellectual interests ranging from ancient history to astronomy, the library contained several thousand volumes shipped around the Horn from Harper's in New York City. Although he had left the center of Oregon politics, Applegate stayed up-to-date. He subscribed to the Oregon newspapers, the *San Francisco Bulletin*, the *New York Tribune*, and the *Congressional Record*.[6]

Slavery had driven Applegate from Missouri with his farm unsold and the bacon of three hundred hogs still hanging, and it remained the political issue on which he was the most uncompromising. When Oregon became a state in 1859, he opposed a constitutional provision that denied the vote to free blacks. And he was reputed to have had a hand in preventing Oregon from supporting the Confederacy. Shortly after the Civil War began, Oregon senator Joseph Lane hoped to foment a rebellion that would carry off the whole West Coast as a slaveholding "Pacific Republic." He was allegedly transporting rifles and ammunition to fellow conspirators when a road accident stopped him near Yoncalla. Applegate visited Lane while he was recovering and talked him out of his scheme.

Still, secessionist feelings ran strong in Oregon, largely through the workings of a militant pro-slavery group known as the Knights of the Golden Circle. When Applegate's daughter Gertrude eloped with Golden Circle member Jimmy Fay, Jesse sliced his daughter's name out of the family Bible. Even after the war was over and Gertrude came home to die of tuberculosis, her father never restored her name to the Good Book.[7]

Meanwhile, Applegate's fortunes were slipping. In 1860 he set his worth at $15,000 in real estate and $10,000 in personal property. Ten years later he was down to $4,000 in real property and a mere $952 in personal. By contrast, his brother and neighbor Charles, who faced the same weather and market conditions, claimed assets of $20,000 in real estate and $6,955 in personal property that year, more than five times Jesse's net worth. Jesse had signed over some assets to his children and one grandchild, but even when those transfers are accounted for, his wealth came to a fraction of what it had been in 1860.

Jesse had made the mistake of lending money to Samuel E. May, who won election as Oregon secretary of state in a campaign funded by $60,000 in personal bonds.[8] Accused of embezzling money in office, May won acquittal, but his bondsmen, including Applegate, had to forfeit their funds. Applegate lost what little property he had left, and the legal battle with a fellow bondholder threatened his children's title to the land he had passed on to them.[9] To make matters worse, Applegate was in debt for $25,000 to Lower Klamath Lake rancher Presley Dorris.

Brought down in the world and desperate to recover his wealth, Jesse went back to earning a living as a surveyor. In the course of that work, he met a wealthy California rancher with ambitions for a cattle empire in the Modoc country, a man who shared Applegate's Christian name: Jesse D. Carr.

• • •

On the face of it, the two Jesses were unlikely business partners. Applegate was anti-slavery, first a Whig then a Republican. Carr hailed from Tennessee, opposed the Emancipation Proclamation, and devoted himself to Democratic politics his whole life long, mostly behind the scenes. Applegate saw public service as service, and he was contemptuous of politicians who gorged at the public till, a skill at which Carr excelled.

Applegate was so self-conscious of his appearance that never in his life did he allow a photograph of himself to be taken. Only sketches have survived. One shows a man with an oddly small head, a hooked nose, big ears with long lobes, a clean-shaven face under beetling brows, and close-cropped wiry gray hair. All this was set atop a long, loose-limbed body of the sort Walt Disney's animators gave Ichabod Crane. However you slice it, Applegate was no looker.[10] Carr, though short and increasingly rotund as the years mounted, was modestly nice-looking behind his trimmed beard. He suffered, however, from a congenital palate defect that weakened his voice, hampered public speaking, and relegated him to backroom roles in business and politics.[11]

Most important, the two Jesses shared the desire to make a financial killing. Applegate was so stung by his fall in fortune that, in a letter to a friend, he wrote, "I feel myself fast sinking in the direction of the Digger [Indian]. It is true I do not run naked and eat snails, but I dig pretty constantly to escape that necessity."[12] As for Carr, he had known the bitter taste of ruin as a sutler during the Mexican War, an episode, he told a newspaper reporter, that "left me more flat broke than I ever was before. . . . I swore I would never be broke again, and I never will."[13] Carr had built up his fortune by lending money, then making himself so scarce that repayment was difficult and interest mounted. He also speculated in real estate, sometimes with the help of surveyors he bribed to adjust boundary lines in his favor.[14]

The vehicle for rescuing Applegate from ruin and ensuring Carr against destitution was an enormous ranch in the Modoc uplands. The two Jesses planned to gain control of some 150,000 acres that stretched from the northern and eastern shores of Tule Lake, including the lower reaches of Lost River, across the hills to the eastern side of Clear Lake, its Willow Creek tributary, and the Lost River outfall. Not that Carr, who was putting up the money for the plan, intended to buy all this massive acreage outright. Rather, he planned to lay claim to every seep, swamp, creek, and puddle under the federal Swamp and Overflow Act of 1850, fence these precious water sources, and effectively control a much larger area than he actually had title to. "Land is no good without water," Carr later told a newspaper reporter. "That's perfectly simple, isn't it?"[15]

Carr needed a surveyor to help lay the claims—fraudulent if need be—and a ranch manager to keep the growing spread humming while he himself ran the tens of thousands of acres he owned near Salinas, California. Applegate fit the bill as both surveyor and manager. Eager to distance himself from his legal and financial troubles in Oregon, Applegate moved over the state line with his wife, Cynthia, and various family members and settled into the ranch headquarters on the northeastern shore of Clear Lake. Although Carr owned the spread through his Jesse D. Carr Livestock Company, locals often called it the Applegate ranch. It was a fine place, one that reflected the two men's ambitions: two stories of well-caulked hewn logs, a clapboard roof, and stable, shop, and strong corral nearby.[16]

Applegate and Carr's grand plan faced two major obstacles. One was settlers flooding into the Tule Lake Basin and Lost River. Then there were the Lost River Modocs who had walked off the Klamath Reservation. Both settlers and Indians had to go. Jesse Applegate looked to pit the one against the other and get rid of them all.

• • •

Adopting the persona of wise elder statesman, Applegate took up the pen in the settlers' cause. He wrote a long letter to old Oregon friend A. B. Meacham, then the state's superintendent for Indian Affairs.

Applegate told Meacham that both settlers and Indians in the Lost River country were in "a high state of excitement. . . . As the indians are very saucy and in some instances menacing, and the widely scattered settlers . . . are at the mercy of the marauders[,] a state of terrorism exists among them hard to realize except by those exposed to a like danger." Since petitions to both the U.S. Army and the Bureau of Indian Affairs had been ignored, plans were afoot among the settlers to raise a Ben Wright–style militia against the Modocs. Applegate knew that Meacham had proposed a small Lost River reserve for the Modocs, an idea the Natives liked. He cautioned Meacham against it. "Such an arrangement will not generally satisfy the whites," he wrote, because "most of them require absolutely the removal of the Indians from the country or their strict confinement in strict limits, which could not be done upon a small reserve in the heart of the settlements." To make matters worse, the reservation would soon become "the resort and refuge of every vicious and Vagabond Indian in the country and soon become a greater nuisance to the settlements than even the present unauthorized maraudings of the modocs."[17]

Meacham punted Applegate's letter to the army's Department of the Columbia in Portland, which in turn sent it back to Fort Klamath. The fort was then under the command of Captain James Jackson, the very officer who would lead the Lost River raid less than a year and a half later. Applegate's claims of military inaction rubbed Jackson the wrong way. "The charge of Mr. Jesse Applegate that the 'petition' of settlers of Langell Valley, 'for protection' had been 'wholly disregarded by the military' is *untrue*," he informed his superiors. "No such petition has been made." Applegate's claim that the settlers were about to take military matters into their civilian hands was equally false: "No proposition has ever been made to raise a force of settlers for his [Kient-poos's] suppression."[18]

Undaunted, Applegate kept up the pressure. In early January 1872 three settlers appeared at Fort Klamath to give depositions to an infantry lieutenant on crimes attributed to the Lost River Modocs. They were accused of knocking down fences and making off with hay, stealing household utensils and halters, demanding money, and threatening lives. The young officer duly noted the claims and passed them on to his commander, who then forwarded the information to Brigadier General Edward R. S. Canby, the commander of the army's District of the Columbia.[19]

Soon thereafter, sixty-five settlers signed a petition to Governor Grover written with the free-form spelling and random punctuation of men whose literacy was limited: "Immediately have a band of Renegade and Lawless Modock Indians Removed from Our Settlements, and confind on the Reservation. . . . They are Extreamley saucey, and Menacing in theire repeated threats against the settlers, and their Stock, They set up a Claim to our Homes, They freaquently Draw Pistoles, and guns, on inoffensive Citizens."[20]

At the same time, Applegate composed another letter to Meacham. "I am as you know much in favor of treating Indians with forbearance and humanity," he claimed. The Modocs, though, were a rough bunch, "not of the quiet, orderly description that the majority of Oregon Indians are." Escaping the reservation had emboldened the Lost River band to believe that the Bureau of Indian Affairs and the army were weak. "Their arrogance and impudence have been ever greater," Applegate asserted. "This state of things, discourages new settlers and keeps those in the country in a feverish state of uneasiness and alarm, and instead of their increased numbers driving the Indians into better behaviour, the numbers of the Indians are being constantly recruited by the bad and discontented fleeing to them from the neighboring Reservations, and they being concentrated in a body, they actually hold the settlements on Lost and Link Rivers at their mercy, and being perfectly aware of this fact, they use it to their own advantage."

Removing the Modocs from Lost River would work not only to the benefit of white settlers but also to the greater good of the Natives. "If the humanitarians who now control Indian Affairs have no regard for the lives of white men, women and children, there are reasons for the removal of these Indians to their Reservations which may be in accordance with their tender sympathy for the welfare of the Indians themselves," Applegate wrote. "Poets and moralists agree that the 'untutored savage' is also a 'wild man' and like other wild animals they chafe and fret under any kind of restraint, they will prefer the liberty and license of the 'City of Refuge' to even the wild restraints of a pious life on the Reservation." With an eye to saving the souls of the "poor Indians," he concluded that "they had better be removed out of harm's way and the City of Refuge on Modoc [Tule] Lake broken up."[21]

A few days before Applegate's letter dropped onto Meacham's desk, there came a new petition from forty-three settlers demanding the removal of the Modocs from Lost River. Like the earlier petition to Governor Grover, this document complained of years of annoyance from Modocs who refused to abide by the Council Grove Treaty. The question was clear: "Shall a petty Indian chief with 20 desperadoes and a squallid band of three hundred miserable savages any longer set at defiance the strong arm of the government[,] driving out citizens from their homes, threatening their lives and destroying their property."[22]

Where the petition to Grover qualified as but vaguely literate, this new document was polished and articulate. One suspects that a well-educated Applegate had a hand in it. And the petition, as well as Jesse's letter, had the desired effect. Meacham dropped the Lost River reservation idea and agreed to the forced removal of the Modocs.

There matters stood when Meacham discovered he was out of a job.[23] It fell to T. B. Odeneal, the new Oregon Indian Affairs superintendent, to make the next move.

• • •

Odeneal had Elmer Otis, then commander of the army's District of the Lakes, write a recommendation that the Modocs' permission to remain at Lost River be canceled and the Indians moved back to the Klamath Reservation. F. A. Walker, the commissioner of Indian Affairs, agreed with Odeneal: "You are instructed to have the Modoc Indians removed . . . to the reservation."

Finding it "impracticable . . . to go in person to the Klamath country" to give Kientpoos the news, Odeneal dispatched Ivan and Oliver Applegate, Jesse's nephews, and new Klamath Reservation Indian agent Leroy Dyar to Lost River. Kientpoos refused to leave. His reasoning was simple: reservation Indians were cold and hungry. The chief wanted nothing of the sort for his people.[24]

Odeneal informed Commissioner Walker that the Modocs had turned down the opportunity to leave Lost River voluntarily. He wanted to jail Kientpoos and the other Lost River leaders and force the rest of the Modocs onto the reservation. Autumn, when the Modocs returned to their winter villages, was the time to make the move.[25] Walker gave Odeneal permission: "Your recommendations . . . are approved, and you are directed to remove them to the Klamath reservation, peaceably if you possibly can, but forcibly if you must."[26]

• • •

As autumn approached, the new Fort Klamath commander, Major John Green, began reconnaissance of the Lost River country. The army felt much less urgency about the Modoc issue than did the settlers. Still, the ever-prudent General Canby ordered Green to have a look around.

Green left the fort on September 9 and camped on Lost River opposite Kientpoos's village at noon five days later. The patrol's presence agitated the Indians even though Green sent his interpreter ahead to say he meant no harm. An English-speaking Indian acting as a go-between asked the major whether he wanted to meet with the chief. Green said he was carrying no message, but he would receive Kientpoos if the chief wished to talk. Kientpoos did not appear, however. Green learned later that Kientpoos's mother was dying and the chief was attending to the rituals of her passing.

Green's purpose was to determine just how much trouble these Indians were causing. "I inquired of the people living in that country what the conduct of these Indians had been, some told me they were the best Indians they ever saw and others that they were the worst, but none could point out any especial depredations," he wrote in his official report.

This pattern continued when the major led his men along Tule Lake and over to Clear Lake and the cattle ranch Jesse Carr was building with Jesse Applegate. Green reported that "I learned from Mr. Jesse Applegate that the Modocs were a bad set of people, robbing them, but he could not point to any particular robbery they had committed."[27]

Despite Green's negative report on the settlers' inflated claims, Applegate knew that it was only a matter of time, that in the end he held the stronger hand. Odeneal had committed to moving the Modocs off Lost River. His nephews, Oliver and Ivan, worked on the Klamath Reservation, where they could report what was happening and shape events as needed. All Applegate had to do was let matters take their violent course and focus on the wealth headed his and Jesse Carr's way. When he received word of the Lost River gunfight, a vision of all that wealth in the offing must have danced in Jesse's knobby, close-cropped head.

7

Gray-Eyed Rancher to the Rescue

John Fairchild came to Northern California over twenty years
ago.... When he undertook to make this [ranch] a business he
arranged with the Modocs to do it to their satisfaction, and by a
regular trade purchased the privilege of them.... He understands
human nature as well, even the Indian aspects of it, and soon got to
be on reliable terms with them. He carried out all his agreements
faithfully, and they did as well by him.

—"Description of Modoc Land," *New York Times*, June 16, 1873

John Fairchild reacted differently than did Jesse Applegate to the
news of the raid on the Modocs. He rode from his ranch west
of Lower Klamath Lake to see for himself what had happened at Lost
River. The charred frames of the Modocs' winter houses and a litter
of spent cartridges and broken weapons told him that it had been as
bad as he feared. Then, while he rode back to his spread, the rancher
focused on the problem at hand: how best to protect Indians who
worked and lived on his land.

The Modocs who fled into the Lava Beds after the Lost River raid
were not the only members of their nation. About half the people who
called themselves Modoc were living at Yainax on the Klamath Reservation, under the leadership of aged chief Old Schonchin. Most of the
rest were with Kientpoos at Lost River, then in the Lava Beds. Another
community, the Hot Creeks, numbering fourteen men of working and
fighting age plus their families, for a total of around forty people, was
living along the small watercourse of that name on the range where
Fairchild and his neighbor Presley Dorris ranched. Hot Creek men
worked as cowhands on those ranches and other spreads in the vicinity,

and some of the women, like Miss Joe, a cousin of Kientpoos, worked in Fairchild's house. The Hot Creeks were assimilating into American society through employment with Fairchild. Many of them, both women and men, had learned at least serviceable English, for example.[1]

Nothing in Fairchild's background showed him to be a bleeding-heart humanitarian or nascent Indian-rights activist. Rather, he was a quick-witted rancher with a good head for business and an endless love of fine horses. Fairchild saw in the Modocs a people who knew every nuance and detail of this landscape with its demanding climate, unique topography, and roving grizzlies and wolves. Understanding that the Natives possessed aeons of knowledge and skills rooted in this country, Fairchild hired the Hot Creeks to work for him, to lend him their expertise in return for protection and sustenance. The bargain worked.

· · ·

The Mississippi into which Fairchild had been born in early 1828 was a rough and violent frontier where white overseers lashed black slaves working cotton fields cut out of deep forests teeming with bears and rattlers.[2] Mississippi still had its complement of Indians, though not for long. Andrew Jackson was elected president in the year of Fairchild's birth, and his administration soon pushed through the Indian Removal Act of 1830, which forced all Indigenous nations east of the Mississippi River into what is now Oklahoma. Mississippi's Choctaws were the first to be shipped out, the vanguard for what came to be known as the Trail of Tears. The Choctaws' route took them right through the small town of Raymond, west of Jackson on the road to Vicksburg, where Fairchild's family lived. Alexis de Tocqueville, the French commentator on the early days of American democracy, found the scene of the Indians' forced passage wrenching. "It was then the heart of winter, and the cold that year was unusually bitter. The snow on the ground had frozen, and enormous chunks of ice floated on the river. The Indians traveled in families. Among them were the wounded and the sick, newborn infants, and dying elders. They had neither tents nor wagons, broken, exiled, only scant provisions and some weapons," he reported. "Not a sob or a cry was to be heard despite the large number of people; all were silent."[3]

Still a boy when his commercial-merchant father died, Fairchild completed only a few grades of school. As a teenager he took over management of an uncle's cotton plantation with its army of enslaved African field hands. No doubt Fairchild learned many of his managerial and agricultural skills on the plantation, yet something in this southern, slaveholding life galled him enough to move on.

Fairchild escaped in the spring of 1849, the first traveling season after the discovery of gold in California. Now twenty-one, the handsome young man with piercing gray eyes traveled to Fort Gibson in Indian Territory, close to the modern town of Muskogee, Oklahoma, looking to find a way west. He threw in with a group of Arkansans and Cherokees heading to the gold fields under the leadership of J. N. A. Carter.[4] Like most of the Arkansas-based emigrants of that first gold rush year, Carter's company took the southernmost route through a West still largely unknown to English speakers. After traversing Oklahoma, the travelers struck out across the Texas Panhandle, home country of the dreaded Comanches, for Santa Fe, New Mexico. Following the Rio Grande downstream, they left the river at what is now Garfield, crossed the Animas Mountains into the New Mexico Bootheel, and climbed Guadalupe Pass over the border into Mexico. In the next stretch the emigrants traversed a ferocious desert of unrelenting sun and no water littered with desiccated ox carcasses and human corpses. After the surviving men and animals made their dry, hot way to Tucson, they headed west to the friendly Pima Indian villages on the Gila River and followed that watercourse to the Colorado. Yuma Indians helped swim the travelers and their wagons and animals across into California and its promised wealth.[5]

Fairchild first hunted for gold in the Sierra Nevada foothills, then moved north to the Salmon River, at the foot of the Marble Mountains, close to the Oregon border. During the unusually severe winter of 1851–52, Fairchild discovered there were more ways to make money in a gold rush than panning an icy stream. With the miners snowbound and provisions exhausted, a duck fetched $5 and a deer $100—roughly $150 and $3,100 in contemporary money. Renowned as a sharpshooter, Fairchild bankrolled himself by hunting game through that starvation season. When the snows melted, he moved on to buying hogs and cattle along the Rogue River in southern Oregon and driving the animals to the northern California mining settlements to slaughter, butcher, and market.

Next Fairchild partnered with Cy and John Doten to drive cattle into the extensive grasslands of Butte Valley, north and east of Mount Shasta. There was one drawback to this beckoning rangeland: the Modocs. Instead of picking a fight with the Indians, Fairchild paid them in cattle, horses, and provisions for the privilege of running cattle unmolested. Presley Dorris, his ranching neighbor, followed Fairchild's example, ensuring free run for his stock and extra Native hands for the unending work on the range.

After Fairchild's partnership with the Dotens dissolved in litigation, he settled on Cottonwood Creek and erected ranch buildings—hewn-log house, barn and large sheds, as well as orchard and vineyard—near where the stream emerged from the bedrock of Mahogany Mountain. Married now and with children coming in quick order, he bought 2,560 acres from the government and under California's Swamp Land Act laid claim to another 10,000 acres along Lower Klamath Lake, where he cut hay. That rich grass Fairchild fed to his herd of 500 to 600 horses and some 3,500 to 5,000 cattle, most of the latter half-wild range stock left over from the days when California was part of Mexico. Fairchild's passion was horse breeding. He ran several fine stallions with his herds, and he owned an enormous jackass for which he paid $2,000, more than $35,000 in today's money, a great deal of money even for a big burro. The giant mules the jackass sired brought prices as big as they were.[6]

All the while, the Hot Creek Modocs were working for Fairchild and sometimes Dorris. Americans had no interest in learning the strange and challenging sounds of the Plateau Penutian tongue the Indians spoke and calling the Modocs by their rightful names. Instead, they dubbed the Indians with anglicized nicknames that, like the classical Roman and Greek names attached to African slaves, also served to keep the Natives in their racial place. Some may have been corruptions of Modoc names, while others voiced individual characteristics Americans found memorable. Shacknasty Jim could be a reference to that Modoc's mother's sloppy housekeeping or a twisting of *ski-et-tete-ko*, meaning left-handed. *Slat-us-loks* became Steamboat Frank, allegedly the son of a fat mother who huffed and puffed like a Mark Twain riverboat.[7] Ellen's Man, a moon-faced young fellow, was named after his older wife. Bogus Charley got his moniker from living on Bogus Creek, and Boston Charley for being light-skinned and fluent in English, which Indians often called Boston after the Yankee ships that plied the Northwest Coast at the height of the fur trade.

Fairchild worked daily with Modocs, respected their skills, and trusted them, yet he was a lifelong pro-slavery Democrat and so outspoken a supporter of the Confederacy that a warrant was sworn out for his arrest during the Civil War. A cousin in the Union military in San Francisco blocked the warrant and warned Fairchild. Thereafter, the gray-eyed rancher became more circumspect about broadcasting his sympathies. Still, he named his favorite riding stallion Joe Lane, after Oregon's first governor and later senator, the North Carolina–born Democratic politician who hoped to build a mini-Confederacy on the Pacific Coast until Jesse Applegate allegedly talked him out of the idea. Yet, given his good relations with the Modocs, Fairchild was no simple white supremacist. Rather, he was something of a libertarian, a man who believed in live-and-let-live and put loyalty to friends at the center of his ethics.[8]

On that December day when he rode back from the burned Lost River villages to his ranch and the nearby huts of the Hot Creeks, Fairchild was forty-four years old, lean and suntanned, a striking man with a prematurely gray, squared-off beard and blazing gray eyes. Behind those bright eyes his brain was turning. The Klamath country teemed with blue-coated cavalrymen uncertain who their enemy was, armed settlers frightened by the prospect of a general Native uprising, and weapons-brandishing, whiskey-fueled vigilantes ready to end the Indian problem by ending every Indian. Fairchild made up his mind to protect the Hot Creeks.

His ranch was caught between proverbial rock and hard place. The hard place lay to the north, among Oregon's trigger-happy settlers. The rock loomed to the south, in the Lava Beds with Kientpoos's Modocs. Only a half day's ride away, the Modocs could, if they wished, raid Fairchild's ranch and the neighboring Dorris spread. Or they might slip in among the Hot Creeks at night and persuade them to throw in with the resistance.

The Hot Creeks made it clear to Fairchild that they had no interest in joining forces with their Lava Beds cousins. Although Hooker Jim, who had led the revenge raid along Tule Lake, was a Hot Creek, he had moved into the Lost River band when he took Curley Headed Doctor's daughter as his second wife. Despite that connection, the Modocs on the Fairchild and Dorris ranches saw the coming Lava Beds fight as somebody else's business. The most assimilated of all the Modocs agreed among themselves that their best strategy lay in taking themselves to Yainax on the Klamath Reservation.

The headman of the Hot Creek band was Old Sheepy, now well over eighty years of age and too frail to travel the dozens of rough miles from Fairchild's to Yainax. The Modocs and Fairchild decided it best if Old Sheepy remained behind, under the rancher's protection, with several Modoc women staying back to take care of him. Leadership of the band passed to Shacknasty Jim, a young man with proven skills and a pregnant wife.

Fairchild alerted Leroy S. Dyar, head agent at the Klamath Reservation, and Captain James Jackson of Fort Klamath that he and the forty-some Hot Creek Modocs were heading north.[9] Neighboring ranchers Presley Dorris, Samuel Colver, Nate Beswick, and N. B. Ball agreed to ride along. All of them came well armed.

•••

Meanwhile, the good citizens of Linkville were bellying up to the muddy village's one bar and telling tall tales of murders, atrocities, brutalities, and tortures attributed to the Modocs. When they received the news that more than three dozen Indians accompanied by a handful of despised, Modoc-loving California ranchers were heading toward the reservation, eight or ten would-be vigilantes saddled up and rode south. The settlers resolved to waylay the refugee Natives and their escorts at Whittle's Ferry on the Klamath River and grab as many Modocs as possible for a Linkville lynching. To them, a Modoc was a Modoc. It mattered not a whit that the fourteen Hot Creek men had nothing to do with the Lost River fight or the Tule Lake settler killings.

Two other Linkville residents, Harris and Howard, overheard the whiskey-primed talk of their friends and neighbors and raced ahead to warn Fairchild and Dorris. Their weapons held close and ready, the two ranchers confronted the would-be lynchers at the ferry. By this time the dropping alcohol level in the Linkville men's blood and the falling thermometer were cooling their murderous ardor. It hardly hurt that crack shot Fairchild was brandishing a rapid-fire Henry rifle and that Dorris was a tough, no-nonsense Mexican War veteran. Soon the two California ranchers talked the Oregon men into going home.

One thing Dorris and Fairchild did not figure on was Fritz Muntz, a German immigrant and Linkville vigilante who wanted revenge for the Modocs' killing of countryman Wendolin Nus during the Lost River raid. As the two ranchers talked sense into the other would-be lynchers, Muntz circulated among the Modocs and let them know what exquisite tortures the mob up in Linkville was preparing. The Hot Creeks understood what he was saying; many of them spoke English better than Muntz did. They understood Dyar, the Klamath Reservation Indian agent, as well. He announced that a necktie party was indeed waiting in Linkville and that the wisest course was to wait at the ferry until midnight then make a quick dash to the reservation. At that foreboding news, panic moved through the Indians in a tide.

Fairchild and Dorris tried to convince their Modoc hands and families that the whole party could indeed sneak past Linkville without a fight. The Hot Creeks remained unpersuaded. While the Californians and Dyar went off to confer in Bob Whittle's riverside cabin, the Indians slipped away into sagebrush and rocks, taking every loose horse they could round up. A few of the men and most of the women and children returned to Fairchild's. The rest of the men took off for the Lava Beds, to join Kientpoos and their Lost River relations. Over the next few days most of the Hot Creek Modocs abandoned the ranch that had been their home and made for the Lava Beds.[10]

• • •

In their zeal to eliminate the Modoc threat, the Linkville settlers boosted its strength. Modoc fighting men in the Lava Beds had numbered no more than thirty-five to forty. The fourteen Hot Creeks who sought

Holy Lands Here and There

refuge with them swelled that number of fighters to some fifty or fifty-five. And the Hot Creek leaders who joined Kientpoos would, with their knowledge of American ways and fluent English, come to figure prominently in this drama. Had Shacknasty Jim, Steamboat Frank, Bogus Charley, and Ellen's Man made it to the Klamath Reservation and not the Lava Beds, the Modoc War would have played out differently.

Now it was only a matter of time before Fairchild, the rancher, and Shacknasty Jim, the ranch hand, faced off in battle. It was not an outcome they chose, but a situation into which they were driven by forces outside their ken and control. The gathering momentum of this Indian war that never had to happen was following its own tragic trajectory.

PART 2

True Fog, Real War

In America, the aboriginal barbarous tribes cannot be forced to change their habits, or even persuaded to successful emigration: they are melting away from year to year. . . . It is as clear as the sun at noon-day, that in a few generations more the last of these Red men will be numbered with the dead.

—Josiah C. Nott and George R. Gliddon, *Types of Mankind*

8

Glove and Fist

We do not contest the ever-ready argument that civilization must
not be arrested in its progress by a handful of savages. . . . [T]he
Indian must not stand in the way. . . . We would only be understood
as doubting the purity and genuineness of that civilization which
reaches its ends by falsehood and violence, and dispenses blessings
that spring from violated rights.

—Report to the President by the Indian Peace Commission,
January 7, 1868

Like John Fairchild and Shacknasty Jim, Edward Richard Sprigg
Canby found himself trapped in a series of unfortunate events.
The commanding general of the army's Department of the Columbia
was cautious and careful, someone who liked to know in detail, before
he took action, whom and what he was up against. Canby had long
seen the Modocs as a simmering problem. Still, he wanted to address
the issue only when the army could field enough soldiers to force the
Lost River Indians onto the reservation, ideally without a fight.

Back in September, Canby had laid the groundwork for this plan
with a heads-up to Lieutenant Colonel Frank Wheaton, newly installed
commander of the army's District of the Lakes, at his Fort Warner
headquarters about one hundred miles east of Fort Klamath. The alert
told Wheaton that Oregon Indian Bureau superintendent T. B. Odeneal was likely to want the Lost River Modocs removed in November.
Although Canby did "not consider it probable that the Modocs would
offer any resistance, or that the force at Fort Klamath will be insufficient to control them, it is possible that they may resist and require a
greater exhibition of force, than can be furnished from that post." In

case the Modocs fought back, Canby placed the forces at Fort Klamath under Wheaton's temporary control.[1]

Wheaton let Canby know that he had instructed Major Green at Fort Klamath to let him know promptly of any change in the Modocs' attitude. Wheaton himself was prepared to move on Lost River with every mounted soldier at his disposal and "compel Captain Jack's [Kientpoos's] immediate compliance."[2]

Wheaton's attitude had lost none of its optimism in a follow-up letter to Odeneal: "I trust there will be no serious difficulty in inducing these Indians to make the desired move, but if there should be, you may rely on my full and hearty co-operation."[3] That letter was dispatched on the very day that Captain James Jackson raided Lost River. Two days later, a still-clueless Wheaton sent an order to Major Green at Fort Klamath to bring the Modocs in once reinforcements arrived and boosted Green's manpower.[4] Wheaton had no idea that what he was preparing for had already happened, and that it had come off badly.

Through no fault of his own was Wheaton behind the curve. No telegraph ran between Fort Klamath and Fort Warner. The terminal closest to Fort Klamath sat in Jacksonville, Oregon, more than eighty miles to the west. Green could have alerted Wheaton by courier, but he neglected to take that measure when he ordered his men out against the Modocs. Since Wheaton had no idea what was about to occur, he was unable to alert Canby. The general himself found out a full four days after the fact, on December 3, by means of letter from Governor LaFayette Grover. Invoking an I-know-something-you-don't tone, the governor informed the general that "a serious outbreak of the Modoc Indians had occurred in the Lake Basin in southern Oregon, and that the settlers about Tule Lake had been slaughtered." The governor had dispatched Brigadier General James T. Glen of the Oregon militia to assess the situation, report back, and raise volunteer forces. He was hoping, too, that the army would help out.[5]

Canby wrote right back to assure Grover that things could not be as bad as the governor made them out to be. After all, he himself had placed all the forces at Fort Klamath and Forts Bidwell and Harney—a total of four companies of cavalry plus three of infantry—under Wheaton's command to ensure that the Modocs would move.

"I have received no reports from the commanding officer in the Klamath Country in relation to these hostilities," Canby wrote, "and in the absence of such reports there is reason to hope that the difficulties are not so serious as now reported, and that there has been no loss of life among the settlers on that frontier." Politely—Canby was rarely other than polite—the general was telling the governor to tone it down. Yet, just in case, he was moving two companies of infantry from the mouth of the Columbia River to the Tule Lake region.[6]

When Canby finally did hear from Major John Green the next day, he surely felt egg dripping from his clean-shaven face. Green was eager to portray his move against Lost River as prudent rather than impetuous. Indeed, if it had not been for his own sense of fair dealing, the major assured the general, the Indians would have surrendered meekly: "The troop rode its march as expected and completely surprised the Indians and could almost have destroyed them, had it not been fair to give them a chance to submit, without using force."

Green assured Canby that the army was already rallying to crush the rebellion. The cavalry reinforcements from Fort Warner were expected to arrive shortly. Klamath Indian scouts were also headed toward the Lava Beds to face off against their Modoc cousins. And, to keep the settlers safe, Green had distributed twenty rifles, ten carbines, and ammunition to the settlers and sent another ten carbines each to the Yainax and Klamath Indian agencies.[7] "Don't worry a bit, general," Green seemed to be saying. "I've got this little problem under control."

• • •

Green was wrong: this fight filled a much bigger frame than he understood from the perspective of his little frontier fort. The standoff in the Tule Lake Basin offered a test case for the effectiveness of what had been ballyhooed across the nation as a completely new approach to dealing with the Indians of the West. And upon the outcome of this test rode the political fortunes of no less a figure than President Ulysses S. Grant.

Once the Civil War ended and the United States could focus its expansionist energies westward, the so-called Indian problem moved again to the center stage of American politics. There were other issues, of course, all of them pressing: reconstructing the defeated South, paying off the enormous debt left by the war, reintegrating veterans into society, and determining the political fate of emancipated Africans. Still, the West regained its shine as a beacon drawing the nation to new prosperity. The stumbling block was Indians. Scarcely an American in the mid-1860s saw the continent's Native peoples as anything other than an obstacle to be removed before civilization's inevitable, and innocent, progress from sea to shining sea. The question turned on how to effect the dispossession, not whether.

Extermination, the nineteenth-century word for genocide, had long been one solution. Even while the Civil War raged, a pilot project in the western extermination strategy rolled out at southeastern Colorado's Sand Creek on November 29, 1864, eight years to the day before the Lost River raid. John Milton Chivington, a onetime Methodist minister and the first grand master of Colorado's Masons, led seven hundred volunteers in an assault on a village of Northern Cheyennes and Arapahos. Chivington was clear about his purpose, and its holiness: "I have come to kill Indians, and I believe it is right and honorable to use any means under God's heaven to kill Indians."[8] The Cheyennes and Arapahos at Sand Creek thought themselves at peace; Chief Black Kettle even flew the Stars and Stripes over his lodge. The militia attacked anyway. Since most of the younger Indian men were away hunting buffalo, the death toll of as many as three hundred fell most heavily on women, children, and old people. To add an extra measure of barbarism, Chivington's men scalped and mutilated the dead and took the trophies home. Denver greeted the returning Chivington and his men with the same enthusiasm Yreka had shown Ben Wright after the Modoc massacre of 1852. Trophy Indian body parts, including tobacco pouches and purses fashioned from severed genitals, on display in a theater and various saloons drew ghoulish crowds of gawkers.[9]

The dark truth of Sand Creek, beyond the slaughter itself, was that the short-lived public uproar at the news and the congressional investigation of Chivington's actions—which resulted in no criminal prosecution—had more to do with party politics than outrage at genocide. Chivington was a Republican with ambitions backed by fellow

Republican and Colorado governor John Evans. The *New York Herald*, a Democrat-leaning paper, publicized the atrocity not to help Indians but to thwart Chivington's and Evans's political careers and impugn the Republican administration of Abraham Lincoln.[10]

Sand Creek, however, left a lingering bad taste in the public mouth made all the worse by rampant corruption among whites running Indian reservations. The agents, mostly political hacks who got their jobs through patronage, took huge kickbacks on food and supplies while the Indians sickened on bad beef and shivered half-naked through winter's blizzards. When desperate Natives left the reservation, as the Modocs had done, they provided more quarry for Indian killers of Chivington's bent.

American humanitarians came to see the moral degeneracy of the agents as the crux of the issue. Were the agents good men who dealt honestly with their charges, then Indians would go willingly onto the reservation and stay there, well fed and adequately clothed. Then they could be trained in the arts of civilization: agriculture, literacy, temperance, individualism, and, of course, Christianity. The application of Christian moral principles and the shining example of upstanding Christian men would lift barbarism from the savages and allow them to be assimilated into American society as pious, baptized, yeoman farmers. Or so the reformers argued.

This approach came to be known as the Peace Policy. Sometimes it was called the Quaker Policy, because of the preeminence of that denomination in promoting the idea. The Peace Policy's proponents took new heart in March 1869, when U. S. Grant recited the oath of office. His less-than-eloquent inaugural address offered two sentences of twisted syntax and pregnant meaning: "The proper treatment of the original occupants of this land—the Indians one deserving of careful study. I will favor any course toward them which tends to their civilization and ultimate citizenship." This ambiguous aside offered the Quakers and their religious kin a slice of hope that the new president had come on board. Grant had, although his reasons were more practical than humanitarian or religious. The post–Civil War army had been pared to a skeleton force by a Congress unwilling to pay the price of keeping more soldiers in the field. If the Indigenous nations could be talked onto reservations run by upstanding churchmen, then so much the cheaper and the better.

Grant's Peace Policy, however, had a distinctly military flip side. A general order promulgated for the Great Plains region in 1869 and extended to the Department of the Pacific in 1871 made this clear: "All Indians when on their proper reservations are under the exclusive control and jurisdiction of their agents. They will not be interfered with in any manner by military authority." Off the reservation, though, everything changed. "Outside the well defined limits of their reservations they are under the original and exclusive jurisdiction of military authority. . . . All Indians . . . who do not immediately remove to their reservations will be . . . treated as hostile, wherever they may be found, and particularly if they are near settlements or the great lines of communication."[11]

As a saying of the time went, the United States government approached Indians with a Bible in one hand and a Sharps carbine in the other. The Modocs had refused the Bible. Now it was the Sharps carbine's turn.[12]

• • •

In its first editorial on the situation, the *New York Times* saw the conflict as both trivial and momentous. It was small in scope—the *Times* editorial writer described the fight as "a speck of war 'scarcely bigger than a man's hand'"—yet the consequences it threatened, specifically an uprising by all the tribes along the Pacific Coast, were "of a serious character." Blame lay with the Modocs, of course. The Indians "have from the beginning been the aggressors. For several months past they have been sullen without cause." Ordered back onto the reservation, the Modocs chose to fight instead.

Grant's Peace Policy had not failed; rather, official incompetence let the matter get out of hand. "The Indian policy of President Grant, if properly carried out, would render such affairs impossible, and that it has not done so in this case has been plainly due to the errors of subordinate agents. We hope that these, if found equal to the duty, will be required to repair their mistakes, or that they will be replaced by others of more discretion and nerve."[13] The problem was not bad policy but bad personnel.

It fell to General Canby to prove the *Times* right and justify the iron fist in a velvet glove that was Grant's Peace Policy. He understood the political environment surrounding the Lost River Modocs. Even though Major Green had violated the order to move against the Modocs only with sufficient force, Canby refused to point an accusatory finger at his subordinate when he spelled out what had happened for his commander, Major General John M. Schofield, head of the Department of the Pacific. Green had to act fast, because "the Modocs were under evil influence from the unauthorized a[nd] illegal interference of interested parties (whites) who had counselled them to resist removal." The one-troop raid likely would have worked except that, Canby argued, the Modocs had pulled in all their fighters to prepare for the coming attack. In fact, the Modocs posted no sentries outside the Lost River villages, and Troop B caught them flatfooted. Ignoring these facts on the ground, however, Canby let Green off the hook by blaming the gunfight on the Indians: "I do not think that . . . he . . . should be judged wholly by the result. If the mission had succeeded the conception and the execution would probably have been as highly commended as they are now censured."[14] The major was given a pass for fatally poor judgment.

Canby knew that prevailing political myth protected him and his subordinate officers against the consequences of even their worst decisions. No matter who did what to whom for whatever stupid reason, the Modocs would take the rap.

Still, with the war he had hoped to avoid now dropped in his lap, Canby needed to end it as swiftly as he could. He had to show that the army could drive the Lost River Modocs back onto the reservation, where they belonged. Canby was sure that victory over the Modocs was but one frontal assault away.

9

Modoc Steak for Breakfast

It has been laid down and acted upon, that the solitudes of
America are the property of the immigrant children of Europe
and their offspring. . . . Public sentiment with us repudiates
possession without use, and this sentiment is gradually
acquiring the force of established law.

—John Louis O'Sullivan, *New York Morning News*, October 13, 1845

Brigadier General John Ross of the Oregon militia drank from
the same well of mythic confidence as Canby. He assured Governor Grover that a lengthy conflict with the Lost River Modocs was
unlikely: "My opinion is that if . . . sufficient force is brought to bear
& prompt action taken, the war can be brought to a close in thirty
days."[1] The several dozen Oregon civilians who volunteered against the
Modocs signed on for only a month. They expected to be done with
kicking the defeated Indians' backsides onto the reservation and packing the ringleaders off to the gallows by the second week of January.

Lieutenant Colonel Wheaton, Canby's field commander, shared
Ross's strategic assessment. "I do not believe we need anticipate a continued resistance from this little band of Modocs," he wrote Canby.
"Field operations against the hostile parties of the Modocs will be continued until their submission is complete."[2]

Canby himself thought that the two companies of the Twenty-First
Infantry he was sending south from Fort Vancouver might be overkill,
what with all the cavalrymen already headed to the Lava Beds from
Forts Klamath, Warner, Harney, and Bidwell. The general communicated confidence in the superiority of the force to Major General Schofield. Schofield, in turn, radiated the same assurance to Commanding

General of the Army William T. Sherman: "Genl Canby does not apprehend serious trouble."[3] Confidence brimmed so high that when Captain Reuben F. Bernard received orders from Wheaton to head to the Lava Beds from Fort Bidwell, a distance of about 110 miles, he and his men rode out with but eight days' rations and supplies.[4] The myth of American superiority had such power that even undersupplied warriors felt certain of victory.

On the surface at least, the confidence glowing from Ross, Wheaton, Canby, and Schofield appeared justified. After all, the American force gathering around Tule Lake to dislodge the Modocs from the Lava Beds would number close to three hundred fighting men.[5] The Modocs could field only fifty to fifty-five fighters, some of them mere teenagers barely big enough to shoulder a Springfield. Americans outnumbered Natives six to one.

Closer examination of the logistical and tactical specifics might have tempered that confidence, however. Grain was in such short supply that Wheaton preferred infantry troops over cavalrymen and their horses. Wagons for ferrying supplies were hard to come by, and many of the mule teams were wild, unbroken, and in such poor health that the Fort Klamath quartermaster discovered one animal lying dead in the corral. Solid cavalry horses were also hard to come by. "I inspected the horses . . . [of Troop B, First Cavalry], and found just six, fit for service in the field," wrote a clearly appalled Lieutenant Robert Pollock.[6] Fort Klamath also lacked uniform greatcoats, boots, and the ever-popular number-4 drawers.[7]

This was an army, too, that in the lean years following the Civil War had not yet settled on a standard-issue weapon. Many soldiers carried Springfield breechloaders, some of them refitted muzzle-loaders left over from the Civil War. Others had repeating Spencers, yet others single-shot Sharps carbines and the occasional Henry repeater. The different weapons fired cartridges of different calibers and charges, some centerfire and some rimfire, a reality that worsened the overall shortage of ammunition. Cartridges were so expensive that few soldiers during peacetime got the opportunity to fire their weapons more than a rare now and again.[8]

Wheaton found his men woefully short of ordnance, writing Canby that "nearly all of the Spencers having been issued to citizens the day after Jacksons fight, at the Modoc Camp, and the supply of Sharps and springfield utterly inadequate, some of the troops today have but 5 & 10 rounds apiece: As [Fort] Bidwell was the closest point, I have sent Col Bernard to that point for ammunition, and it will be here as soon as possible."[9]

The men who wielded this makeshift arsenal were as mismatched as their weapons. Only about half the soldiers who enlisted during the West's Indians wars were American-born, mostly young men raised in one rough tenement or another, boys running away from hard-luck farms, the occasional Confederate veteran unable to make it in a Yankee world, and small-time criminals looking to hide out from the law. Recent immigrants accounted for half the enlisted ranks fighting Indians in the West. Coming mostly from Ireland, Germany, and England, a fair number were veterans of foreign armies who signed up because jobs in the post–Civil War civilian economy of the United States were scarce. Enlistees must have felt desperate, indeed. Base pay was such a pittance—thirteen dollars a month for a private, less than forty dollars in today's currency—that men in the lower ranks effectively worked for food and shelter, or three hots and a cot. That small salary was paid in paper greenbacks that local merchants discounted at 15 to 50 percent of face value off gold or silver coin, leaving soldiers even more impoverished. Uniforms were Civil War leftovers well on their way to the rag pile. Mess consisted of a steady diet of hash, stew, stringy range beef, salt bacon, coffee, and coarse bread seasoned with salt, vinegar, and sugar. Soldiers who hungered for vegetables had to grow their own, so greens, roots, and tubers were almost never available on campaign. Because the single blanket issued to each soldier was too thin to keep out the deep freeze of plains and mountains, enlisted men slept with a buddy and shared covers.[10]

Just getting to the remote battlefield of the Lava Beds was a tough, draining ordeal. Consider the journey of the two companies of Twenty-First Infantry from Fort Vancouver. The soldiers boarded a riverboat on December 3 to cross the Columbia to Portland, where General

Canby himself greeted them. Next they took an overnight train to Roseburg, Oregon. So far, so good. The hard part began as the troops headed over the southern Cascades on foot. It took seven days' hard march to get up the Umpqua River Valley through mud so deep that the quartermaster, Lieutenant William Henry Boyle, foundered to his waist. The muck got even worse once the troops passed through Jacksonville. "The rains began to pour down and the roads became so soft that it was impossible to draw an empty wagon up the mountain side, and we had to double the teams on the wagons, and get the men to assist, to enable the teams to keep pace with the men. The men were footsore," he recalled. "On the evening of the 13th we camped on the side of Cascades . . . and the snow fell that day to a depth of about one foot. All the next day, through the driving snow, the troops marched on."[11] Reaching Linkville took ten days of this cold, wet, muddy slog. There the men rested before another two days' hard march brought them to a windy camp along Lost River on December 21, eighteen tough days after having left Fort Vancouver.

Conditions were different, but no better, for the cavalrymen who were ordered to the Lava Beds from posts to the east. Joel Trimble, a former enlisted man who had risen to cavalry captain, rode with his men from Fort Harney, which lay sixteen miles east of the modern town of Burns in the high desert of eastern Oregon. Under orders to cover the three hundred miles under "light marching order"—that is, on horseback alone, without the wagons that could transport tents, extra blankets, and additional food—the yellowlegs of Troop H, First Cavalry, crossed a wintry landscape. "Thus we moved on day by day," Trimble wrote later, "varying the monotony by an occasional dousing in slightly frozen streams, climbing over the rugged bluffs, skirting the shallow lakes, winding over the great alkali plains that are even in summer white as snow." At day's end officers and men tried to warm around sagebrush fires. In the mountains, sagebrush gave way to fir, pine, hemlock, and snow so heavy that the loads on the horses and mules had to be lightened and the animals led by their bridles. The men wrapped their boots in spare grain sacks to shed snow, lest it melt and soak their feet. They slept on hemlock branches laid close to the fire. "All stretch themselves beside the smoldering logs in chilly slumber.... In the dark, cold morning... we move out, but do not mount; horses will wade through snow two feet deep by alternating the lead, but beyond that man must break the way. So on we go, up and down the mountain, plunging sometimes armpit deep, dragging our unwilling beasts and often stopping to rescue a comrade or his horse from total submersion." It took more than two weeks of this rough riding for Trimble and Troop H to make it to the Lava Beds.[12]

Given the meanness of life in the army of the Indian wars, some enlistees decided they had had enough. At least one-third of men in the ranks deserted before their enlistments were up. Settlers, who had a low opinion of the military as a whole, often sheltered deserters against the army, which did not try all that hard to find them. The army fretted less over the loss of personnel than the cost of continued recruiting and of replacing equipment, such as weapons and horses, that deserters stole and sold to finance their escape.[13]

As desperate and dodgy as they were, Regular Army soldiers were far more reliable than the Oregon militiamen headed toward Tule Lake. With their thirty-day enlistment and desultory training, the volunteers were of the same undisciplined, secretly murderous sort as the hot-to-kill miners who rode with Ben Wright in 1852. They looked forward to giving the Modocs a good whipping and enjoying the spoils of battle. Since the war was taking its time getting started, the supply of beans ran low, the coffee was all gone, and if it were not for provisions from the Regular Army, the volunteers would have been subsisting on half rations. There was, however, occasional solace. One militiaman told of a keg of whiskey the volunteers deemed so terrible they passed it on: "We gave this morning a treat to the whole command [of] regulars... which consumed the whole of it."[14] In war, even bad booze can win friends.

• • •

For all his faith in the superiority of civilized soldiers, even those miserable Oregon volunteers neither he nor General Canby had asked for, Wheaton was in no great hurry to assault the Modocs. He wanted to be sure that all the matériel he needed was on hand. Because transport was slow and weather bad, he had to wait. Wheaton lay heavy strategic emphasis on two mountain howitzers that were making their heavy-weight way to him from the Fort Vancouver armory. Since the Indians were forted up, Wheaton thought it would be an easy matter to shell them into submission. "The Howitzers and ammunition for small arms will reach me at about the same time," he wrote Canby, "and we will be prepared to make short work of this impudent and enterprising savage [Kientpoos]. I feel confident the Guns will astonish and terrify them and perhaps save much close skirmishing and loss of life."[15]

Even as Wheaton was longing for shock and awe to animate his battle plan, the Modocs offered an object lesson in close observation of the army's every move. The much-needed rifle ammunition requisitioned from Fort Bidwell was making its way toward the Lava Beds in a wagon escorted by only five troopers. About a mile from Captain Bernard's camp near the southeast corner of Tule Lake, the Modocs sprang an ambush and quickly shot down two soldiers, five horses in the wagon's team, and a mule. The three surviving soldiers scattered as the Modocs swarmed the wagon. Before they could make off with the prize, a troop of yellowlegs from Bernard's camp galloped in, shooting as they came, and drove the Indians off.

That quick action saved the ammunition. It also brought the cavalrymen face-to-face with the reality of this war. Private Sidney Smith, one of the two dead, was found shot through the head, leg, and abdomen, stripped naked, and scalped. One ear had been lopped off, and the other partly severed.[16] The Modocs were playing for keeps.

• • •

John Fairchild had gotten the same message, albeit in a less brutal manner. A few days after the Hot Creek Modocs had fled his ranch, Fairchild and neighbors Presley Dorris, N. B. Ball, and Nate Beswick rode into the Lava Beds to find Kientpoos and talk with him. The chief was eager, accommodating. He repeated his bewilderment at the surprise attack on Lost River, and he made it clear that he had nothing to do with killing settlers along Tule Lake. Still, Kientpoos said he would fight rather than go back to the reservation. He told his white friends to warn the soldiers that if they came, he would take them on.[17]

As he rode back to his ranch, Fairchild must have realized that

Kientpoos was trapped without the slimmest avenue of escape. If he surrendered, the settler killers would be hanged; Governor Grover and Major Green had made it clear they would accept nothing less. Such a capitulation would show that Kientpoos could not protect his own and would cost him his status as headman. In the radical democracy of the Modocs, a leader lost authority the instant he proved ineffective. Resistance, however much it might bolster Kientpoos's standing within his community, meant taking on the vastly more powerful forces arrayed against him. With just fifty-some fighters, the odds were impossible. Either way, Kientpoos and his people lost.

Fairchild knew that the world he had built on his ranch had also come to an end. Already he had sent his wife and children into Yreka for the duration, barricaded and fortified his house, and armed his remaining cowhands. Fairchild was trapped on the American side of the divide as surely as Kientpoos was on the Modoc.

And so, on December 27, when Yreka's residents met to form a volunteer unit, they elected Fairchild captain. The group comprised only twenty-odd men, most of them vaqueros who worked the Fairchild and Dorris ranches, assembled under the grand moniker of Independent Company of California Volunteers. Fairchild, longtime patron of the Modoc people, had agreed to fight against them.[18]

· · ·

Wheaton called his field headquarters at Crawley's homestead along Lost River "a miserable shanty" made meaner yet by wind, snow, rain, and no fuel but sagebrush.[19] Yet, despite the discomfort, he had to like the military hand he was to play.

With Wheaton at Crawley's were the two companies of the Twenty-First Infantry who had made their muddy way down from Fort Vancouver, and Troop B, First Cavalry, who had come through the snowy desert and mountains. They were joined by a handful of Indian scouts, many of them Paiutes, and an irregular company of nineteen Klamaths. Captain Bernard and Troop G, First Cavalry, as well as ten Paiute scouts were camped at the southeast corner of the lake, on the ruined homestead of settler Louis Land. Across the lake and back from its southwest shore another eight miles at the Van Bremer brothers' ranch were Troop F of the First Cavalry and the two companies of Oregon volunteers. One of the volunteer companies was headed by Oliver Applegate, the Indian Bureau employee who led the vigilantes at the Lost River raid, and it included some twenty Klamath and Modoc Indians off the reservation as well as ten whites.[20]

While he waited for the howitzers, Wheaton planned for the decisive battle that would begin upon the guns' arrival. An experienced combat officer, Wheaton knew the Lava Beds were too rough for a cavalry charge, but beyond that he displayed little concern with terrain. Sitting on the far side of Tule Lake and lacking any firsthand knowledge of the country his men were to fight over, Wheaton saw the engagement to come as a set-piece battle featuring a classic pincer movement. What he failed to understand was how the Modocs would use the land to give themselves a substantial edge.

If you climb the precipitous bluff at the western edge of the Lava Beds—a steep but well-trod trail exists there even today, the very one both Americans and Natives used more than 150 years ago—then turn around and look back, the country beneath your gaze looks soft, even easy. In a few places where the lava opens its broken surface to the sky, the landscape is black. Elsewhere, sagebrush blankets the slow-rolling land in a muted gray-green. That vegetation masks the many pits, holes, ditches, gullies, rifts, ravines, and rills in the lava substrate, features that make just walking from here to there a struggle. I know; I have done it. Making that walk while someone on the higher ground of the Stronghold is shooting at you, firing those heavy, big-bore slugs that can tear off most of a limb if they strike bone, becomes a perfect nightmare.

Wheaton had taken no close-up look at the battleground. Instead, he trusted in his mythic certitude about the superiority of civilized American soldiers over Indigenous foes. This fight came down to getting close and squeezing the Modocs hard.

Most of the squeeze would come from the west. Wheaton moved both of Major Edwin Mason's companies of Fort Vancouver infantry to the Van Bremer ranch to join Major Green and his cavalrymen, the Oregon militia under General Ross, and the California volunteers led by Fairchild. Captain Bernard, his cavalry troops, and the Klamath scouts remained to the Modocs' east. The night before the day of battle, Bernard was to slip in close to the Modocs and wait for the push from the west at first light. From that direction, the infantry, the dismounted cavalry, and the militiamen would come down off Sheepy Ridge from a night camp on its flat top and advance on the Modocs, skirmishing as they covered the three miles to the heart of the Stronghold. At the same time, Bernard would move his troops and scouts toward the Modocs. The goal was for the western and eastern assault forces to meet up south of the Stronghold, then advance north to force the Modocs out of the rocks and up against Tule Lake. Should there be any canoes on the shore, Bernard was to capture them and close the exit route over water, trapping the Modocs on the shoreline.

Wheaton was prepared to crush any resistance remaining after his inevitable victory. "If during or after the attack on the Modocs they should escape from their Rocks and Caves," he wrote Canby, "Major Green will promptly pursue with all the mounted forces and kill or capture every hostile Modoc of Capt. Jacks murdering band unless they unconditionally surrender."[21]

As the third week of January 1873 began, all the troops, militiamen, and scouts took their assigned positions. The newly arrived supply of ammunition was distributed. Each soldier carried a hundred rounds in his haversack and had another fifty in close reserve. Three days' rations of bacon and hardtack were prepared and handed out, along with two blankets per man. Every fighter also carried a canteen, which he was to fill in advance of battle. The horses and mules that hauled the reserve ammo and the howitzers were to be fed and watered before camp was broken. By Tuesday, January 15, all the men, gear, and animals were ready.

Spoiling for the triumph to come, Wheaton telegraphed his enthusiasm dispatch to Canby: "I am happy to announce that, after all our annoying delays, we are now in better condition than I ever saw troops for a movement against hostile Indians. . . . Now our artillery pack train and howitzer details are admirably drilled, we leave for Captain Jack's Gibralter to-morrow morning and a more enthusiastic jolly set of regulars and volunteers I never had the pleasure to command. . . . Our scouts and friendly Indians insist that the Modocs will fight us desperately, but I don't understand how they can think of any serious resistance."[22]

• • •

The saying goes that no battle plan survives initial contact with the enemy. The beginning of what would be known as the First Battle of the Stronghold proved the sagacity of this precept. General Field Order No. 3 detailing the mode of attack made it clear that surprise was important, that "every precaution [is to be] taken to prevent the Indians from discovering our numbers and precise location."[23] That advantage was lost as soon as the troops moved.

On the west, Captain David Perry and F Troop, First Cavalry, rode out of the Van Bremer ranch at 4 a.m. on January 16. Their goal was to secure the top of Sheepy Ridge by the middle of the afternoon. As the yellowlegs rode up the ridge, they entered a thick blanket of fog. Modoc sentries on the bluff fired at the soldiers' spectral forms moving through the mist. By the time Perry and his men rallied for a counterattack, the Indians had melted away down the bluff's east side, carrying the message back to the Stronghold that something was brewing on the west.

As Perry was moving into position, so too was Captain Bernard. His two troops of cavalry and the Klamath irregulars, about one hundred fighters in all, planned to head almost fifteen miles west from their camp on Land's ranch and slip unnoticed into a position no more than two miles from the Stronghold. The same fog that had turned Perry's yellowlegs into ghosts on the other side of the lake so confused Land, who was acting as Bernard's scout, that he led the troops too close to the Modocs. As barking dogs and yelling men alerted Bernard, an experienced Apache fighter, that his men were within rifle range of the Stronghold, he ordered them to retreat. Already, though, the Modocs were pursuing the soldiers. A firefight broke out, and three of Bernard's men went down. Gathering the wounded, the troops fell back to the prominence soon to be known as Hospital Rock. There they set up an armed camp for the night.[24]

Now the Modocs knew something was stirring on the east as well as on the west. Any element of surprise had evaporated.

As Bernard's fighters settled in, the western force climbed Sheepy Ridge. They made camp on top, lit night fires of sagebrush, ate cold rations of greasy bacon and brittle hardtack, felt the January cold creep through blankets and clothes. "There was little sleep that night," Oregon militia officer William Thompson remembered. "The frozen ground with a pair of blankets is not a bed of roses, and is little conducive to sleep and rest."[25]

Some Oregon militiamen took to boasting to convince themselves that tomorrow would be an easy romp of Indian killing and trophy taking:

> One brave captain of volunteers said to another, "I have but one fear, and that is that I can't restrain my men, they are so eager to get at 'em; they will eat the Modocs up raw, if I let 'em go."
>
> "Don't fret," said Fairchild; "you can hold them; they wont be hard to keep back when the Modocs open fire."
>
> "I say, Jim, are you going to carry grub?"
>
> "No. I am going to take Modoc *Sirloin* for my dinner."
>
> "*I* think," said a burly fellow, "that I'll take mine *rare*."
>
> Another healthy-looking chap said he intended capturing a good-looking squaw for a—dishwasher. (Good-looking squaws wash dishes better than homely ones.)[26]

"Dishwasher" was a frontier euphemism for prostitute. Nubile Native women numbered among the spoils of battle the Oregonians were hoping for.

Well before dawn, the soldiers and militiamen rolled out of their frozen blankets and made ready to descend to the Lava Beds. With the battle expected to take only a few hours, most of them left their knapsacks and blankets on the top of the bluff under a small guard detachment. First over the edge went Captain Perry and his dismounted cavalrymen, who had the task of securing and holding the route to the battlefield. They encountered no resistance and gave the all-clear. Behind them, and led by Major Green, came the two companies of infantry, Fairchild with the California volunteers, the Oregon militiamen, and finally the two mountain howitzers. Once the big guns reached the flat at the bottom, Perry and his cavalrymen descended and formed the rear of the column.

Thick fog still blanketed the Tule Lake Basin. Under this cold coverlet the men moved to the lake and filled their canteens, then formed a skirmish line to advance toward the Stronghold. Captain Bernard's smaller force came out from Hospital Rock and edged closer to the Modocs in their lava fortress.

The howitzers were unpacked from the mules behind the skirmish line and set up. Gunners launched three rounds in the general direction of the Stronghold. The shells arced through the fog, fell, and detonated, scattering shards of basalt and scoria here and there, harming no one and breaching nothing.

The time was half past 6 a.m., Friday, January 17. The First Battle of the Stronghold had begun.

10

A Look Inside

Praise Allah, but first tie your camel to a post.

—Sufi saying

The fog that lay heavy on the Lava Beds formed one element of Curley Headed Doctor's plan. This old-school Modoc shaman recognized that the fight with the Americans turned as much on matters of spirit as on strategy, tactics, and logistics. Even before the attacking soldiers, militiamen, and scouts advanced, Curly Headed Doctor had been readying for the assault.

The women plaited a rope of tule fiber hundreds of feet long, then dyed it red. This barrier Curley Headed Doctor lay around the center of the Stronghold and proclaimed that no white man could cross it and live. He erected a shaman's pole on a high point, decorated it with the skins of white dogs, a hawk's tail feathers, an otter pelt, and the fleece of an ermine. Then he led the dance.

It was a simple pattern of left step and right drag in time to a chant the dancers sang. They circled a fire and lay offerings of meat and roots on its flames. Curley Headed Doctor inhaled the sacrificial smoke and then fell into a deep trance marked by the jerking and twitching that evidenced transport into the spirit realm. When he revived, the shaman declared each Modoc fighter impervious to the soldiers' bullets.

A survivor of the Ben Wright Massacre, Curley Headed Doctor was ready for the world to be made right again. He had prepared long and hard for this transformation.

• • •

Say "Ghost Dance" and modern readers think first, and rightly, of the Paiute prophet Wovoka and the religious movement among the Plains

Indians that ended with the murder of Sitting Bull and the massacre of as many as three hundred Lakota Sioux at Wounded Knee, South Dakota, in 1890. That was, however, only the final phase of a revival whose roots reach back into the 1840s and worked its way into the Modoc spiritual world well before Kientpoos and the Lost River people fled into the Lava Beds.

The Modocs of that earlier era took part in what anthropologist Leslie Spier named the Prophet Dance. This religious movement reached Indigenous communities across a wide area—from what is now northeastern California and northern Nevada to well above the Babine River in British Columbia and across the plateau and high-desert country of the upper West all the way to Montana. The Prophet Dance emphasized the relationship of the living to the dead, and it turned on the re-creation of right order following the world's apocalyptic destruction.[1]

In the late 1860s, with settler incursion into the West cresting in an Indian-killing, game-destroying, disease-bearing flood, the ritual emerged in new form. It began among the Paiutes along the Walker River in northern Nevada with a shaman named Tävibo.[2] From there it spread to most of the Indian tribes in northern California and southern Oregon. A Walker River Paiute named Frank Spencer brought Tävibo's ritual dance to the Yahooskin Paiutes on the Klamath Reservation. The Walker River people were dancing to bring the dead back after a great earthquake destroyed all the whites, Spencer told his tribal cousins; the Paiutes at Klamath should do the same. And they did, dancing in a circle in a simple move where the left foot led and the right dragged behind, chanting about the return of the dead. Next Spencer evangelized his message of resurrection among the Klamaths and Modocs on the reservation.

During the spring before the Lost River raid, Doctor George, a reservation Modoc shaman, brought Spencer's revivalism to Kientpoos's villages. Doctor George had a dramatist's feel for ritual. At his direction, the dancers painted three horizontal stripes of red, white, and black on each cheek. To the east of the central fire on the dance ground he erected a pole of the sort used in shamanic initiations. He stretched a rope of twisted tule around the area, declaring that no one who wanted to interfere could cross it. The dancers linked hands to form a circle and moved counterclockwise around the fire, dancing and chanting.

Everything had to be done the right way. "Put up a long pole, put a fire to one side of it, and dance. If some of you fall down, you must go and meet the dead," Doctor George insisted. "You must sing like me and believe, or you will be turned to rock." The risk was worth it. "The dead are coming back when the grass is about eight inches high. White people will die out, and only Indians will be left on earth. Whites will burn up and disappear without leaving any ashes. Deer and other animals will all come back. A good many of you have relations who have died. They will all come back, and people will never die anymore. Those who will come back have died once, but they will never die anymore. You must think of nothing but the dead people coming back."[3]

For five nights the Modocs danced along Lost River, then Doctor George returned to the reservation. Curley Headed Doctor paid professional attention to what he saw in the course of those five nights. When the time came, he resurrected the dance to solidify the fighters' spirits against the attack that was sure to come. The shaman convinced his people that the spirits of the other world, the ghosts of the dead, even the elemental forces of the Earth itself were fighting on their side. He chose a dancing ground that was exposed to gunfire yet gave the dancers a clear sight of most of the sacred peaks of the Modoc world—Horse Mountain, Petroglyph Point, Sheepy Ridge, Bryant Mountain, and the Medicine Lake Highlands—and drew their power to the Modocs.[4] The shaman called upon the forces of nature to serve as the Modocs' allies. In the words of a Paiute Ghost Dance song:

Fog! Fog!
Lightning! Lightning!
Whirlwind! Whirlwind![5]

•••

The dance served another, political purpose: it created much-needed unity among a divided people.

The Modocs who found themselves in the Lava Beds were hardly of one mind. The split between the Lost River villages, one on each side of the stream, embodied the division. The larger village was led by

Kientpoos, whose strategy centered on passive resistance to encroaching American power. He refused to return to the reservation, and he constantly stalled for time, hoping that if he delayed long enough the advocacy of friends like Yreka lawyer Elijah Steele might one day make the Lost River reservation a reality.[6]

Kientpoos, too, held to the idea that Americans and Indians could share the land. In late 1871 he told Ivan Applegate, "I want to live in my own country. I will live on the East side of Lost River. People in Yreka tell me this is my country . . . from Pit River to Lower Klamath Lake—whitemen may have timber, grass, and cold water, but the Fish, Ducks, Roots, and warm Springs we want, we will keep these."

Applegate asked whether Kientpoos and the Modocs would keep to the boundaries of their reservation, always a sticking point to settlers like the Applegates who wanted Indians to stay far, far away. Kientpoos saw a different future. "We want to live in this Country," he answered, "to travel and camp anywhere in it, to live among our white neighbors."[7]

Ivan's uncle Jesse would have nothing to with Kientpoos's multiracial vision. Nor, in fact, would some of the Lost River Modocs. The smaller village across the stream from Kientpoos's was home to hard men like Curley Headed Doctor and his son-in-law Hooker Jim. They held that a fight to the finish with the settlers was inevitable. The sooner it came, the better.

The split between the two factions became obvious after the Lost River raid. Kientpoos led his people across the Tule Lake to the Lava Beds and its stronghold even as Curley Headed Doctor, Hooker Jim, and friends left a trail of dead settlers. Now both factions, along with the Hot Creek Modocs from Fairchild's ranch, were sharing the Stronghold. They did not, however, share the same vision of the future.

The news on January 16 that military forces were massing for an attack on both sides of the Lava Beds divided Modoc from Modoc. Kientpoos advocated surrender. He was joined by none other than Scarface Charley, who had displayed his toe-to-toe bravery in the duel with Frazier Boutelle. Curley Headed Doctor and Hooker Jim, however, argued vehemently against giving up. They knew that surrender would send them to the gallows. Why would a man choose to die stretched and strangled when he could perish like a Modoc, a gun in his hands? And what if this confrontation was the end of days prophesied in the Ghost Dance, the time when the whites would disappear and all the dead Modocs would reappear to renew the world as it once had been? The time had come for apocalypse.

Schonchin John sided with Curley Headed Doctor and Hooker Jim, at least for the moment. He was Old Schonchin's younger brother, a bitter man in his fifties who had survived the Ben Wright Massacre and coveted Kientpoos's leadership position. He knew that Kientpoos actually had little stomach for a fight and hoped that he himself would emerge as the community's next leader. The Ghost Dance was fine with him when it served his ambition.

The Modocs in the Lava Beds lined up behind Curley Headed Doctor, Hooker Jim, and Schonchin John in the open, democratic way that was their custom. The vote among the fighters was fourteen for surrender, thirty-seven for resistance. And, as was also Modoc custom, Kientpoos went along with what his men chose, and Scarface Charley with him. War it would be.[8]

The Ghost Dance led by Curley Headed Doctor through the night before battle called upon the spirits to defend the Indians. The souls of those who had passed on were simply awaiting their chance to return once the inevitable apocalypse came to pass. And the shaman could show that his prayers had aligned the elemental forces of the Earth in the Modocs' defense:

Fog! Fog!
Lightning! Lightning!
Whirlwind! Whirlwind!

And it came as Curly Headed Doctor had bidden, thick ground fog pouring in over the Lava Beds, this country the Modocs knew in all its turbulent detail.

• • •

The proverb from Sufi Islam—"Praise Allah, but first tie your camel to a post"—is a reminder of two balanced aspects of human life. "Praise Allah" invokes the need to honor the cosmic, to seek right relation with the universe. With his Ghost Dance and medicine pole, Curley Headed Doctor was attending to that facet of the Modocs' existence. The other half of the proverb, "but first tie your camel to a post," reminds the faithful to take care of business. This, too, the Modocs were paying attention to.

Soon after the Lost River people arrived in the Lava Beds, they rounded up some hundred head of cattle, probably strays from Presley Dorris's ranch, herded them into the small, deep basin on the western edge of the Stronghold, and fenced the animals in by piling rocks across the narrow entrance of this natural corral.[9] Water could be had from Tule Lake as long as the Indians held the shoreline. The lake also supplied food in the form of waterfowl, which thronged on the winter waters by the hundreds of thousands, as well as fish and freshwater clams.

Then there was the Stronghold itself, a plateau some 165 yards in diameter raised slightly above the surrounding landscape. It contained eight collapse pits, vertical-walled holes from three to almost twenty yards across and four to nine yards deep. As accommodations the pits were none too luxurious, their floors cluttered with angular boulders tumbled down from the roof and walls. Still, people could crawl in among the rocks for protection against snow, rain, and wind.

These crude and crowded shelters—which became the "caves" of military reports and newspaper accounts—housed nearly 160 people. Only fifty to fifty-five of them counted as fighters, a loose term that included even adolescents and boys big enough to survive a muzzle-loader's mule-kick recoil. The hundred or so remaining Modocs represented both sexes and all ages, from infants to frail elderly, including Shacknasty Jim's pregnant wife, Anna. However much U.S. Army units like Trimble's cavalry and Boyle's infantry endured in slogging from their duty stations to the wet and windy camps of the battle front, they were grown men in good physical condition, unimpeded by concerns about keeping their families and elders safe. The Modocs, by contrast, were less a military force than a besieged village.

The Modocs' main defensive positions took advantage of the cracks and crevices that ran along the edges of the Stronghold's plateau and on the tops of the volcanic domes just beyond. These natural trenches formed one line along the northwest corner—precisely the direction from which Wheaton was planning to send the bulk of his assault force—and another between the Stronghold and Tule Lake. The Modocs cleared the trenches of loose debris to allow defenders to run fast from position to position. Faced with defending a perimeter of nearly a mile, they calculated how best to distribute their fifty-odd rifles to cover the western, eastern, and lakeshore approaches to the Stronghold and built low rock walls to reinforce gun positions on high points. A sniper could poke his rifle barrel through a slit in the rocks and pick off approaching soldiers, then fade unseen back into the landscape. Women were prepared to load the cumbersome single-shot weapons and keep a ready rifle in each shooter's hands at all times.

The Modocs knew that any assault had to come from the west or the east. Except for a narrow band along the shoreline, the lake blocked the north; the land to the south was too tumbled and chaotic. Yet the Indians knew of one more strategic feature on the south: a smooth and level trail about fifty yards across that led from the natural corral to the easier terrain beyond the lava flows. The Modocs used this trail to drive cattle into the corral. And, if worse came to worse and Indians had to run for it, they could use this pathway to escape.[10]

And so, when the mountain howitzers launched their three signal rounds into the mizzly dawn of January 17, the Modocs were prepared. Allah had been praised, the camel tied. With the help of the dead and the Earth itself, their back-of-the-hand knowledge of the ground they would fight over, and the strategic preparations they had made, the Modocs were about to prove as fearsome as they were desperate.

11

First Fog of War

War is the province of chance. In no sphere of human activity is such
a margin to be left for this intruder. . . . He increases the uncertainty
of every circumstance, and deranges the course of events.

—Carl von Clausewitz, *On War*

It made John Fairchild uneasy, this eerily cold day with fog so thick
he could see only a few yards into the murk. He and twenty-five
other California volunteers anchored the left of the skirmish line as it
moved forward. Every rock loomed like a mountain, and the mist muffled each man's anxious breathing. To the volunteers' right—not that
Fairchild could see them—came the infantrymen under Major Mason.
Even farther along were the Oregon militiamen, including Oliver Applegate, and, on the extreme right, most of the dismounted yellowlegs.
A cavalry detachment stayed behind to guard the howitzers. The big
guns, anticipated for so long, proved useless. Unable to sight in the fog
and afraid of blasting their fellow soldiers, the gunners held their fire.

"Go slow, boys, go slow," Fairchild called out to his men. "You'll raise
'em directly. . . . Go slow, boys; keep down, boys—keep down *low*, boys!"[1]

The Oregonians kept up their loud bragging from the night before.
"I knew them black devils would run when they learned that we vol-
unteers would get after them," one of the webfeet called out. "We want
Injuns. Show us your Injuns and we will show you some dead ones."

A rifle flashed and boomed. Californian Nate Beswick went down,
swearing, "Damn your souls! Get me out of here! Can't you see I'm
shot? My thigh is broke."[2]

The militiamen took cover behind rock or sagebrush. Two crept out
to help Beswick and themselves drew fire from unseen Modocs. Jerry

Crooks was hit in the thigh, Judson Small in the shoulder. Then Fairchild saw George Roberts, his second in command, take a round to the forehead. Roberts remained alive for the moment, but the wound soon proved mortal.[3]

Fairchild realized that the fog gave every advantage to the Modocs. They could see no better than he could, yet they knew this stretch of broken lava intimately. If a volunteer gave away his position, an incoming bullet from a Native rifleman flew in his direction within seconds.

The Modocs were directing fire at the Oregon militiamen as well as the Californians. William Franklin Trimble, a soldier in Oliver Applegate's unit, took a round through the heart, and George Chiloquin, a Klamath scout, was knocked down by a bullet that ricocheted off his heavy buckskin coat and did no more than bruise him badly. As soon as the Oregonians realized that these Indians shot back, they lost all stomach for the mayhem they had hoped for. This battle would be no raucous Sand Creek, with Modoc sirloin for breakfast and slim brown girls for pleasure. Instead, the militiamen retreated to cover, dragging their dead behind.[4]

Things were proceeding no better on the east. Captain Bernard moved his yellowlegs and Klamath scouts up until Modoc fire forced them to duck and cover. A quick charge dissolved once the soldiers ran into what they called a chasm, then fell back to a more secure position 150 yards to the rear. Seeing the whites hunkered down, the scouts found little reason to fight. They were arrayed against people among whom they had in-laws, friends, hunting and fishing buddies. They fired over the Modocs' head and called out in their Native language to the distant Indians, who called back.

In the early afternoon, the regulars on the west, with no help from the Oregon militia, advanced bit by bit some three hundred yards until they reached the same chasm that had stopped Bernard's men. Then they, too, fell back and took cover.[5]

• • •

The word *chasm* suggests a landform monumental and immense, a yawning abyss, the very gape and maw of the underworld. Walk the Lava Beds surrounding the Stronghold, and you will find no chasm. The surface lava flow does boast depressions that average twenty feet deep, perhaps a hundred across, and about a quarter of a mile long, with sloping sides that range from gentle to precipitous. In a military world of mass charges across open ground, such depressions should have stopped no well-led and motivated army. But these very features stymied the officers, soldiers, volunteers, and scouts in the Lava Beds on January 17.

The men faced with crossing that putative chasm were not simply out for a hike in what is now a national monument, more concerned about rattlesnakes than terrain. Under fire from gunmen they could not even see, every feature of the landscape grew into something frightening and formidable. Gentle slopes rose into escarpments, depressions became the canyons of the Colorado, and collapsed lava tubes gaped like tunnels to the underworld. And the advancing fighters had good reason to fear the Indian gunfire raking this rough terrain.

The Springfield breechloader used by many on both sides fired a .50-caliber slug that weighed a massive 450 grains, a little more than an ounce. One such projectile equaled more than eight of the 55-grain bullets that leave the muzzle of the M16 and M4 assault weapons in the current United States military arsenal. Even at the slow muzzle velocity of the Springfield, around 1,300 feet per second, that massive slug blasted a fearsome tunnel through skin, muscle, and viscera. And should a bone be struck, it would splinter into sharp fragments that scattered through flesh like shrapnel or sprayed out through the exit wound. Such a wound in a limb was unlikely to bring sudden death unless a major blood vessel were torn. But if you lived long enough to reach the field hospital, you ended up on a surgeon's amputation table, where crippling was certain and survival iffy.

It is easy to see how the army veterans imagined ravines as chasms when they thought of what a Modoc bullet could do to them. How much easier to pronounce the terrain impassable, shelter behind a boulder, and long for the order to retreat.

• • •

That order did not come quite yet. Stymied from closing Wheaton's pincer from the south as planned, Major Green decided to join the western and eastern forces on the north side of the Stronghold along Tule Lake. The Oregon volunteers refused to move, so Green ordered

Fairchild and his California volunteers, Mason and his infantrymen, and Perry and his dismounted yellowlegs to edge along the shoreline and hook up with Captain Bernard's force on the east. Dodging from rock to rock and sagebrush to sagebrush, volunteers and soldiers soon found themselves pinned down by Modoc riflemen only fifty yards away on the Stronghold's high ground. By now it was three o'clock in the afternoon, the fog was lifting, and the only way to survive was to lie low.

Rough, taunting humor came from the Modocs who recognized men pinned down behind the rocks. Steamboat Frank, who had a big voice and excellent English, called out to Scarface Charley, "Hello, Charley, here is some Yreka boys; don't you see them?"

"Yes," Charley called back.

"Boys, what do you want? What makes you come here to fight us?" Frank hollered.

Fairchild, Dorris, and the other Californians who had seen four of their friends and neighbors shot down must have been asking themselves the same question.

Frank called out again. "Charley, there is old Dorris. Dorris, what do you want here? Say, Dorris, how long are you going to fight us?" He kept on taunting the silent rancher. "What's the matter with you, Dorris?" he yelled. "Can't you hear? Ain't you got ears? Can't you talk? Ain't you got a mouth?"

Dorris stayed silent and hidden. Curiosity proved too much, however, for a nearby cavalryman who popped up for a quick look. A scant second later, a rifle round blasted through his head, spraying brains and blood.

Captain Perry, a few yards away, heard the awful thwack of lead against skull and the deadweight slump of a man becoming a cadaver. He pushed up on one arm to see. A waiting Modoc rifleman sent a slug through Perry's other arm and into his side. The wounded officer fell back and moaned, "Oh, I'm shot!"

"You come here to fight Indians," a shrill woman's voice mocked, "and you make noises like that; you no man."[6]

• • •

By about four o'clock, the advance had utterly ceased to advance. Green made his way to the lake shore where the Modocs had the soldiers and volunteers pinned down. He urged his men to charge. They refused to leave cover against Modoc fire at such close range. Furious, Green leapt atop a rock in full view and launched into a tirade so profane and colorful that no newspaper dared report it word for obscene word. For emphasis, the major pulled the glove off one hand and snapped it rhythmically into the palm of the other, still-gloved hand. Several Modocs aimed at Green and squeezed off what must have looked like an easy shot. The major ignored the whizzing slugs, as if they were no more lethal than angry bees, and continued his profane sermon to its unprintable end.

All that bravado led to whispered tales among the Modocs that the major's glove worked strong magic. And, remarkably, it later won Green the Congressional Medal of Honor, one of the Modoc War's most ironic twists. Here was the man whose impetuous order had sparked the conflict, earning the nation's highest military honor for the same impetuosity.

Not that Green's profane moments under fire on the Tule Lake shoreline did any good. His men hunkered where they were, and the Modocs took occasional, fruitless potshots. The battle had ground to a standstill.[7]

•••

Lieutenant Colonel Wheaton came down off Sheepy Ridge to assess the situation. He found the Oregon militiamen close to the bluff's base, licking their wounded pride. The howitzers remained unlimbered yet unused. The infantrymen under Major Mason refused to budge, afraid of drawing Indian fire. The California volunteers and dismounted cavalry whom Green had hoped to rouse to action remained pinned down along the lake. Bernard's force on the east sat in pretty much the same spot where it had begun the day, and the Klamath irregulars kept up their long-distance banter with the Modocs in the Stronghold. Even Wheaton knew it was over. He ordered the retreat.

Pulling back did not go well, particularly for the Oregonians. A rumor that the Modocs had captured Sheepy Ridge and were waiting in ambush panicked the militiamen, who for hours were too afraid to climb up and see for themselves. Instead, they huddled at the prominence's base, cold and hungry and terrified. When, about two in the morning of January 18, a small detachment braved the trail to the top, they found no Modocs, only the soldiers guarding the baggage, men as terrified as they themselves were. With the all-clear given, the volunteers scrambled up the steep grade. John Ross, their commander and no longer a young man, was so beaten down that he held onto the tail of a mule and whacked it across the rump to keep the beast pulling him uphill.

Neither volunteers nor soldiers had slept in at least twenty-four hours or eaten in nearly a day. Once they reached the top, they scrounged what food and shelter they could find and slept where they fell.[8]

Things went a little better on the east. The Indians held their fire as the California volunteers and dismounted cavalry fighters withdrew. Kientpoos, Scarface Charley, Schonchin John, even Curley Headed Doctor and Hooker Jim likely felt that the victory was as decisive as it needed to be without more killing. The soldiers and volunteers left the dead where they lay, planning to retrieve them later, and carried their wounded suspended in blankets with a man at each corner. The tired stretcher bearers bumped and smacked their wounded comrades against unseen rocks and trees, raising groans and moans and awful cries.

Jerry Crooks, the California volunteer with a leg broken by a rifle bullet, was given a horse to ride. Every time the horse bumped the damaged leg against an obstacle, Crooks was racked by an agony of splintered bone and tunneled muscle. He proved himself an enterprising casualty by looping a rope over his foot. When he spotted a hazard that the horse was sure to hit, he hoisted his broken limb out of harm's way.[9]

It was one o'clock in the morning by the time all the fighters on the east, white and Klamath, collected on the Land ranch. Hungry and exhausted, they dropped where they stood and slept on the bare ground. After a day of fear and death, their repose was less than peaceful and refreshing. In sleep "they could hear the whizzing of the balls," Captain Bernard wrote soon after, "and the War-whoop of the Indian, for the next twenty-four hours; besides, two thirds of the command was so badly bruised and used up that they are limping about yet."[10]

True Fog, Real War

Next morning Wheaton realized that ordering a new attack with men so tired and broken was futile. The First Battle of the Stronghold had reached its official end. Now came the time to figure out why the outcome Wheaton, all his officers, and their superiors thought fore-ordained had instead gone so terribly awry.

12

Celebration and Postmortem

"Friends," said Red Cloud, "it has been our misfortune to welcome
the white man. We have been deceived. . . . My children, shall the
glittering trinkets of this rich man, his deceitful drink that overcomes
the mind, shall these things tempt us to give up our homes, our
hunting grounds, and the honorable teachings of our old men?
Shall we permit ourselves to be driven to and fro—to be herded
like the cattle of the white man?"

—Charles Eastman (Ohiyesa), *Indian Heroes and Great Chieftains*

The only elation anywhere in California's northeastern corner
on the morning of January 18, 1873, was to be found within the
Stronghold. The victory vindicated the spirit power Curley Headed
Doctor called down in his Ghost Dance. Just as the shaman promised, no white soldier had crossed the red-dyed tule rope. To make
the victory even sweeter, not a single Modoc fighter had fallen. With
but fifty-odd rifles spread over a mile of perimeter, the Modocs had
stopped an attacking force three times bigger than their own garrison, defended the hundred or so noncombatants inside the Stronghold, and claimed victory.

They also emerged better armed. Eager for retreat, the army and
militias had left most of their dead on the field. As soon as the next
morning's sun rose, Modoc women picked the corpses clean of uniforms, rifles, and ammunition, and they gathered the blankets, cartridge
boxes, and weapons retreating soldiers and militiamen had thrown away
in panic. No longer would some of the Modocs have to rely on Kentucky long rifles from Daniel Boone's time and pre–Civil War muzzle-
loaders. Now they carried breechloading arms as good as the soldiers',
and they had the ammunition to keep them firing.

"A few days like this," Captain Bernard commented wryly, "would be all the Modocs would want to supply every man they have with the most improved arms, and a hundred rounds of ammunition for each."[1]

The political stock of the Modoc leaders who favored all-out war—Curley Headed Doctor, Hooker Jim, and Schonchin John along with Ellen's Man, Steamboat Frank, and Shacknasty Jim of the Hot Creeks—rose high. Kientpoos and Scarface Charley, who preferred peace, took less solace in their band's success. This win could be only a temporary success, they knew. In the long-gone days of Old Schonchin, the ever-rising tide of settlers overcame the Modocs' resistance. Surely now, with their soldiers beaten, the Americans would boost the force against them to a size that even the strongest shamanic ritual and a reinforced armory could not withstand. The days of Modoc victory, they feared, would prove short and few.[2]

• • •

As soon as a chagrined General Canby digested Lieutenant Colonel Wheaton's initial report of the January 17 defeat, he ordered reinforcements to the Lava Beds: two companies of artillery and three more of infantry from California, a cavalry company and an infantry company from Oregon. "In all about three hundred and sixty (360) men," Canby figured, more than doubling the number of Regular Army boots and hooves on the ground. He was also on the lookout for Indians with more willingness to fight the Modocs than the Klamaths. "Can you organize a force of Indians that can be trusted?" he asked a lieutenant in Oregon.[3]

Humbled, Wheaton tried to explain to his commander what had gone wrong, putting part of the blame on the terrain: "We fought the Indians through the lava-beds to their stronghold which is in the centre of miles of rocky fissures, caves, crevices, gorges, and ravines, some of them more than one hundred (100) feet deep." Given the difficulty of fighting on such ground, Wheaton argued that he had far too few troops, even though they dove enthusiastically into the battle: "In the opinion of any experienced officer of regulars or volunteers, one thousand men would be required to dislodge them [the Modocs]. . . . No troops could have fought better than all did in the attack advancing promptly and cheerfully against an unseen enemy, over the roughest country imaginable. It was utterly impossible to accomplish more than to make a forced reconnaissance developing the Modoc strength and position." He put the loss in killed and wounded at about forty, including two officers.[4]

Before the battle, Wheaton had assured Canby that victory would be both certain and swift. Now the same senior officer claimed that he and his men had fought against an insurmountable foe situated in an impregnable fortress—wild warriors dug into an even wilder land. Wheaton spun the defeat as not a loss but a "forced reconnaissance." And he invented an arithmetic of factoids to support his explanation for this epic fail. The ravines were five times deeper than they are, Indian forces three times larger than they were, and American casualties inflated by eight—ten dead and twenty-two wounded, in point of fact.

Wheaton was hardly the only leader on the American side who succumbed to the temptation of fiction and factoid. Since the myth of white superiority over Indians had been dealt a roundhouse punch to the gut on January 17, supporting evidence needed to bend.

The most colorful accounting came from the Oregon militia leaders. To hear Oliver Applegate tell it, his militiamen had been wreaking havoc since before the main battle. Five days beforehand, Applegate and forty of his volunteers in Company B accompanied Captain Perry and fourteen cavalrymen on a reconnaissance—planned, this time—of Sheepy Ridge. When American scouts flushed Modoc pickets, a firefight broke out. "There are good evidences that 3 Modocs were killed or mortally wounded," Applegate claimed.[5] Following the January 17 battle, in his official report on Company B's actions, Applegate swelled the body count of this brief engagement: "The Modocs probably lost four or five men in killed and wounded but as they were removed as fast as hurt, it was not possible to ascertain with any certainty what their casualties were."

Applegate maintained that he and his stalwart militiamen continued their grim reaping of Modocs during the assault on the Stronghold: "Three Indians were shot falling headlong into the crevices. Their fall was witnessed by many of the men. . . . During our approach to this point several of the Men saw the feet of an Indian protruding from beneath the rocks and covered with blood. Not having the time an investigation was not made but from appearances he was evidently killed."

Applegate embellished the landscape of battle as well. He and his men fought among "crags" and deep "canyons," and their forward rush to the Stronghold was stopped, he said, by precipitous "cliffs" where, in fact, there are none.[6]

Captain Hugh Kelly, Applegate's counterpart with Oregon militia Company A, served in civilian life as editor of the Jacksonville, Oregon, *Sentinel*. Kelly used his journalistic expertise to report an account of the battle that made the geography even more infernal than Applegate's invention and swelled the number of Modocs far beyond Wheaton's estimates. "The extent of country over which the Indians were scattered was full of deep holes and frightful chasms, varying from ten to one hundred feet in depth" he wrote. "No one who was in the fight pretends to say the Modoc force numbered less than two hundred, and some place the number as high as five hundred. One thing we know, that while they were fighting our troops over a circle five miles in diameter there were seventy counted in one bunch."[7]

John Fairchild had no truck with the Oregon volunteers' inventions. The California Volunteers had sustained the highest casualty rate of any unit in the fight—two mortally wounded and two maimed among but twenty-six men. A tired, angry, and normally laconic Fairchild stomped into the Oregonians' camp and lit into the men who had boasted of what they would do to the Modocs.

"How did you like your 'Modoc sirloin,' eh? putty good, eh? didn't take it raw, did you? Where's that feller who was going to bring home a good-looking squaw for a—dishwasher?" he railed. "Now, captain, let me give you a little bit of advice; it won't cost you nothing. When you raise *another* company to fight the *Modocs*, don't you take any of them fellows that you can't hold back, nor them fellows who want to eat Modoc steaks *raw*; they aint a good kind to have with you when you get in a tight place. Why, Shacknasty Jim could whip four of them at a time."[8]

Fairchild was under no illusion that terrible terrain or an unexpectedly large Modoc force made the difference in the terrible outcome. It was the Indians' strategic savvy and cool resolve: "As we charged the

Indians, they could hear the commands of our officers and tell where we were, and we could not see them. The first we would know we would receive a deadly volley. I have been in a good many close places but that beat anything I ever saw."[9]

• • •

Captain Bernard was an experienced Indian campaigner, a man whose graying, chest-sweeping beard gave him the look of the grizzled veteran he was. When the Modoc War broke out, Bernard had served for eighteen years. After enlisting as a blacksmith with the First Dragoons in New Mexico and southern Arizona, he rose through the ranks on a well-earned reputation as one tough Apache fighter. Early in the Civil War he won a second lieutenant's commission in the First Cavalry and was breveted three times for battlefield gallantry. After the Confederacy fell, Bernard returned to Arizona and led a series of successful expeditions against Cochise and his Chiricahua Apaches. By the time Bernard finished his military career he had engaged in more than one hundred firefights, skirmishes, and battles against Indians or Confederates.[10]

Reporting to Major Green on his piece of the battle puzzle two days later, Bernard recited the tactical events of the engagement in the manner expected of an experienced officer, citing both the bravery of his men and the difficulty of the terrain. And he added his assessment of what it would take to push the Modocs out: "The place the Indians now occupy cannot be taken by a less[er] force than 700 men, and . . . to take the place with an assault by this force will cost half the command, in killed and wounded."[11]

Over the next three days, Bernard and his men withdrew from the Land ranch at the southeast corner of Tule Lake to the safer Applegate and Carr spread on Clear Lake, eight miles east. They were camped there when a group of Modocs slipped out of the Stronghold, way-laid two wagons ferrying grain from Land's to Applegate's, and drove off the escort. Bernard led his entire company on a ten-mile gallop to the ambush site and pursued the Indians into the Lava Beds. One fighter, Greasy Boots, was caught out in the open, ridden down, and shot dead. In the entire month of January 1873, Greasy Boots was the one and only Modoc the army killed.[12]

Perhaps this small success after so much difficulty changed the captain's perspective. Or, perhaps, camping on the ranch Jesse Applegate operated for absentee land baron Jesse Carr somehow aroused his suspicions about the real causes of this conflict. In either case, Bernard put pen to paper to give his assessment of the situation.

Bernard, like Fairchild, recognized the unusual determination of the Modocs. Yet Bernard went Fairchild one better and, for the record, put justice on the side of the Modocs.

Moving the Modocs off their own land onto a reservation within traditional Klamath territory was doomed to fail, the captain argued in an impassioned letter to Samuel Buck, adjutant general of the army's Department of California. The Modocs who bolted under Kientpoos's leadership because of the intolerable conditions on the reservation had been doing just fine on their own along Lost River, without government help. Then "avaricious land-grabbers, stock-men and Indian agents made representations, and got an order to have them moved back to the Reservation, peaceably if possible, and forcibly if necessary."

Even after the Lost River raid, Bernard pointed out, Kientpoos's Modocs retreated to the Lava Beds without harming anyone but the soldiers who had set upon their village. The Modoc village across Lost River, the one that was led by Curley Headed Doctor and Hooker Jim and that had been attacked by Oliver Applegate's settler posse, took the fight south as they escaped. They killed settlers on land they saw as their own yet spared women and children.

"These Indians have acted more humanely, in every instance, than we have. The only thing they claim or ask is a home at the mouth of Lost River, where they were born and raised," Bernard pointed out. "They have fought like men fighting for their rights, and if any man or men should have, or could gain their rights by fighting for them, the Modocs are more than entitled to what they claim."

Granting the Modocs those rights ran counter to the financial interests of certain settlers: "But for the gratification of a few cattle-men, land-grabbers &c, the Modocs must be compelled to kill and wound soldiers and citizens to twice their numbers, costing the Government and private parties hundreds and thousands of dollars."

The Modocs were, Bernard argued, freedom fighters in the long American tradition of rebellion against tyranny: "Men that would not fight under such circumstances, are not worthy of life or liberty."

With his assessment that taking the Stronghold would cost 350 killed and wounded, Bernard argued that continuing this profit-oriented war against the Modocs would cost far too much in blood and treasure: "It seems cruel that human life should be sacrificed for the gratification of a few unscrupulous dollar hunters." Peace was the better option, and Bernard outlined possible terms. Give the Modocs a thousand acres at the Lost River mouth, plus a mile-wide stretch along the precipitous western shore of Tule Lake plus the whole of the Lava Beds. And, just to be safe, site an army camp nearby, as much to protect the Indians against whites as vice versa. "The whole country of cowards will cry out for the blood of the [Modoc] murderers, this they never should have," he wrote. Rather, "Let peace be made with these Indians."[13]

• • •

Bernard's dissent wound its way up the chain of command to Canby's desk, where it attracted little notice.[14] The brigadier decided, instead, that, besides sending reinforcements, it was time to change leadership. Canby ordered Colonel Alvan C. Gillem, the commanding officer of the First Cavalry, to replace his subordinate Lieutenant Colonel Wheaton and take personal command of the troops in the Lava Beds.

Wheaton let Canby know by telegram that he was none too pleased with his removal: "I am greatly disappointed and pained at not being permitted to retain this command in the field—I am perfectly familiar with the situation and Confident that we can easily kill or capture every hostile indian in arms."[15] Still, he had no choice but to pack his bags, saddle up, and make the long, cold ride back to Fort Warner.

Canby gave Gillem his take on the situation he was inheriting. Canby was certain that "some of the reckless and desperate young men of neighboring tribes have probably joined them [the Modocs]," although he was at a loss to say where these Native reinforcements had come from. The new commander's charge was to contain the Modoc fight, particularly given "the uneasiness and apprehension that prevails among the settlers."

On the rightness of the war he was to run, Canby assured Gillem, the new commander should be at ease. "You will find great conflict of opinion as to the character and conduct of the Modocs, and of their treatment previous to the present revolt. My opinion is that they have been dealt with very considerately by the officers of the Indian Department, and that forbearance was carried to the extremity of proper limit, and that they should now be regarded and treated as any other malefactors," he wrote. "The operations against them should be pressed earnestly and persistently, and all who may be implicated in murder or outrage should, if captured, be turned over to the civil authorities for trial and punishment."[16]

Canby was doubling down on the iron fist within the Peace Policy. Because the Modocs had resisted, they needed to be eliminated from land that had been theirs by killing as many as possible and exiling the survivors to some reservation far, far away. Canby was readying the forces to launch this implicitly genocidal war.

At the same moment, events were taking a different turn on the other side of the continent. An unemployed Indian Affairs bureaucrat saw in the military's defeat a rare opportunity to win himself a job. His chance lay not in war but in peace.

PART 3

Firing into a Continent

Once, I remember, we came upon a man-of-war anchored off the
coast. There wasn't even a shed there, and she was shelling the bush.
It appears the French had one of their wars going on thereabouts.
Her ensign dropped limp like a rag; the muzzles of the long six-inch
guns stuck out all over the low hull. . . . In the empty immensity
of earth, sky, and water, there she was, incomprehensible, firing
into a continent.

—Joseph Conrad, *Heart of Darkness*

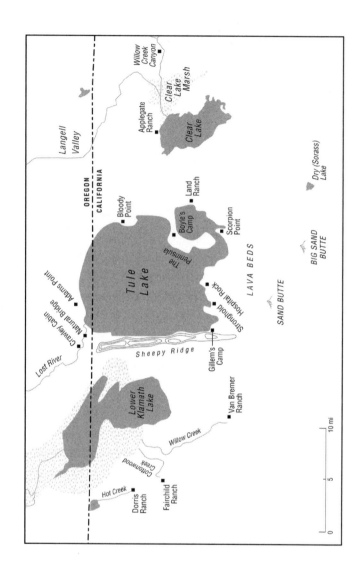

MAP 2. The Modoc War battlefield, November 1872–June 1873.
Courtesy Erin Greb Cartography.

13

Give Peace a Chance

Extermination is no longer even a question of time—the time has
already arrived, the work has been commenced, and let the first white
man who says treaty or peace be regarded as traitor and coward.

—*Yreka Mountain Herald*, August 7, 1853

Through the long months since he had been sacked from his position as Oregon's superintendent for Indian Affairs and replaced by T. B. Odeneal, A. B. Meacham was both rankled and unemployed. Since he blamed his professional downfall on Odeneal, Meacham had to have been pleased when the new superintendent's ill-timed raid on Lost River drove the Modocs into the Lava Beds. That was where things stood when Meacham left his home in Salem, Oregon, to travel to Washington, DC. He had been chosen to represent his state in the Electoral College and confirm the reelection of Republican Ulysses S. Grant as president.

As Meacham was tending to his political duties, the Modoc victory on January 17 played as a hot item in the major eastern newspapers. A story in the January 21 *New York Times* told the tale in its inflated headline: "THE MODOC WAR. An Eight-Hour Battle—The Troops Defeated, with a Loss of Forty Killed." Four days later, the *Times* ran a follow-up story with an alarming lead: "The intelligence from the seat of the Modoc war is to the effect that Capt. Jack is evidently contemplating a raid upon the white settlement at Butte Creek within forty miles of Yreka."[1]

The Democrat-leaning *New York Herald* argued that the First Battle of the Stronghold eroded the foundation of Grant's Peace Policy. It was all very well and good to advocate reservations for Indians, but if Natives resisting removal could so easily defeat the troops sent to chase them back where they belonged, was the policy itself not weak and bankrupt? "This result [the January 17 defeat] shows that Captain Jack, and his Lieutenants, Scar-Faced Charley and Shack-Nasty Jim, not only mean to fight, but have the power to do it with effect," the *Herald* editorialized. "Yet it seems strange that, after all these weeks of preparation, involving, as it has, thousands of dollars of expense, our troops should have been so shamefully beaten."[2]

Meacham saw opportunity in the Grant administration's predicament. Ever the politician, he realized that the government might now be willing to consider a less expensive, negotiated settlement to this embarrassing conflict. Meacham had experience with the Modocs and one definite, if temporary, triumph in jawboning Kientpoos and his people onto the reservation without firing a shot. If he could put his idea before the right people in the president's cabinet without looking too eager for vindication and per diem, Meacham might land the assignment to lead the negotiation.

Meacham turned for help to notable Oregonians who happened to be in the nation's capital at the same time. They were led by Lindsay Applegate, Jesse's brother and former Indian agent on the Klamath Reservation, and the respected journalist S. A. Clarke, who had helped found Portland's *Oregonian*. Applegate, Clarke, and the others composed a letter to Columbus Delano, who as Interior Department secretary was the cabinet officer responsible for the Indian Bureau. The letter's proposal was simple. The army could eventually exterminate the Modocs, but the cost would be prohibitive and the brutality of annihilation could ignite a wider Indian war across the Pacific Northwest. How much better it would be to persuade the Modocs to surrender and remove them to a neutral reservation along the Pacific coast: "A peace commissioner should hasten to the scene of trouble as coming from the 'Great Father' of all the people, both whites and Indians, with full authority to hear and adjust all the difficulties. On account of his personal acquaintance with those Indians and their implicit confidence, we would respectfully suggest and recommend Hon. A. B. Meacham."

Firing into a Continent

Delano received the letter on January 27, met with Meacham the following day, and offered him the job on the spot. Meacham accepted with coy reluctance. He agreed to take the position only, he claimed, because he wished to end the grief of the Tule Lake families who had lost husbands and sons. "My heart was in sympathy, too, with the poor bereaved wives and mothers, made so by Modoc treachery," he wrote later. "The sands of the sage-brush plains had drank up the blood of a score of manly hearts; immersing the lava rocks in blood could not make the dead forms to rise again."[3]

• • •

For the peace effort to move forward, two matters needed attention. First, the military had to call off the dogs of war. Delano met with President Grant and Secretary of War William Belknap and convinced them that this peace commission proposal would work. Soon thereafter, Commanding General of the Army William T. Sherman telegraphed General E. R. S. Canby. He made it clear where his new orders came from: "I am instructed by the Secretary of War to telegraph you that it is the desire of the President that you use the troops to protect the inhabitants as against the Modoc Indians, but, if possible, to avoid war."[4]

By return telegram Canby told Sherman he had ordered Colonel Alvan Gillem to stand down, and he let his ever-belligerent superior know that negotiating peace with the Modocs would fail. "I am satisfied that hostilities with the Modocs would have resulted under any circumstances from the enforcement of the [Indian Bureau] Commissioner's order to place them on the reservation," Canby wrote. "They were determined to resist, and had made preparations to do so." War with the Modocs had always been an issue of when and where, not whether. "I have been very solicitous that these Indians should be fairly treated," he asserted. "I think they should now be treated as any other criminals, and . . . there will be no peace in that part of the frontier until they are subdued and punished."[5]

Sherman promised to lay Canby's opinion before President Grant. In the meantime, "Let all defensive measures proceed, but order no attack on the Indians till the former orders are modified or changed by the President, who seems disposed to allow the peace men to try their hands on Captain Jack."[6] Sherman, the hellish warrior, was as skeptical of peace as was Canby.

Canby's take affected the second issue to be resolved: the commission's roster. Delano wanted a three-member panel, with Meacham as its chair. For the other two positions Delano proposed Odeneal and J. H. Wilbur, a Methodist minister who served as Indian agent on the Yakima Reservation in Washington State.[7] Meacham refused to serve with either man. The last thing he wanted was vindication for Odeneal, and he disliked Wilbur for dabbling in Oregon affairs that were Meacham's business.[8] Meacham suggested instead Samuel Case, Indian agent at the Siletz Reservation and an old friend, and Jesse Applegate, likewise a long acquaintance and a fellow Republican. Delano agreed.[9]

Affecting generosity that belied his self-interest, Applegate refused to take compensation beyond out-of-pocket expenses.[10] Of course, he had bigger fish to fry: removing the Modocs and then buying up or burning out every homesteader in the ethnically cleansed neighborhood. Although Meacham probably had only a dim idea of how greedy Applegate and silent partner Jesse Carr were, he saw Applegate's economic self-interest as leverage and boasted about it to a reporter: "Meacham knew Uncle Jesse and his partner (another man by the name of Jesse) had a little interest in certain swamplands in which he might he able to lend assistance."[11]

The Peace Commission had a fourth, de facto member as well, one designated by the struggle between the War and Interior Departments over which was better at getting rid of Indians. H. R. Clum, the acting Indian Bureau commissioner, made this reality clear in his charge to Meacham: "The Commission before entering upon the active discharge of its duties will confer with General E. R. S. Canby, and for this purpose will arrange to meet him at the most available point. The Commission will also confer in subsequent proceedings, and will act with Gen. Canby under his advice, as far as possible, and always with his cooperation."[12]

The commission's two tasks—to determine the causes of the Modoc hostilities and to find the best way to end the fighting and restore peace—now fell to an unlikely group of four. All hailed from Ore-

Firing into a Continent

gon, even though the theater of war had moved into California. One wanted to repair his damaged professional reputation, another wished to ensure the removal of Indians from land he coveted for a cattle barony, the third was a functionary selected to make no waves. The fourth supposed peacemaker—and effective holder of a veto over the commission's doings—was a professional soldier committed to defeating and punishing the Modocs. As to the long-term welfare of the Natives and their continued existence as an independent people, no one on the Peace Commission was giving that the least thought.

• • •

Two men who had a stake in the outcome of the conflict beyond personal gain were even then making their way to the Stronghold. Through One-Eyed Dixie, a Modoc woman who acted as go-between, Kientpoos asked John Fairchild and Presley Dorris to come talk peace. The headman's only condition was that no detachment of soldiers accompany the two ranchers. Displaying stunning trust, the two Californians agreed to meet on the Modocs' turf.[13]

Kientpoos's diplomatic overture revealed the fracture lines within the Stronghold. Curley Headed Doctor and Hooker Jim, who had settlers' blood on their hands, saw peace talk as the opening act of a Modoc surrender that would send them to the hangman. They argued heatedly with Kientpoos, even threatened to kill him if he met with Fairchild and Dorris. Because the Ghost Dance and the red tule rope had defeated the soldiers on January 17, many of the Modocs in the Stronghold sided with the shaman and his hotheaded son-in-law. This group included the Hot Creeks under Shacknasty Jim, who maintained their identity as a community separate from the Lost River Modocs. Schonchin John waffled depending on his self-interest, sometimes supporting Kientpoos and sometimes opposing him. In the end Kientpoos could count on the continuing loyalty of only his family and closest friends, among them Scarface Charley. Both men were realists. In time, they knew, the United States and its army would mount sufficient force to crush them, Ghost Dance and tule rope and all. And so, despite nightlong shouting matches replete with death threats, Kientpoos and his allies met Fairchild and Dorris.

The two ranchers were accompanied by First Lieutenant John Quincy Adams as the army's spokesperson, two other local settlers, and the scout Donald McKay, mixed-blood offspring of one of Oregon's old Hudson's Bay Company families. The assembled Americans shared tobacco and pleasantries with the Indians and conveyed Lieutenant Colonel Frank Wheaton's offer: unconditional surrender of all Modocs, with the Tule Lake settler killers to be tried on murder charges in Oregon. Perhaps Kientpoos smiled, perhaps he laughed aloud, perhaps he told Fairchild and Dorris they might remind Wheaton that a defeated commander was in no position to dictate terms. The two ranchers let Kientpoos know that the Peace Commission on its way to the Lava Beds would take up the diplomatic approach to ending hostilities. Up to speed now on what the next step would be, Kientpoos, Scarface Charley, and the other Modocs went their way, and the whites theirs.[14]

This meeting accomplished nothing, yet it signified what might have been. Only two weeks earlier Fairchild and Dorris had traded rifle rounds with the Modocs they were now talking with. Both sides understood that circumstances had pushed them into an unwanted war and that new circumstances might carry them to a peace not unlike what they had known together before. Had Fairchild or Dorris been appointed to the Peace Commission, that trust and respect could have provided a foundation for a negotiated settlement. Yet within the political mythology of the time, naming one or both ranchers to the commission was impossible. Fairchild was a Mississippi Democrat who rode a stallion named Joe Lane after Oregon's pro-slavery, pro-secession governor and senator. Dorris came across as less partisan, but like Fairchild he had worked side-by-side with Modocs as ranch hands and house help, paid rent to use their land for grazing, and vouched for their honesty and good intentions. The two ranchers had blurred the line between white and red; they represented an old way that was fated to vanish.

• • •

Meacham had come to Washington, DC, to cast an electoral vote for Ulysses S. Grant. He made ready to leave in a wholly new role, one that would raise his status in Republican politics and put him in the front rank of civilization's inexorable march across North America. Prepared for triumph, Meacham packed his bags and on Wednesday, February 5, boarded a train west.

That same day there arrived near the Lava Beds another figure who would play a leading role in the unfolding drama. He was the special Modoc War correspondent of the *New York Herald*, come all the way from Gotham itself, a onetime yachting editor named Edward Fox.

14

The News That Fits

To the prosaic observer, the average Indian of the woods and prairies
is a being who does little credit to human nature—a slave of appetite
and sloth, never emancipated from the tyranny of one animal passion
save by the more ravenous demands of another . . . . I could not help
saying, "These people must die out—there is no help for them. God
has given the earth to those who will subdue and cultivate it, and it
is vain to struggle against His righteous decree."

—Horace Greeley, *An Overland Journey*

The *New York Herald* had become America's leading newspaper
by understanding the power of on-the-ground reporting via
telegraph and feeding the popular taste for violence, vice, and crime.[1]
Indeed, James Gordon Bennett Jr., the paper's editor since 1868, was
the perfect journalist to guide America into its Gilded Age. Ostenta-
tious, wealthy, and entrepreneurial, he wanted to make news rather than
just wait for it, and he was willing to foot the bill. Only a few months
before the Modoc War broke out, the strategy achieved its greatest
success when reporter Henry Morton Stanley crossed East Africa on
Bennett's dime and found the long-missing medical missionary David
Livingston deep in the bush. Stanley's acclaimed article and follow-up
book cemented the *Herald*'s reputation as the newspaper that nailed
the story no one else even tried for.

Bennett saw a new opportunity for daring firsthand reporting in the
Modoc War. Most Indian wars in the West were fast-moving conflicts
fought in scattered skirmishes of unpredictable location. The Modoc
War was different, more of a set-piece siege. And now, with a cease-fire
in effect and the Peace Commission formed, hostilities were on hold.
An enterprising reporter might use the lull to gain access to Kientpoos

and his lieutenants and interview them. That could be a journalistic coup to rival Stanley's trip into uncharted East Africa. It would boast the same reportorial essentials: journalist-hero penetrates remote wilderness inhabited by dark and dangerous warriors and comes home with a thrilling, up-close-and-personal story.

To pull it off, Bennett needed the right man. On the *Herald*'s staff was a strapping, long-haired Englishman who came from a family of means and had served in the British army as an officer before going into newspapering. And Bennett knew he could get his facts straight and write well. After all, Edward Fox was the yachting editor.[2]

From Bennett's perspective, the choice made complete sense. Bennett was so accomplished a sailor that he won the first-ever transatlantic yacht race. There was no section of the paper he scrutinized more closely than the nautical news, pouncing on the least error of maritime technique or terminology.[3] This day-by-day scrutiny convinced him that Fox was the right man for the Modoc assignment.

Bennett, like all leading newspaper editors of the time, saw no place for Indians in an expanding America. They stood as obstacles to the future, primitives to be swept aside in the rush toward progress. All Edward Fox had to do was report the Modocs' extinction with all the adventure and action he could muster. His assignment amounted to blood-and-thunder pulp fiction with no backstory.[4]

• • •

Arriving at John Fairchild's ranch on February 5, the same day Meacham left Washington, DC, Fox filled the *Herald*'s bill with the story he filed the very same day. Just getting to the Lava Beds had been an arduous journey, he reported. Having reached Sacramento by transcontinental railroad, Fox learned that snowfall up north had made the roads nearly impassable. He grabbed another train to Redding, a seventeen-hour journey, slept but a few hours, and caught a stagecoach to Yreka that had to plow through eighteen inches of snow. Discovering that there was no inn between Yreka and the Lava Beds, Fox bought a rubber sheet and all the blankets he could find in case he needed to camp on the way over the mountains. Luckily for him, he did not have to. Although the stagecoach sank to its axletrees in the snow-softened track, the driver made the thirty-eight miles from Yreka into Butte Creek Valley in only one day. There he and his passengers spent the night on a hospitable ranch. By late afternoon the next day, the coach covered the remaining snowy ground to Fairchild's ranch, which was serving as a headquarters location for the military. In his first story, Fox declared the place "*Herald* Headquarters" as well.[5]

Despite its grand name, this assignment was pure hardship, as Fox made clear. In the cold, bitter, high-country winter, he had to sleep on the floor of an unheated outbuilding among fourteen men crammed into but fifteen square feet. The food was even worse. "We have two meals per diem, one at 8:00 A.M. and the other at 4 P.M. These meals are decidedly simple in their nature and are served with a fair allowance of dirt," he reported. Although the likable Fairchild had more than three thousand head of cattle, "the lacteal produce of the bovine race has never been used in the ranch, and even the butter that graces the hospitable board is brought all the way from Yreka. The staple article at both meals is beef, fried in grease in the morning and boiled in fat in the afternoon. Flour made up to the style of hot biscuits is also used at each meal, as vegetables have not yet made their appearance here. The fluid in use is called coffee and has a brown appearance resembling a liquid we have seen before bearing the same name."[6]

Like Henry Morton Stanley, Fox made himself as much the subject of reporting as the Modocs, Fairchild, and the men he slept among. Still, he was a hardworking reporter who wasted no time. Knowing that readers expected action and adventure, the *Herald*'s man on the scene re-created the events of January 17 from Lieutenant Colonel Frank Wheaton's orders and the initial reports of the field commanders. In only three days of reporting and writing, he pulled together a surprisingly accurate and detailed account of the battle that ran several thousand words—no mean feat in an age of pencils, foolscap, and telegraph. With Meacham still making his way to the Lava Beds and the Peace Commission yet to begin its work, Fox interviewed an unidentified Modoc woman—probably One-Eyed Dixie or Artina Chockus, who lived near the Fairchild ranch and had stayed behind to care for the frail Hot Creek leader, Old Sheepy. The woman was acting as a messenger between the Stronghold and army headquarters, and the information she gave Fox allowed him to report on the division in the Indian camp. Californians, Fox also reported accurately, were generally better disposed to Modocs than Oregonians, who "were bitter against the Indians" and blamed the conflict on men like Elijah Steele, the Yreka lawyer and advocate for Indians. He ferreted out Jesse Applegate's potential conflict of interest as well: "He is a large real estate proprietor in Oregon and has considerable interests in some land lately taken up in this neighborhood under the Swamp or Overflowed Land Act." And at this early time in his reporting, Fox tilted toward the Modocs: "There is . . . little doubt that the Indians have been badly treated, and if the whites had kept faith with them, there would have been no disturbance at all."[7]

• • •

Fox was by no means the only member of the fourth estate on the scene. Alex McKay, a Yreka surveyor, reported for the *San Francisco Evening Bulletin*. Robert D. Bogart, thirty-year-old veteran of the United States Navy and former reporter with the *New York Sun*, came north to file stories for the *San Francisco Chronicle* that also ran in the *Daily Alta California*. Today the only surviving daily in the city, the *Chronicle* of 1873 was a scandal rag whose founding editor would later be shot by a local businessman for defaming his family. And the same stagecoach that brought Fox to the Lava Beds also carried H. Wallace Atwell. Forty years old and described as both burly and slovenly, Atwell had been the editor of the *Woodland News*, then editor and publisher of the *Marysville Defender*, a small Sacramento Valley paper he sold to take a reporting job with the bigger *Sacramento Record*. Atwell was also a successful commercial writer whose *Trans-Continental Railroad Guide*—written under the pen name Bill Dadd the Scribe—sold well among train travelers headed west.[8]

For the time being, all the reporters, ranchers, and soldiers on scene could do was sleep on cold floors, eat greasy beef and doughy biscuits, and wait for the Peace Commission's members. Until they had arrived, nothing newsworthy would happen.

Edward Fox used the downtime to plan ahead. He was casting about for a way to interview Kientpoos one-on-one.

15

Heroic Reporter Dens with Lions

I did what cowardice and false pride suggested was the best thing—
walked deliberately to him, took off my hat, and
said, "Dr. Livingstone, I presume?"

—Henry Morton Stanley, *How I Found Livingstone*

Less than a month later, Edward Fox was sitting in Kientpoos's cave in the Stronghold, taking down the peace-inflected speech of the Modoc leader. Flames from a bonfire lighted the faces of the fifty to sixty Natives and a handful of Americans crammed into the rocky vault. They illuminated, too, the foolscap on which Fox penciled his notes, word by translated word.

Meanwhile, back at the Fairchild ranch, Meacham was fuming. The Peace Commission chairman had made it clear that the press was to receive only the information he deigned to give out. Yet a rebellious reporter had found a way to go around him, slip into the Stronghold on his own, and get the story directly from the Modocs. Meacham had to wonder how he had been made such a powerless fool.

It was, as the saying goes, a long story.

•••

The Peace Commission was slow in getting up and running, largely because bad weather and worse roads delayed Meacham's arrival. On February 15 in Linkville, Jesse Applegate convened the commission's first meeting, with himself, Samuel Case, and General Canby attending. Since Meacham was still on his way, the commission could conduct little business. Oliver Applegate was appointed secretary. And Uncle Jesse read into the record a disgruntled letter from Governor Grover, who wanted to ensure that his state would get its pound of

Modoc flesh: "The people of Oregon desire that the murderers shall be given up and delivered to the civil authorities for trial and punishment." As to the lingering possibility that the Modocs might be granted a reservation on Lost River, Grover reminded the commissioners that the Council Grove Treaty of October 1864 extinguished any Native claim to the land: "For the interests of Southern Oregon and for the future peace of our southern frontier, I will express the hope and confidence that the project of a reservation on Lost river will not be entertained by the Commission, and that the Modocs will either consent to return to their own reservation or be assigned to bounds beyond the settlements."[1]

Applegate tabled the letter because Meacham was absent, not because he disagreed with Grover's position. Indeed, he was on the same page. His nephew Oliver dubbed this the Oregon, or Modoc, Platform: the Modocs surrender unconditionally, the murderers dance their last on the gallows, and the surviving Indians slink off to some reservation far, far away. Applegate and Case stood firm on this position, and they planned to lobby Meacham for his support once he arrived.[2]

The commission adjourned, spent the night in Linkville's lone hotel, and left for the Lava Beds the next day. The weather was mucky, the road mired. Fox, who had gone to Linkville to report on the commission meeting, drew on his yachting expertise to add color to his account of the wagon ride back to Fairchild's: "During the first two miles the sidlings were so bad and the ruts to port so deep that General Canby got out and walked, while I hung on the starboard side, holding fast to the weather rigging. As ballast, I proved a success, and probably saved the ship capsizing on two or three occasions." The big Englishman from the big city had brought along a sense of humor.

On the rutted, muddy way south, Canby chatted up Matilda Whittle, an English-speaking Modoc woman married to Bob Whittle, who operated the Klamath River ferry. She agreed to carry a message into the Lava Beds and the Stronghold if the Peace Commission wanted.[3]

•••

Fox had already discovered that the locals on the California side of the state line had a low view of the Peace Commission. The problem was not the settler killings; that was Oregon's business. The issue was the commission's personnel: the Modocs openly despised Meacham, who finally arrived on February 18. They hardly needed reminding that Meacham had forced them back onto a reservation where they went hungry and cold. Nor did they buy Meacham's explanation that their mistreatment was due to poor management by Indian agent O. C. Knapp. The reservation was Meacham's lookout, and he looked away. As for Jesse Applegate, his lobbying among settlers and state politicians against the Modocs was well known, and his nephews Ivan and Oliver led the cavalrymen and the settlers' posse into the Lost River villages. Wherever the Modocs turned, an Applegate stood in their way.[4]

Robert Bogart, the reporter covering the Lava Beds for the *San Francisco Chronicle* and the *Daily Alta California,* had an opinion of Oregon's illustrious pioneer family as low as the Modocs'. Like many newspapermen of the time, he conflated reporting with commentary to create controversy. The Applegates offered a perfect target: "Three years ago, when the Applegates had all to do with feeding the Indians, the complaints were so numerous as to cease to attract attention."[5] The Modocs distrusted Jesse Applegate too much to negotiate peace with him: "The Indians have no confidence in any of the Applegates, and it is not believed here that they will meet old Jesse at all. He is regarded as the chief cause of all their troubles. . . . The Oregon War Ring, with the Applegates at its head, will take good care that peace is not brought about too hastily, and will also take care that no investigation is made of the management of Indian affairs in the past."[6] The Indians received undersized, threadbare blankets and far too little food, for which the government paid hugely inflated prices that profited the Applegates.

The Applegates took such personal attacks personally. Lindsay Applegate, leader of the clan, was intent on confronting Bogart. His son Oliver wrote to dissuade him, saying that family reinforcements would be counterproductive: "There are Applegates enough now at the front to make it seem like they are trying to 'run' the thing."[7] He had that right.

• • •

All the while, Canby made it clear that he was hoping for peace yet preparing for war. The general saw the army's role in the cease-fire as confining the Modocs to the Lava Beds and preventing them from resupplying. At the same time, he was searching out additional army units and dispatching them to the military camps around Tule Lake. And, ever an admirer of artillery, Canby was adding four Coehorn mortars to the mountain howitzers in his arsenal. These squat, portable weapons lobbed a shell high into the air and dropped it almost straight down—just the thing for bombing the Modocs in their caves, trenches, and hidey-holes.[8]

On the peace side of the ledger, Canby realized that Oregon's official demand to put the Modoc killers on trial could lead to a conflict of state versus federal rights. He saw, too, that the Applegates were staking their considerable family reputation on hanging the Modocs in Oregon. Canby decided, without consulting the other commissioners, that someone more sympathetic to the Modocs' position—preferably a Californian—was needed to counterbalance the vengeful Oregonians. And he knew that communication with the Indians had to be opened before they could be persuaded to surrender.

That was where Matilda Whittle came in. In a meeting with the Peace Commission chaired by Meacham and closed to the press, Canby argued for sending Whittle and some other trusted Indian woman into the Stronghold to request face-to-face negotiations. The message they were to carry struck a paternalistic note: "That the president of the United States, General Grant, had heard about the war and was very sorry his children were fighting. He looked upon all people of every color as his children, and he did not want them to spill each other's blood." Talking was better than fighting, but if the Indians wanted to fight—the message warned—the president had more than enough soldiers to crush them.

The other woman entrusted to carry the commission's message turned out to be Artina Chockus. She was a Hot Creek Modoc, a niece of Old Sheepy, and one of the women who stayed behind on Fairchild's ranch to care for the frail chief. Both Whittle and Chockus knew that, despite their ethnicity, walking unarmed into a war camp posed no small danger. They dressed the peacemaker's part: Chockus in paint, with a white handkerchief tied around her head, and Whittle in a close-fitting red dress, a white cloth snugged about the bodice. As the women left Fairchild's ranch in the late morning, Matilda removed all her jewelry and entrusted it to her husband. No sooner had the two Indian women ridden off, Fox reported, than the ravens around the campfire set to ominous croaking.

Late the following afternoon, the two women rode back over the ridge and down toward Fairchild's. Jesse Applegate walked out to meet them and ensure that whatever they said went unheard by the reporters nearby. He ordered the two to speak not a word until they had talked with himself, Meacham, Canby, and Case. Fox asked to listen in on the conversation; the commissioners put him off.[9]

That refusal strengthened Fox's dislike for Meacham and his controlling ways: "The commission have been very careful as to what information they furnished the correspondents of the different newspapers, and what they did give them was furnished as a special favor. One of the commissioners was kind enough to promise me all the current news on the condition that I should submit my correspondence for the approval of the commission before mailing it to its destination. It is needless to say that I was unable to avail myself of this very kind offer."[10]

The *Herald* reporter kept watch as the two Modoc women were hustled into closed conference with the commissioners. "The star chamber was thereupon convened," Fox reported, "and the grand inquisitor, Mr. Meacham, put the squaws through a most interesting 'course of sprouts.' After about two hours' talk the session was closed, and they all came up to the ranch."[11]

The Modocs in the Stronghold, Meacham said, received the two women hospitably and wanted to talk peace. They were out of clothing and food and afraid of treachery of the sort Ben Wright worked back in 1852. Still, the Modocs were willing to talk. They proposed no terms of settlement, preferring to hear what the whites offered.

Sensing there was more to the story, Fox found Bob Whittle and pushed him to talk. His wife had told him, Whittle said, that Kientpoos had his own preference for negotiators, none of whom sat on the Peace Commission. The headman wanted Elijah Steele, the lawyer and former Indian agent who had negotiated the unratified 1864 treaty, or A. M. Rosborough, Steele's law partner and a judge in Yreka.

Late that same day a telegram from Interior Secretary Delano arrived to inform the Peace Commission that Rosborough had indeed been named as a fourth member, a result of Canby's behind-the-scenes politicking.[12] And the following morning Matilda and Bob Whittle made a one-day ride to and from the Lava Beds to advance the negotiation. Kientpoos remained picky on whom the Modocs would parley with, according to Bob Whittle: "They wanted to talk to their friends, Fairchild, Steele, and Rosborough; did not know these commissioners [Meacham, Case, Applegate, and Canby]. . . . Wanted especially to see Fairchild."[13] Since Fairchild was the one man trusted by both Americans and Modocs, the commission decided to send him to the Stronghold along with the Whittles and Artina Chockus to arrange a grand conference.

Fox saw the opening he had been waiting for; he asked Meacham for permission to go along. Meacham refused: "Mr. Meacham and the commissioners appear to be throwing every obstruction in the way of a public investigation of this matter, and ordered Whittle and Fairchild on no account to allow any reporters to go with them. This is not the first attempt that has been made to prevent the press from obtaining direct information."[14]

Nor would it be the last.

• • •

Channeling his inner Henry Morton Stanley, Fox got to thinking. What authority did Meacham have over a reporter's comings and goings in a free country? None, Fox decided. So if he could get to the Lava Beds under his own power, there was simply nothing Meacham could do about it. He had to make the effort: "There must be some mystery that these gentlemen were attempting to hide from the public."

Fox concocted a strategy as sly as his surname. The day before Fairchild, Whittle, and the two Modoc women were to leave for the Lava Beds, the reporter announced loudly that he was riding south to the Van Bremer ranch to dine with the officers of the newly arrived Fourth Artillery. After the meal, Fox dropped by the sutler's to pick up a couple of pounds of tobacco and fill his whiskey flask—just in case.

The *Herald's* man was up at dawn and out the door into three inches of new snow. Gobbling a quick breakfast and saddling his mount, Fox headed north along the track leading toward the Fairchild ranch. He passed the spot where another track branched to the east across a small creek toward the Lava Beds. Seeing no tracks in the snow headed that way, Fox continued north, slowly, until he spotted four riders coming his way. Fairchild and Chockus rode in front, the Whittles twenty yards behind. Fox turned his horse, walked it alongside Fairchild's.

"Where are you going?" the gray-eyed rancher asked, surely surprised to see this big-city boy out and about on a frigid morning.

"To the Lava Beds with you," the reporter answered.

"Well, personally I have not any objection, and in fact I would be glad to have you with us; but as I am only accompanying Whittle, you had better see him."

Fox did just that. When Whittle asked "Where are you off this morning?" the reporter answered, "I hardly know—just taking a little ride."

"I am sorry the commissioners would not let you go with us."

"Yes," Fox agreed, "it was rather mean of them. But I have an idea of going without their permission, as I do not see what authority they have to govern my traveling in any part of the country I deem proper."

Whittle was politic: "That is so, but you cannot go with me."

"But if I choose to ride along after you, there is nobody who can prevent my going into the Lava Beds."

"If you go there, you will have to find the way yourself as, if you follow me, I shall turn back."

"You need not do that; nobody can blame you if I follow you."

"Yes, they will," Whittle said. "If you had asked me before I was engaged by the government, I would have taken you, but as it is, if you go I go back."

"Is there no way I can fix it?" Fox was pleading.

"None that I know of," Whittle answered.

"Well, if that is the case, I suppose I must defer my visit."

"I am very sorry," Whittle said, "but it cannot be helped."

The four emissaries crossed the creek and started up the slope to the east. Fox continued north, back toward Fairchild's. The horse prints cut clean and sharp into the new snow caught his eye. "It suddenly flashed across my mind," Fox wrote, "that those tracks would lead me to the Lava Beds, and the commissioners could then throw no blame on Whittle."

The reporter reined his horse about. Seeing that the four riders were already out of sight over the first hill, Fox followed their trail. He kept his pace slow, lest he come up on them suddenly. Near the top he dismounted and peered over the crest. The four had already passed out of sight. Fox continued down to the shore of frozen Lower Klamath Lake. Now the reporter could see his unwitting guides about two miles ahead. He followed at a speed that kept distance and landscape between them and him.

As Fox rode, he realized he was following the track of the Applegate Trail where "the fathers of these very Modocs whom I desired so much to see had taken a prominent part in butchering hundreds of victims. This train of thought had rather an unpleasant effect on my peace of mind, and the close proximity of two large ravens that kept slowly hovering over my head did not tend to enliven my spirits."

Sensing eyes watching his every move, Fox crested the next ridge at a trot and spotted the four on the flat below. At the same instant they turned and saw him. He had no choice but to ride down in full view.

"So you were determined to come? Well, well," Whittle said, "now you have come; you had better keep up close, as we have been seen by the Modocs before now. If I had seen you a couple of minutes further back I would have turned back, but as we have been seen, it would be unwise to return now."

Chastened, aware that his fear of spying Modoc eyes was all too real, Fox rode alongside Fairchild and Chockus. At the top of the Sheepy Ridge overlook, the two women dismounted, piled sagebrush, and set it alight. Soon Artina spotted an approaching Modoc, then two others. Fox missed the name of the first Native to arrive atop the bluff. The second man was the notorious Hooker Jim, leader of the settler-killing war party that took revenge for the Lost River raid. He took Fox's hand in a grip the reporter called "sullen." Jim's scowl was made all the more dramatic by black paint smeared across his face from the eyes down, a sign of mourning. He was dressed in a flannel shirt and "a pair of gray pants considerably the worse for wear," and armed with an old-fashioned muzzle-loader and a powder horn. Steamboat Frank, the third Modoc up, was better armed: a Spencer carbine and a full cartridge belt emblazoned with the letters "U. S.," booty from the January 17 battle.

Fox filled and fired his pipe and passed the smoking briar around the circle. The Modocs spoke in their tongue with the two women. Steamboat Frank, a Hot Creek who had worked for Fairchild, turned to the rancher and told him in good English that Kientpoos was too sick to leave his cave. Instead, the chief wanted Fairchild to come to the Stronghold to talk. Whittle asked whether he and "the paper man" were also invited. Frank said they were. And so the party of five emissaries, one tagalong reporter, and three Modoc fighters descended the steep trail, leading their horses down. At the bottom they remounted and rode toward the Stronghold.

Soon they came upon a half-dozen Modoc men warming themselves at a sagebrush campfire. "They were a wild looking group, nearly all clad in woolen shirts and secondhand soldiers' clothes. They were all armed to the teeth and painted. Some were in mourning, but the majority had their faces daubed with the reddish-brown mixture which they use as war paint," Fox wrote. Fairchild introduced the reporter as "the paper man from afar off, from the big town by the sea, Boston Illihee." Pacific Coast Indians commonly called Americans Bostons because the first Americans they had met were New England ship's captains. Fox again passed his lighted pipe from man to man.

A half mile farther along, the travelers came to a much bigger gathering. "A large party of the Modocs were standing and lying around a fire, built on the summit of a rocky bluff. . . . There were about fifty or sixty bucks, squaws, and papooses in the group, and the squaws, attired in their red petticoats with their papooses on their backs, gave one the picture of what might be taken for a gypsy encampment."

Fox had become acutely aware that his plan was working, perhaps too well. He had entered the dangerous world of a race he judged to be primitive, one he described in pejoratives like "buck" and "squaw." It unsettled Fox further that Hooker Jim took a shine to his Ulster overcoat and wanted to trade for it. He worried, too, that his ten-inch-long hair could become the desired trophy of a warrior with a scalping knife. Yet Fox had no choice but to follow the Modocs into the Stronghold.

Tame, who would be Fox's host for the night, showed him where he was to sleep: "The accommodation was certainly limited, as the reed matting [hanging] over a few tent poles stuck in the ground in an oval shape did not cover an area of more than ten feet by eight. The fire was built against the rocks in the open air, and under two rocks that had fallen together and formed two sides of an equilateral triangle." Inside the flimsy shelter Fox met Tame's wife, Wild Gal ("rather better looking than the average run of Modoc squaws"), and her daughter: "Miss Wild Gal Tame, a pretty little papoose about three or four years of age, sat on her knee playing with a dead mouse."

This introduction to Modoc domestic reality lasted only until Fox was invited to a council in Kientpoos's cave. This was a much bigger accommodation than Tame and Wild Gal's dwelling, a more or less round subterranean cavern, some forty feet in diameter by Fox's estimate. The hollow was filled with fifty or sixty Modoc women and men; the latter all carried rifles, whose barrels glinted in the firelight. At the center sat Kientpoos wearing a blanket around his lower body, a gray flannel shirt, and a white kerchief on his head. He offered his hand, cordially, to Fox, as did Scarface Charley, Shacknasty Jim, and Black Jim. Fox, as well as Fairchild, the Whittles, and Chockus, took a seat with them on a mat to Kientpoos's left. On the headman's right sat Bogus Charley, Steamboat Frank, Schonchin John, and Hooker Jim.

Fox was the only true newcomer; everyone else knew one another. "When all were quiet, John Fairchild got up and introduced the *Herald* correspondent by name to the assembled Indians and told how I came from afar off, from Boston Illihee, and wrote for a paper that told all the white people what was doing in all parts of the world. He said I had heard what the white people said about the Modoc troubles, and that I wanted so bad to hear the Modocs' story that though the commissioners had forbidden him to take me in, I had followed their tracks in the snow to the top of the bluffs. Bogus Charley . . . then translated this speech to the sachems."

The Indians, Fox reported, grunted their approval. They did the same when Fairchild read the letter he had been instructed to bring into the Stronghold. It said little, except that the commissioners were Applegate, Meacham, Case, and now Rosborough and that any substantive talk would be postponed until Rosborough and Steele arrived from Yreka.

Fox passed his pipe and tobacco around, and Fairchild asked the Indians to say their piece. Schonchin John was first to stand and speak. Fox transcribed sentence by sentence, as the aspiring headman's words were translated by someone left unnamed. All the bilingual people in the cave were native Modoc speakers, and the English that emerged from their lips through Fox's pencil sported the short sentences and fractured grammar of dime novels. Yet even through these twisted filters there emerged a political savvy, an astuteness, on the part of these people conventionally described as savage and primitive.

Right off, Schonchin John saw the public-relations advantage to getting the Modocs' story into the *New York Herald*. "Well, glad to see men; glad to see the paper man from afar off; my heart feels good when men talk," he began. "You tell me a name; I know him; Mr. Meacham; I see him; he says I am big chief. . . . Man from afar off, hear Indian speak. Hear him speak truth."

The older man's tone changed when he portrayed the Lost River raid as an unprovoked attack set by a lying Ivan Applegate: "What the matter? Bad work. . . . I don't know what the matter with [Captain James] Jackson [who led the cavalry unit]. He come early morning; soldier men coming, pistol in hand; like to see Captain Jack; all carry gun."

As Schonchin sat down, Bogus Charley stood and took up the story. He, too, blamed Jackson's action on Ivan Applegate. And he laid the shotgun killings of noncombatants on the settler vigilantes led by Oliver Applegate.

By now the sun had fallen, and the council broke for dinner. Fairchild, the Whittles, and Fox returned to Wild Gal and Tame's tule-mat shelter to eat cold meat and biscuits they had packed in their saddlebags. Wild Gal boiled water and made coffee. Scarface Charley, Schonchin John, Bogus Charley, and some others dropped by. Munching bits of bread, the three men told of their hard, cold, hungry time on the reservation. They also shared their low opinion of the Oregon militia in the January 17 battle: "They [the volunteers] lay on their backs and shot up in the air. They asked me all about the *Herald* and were evidently much amazed and astonished at the magnitude of the establishment connected with that paper," Fox reported.

The Modocs then invited Fox to watch Curley Headed Doctor use a shamanic ritual to cure Kientpoos. When the reporter arrived at the cave, the headman was lying beside the fire, his head close to his young wife, "a nice-looking woman with a magnificent eye, soft and full of expression." While a number of men danced and sang, the shaman worked himself into a frenzy, rolled Kientpoos over onto his belly, and sank his teeth into the headman's shoulder blade. Remaining attached, Curley Headed Doctor writhed and twisted, and another man jumped on top to hold the shaman in place. When the second man rolled off, the shaman unhooked his teeth, rushed to the mouth of the cave, and vomited. "All the Indians ran up after him to see what he threw up, as their belief is that he had sucked all the disease out of the sick man, and they wanted to see what it looked like. My curiosity did not lead me to join in the prospecting party, so I sat and watched them bathe Jack in cold water."

Sure that such rough and superstitious treatment would kill the chief by morning, Fox returned to Tame and Wild Gal's shelter. He barely slept, partly because of the penetrating cold, partly from fear of what would befall the white visitors if Kientpoos died in the dark.

After sunrise, back in the big cave, Fox was surprised to find the headman alive. In fact, Kientpoos "was sitting up, supported by his squaw, who had her arms around his waist, and he looked a little better this morning, as if the treatment he received on the previous evening had really done him good."

The chief felt good enough to talk. "I know Mr. Meacham. . . . I don't know which way he comes from now. . . . I afraid I don't know him; maybe he don't feel good. I got one heart; maybe Meacham got two hearts. My thoughts straight," he said. "I want you, Mr. Fairchild, tell how you know me long time, hear me speak truth. I don't know what I done bad. I tell truth. I am Yreka man. I conceal nothing."

When Fairchild, concerned that Kientpoos was losing control of his community, asked whether he could get his men to lay down their arms, the chief demonstrated his awareness of the political fractures dividing the Americans. "My boys think as me; I say quit, they all quit. Mr. Meacham maybe got two tongues; I speak with one tongue. These are all my people. I make good sense, give them my sense. Meacham got too many friends," he said. "Maybe half white good, maybe half bad. All boys here one mind; want whites all one mind."

Kientpoos even said he was ready to give up the old life, to find his place in this America that was sweeping the Modocs aside. "I want no Indian law," he said, "got no Indian law. Want same law for Indian and white man. Indian want to be same as white man. When Mr. Meacham done talking, if he tells no lies, I be same as white man."

Returning yet again to the root causes of the Lost River raid, the Modoc leader accused Captain Jackson of unwarranted aggression and Ivan Applegate of deceit and murderous treachery: "Ivan say, 'Clean them all out today, kill these Indians.'"

Displaying the skill of a politician who valued good press, Kientpoos made sure Fox felt welcome and wanted. "The man with good eye, he come to see me; he not afraid. Indian glad to see him, want paper man come again. He hear same story, hear me speak truth."

Fairchild and Kientpoos turned to setting the time, place, and guest list for a big meeting. Soon they decided that the meeting would take place on the grassy flat at the foot of Sheepy Ridge. There would be no soldiers, only the Peace Commission, including General Canby, plus Fox, Steele, and a couple of assistants. The meeting would occur once Rosborough and Steele arrived at Fairchild's.

It fell to Schonchin John to give the closing oration. This old man had seen the destruction of his people by disease and gunfire during the settler invasion and was one of the handful who had survived Ben Wright's massacre. Schonchin knew how bitter genocide tasted. At this moment, though, all was sweet: "I feel good now as if I stood in high place, saw all peace." This war could end: "Don't want to see more soldiers. I tell you truth, white men. Come and see me, all right. That's all."

As the Whittles, Chockus, Fairchild, and Fox left the Stronghold bearing good tidings to the waiting Peace Commission, the Modocs

Firing into a Continent

crowded the rocks and called out the names of those departing. "Good-bye," they said in English, "come again," over and over.[15]

• • •

Writing into the night at the Van Bremer ranch, Fox finished the story he had begun in the Stronghold. He sent it by courier to Yreka to be telegraphed back to New York at a cost of $500 to $600—in the neighborhood of $10,000 to $12,000 in today's money. Four days later he filed a second, reflective piece that covered much the same ground in greater detail.

One substantive difference between Fox's two stories was his assessment of the Peace Commission's prospects. The first article directed blame for the war's origins away from the Modocs. "From what I have seen of the Indians in the Lava Beds, and from what I have learned of their history," Fox wrote, "I think they have been badly treated and that the origin of the war can easily be traced to a few Oregonians." Small wonder then that the Modocs had no confidence in Meacham or any Applegate: "It is very doubtful . . . whether the present peace commission will do any good with these Indians, as I am satisfied from what I have seen in the Lava Beds that they distrust them."

The second version omitted this judgment entirely. Rather, Fox patted himself on the back for advancing progress toward peace. Steele had only just arrived at Fairchild's in the company of his law partner and now commissioner, A. M. Rosborough. "I had the pleasure of hearing from Mr. Steele," Fox wrote, "that my visit to the Lava Beds, he was certain, had done more to establish confidence between the Indians and the whites than anything that the peace commission had yet accomplished."[16]

Despite the self-congratulation, Fox aired the Modocs' grievances and repeated reports that Indian agents on the Klamath Reservation, Applegates among them, had cheated and starved the Indians. The Indians held, too, that the killings of Tule Lake settlers were retribution for the unprovoked cavalry attack on Lost River according to the Modoc law of war: "They hold themselves innocent of any crime, as after the white men attacked they do not consider it wrong to kill white men and . . . they spared women and children."[17]

None of this insight into the conflict interested the American press or its readership, however. What mattered was the reporter's heroic exploit, his bold entry into a den of Native lions, his vivid descriptions of war paint and red petticoats. Fox's own newspaper crowed, "This feat of Fox has placed the *Herald* in the van, and distanced all competitors in the race for news!" The *Trenton Gazette* praised Fox's interview as chivalrous proof of the moral superiority of the civilized over the savage. The story, the paper said, "reads more like some knight's tale, related at King Arthur's Round Table, than a mere matter-of-fact piece of modern newspaper enterprise."[18]

As far as the reading public was concerned, Fox wrote not about the Modocs. He wrote about himself. And even if the Indians had grievances, they still had to be removed, by any means necessary.

16

Talking for Peace, Lying for War

Report comes this morning that the war must continue. Steele barely
escaped with his life from the Lava Bed[s] and says when he goes
again it will be with a gun. So that the war in all likelihood goes
on and we must look out. The storm is raging.

—Oliver Applegate to Ivan Applegate, March 5, 1873

Two issues, General Canby recognized, stood between the Modocs
and their acceptance of a negotiated peace. The first was the fate
of the Indian raiders who had swept around Tule Lake after the Lost
River raid and killed a dozen or so American settlers. The Modocs saw
the killings as justified retribution for the shooting of noncombatant
women and children by other settlers, and they were not about to give
the responsible men up for the gallows. To the Oregonians these same
killings were wanton, unjustified savagery of the kind Indians practiced
routinely, and the killers deserved swift, lethal justice.

The second issue was the destination of the Modocs if they surrendered. The Oregonians wanted the Indians hauled off to some remote
place no white man would ever want. As for the traditional Modoc
land along Lost River—some of the most attractive acreage in the
entire Klamath Basin—they wanted that turned over to white settlers and homesteaders.

Jesse Applegate and Samuel Case had signed on to executing the raiders and sending the Modocs far away. Meacham appeared to endorse
the Oregonian plan,[1] but he remained open to alternatives.

Once Canby arranged for Rosborough to be appointed to the commission, the political arithmetic changed. As a California jurist, Rosborough had only an abstract concern about homicides in Oregon. And,

since the Applegates and their allies accused the judge of belonging to the Yreka cabal that armed and incited the Indians, Rosborough had every reason to want the Modocs settled in a fair and beneficent place and thereby thumb his Californian nose at the Oregonians. The commission's calculus now became two—Applegate and Case—against one—Rosborough—with a single swing vote—Meacham.

Sensing a political opening, Canby outlined an idea to General Sherman: "The Commission has proposed as the readiest solution of the Modoc question, that they surrender and put themselves under the protection of the United States as prisoners of war, until a suitable location can be found for them, with the assurance that if they accept the terms offered, they will be protected, subsisted and transported to their new homes and cared for, until they are able to provide for themselves."[2]

Canby's plan represented smart politicking. It blunted Oregon's desire to hang the Indians by putting them beyond the state's grasp. To gain that protection, the Modocs had to accept removal to a reservation to be named later, surely not Lost River and likely somewhere other than in Oregon. And he put the plan in the hands of an emissary the Modocs trusted: the tall, Lincoln-esque lawyer Elijah Steele.

Steele left for the Lava Beds on the morning of February 28. He saw his mission as a way of obtaining a fair deal for the Modocs, and no more. "I have been so long on the frontiers, and have seen the Indians in their native disgusting state, that I have no special regard for them, other than making out justice, and I have none of the poetry entertained by many who do not know them," Steele wrote later. "The Modocs are generally a whiter tribe of Indians than any other I have met with."[3]

Alongside Steele rode Fairchild and the three California newspapermen—H. Wallace Atwell, Alex McKay, and Robert Bogart. The journalists were hoping for a scoop to rival the derring-do of the *New York Herald*'s Edward Fox, who so far had outdone them mightily. Since the Whittles had left Fairchild's to return to their ferry business on the Klamath River, their place as translators and go-betweens was taken by another interracial couple.

Frank and Toby Riddle had gotten together in the way most whites and Natives forged unions along the California-Oregon frontier of the time: Frank bought Toby for two horses.[4]

• • •

The romantic myth of the West skips over the reality that the frontier was a sexual war zone. Americans who came to northern California and southern Oregon to work the mines brought with them mythic stereotypes built from many years of genocidal violence and a studied ignorance of Indigenous cultures. Sure that Native women eagerly offered their favors to any and every importuning male, gold rush miners felt no compunction against rape and forced concubinage, and they killed with impunity any Indian man who got in the way. Prostitution became one of the few modes of survival open to Indian women pushed into poverty by the emigrant invasion.[5]

Sexual violence shredded Native cultures as surely as did smallpox, the extermination of game and fish, polluted springs and streams, and gunshot. The Indians' sense of morality, community, and sexual ethics was assaulted even as venereal disease slashed birth rates, adding yet another threat to survival. Sex was a weapon in genocide's armory.

Against this backdrop, the Riddles' story played out. Frank was only eighteen when he left his loveless, slaveholding family in Kentucky and struck out for California, working first in Sacramento then drifting to the gold fields around Yreka. After six years of mining, about the time Toby took up residence with him in 1862 in exchange for those two horses, Frank changed to farming and ranching and moved to Bogus Creek, east of Yreka, the same stream that gave Bogus Charley half his white nickname. The Riddles' only child, a son, was born late the following year. The two names given to the boy show how he straddled the frontier between Indian and white. To the Modocs he was Charka, which means "the handsome boy." Whites knew him as Jefferson Davis Riddle, named after the Confederate president in fealty to his father's Kentucky loyalties.

When his son was six, Frank Riddle sold the Bogus Creek ranch and moved his family north to trap and hunt along Lost River upstream of Kientpoos's village. He was skilled at woodcraft. By one accounting, he killed 743 deer and elk and 132 bears in his career.[6]

It was along Lost River that Toby and Frank came to the attention of Meacham while he was the state's Indian superintendent. Toby was Kientpoos's cousin, and she and Frank translated for Meacham when he showed up uninvited at Lost River to force the Modocs back to the Klamath Reservation. Now, three years later, Meacham tapped the Riddles to replace the Whittles as the Peace Commission's translators and go-betweens.

So it was that Frank and Toby Riddle saddled up early on February 28, left son Jeff at Fairchild's ranch, and rode out for the Lava Beds with Steele and the three California newsmen. They were to translate the offer Steele was conveying to the Modocs for Canby, an offer that might bring this war to a prompt and peaceful close.

• • •

The Yreka lawyer returned at the head of a group larger than he had left with, his mood euphoric. Raising his hat as he approached the tents of the army camp, Steele shouted, "They accept peace." As if to signal agreement with the terms the Peace Commission had offered, several prominent Modocs came along back to Fairchild's: Princess Mary, Boston Charley, Bogus Charley, Hooker Jim, Long Jim, Curley Headed Jack, Shacknasty Jim, Duffy, and Weium (aka Tame, Fox's host on his visit to the Stronghold). Steele's euphoria swept through the encampment. Newspapermen drafted enthusiastic reports for their editors, Meacham readied a wire of self-congratulatory success to his superiors, and couriers were ordered up to ride to Yreka and bear the news to the telegraph office.

Fairchild, however, held to a dissenting opinion of what had happened in the Stronghold. "I don't think the Modocs agreed to accept the terms offered," he said. "True, they responded to Steele's speech, but *not in that way*. I tell you they do not understand that they have agreed to *surrender yet, on any terms*."[7]

Steele argued with Fairchild, summoning as proof the notes that Atwell had made in the Stronghold. Those notes were a translation of words spoken in English, translated into Modoc, answered in Modoc, and translated back into English—a game of telephone played in two languages by non-native speakers.[8] Atwell tipped toward Steele's opinion that the Modocs were enthusiastic about surrender, even as the other two reporters, McKay and Bogart, favored Fairchild's skepticism. To settle the matter, Meacham, Canby, and the other commissioners questioned the Modocs who had ridden in with Steele. "They were reticent, saying they came out to *hear* what was said, and not to *talk*," Meacham reported. "No expression could be obtained from them."[9]

Steele was so convinced of his accurate reading of the Indians' temperament that he proposed returning to the Lava Beds the next morning to begin negotiating the details of the Modocs' surrender. Atwell wanted to go along; the skeptical Bogart and McKay chose to remain behind. Fairchild also said no, shaking his bearded head with gray eyes closed. Any misgivings Frank and Toby Riddle felt did not stop the two from going back as translators.

Soon after sunrise, the party rode out: Steele, Atwell, and Frank and Toby Riddle. Princess Mary and six of the Modoc men who had come in the day before went on ahead. They would reach the Stronghold first. They were carrying disturbing information they wanted to share with families and friends well before the Americans arrived.[10]

• • •

As soon as Steele strode into the Stronghold leading his horse, he sensed a communal bristle among the Modocs that pricked his own hair. As the three white men unsaddled, tied their horses, and walked to Wild Gal's to take their supper, the Indian men they passed threw sullen glares. After the emissaries ate, they made their way to Kientpoos's cave to talk peace. The rocky cavern was packed with Modocs wrangling loudly around the fire. As soon as the whites ducked under the overhanging rock and entered the cave, the Indians fell silent. "The whole circle of dusky warriors looked dark, gloomy and forbidding," Atwell reported.

Steele stepped up to shake hands with Kientpoos. As palm grasped palm, the Yreka lawyer knew everything was wrong. Kientpoos wore a woman's cap, a sign that he had been fooled and knew it. Feigning nonchalance, Steele cut up a hank of twist tobacco and passed it around the huge circle. He read to the Indians the terms proposed by the Peace Commission and General Canby. The Modocs would be transported to Angel Island, in San Francisco Bay, and remain there while Kientpoos and a few other leaders took the train to Washington, DC, for an audience with President Grant. Once the Modoc leaders returned and a new reservation was chosen, probably in Arizona, the entire tribe would be moved there and settled. When Steele finished reading and the Riddles translating, only Scarface Charley and two other men said yes. The rest of the Modocs remained silent and sullen.

Kientpoos rose. He accused Steele of duplicity, said he himself had not sold his land and would never leave it. Then Schonchin John seized the floor. He, too, called Steele a liar and asked the lawyer whether, after bringing such a message, he was afraid to sleep in the Stronghold. Both brave and brazen, Steele answered that he was an old man unafraid of dying, which did not hurt very much anyway. Toby Riddle detailed the Peace Commission's proposition in the Modoc language and urged acceptance, an admonition that drew only derisive laughter from the other Indians.

When Steele and Atwell rose to return to Wild Gal's for the night, Scarface Charley whispered, "Sleep here (pointing to his bed), and I will sleep with you tonight." The two white men unrolled their blankets and lay down against the cave wall, alongside Scarface Charley and Princess Mary. Kientpoos himself stretched out at their feet.

In the morning the council resumed, its mood even darker. Schonchin John was the first to speak. "I have heard the talk; Captain Jack has heard it. He don't know anything about another country, don't want to go there," he said. "It looks like . . . another heart had entered into the talk now. . . . I want everything wiped out, and we live as we used to. That is the way I want to settle this matter. I want to know the names of the bad men that want to hang us. I want to know where they live. I want to know why they are mad." He asked, "Why won't those men quit and have peace—those Oregon men? I don't trouble them. . . . Why don't they quit fighting? What is the reason these men won't make friends? Why won't they quit fighting as long as we have?"

Steele answered that protecting the Modocs against Oregon's vengeance seekers was impossible. "The Oregonians are very mad at your people, and if you live here they will kill some of your men," he said. President Grant knew the Indians were not to blame, and to protect them, he wanted the Modocs to go with General Canby to a safe, new home. There was no real alternative: "You can have your own land, raise grass, melons, grain, horses, and cattle, and live like white men. If you do not agree to this, but stay here, it will be war, and you will all be killed."

"The talk that we have been having has taken such a turn I hardly know what to think of it," Kientpoos answered. "I thought everything was to be wiped out and we were to live as we did before. . . . These are all my people; I have no other, and they are like me; we talk with one mouth. . . . [T]the Oregon men want to fight, and the others do not. It is a curious thing to me that your great chief cannot rule your people alike. I am not like the Oregonians. . . . Let them have that side of the lake and I will keep this side. I don't know of any other country. . . . This is my home; I was born here. I have always lived here and I don't want to leave it."

Steele felt everything collapsing around him. "My heart is sick about your talk," he told Kientpoos and Schonchin John. "You want me to trust you all the time but you trust me none."

Sensing that the impasse was total and the Modoc anger boiling over, Steele realized it would be no small trick to get himself, Atwell, and the Riddles out the Lava Beds alive. An escape route opened when Kientpoos offered to meet again at the base of Sheepy Ridge in two days' time. He was picky about the guest list. Meacham and Applegate simply had to be there. Canby, Case, Fairchild, the Riddles, and Atwell could attend, but without Meacham and Applegate there would be no meeting. Kientpoos's insistence convinced Steele that the Indians intended to kill the two commissioners they despised the most. Fearing for his own life enough to make a deal he never intended to keep, the lawyer agreed to the meeting.

Steele, Atwell, and the Riddles saddled their horses and led them out of the Stronghold, then swung up into the saddle. Although he had been invited to the upcoming meeting, Atwell, too, had no plan to come this way again, however dramatic the story: "I shall most certainly decline to serve the *Record* on any such terms."[11]

• • •

Something big had happened between Steele's first visit and his second. The Modocs shifted from initial enthusiasm to a sense of betrayal so strong they were ready to kill. Whatever Princess Mary and the six Modoc men who returned to the Stronghold in advance of Steele, Atwell, and the Riddles passed on to their people poisoned the mood.

Atwell discovered what that something was. "Charles Blair, of Linkville, Oregon, who was here on Sunday, told the Modocs . . . that he had a paper to take and hang nine of them, some of whom were present then," the reporter wrote. "This has raised hell among them."

Blair had boasted openly he did not want the war to stop, and his lie about the warrant for nine hangings was a surefire way to upend peace. He was hardly alone in his desire for continued hostilities. Blair pledged allegiance to a war ring "composed of men who do not want peace, for there is money in this difficulty. Grain at forty cents a pound, and other things in proportion, will give some idea of the profits realized. All these men who are pecuniarily interested have brought strong influences to bear against the Peace Commission, and have even obtained the official countenance of his accidence, Governor Grover, who is owned and ruled by them."[12]

Meacham called Blair "a man of disreputable character," and Fox further identified Blair as "a pardoned convict residing in Oregon."[13] Bogart similarly reported that Blair "told the Modocs the lie, adding that the Commission only wanted to get the Jack's party out to hang them all."[14]

Charles Blair qualified as an unlikely candidate to wield such influence, however. He was a penniless laborer with neither real estate nor trade who hailed originally from Ohio. About fifty years of age at the time, Blair was married to a much younger Klamath Indian woman named Nellie, with whom he had at least two children.[15]

So the story Meacham wanted his boss at the Indian Bureau to buy—and that Atwell, Fox, and Bogart reported—was that a no-count frontier redneck had soured the peace talks by telling the Modocs he was

Firing into a Continent

authorized to arrest and hang them. Equally important, the Modocs bought the story from this unreliable source, became convinced of treachery, and determined to turn tables on the commissioners and invite Applegate and Meacham to an ambush.

Given Blair's utter lack of status, power, or credibility, the story holds water only if this Linkville laborer worked for someone much more powerful than he and if he let the Indians know who stood behind him. The Modocs had already demonstrated their political savvy in welcoming reporters into the Stronghold and exploiting the differences between Oregonians and Californians. The Modocs would buy a cock-and-bull story from a freelance ruffian only if that thug enjoyed the backing of big boys—men of the sort who, in Atwell's view, carried Governor Grover around in their back pocket.

The Americans with the most power in southern Oregon—and the most likely suspects for upsetting the Peace Commission negotiations to their advantage—were the Applegates. Jesse Applegate's grand rancho scheme with shadow partner Jesse Carr rested on running the Modocs out of the Lost River neighborhood. War stood the best chance of accomplishing just that. All the while, Applegate was making money by renting land to the army for its camp at Clear Lake and selling grain to feed military horses and mules at inflated prices. War was good for business; peace, not so much.

The Applegates knew Blair well. Not quite three years earlier Blair wrote to O. C. Knapp, then Indian agent on the Klamath Reservation, to complain of the returned Lost River Modocs as "very saucy since they came here. They have been making some threats of killing white men." Blair made no secret of his contempt for his Indian neighbors. "One white man is worth the whole tribe," he wrote. Oliver Applegate thought highly enough of Blair's missive that he included it in his war memoir. Only three days after the letter was sent, Blair and Applegate met with Kientpoos at Blair's homestead to hear the chief's proposal that the east side of Lost River belong to the Modocs. Later, Blair threw in with Lost River settlers accusing the Modocs of every downed fence and lost calf, heifer, and steer in the neighborhood. He added the bald lie that Kientpoos had threatened his life.[16]

Nor would using an Indian-hater like Charles Blair to talk smack to the Modocs be the only example of the Applegates pulling strings behind the scenes.

•••

Right from the time he arrived in the Lava Beds, Robert Bogart of the *San Francisco Chronicle* focused on the Applegates' role in starving and freezing the Modocs on the Klamath Reservation and starting the war. He wrote article after article alleging corrupt profit-taking by Ivan and Oliver Applegate, with a little help from, and a cut off the top to, Meacham.

Jesse Applegate took the charges against his nephews so seriously that he promised to resign from the Peace Commission as soon as the question of war or peace was decided.[17] That was the public face of the matter. Privately, just to make sure that the Applegates' profitable involvement in all matters Modoc fell through a convenient crack, the family saw to it that Bogart disappeared.

In late February, as the *Chronicle* was running story after story naming Ivan and Oliver as reservation profiteers, the two contacted their eldest brother, Elisha, in Washington, DC, and asked him to do what he could. "I went right off and seen the War Office and the other offices," Elisha wrote back. "I was determined to get some authority on the ground friendly to you boys."[18] Soon after Elisha's visit, the *Chronicle* summoned Bogart back to San Francisco, the city where Jesse Carr had launched his career as a financial and political manipulator and still held hefty sway. As Bogart was leaving the newspaper's downtown offices late one evening soon after his return, he was grabbed by a squad of United States Marines, hauled off to the Mare Island naval base, and imprisoned in the hold of the navy ship *Independence*—an arrest so abrupt that a local newspaper called it a kidnapping. Bogart had been picked up on the orders of no less a personage than Secretary of the Navy George M. Robeson, a prominent leader in the very War Department visited by Elisha Applegate. Never one to shrink from using his office to benefit fellow Republicans like the Applegates, Robeson sent the local naval authorities a telegram ordering Bogart arrested and held "at all hazards." The reporter was charged with embezzling $10,000 while in the service as a paymaster's clerk in

December 1868 and of deserting with the stolen money, offenses for which he had already been tried by court-martial and released. After both federal and military hearings, Bogart was held at Mare Island until, again at the order of the Secretary Robeson, he was set free without explanation.[19] Almost ten months had passed, and by then the Modoc War was over.

As soon as the Bogart thorn was removed from his family's side, Jesse Applegate concluded his tenure on the Peace Commission by drafting a brief, irony-dipped summary of the conflict's origins. In a mere three hundred words penned in a rush on March 9, Applegate laid entire blame for a war decades in the making on the Lost River Modocs' refusal to abide by the 1864 Council Grove Treaty. Since the collapse of Steele's negotiations made war the only option, Applegate concluded that "we therefore consider the Commission an expensive blunder."[20]

Meacham shared his colleague's assessment. He telegraphed Interior Secretary Delano: "The mission is a failure. Instruct immedy [immediately]—time is of most importance."[21]

Delano got back to Meacham the very next day, a response that in early 1873 was as instantaneous as telegraph could make it. The secretary's answer set the Peace Commission chairman back on his heels.

17

The Warrior Takes Command

Canby is usually seen near the head of the column, attended by his
staff and a few mounted troopers as escort. Tall and straight, coarsely
dressed in citizen's clothes, his countenance hard and weatherbeaten,
his chin covered with a heavy grizzly beard of two weeks growth,
a cigar in his mouth, which he never lights—using a pipe when he
wishes to smoke—he certainly has an air of superiority.
—A Colorado volunteer after the Battle of La Glorieta Pass,
March 1862

Sitting in the nation's capital some three thousand miles away
from the Lava Beds, Delano had no problem second-guessing
Meacham. "I do not believe the Modocs mean treachery. The Mission
should not be a failure," he cabled back. "Think I now understand their
unwillingness to confide in you. Continue negotiations."[1]

What bothered Meacham as much as Delano's slap-down was the
surprise that Applegate, Case, and Rosborough had in store. Eager to
be done with the foundering Peace Commission, the three of them
voted to surrender the entire matter of peace and war to General Canby.
Applegate packed his bags and headed over the Clear Lake Hills to his
ranch, huffing under his breath that the "beastly Commission" was a
fraud. Case journeyed back to his job at the Siletz Reservation, and
Rosborough returned to the judge's bench in Yreka. Meacham "could
only look on, giving opinions when requested by Gen. Canby."[2]

Delano, too, had lost all confidence in Meacham and was relying
on the general. "Secy Delano . . . expresses a hope that the wisdom &
discretion of Gen Canby will prevent the further effusion of blood
& bring the unhappy controversy to a peaceable solution," General
Sherman made clear to Canby. "The whole question rests with you."

Delano even ordered Meacham to have Canby approve his telegrams before sending. And he asked Odeneal, of all people, to take the commission seat vacated by Case, even though Meacham had vetoed him earlier. Fortunately for Meacham, Odeneal begged off and suggested in his place Leroy S. Dyar, the current Indian agent at the Klamath Reservation.[3] Delano promptly appointed him.

That left Applegate's spot to fill. At the suggestion of California Republican senator Aaron A. Sargent, Delano tapped the Reverend Doctor Eleazar Thomas, a Methodist minister from Petaluma, California, a small town north of San Francisco known for chicken farming. Thomas was the editor of the *California Christian Advocate*, a San Francisco–based weekly that supported Grant's Peace Policy yet focused its editorial energy mainly on stopping Roman Catholicism, promoting temperance, and decrying drunken debauchery in boomtowns like Yreka. Thomas made political sense because he was a Californian and because he represented the humanitarian Protestants who were criticizing the Grant administration for its belligerence against the Modocs. Although Thomas had no practical experience with Indians, he accepted the appointment.[4]

At the same time, Delano decided it was his "duty to authorize Gen. Canby to remove from the present Commission appointed by this Department any member he thinks unfit, or improper, and appoint in his place such person as in his judgment should be appointed." When General Sherman informed Canby about this extension of the brigadier's power, he spelled out its implications: "This actually de Volves on you the entire management of the Modoc question."[5]

The Modoc War was now Canby's war. Who this brigadier general was, and how he saw the world, would shape the fate of the Modoc people.

• • •

No one would ever have described Edward Richard Sprigg Canby as the sharpest chisel in even a small shed. After graduating second from the bottom in his 1839 West Point class, the brand-new second lieutenant was assigned to the Second Seminole War. He fought in the Battle of Palaklakaha Hummock, where the Mikasuki chief Halleck

Tustenuggee pulled off one of his many miraculous escapes. A month later, however, the Mikasukis surrendered voluntarily. Canby drew the assignment of accompanying 120 of the now-peaceful Natives to exile along the Deep Fork of the Canadian River in Oklahoma's Indian Territory.[6]

Since progress up the military food chain in the 1840s was slow, it took the persistent Canby six years to make first lieutenant.[7] And when President James K. Polk fulfilled his campaign promise to incite war with Mexico, Canby was assigned as a junior infantry officer in Winfield Scott's army of invasion. In the Battle of Cerro Gordo, Canby won modest fame by capturing a Mexican artillery battery. Later he earned citations and two brevet ranks in the Battles of Contreras, Churubusco, and the Belén Gate outside Mexico City. Although Canby never displayed dash or strategic brilliance, his battlefield record and commendations helped lift him, rung by slow rung, up the army ladder of command.

In 1860, Canby, now a major, was dispatched to New Mexico to lead the ongoing campaign against the Navahos. His strategy was to corner the Indians and "inflict punishment," as he put it, "signal in its results and lasting in its effects."[8] When some Navahos sued for peace and laid blame for the conflict on the *ladrones*—horse thieves and robbers within the nation—Canby said he would entertain peace only when the good Navahos brought the bad Navahos under control. As Canby saw it, the war party kept the conflict going because it presented endless opportunity for profit by theft. The only way to throw the war party over, he reckoned, was to inflict upon the wealthier elements of the tribe such suffering that they would turn on the poorer *ladrones*. Canby adopted a strategy of harassing the Navahos to keep them always on the move. Beset by a deep drought as well as the army, the Indians were rarely able to spend more than two nights in the same camp, and many of their precious flocks of goats and sheep perished. In mid-January 1861 three Navaho chiefs offered a partial armistice in order to bring the *ladrones* to heel. By March the number of headmen signing the peace treaty grew to thirty-two. Fighting ceased.

In part due to Canby's misperception of Navaho political culture,

Firing into a Continent

however, the peace soon deteriorated. Ignoring the reality that each Navaho fighter was his own master and could enlist with any leader he wanted, Canby insisted on collective responsibility. Since that concept made sense within white culture, Canby assumed it also applied to the Navahos. He had that wrong. Then he made matters worse when New Mexican raiders invaded Navaho country to capture slaves and Canby did nothing to stop them.[9] In addition, the loss of much of their livestock left the Navahos starving, yet the Bureau of Indian Affairs made no effort to feed the hungry. The desperate Indians went back to fighting, and Canby's peace evaporated.[10]

Canby's blithe assumptions about the equality between Indigenous and American political culture would come back to bite him in the Modoc conflict. In the meantime, though, his career moved forward: he won promotion to colonel and command of the Northern Military District in New Mexico. Now Canby faced a much bigger foe: the Confederate States of America.

● ● ●

The Confederates saw New Mexico as a strategic stepping-stone to the Colorado gold fields on the north and to the southern California ports and Sierra Nevada mines on the west. In the summer of 1861, Lieutenant Colonel John Robert Baylor led fewer than four hundred Confederate troops some forty-five miles north from El Paso, Texas, to the pro-Confederate New Mexico hamlet of Mesilla. After a small firefight, the Union force abandoned nearby Fort Fillmore and surrendered. Emboldened by the easy victory, Baylor declared all the territory south of the thirty-fourth parallel to be Confederate Arizona, which encompassed parts of modern New Mexico and Arizona.

The stage was set for invasion. In early 1862, Brigadier General Henry Hopkins Sibley marched thirty-seven hundred thinly clad, poorly armed, and mostly mounted Confederate troops from El Paso's Fort Bliss into New Mexico, following the Rio Grande through the Mesilla Valley and then north.

Canby knew Sibley well. They had been classmates at West Point, married women who were cousins, and fought the Navahos together. The men were near opposites in temperament: Sibley mercurial, impetuous, womanizing, and alcoholic; Canby taciturn, prudent, faithful, and given to no vice beyond the unlit cigar ever in his mouth.

The two military leaders knew they would clash at Fort Craig, an adobe-walled outpost that guarded the wagon road to Albuquerque and Santa Fe. Sibley needed to capture the fort, and the ammunition, medicine, and food within its walls, to equip his force as it headed ever farther from supply depots in Texas. To stymy the Confederates, Canby arrived at Fort Craig with almost four thousand soldiers, among them the redoubtable scout and Indian fighter Kit Carson, and seventy wagons' worth of supplies. Two-thirds of the soldiers, though, were Spanish-speaking New Mexican militiamen, of whom Canby had a low opinion.[11] The colonel put them to work reinforcing Fort Craig. New earthworks were erected to blunt artillery fire and thwart assault. To make the post look even more formidable, sawlogs were painted cannon-barrel black and positioned in gunports in the adobe. Irreverent soldiers called these fake weapons "Quaker guns."

Sibley's plan was to draw Canby out of Fort Craig and cut him off, then attack and seize the undermanned outpost. After various feints, charges, artillery duels, skirmishes, and two days of sandstorm, Sibley's troops camped behind a ridge across the Rio Grande from Fort Craig, well back from the water. As darkness fell, the Confederate horses and mules were growing thirsty and restless.

That night witnessed an attack worthy of the Three Stooges. A volunteer spy company headed by Captain James "Paddy" Graydon, a former saloonkeeper and military veteran, camped on the same side of the Rio Grande as Sibley and the Confederates to keep watch and report back to Canby. Then Graydon got an idea. He selected two old mules from the remuda and loaded short-fused 24-pound howitzer shells on their swayed backs. The plan was to sneak close to Sibley's picket line under cover of darkness, light the shells' fuses, then smack the mules smartly across the rump and send them at a run into the Confederate ranks. Graydon's crew crept unseen and unheard within 150 yards of the pickets, lit fuses, smacked rumps, and beat a retreat—only to turn around and see the old mules following behind at an eager trot. Fortunately for Graydon's men, they ran faster than the aged, burdened animals, and the fuses were short. When the exploding shells sent chunks

Firing into a Continent

of mule flying every which bloody way, the roused Confederate camp panicked and fired blindly into the night. In the melee, thirsty Confederate horses and mules broke free and ran off toward the river and into the arms of Canby's soldiers.

The next morning Sibley sent part of his force toward Fort Craig, while the remainder bolted north toward the ford at Valverde. Their goal was to cross the river to the road, then attack the fort when Canby came out. Wary, Canby stayed inside and dispatched a substantial detachment to intercept the Confederates. The two forces clashed at Valverde in furious battle. A little before midafternoon, Canby rode out to take command of what was looking like a Union victory.

Then everything went wrong. A wave of Texans armed with shotguns, squirrel rifles, revolvers, and lances charged the Union artillery. The battery on the left held, but the one on the right was overwhelmed, with all the horses and most of the officers and men slaughtered. The Confederates turned the guns around and commenced firing on the Union troops. The New Mexican militiamen fled. Canby, who had three horses shot out from under him in the course of the day's fighting, had to pull the surviving units back to Fort Craig to save what he could.

Losses on the two sides were about equal. Although Valverde was chalked up as a Confederate victory, Sibley had failed to accomplish what he most needed: capturing Fort Craig and its supplies. The Confederates were still hungry, underdressed for winter, and low on ammunition, and they had lost some 350 horses and mules, many to Graydon's wild attack. Meanwhile, Canby and his men and mounts were safe inside Fort Craig with plenty of food, firepower, and fuel. Sibley broke off the siege and headed north toward the bigger prizes of Albuquerque and Santa Fe. Canby dispatched fast horsemen ahead of the Confederate advance to order army depots destroyed before the Confederates could capture them. And the colonel stayed where he was and reorganized his force, shedding the New Mexican militiamen.

Once the Confederates found the supplies at Albuquerque and Santa Fe turned to ash, they dissolved into an army of looters. By the time Union forces from Colorado caught up with them in La Glorieta Pass, the Confederates' situation had become desperate. A surprise, over-the-mountain attack crushed the Confederates and destroyed their supply wagons, forcing Sibley to retreat to Albuquerque. There Canby intercepted the ragtag Confederate army. His force was almost twice as large as Sibley's and far better equipped. Yet instead of charging across the Rio Grande to destroy the Confederates, Canby let Sibley retreat downriver. He followed close behind on the opposite bank, harassing the Confederates just enough to keep them moving fast and longing for Texas. Characteristically, Canby was favoring prudence over dash and derring-do.

When Canby's forces loomed so close that the Confederates could see their campfires flickering through the ghostly, wind-rattled cottonwoods along the Rio Grande, Sibley's bourbon-burned brain dissolved into panic. He ordered his men to abandon the river, ditch the few remaining supply wagons, and bolt overland for Texas.

Sibley was sending his men through a hundred miles of the driest, toughest country in the Southwest without guide, trail, or water. The Confederates burned or buried most of their gear and left mules and horses to die where they fell. Men kept dying, too. By the time Sibley's command shuffled into Fort Bliss, more than seventeen hundred men had been tucked into graves or left to wither and whiten in the desert. The remains of the Confederate army retreated all the way to San Antonio in every-man-for-himself disarray.[12]

Canby had defended the New Mexico territory and its strategic access to Colorado and California with only a modest loss of fighting men. That success carried him first to the War Department, then to New York City after the draft riots, and finally to command of the Military Division of West Mississippi.

In that last posting the war's pain became personal. While Canby stood on the deck of the gunboat *Cricket* plying the White River in Arkansas, a Confederate sniper shot him down. The musket ball blew through his left buttock and exited the left thigh just below the groin, leaving a wound tunnel a half-inch in diameter. Canby was lucky; the slug missed major blood vessels, nerves, and bones. Still, the wound was severe, his recovery slow and painful.

When the Civil War ended, Canby, who was now one of but ten brigadier generals in the downsized army, led Reconstruction in the defeated Carolinas, Texas, and Virginia. Worn out by the contention

Firing into a Continent

of running civil affairs under martial law in the South, Canby sought reassignment in August 1870 as commander of the Department of the Columbia. In Washington and Oregon the problem Canby faced was not stiff-necked Confederates but insurgent Natives. This assignment must have looked like a fitting duty station for a senior officer of more than three decades' service who was thinking retirement. There was just the Modoc business to close out.

...

Soon after Steele's hair-raising second visit to the Modoc Stronghold, Canby hoped he might end this last conflict of his career on a peaceful note. Princess Mary, in the company of several men, appeared at Fairchild's, bearing messages from Kientpoos and Schonchin John. Schonchin said, "I have got all my people to say yes, that they are willing to go & not talk bad any more." Mary reported that Kientpoos was sad, crying all the time. According to her, he said, "I say yes to going to a warmer country and this is the first time I have said yes. I dont want my people shot. . . . But I say yes and consent to everything & go away I dont want to live here any more because I cant live here any more in peace." The Modocs asked that their friends and relatives on the Klamath Reservation be allowed to leave with them, and that a few of the headmen travel the country before the community was resettled. Canby agreed. The Indians promised to surrender at a place called Point of Rocks, northwest of the Lava Beds and east of Lower Klamath Lake.[13]

Canby remained unconvinced of the Modocs' sincerity. "I am not fully satisfied that this consent is not a device to gain time and have sent them word, that if they mean what they say, they must come in tomorrow," he telegraphed Sherman.[14] Tomorrow came, and the Modocs did not appear. Instead, messengers let Canby know that burning the dead according to custom was taking longer than expected. The general and the Indians set another date, two days hence. The time passed, wagons went out to meet the Modocs, and the Indians were nowhere to be seen. The wagons packed up and returned, empty.

Informed of what had happened, Sherman advised Canby to remain patient and settle the conflict peacefully if possible. Still, Sherman cham-

pioned extermination as Plan B: "Should these peaceful measures fail
& should the Modoc Indians presume too far in the forbearance of
the Government & again resort to deceit & treachery I trust you will
make such use of Military force that no other Indian tribe will imitate
their example & that no other reservation for them will be necessary
except graves among their chosen Lava Beds."[15]

• • •

A mystery remains as to what was happening inside the Stronghold
at the time of the Point of Rocks offer. The Modocs who passed back
and forth between the Fairchild ranch and the Lava Beds were stu-
diously tight-lipped. And, after Steele's harrowing visit, no American
was willing to venture into the Stronghold to look and listen. Perhaps
Kientpoos was playing for time, as Canby suspected. The headman
was adept at seeming to agree without agreeing and at dragging dis-
cussions on and on. Although no stirring orator or proven war chief,
Kientpoos could count guns, and he knew his people came up way
short in the arms race. Talking, which he might win, was always better than shooting, which he was certain to lose.

Yet it may also be that the seeming deception of the Modocs' surrender offer resulted not from a plan but from shifting political alli-
ances. Kientpoos and his family, as well as Scarface Charley and a
few other prominent men, saw surrender and peace as the better way.
Curley Headed Doctor, Hooker Jim, and the Tule Lake settler killers wanted the apocalyptic war of red against white portended in the
Ghost Dance. The Hot Creeks, led by Shacknasty Jim, favored conflict most of the time. Schonchin John, ever eager to displace Kientpoos and take over as the community's leader, vacillated between war
and peace according to the politics of the moment. It could be that
the twice-made offer of surrender, followed by the Modocs' nonap-
pearance on both occasions, reflected the rising and falling fortunes
of the peace and war factions over those few days.

One thing was clear. In the two talks with Steele and in the messages Princess Mary carried to Canby, the Modocs saw themselves as a
people seeking to find their just place among the other peoples on the
frontier. "I wish to live like the whites," Kientpoos said. "Let everything

Firing into a Continent

be wiped out, washed out and let there be no more blood. I have got a bad heart about those murderers [of the Tule Lake settlers]. I have got but a few men & I dont see how I can give them up. Will they give up their people who murdered my people while they were asleep [at Lost River]?"[16] Allow everything to begin again, and let justice be done to both Native and American. So Kientpoos saw it.

Such was not Canby's take. Blending Protestant patriarchy with military power, he perceived the Modocs as savage children in need of a beating. The brigadier had been making ready to administer that punishment all along.

18

Squeeze Play

Treachery is inherent in the Indian character. I know of a case where
the Indians murdered the man who not two hours
before had given them food and clothing.

—William Tecumseh Sherman quoted in
"The Modoc War," *New York Times*, April 15, 1873

The Indians portrayed in the newspapers and popular novels of the late nineteenth century exhibited two constant characteristics. One was savagery. At the least provocation Indians turned unspeakably brutal: ambush, massacre, scalping, rape of blond virgins, tortures by flame and blade. The other Native characteristic was treachery. A *New York Times* editorial on the Modocs, as but one example, referred to "the innate ferocity and treachery of the Indian character."[1]

General Canby held to this same belief in a letter to his wife about the Modocs: "They are the strangest mixture of insolence and arrogance, ignorance and superstition that I have ever seen, even among Indians, and from this cause results the great difficulty in dealing with them in any way but by force. They have no faith in themselves and have no confidence in anyone else. Treacherous themselves, they suspect treachery in everything."[2]

Elijah Steele, who likely knew the Modocs better than any other American except John Fairchild, begged to differ. Before the war broke out, Steele wrote, the Modocs were known as "a bold and fearless people, warlike, and a dread to our early emigrants and the surrounding tribes, and very punctilious to their word."[3] Fierce, Steele would buy; treacherous, he would not.

Steele's perspective held more empirical water than Sherman's and Canby's. Indeed, the record placed the burden of perfidy on the white side of the ledger. Ben Wright in 1852 used a deceptive flag of truce to dupe and slaughter some fifty Modocs. The Council Grove Treaty of 1864, by which the Modocs, Klamaths, and Yahooskin Paiutes signed away their vast range of mountain, steppe, lakes, and rivers for a much smaller reservation, was less an agreement among equals than acquiescence by weakened Native peoples to the dominant power of American settlers. The Senate took years to ratify the agreement and made unilateral changes to it, yet the federal government expected the Indians to abide by the treaty's terms all the while. The fraudulent survey that set the Klamath Reservation's boundaries shorted the Indians by almost half the promised allotment. To make matters worse, A. B. Meacham talked the Modocs onto the Klamath Reservation with promises of food and shelter, then failed to deliver so thoroughly that the Indians had to slaughter their own horses to eat. Then there was the game played by Ivan Applegate and T. B. Odeneal in the run-up to the Lost River raid. When Kientpoos refused to meet Odeneal in Linkville—suspecting some Ben Wright–like treachery—Applegate said he would be back in two days' time with the Indian superintendent for face-to-face talks. Instead, he returned with Captain Jackson and the Fort Klamath cavalry.

On the Modoc side of the ledger to this time in the story lies only the twice-made, twice-broken promise to surrender at Point of Rocks. On a treachery meter that ranges from white lie to mass murder, the Modocs' failure to turn themselves in barely budges the needle.

Indeed, Canby was adding a new column to the American side of this unbalanced account. When the cease-fire order came down from Grant and Sherman, Canby promised to "make no aggressive movements until further orders" even as his forces worked "to prevent his [Kientpoos's] getting supplies of any kind." Canby saw no problem with reinforcing and resupplying his own force while the Indians remained under siege and lived on what they had on hand. By the beginning of April, Canby boasted nearly six hundred fighting men, about twice as many as he inherited after the First Battle of the Stronghold on January 17. The unreliable Klamath irregulars had been mustered out. In their place Canby was recruiting Indian scouts from the Warm Springs Reservation in north-central Oregon and putting them under the command of frontier mercenary Donald McKay. The Warm Springs Indians were excellent trackers, Canby reasoned, and could be used as a human shield to absorb casualties in a second attack on the Stronghold. The brigadier was also adding weaponry. Besides the four 24-pound Coehorn mortars he had on order, the brigadier requested three hundred hand grenades, and they, too, were in transit. Then there were the boats, Whitehalls to ferry men and equipment over Tule Lake and lessen the distance between encampments.[4]

Meanwhile, the Modocs were living off what beef on the hoof they still had, the waterfowl and fish they could shoot and spear, and water they drew from Tule Lake. They had added no weapons or ammunition since their gleaning of the January 17 battlefield. Most of the Modocs' horses and mules had been captured in January, so that they had fewer than fifty head remaining. And when Canby saw the opportunity to take and hold a sizable chunk of that small herd, he seized it.

This windfall happened more by accident than design. Canby ordered Major James Biddle, one of the newly arrived cavalry reinforcements, to move his Troop K yellowlegs from Applegate's ranch on Clear Lake to the growing military camp at Van Bremer's. The general wanted Biddle and his men to pass by the Stronghold just close enough to scout the Indians. Crossing the sagebrush flats a few miles south of the Modoc camp, the cavalrymen happened upon four Modoc men and one woman grazing thirty-odd horses. Without firing, the charging yellowlegs drove the Indians into the rocks, rounded up the animals, and proceeded to the Van Bremer ranch.[5]

The next day several angry Modoc women came to demand the return of their mounts. Seizing the animals, they said with some vehemence, violated the cease-fire. Meacham chimed in on the Modocs' side, yet Canby refused to give the animals back. He let the women visit their horses, which he promised would be well cared for, and assured the Modocs that they could have the animals back once peace was made and the band surrendered. The disgruntled women had to return to the Stronghold on foot.[6]

As a Modoc herself, Toby Riddle recognized the women's deep feeling of violation. She told Meacham that this betrayal of the cease-fire would ensure that the Modocs kept no further agreement. Meacham

Firing into a Continent

passed this information on to Canby, but the general, who had come to distrust the Riddles, paid it no attention. Perhaps it bothered him that their loyalty belonged first to Meacham. Perhaps, as a Civil War veteran, he disliked Frank Riddle's Kentucky drawl and Confederate sympathies. Perhaps the widespread prejudice against sex across the racial divide filled him with righteous disgust toward the interracial couple. Whatever the cause, Canby turned away from the Riddles. There would soon come a time, likely no more than a few seconds at the end of his life, when he would rue that loss of faith.[7]

• • •

Keeping the Modocs' horses was hardly the only way Canby was changing the military landscape. It concerned him that, with spring snowmelt in the offing, the Modocs might slip out of the Lava Beds in small bands and scatter. Operating like guerrilla commandos, the Indians could raid and kill as they wished, and stay one nimble step ahead of the plodding military. "Time is becoming of the greatest importance, as the melting of the snow will enable them to live in the mountains," he wrote Sherman. "I think that a system of gradual compression with an exhibition of the force that can be used against them if the Commission should again fail will satisfy them of the hopelessness of any further resistance and give the peace party sufficient strength to control the whole band."[8]

Imagine a hangman's noose drawn wide and draped loosely over the condemned's shoulders. This was the military position when the Peace Commission process broke down on Steele's second visit to the Stronghold. Various military units were stationed at Lost River, near the Crowley ranch and the ruined Modoc winter villages; on Applegate's ranch on Clear Lake; and on the Dorris, Fairchild, and Van Bremer ranches north and east of the Lava Beds. The closest soldiers were at least ten miles from the Stronghold.

Now imagine that the hangman snugs the noose until the rough hemp rasps the prisoner's throat. Such was the anxious state Canby wished to induce via "gradual compression." He ordered the detachments at Lost River and Clear Lake to move their camp to Scorpion Point on the southeastern corner of Tule Lake, a little over six miles from the Stronghold on its eastern flank. The remaining units, a larger force in total, were consolidated at the Van Bremer ranch on the west. The plan was to move them over Sheepy Ridge to only three miles from the Stronghold as soon as the right site could be selected. Canby wanted to make the choice himself.[9]

The reconnaissance party assembled to give the general a look numbered one hundred men in all, including Canby and Colonel Gillem, two physicians, Donald McKay, the *New York Herald*'s Edward Fox, various senior and junior officers, and the whole of Troop K, First Cavalry. A six-hour ride brought this large armed party to the top of the bluff overlooking the Lava Beds. There they stopped and dismounted, and Canby and Gillem glassed the sagebrush plain and volcanic flows. A small group of Modocs came toward the foot of the bluff and called out, in English, to the Americans. The Indians asked one man to come down and talk, and guaranteed he would not be hurt. Thomas Cabaniss, a civilian physician working for the army under contract, volunteered. About fifty years old at the time and a graduate of Maryland University Medical School, Cabaniss had come to California in 1849. With the mother lode eluding him, he returned to medicine, settled in Yreka, and came to know and befriend the Modocs. When Kientpoos had broken his arm a few years earlier, Cabaniss set the bone.[10] Recognizing that Cabaniss understood the Modocs and the risk, Canby gave permission. Down the slope the doctor went.

At the bottom of the bluff Cabaniss shook hands with the Modocs and sat down to talk. One of the Indians rode back toward the Stronghold. Cabaniss walked to the foot of the bluff and called out for another man to come down. Ever the reporter who inserted himself into the story, Fox headed downhill. There Cabaniss told him that Kientpoos and Schonchin John wanted to meet Canby and Gillem for a talk under a juniper tree halfway up the bluff. Fox carried the message to Canby and Gillem, who agreed. He himself went back down the steep slope. More Modocs appeared, and Fox found himself shaking hands with Scarface Charley, Boston Charley, Wild Gal, and Weium as well as several other men. Meanwhile, Gillem and Canby descended to the juniper tree, sat down on the ground, and waited.

In the hour that it took for Kientpoos to make his way from Strong-

Firing into a Continent

hold to bluff, Fox learned that the Modocs remained ticked off about the animals taken from them. "The Indians appeared rather nettled about the loss of their horses and were rather particular in their inquiries [about] who were the soldiers that took them away," Fox reported. "I told them they were taken by 100 new soldiers, hoping that the knowledge of such an addition to our forces might have a wholesome effect, but I am grieved to say they did not look very scared."

Instead, one of the unnamed Modocs ran his hand over a human scalp decorating his shot pouch. The gesture so flustered Fox—"it gently raised my hat"—that he resolved to have his long hair shorn once back at the Van Bremer ranch.

When Kientpoos appeared, he headed up the slope toward Canby and Gillem with Scarface Charley, Curley Headed Doctor, and several others in tow. Scarface Charley made a point of putting his gun on the ground before climbing to the two unarmed officers, yet three of the others still carried revolvers. Nothing untoward happened, however, despite the weaponry. More to the point, this first-ever meeting of Canby and Kientpoos ended soon after it began. Fox, who had been out of earshot, stopped Kientpoos on his way back and asked him how the talk had gone. The Indian leader was unimpressed. "Captain Jack said he had not talked much," Fox reported, "and did not think that the soldier tyee [leader, Canby] had much good to offer. He said he [Kientpoos] wanted peace and wanted to remain where he was."

On the long ride back to the Van Bremer ranch, Fox asked about the brief meeting: "General Canby told me he did not think Jack wanted peace unless he could get Lost River. The general is of the opinion that nothing can be done with the Modocs until they have experienced the power of the troops and thoroughly understand their position."[11] Gradual compression it would be.

• • •

The very day after his chat with the Modoc headman, Canby snugged the noose even tighter. Modocs had been wandering in and out of the Fairchild, Dorris, and Van Bremer ranches more or less at will, dropping by to see relatives who still lived there, visiting with ranch hands they knew, and, so reports went, engaging in black-market vice. The rumor was that Modoc women would bed soldiers for sixty rifle cartridges per sexual favor. Canby wanted to put a stop to illicit resupply and recreation and draw a boundary between Indian world and American. He ordered that "All Modocs of Captain *Jack's* band who may come out from the lava bed, except under the protection of a flag, will be regarded as prisoners of war, and all now in this neighborhood will be placed under military supervision, and except such as are domesticated in the families of settlers, and for whom the settlers become responsible, will be collected at some convenient point to be subsisted and cared for. All others will be warned that any attempt to communicate with or give any assistance to the Indians in the lava bed will cause them to be treated as enemies."[12]

Canby tugged the noose tighter still when he ordered all units at Van Bremer's to decamp, pack weapons and gear, and hump over Sheepy Ridge to the wide, grassy flat at its base, less than three miles from the Stronghold. Moving the military closer would pressure the besieged Indians and favor those preferring surrender and peace over struggle and war. Canby saw the Modocs divided between Kientpoos, with Schonchin John at his side, supporting peace, and Curley Headed Doctor, championing war. Bringing his units closer to the Modocs would strengthen Kientpoos over Curley Headed Doctor by displaying the folly of opposing such enormous force: "The troops are now moving into their positions and when they are reached, then communication may again be opened with the Modocs with the hope of better results."[13]

On the last day of March, the military forces on the west began their maneuver. At the bottom of the bluff that would come to be known as Gillem's, soldiers erected the tents of the camp that would also come to be known as Gillem's. It was, in the way army camps are, an orderly place of rowed tents, stone-fence corrals, latrine pits, kitchen, and hospital tent: a village of staked, rowed canvas snapping in the early-spring wind off the lake. The Modocs could hear that sound, the shouted orders of the noncommissioned officers, the neighs and snorts of the horses, the brays of the mules, the brassy notes of reveille and taps. The noose around their necks had been snugged tight at the hangman's precise angle.

19

A Homeland to Be Named Later

The history of the United States is a history of settler colonialism—
the founding of a state based on white supremacy, the widespread
practice of African slavery, and a policy of genocide and land theft.

—Roxanne Dunbar-Ortiz, *An Indigenous Peoples'*
History of the United States

Kientpoos knew that on his side of the battlefront there were
but fifty-plus fighters, a number that included several teenage boys just big enough to lift a Springfield, no more than there
had been back in January. On the other side, however, the numbers
were swelling. For the past two days, troops had been streaming over
Sheepy Ridge, spreading out over the flat at the base of the bluff,
pitching tents, readying gear. There were hundreds of them already,
and more on the way no doubt, plus mountain howitzers and Coehorn mortars. Kientpoos had no experience with artillery, yet he knew
that guns of such size and men in such number gave the Americans
a weighty advantage.

Now, meeting for only the second time with Canby in person, the
Modoc headman looked across at the brigadier. Americans and Indians
sat around a fire in a small basin about halfway between the Stronghold
and Gillem's Camp under a blackening sky. Besides the general, there
were Colonel Gillem and the peace commissioners—Meacham, Dyar,
and Thomas—with Frank and Toby Riddle as interpreters. Kientpoos
had brought the principal men of his community plus a half-dozen
women. Hands had been shaken, a pipe of tobacco smoked. Canby
told Kientpoos he had brought the soldiers closer to make communication between the two sides easier. His strategic intention, he insisted,

was peaceful, not hostile. The Modoc headman remained impassive even as he scoffed within.

Through Toby Riddle, Kientpoos repeated the peace terms he wanted: soldiers gone, reservation on Lost River, amnesty for the settler killers. Canby shook his head. He could promise only that if the Modocs surrendered they would be protected as prisoners of war until a new home was found for them. The Indians would have to trust Canby.

Kientpoos was shaking his head as the first raindrop struck his cheek. It was so cold and the wind so sharp that the water felt like a wet pebble thrown hard. At the same sudden, damp blow, Canby flinched. In such bad weather they could not continue to talk in the open, the general said. He offered to have a tent pitched for future parleys.

Kientpoos smirked. "The rain is a small matter," he said in a ridiculing tone the Riddles did not care to translate. The general had better clothes, the headman went on, yet the Modoc would not melt in this piddling shower.

As the rain soaked him and the commissioners, Canby decided he had endured enough of yet another routine restatement of the Modoc position. He stood up to head back to camp, where fire and shelter beckoned. Kientpoos stood, too. He said words to the effect that if Canby wanted a tent, he was fine with it. The chief left hanging in the air the feeling that he, the Modoc, was more stalwart and stoic than the beribboned American general. The army had more soldiers, yet the Modocs, a people who prized courage and toughness, claimed the advantage in attitude.

Back in camp, Toby Riddle confessed to Meacham misgivings left over from the meeting. At one point Hooker Jim growled at her husband in Modoc to stand aside and get out of the way. Toby dressed him down, and Kientpoos told Hooker to lay off. Just to play it safe in case gunfire broke out, Toby moved closer to the whites, sitting between Canby and Thomas, hoping that her kinship with Kientpoos would shield them as well as her. Meacham lent the Indian woman's fears credence. The setting of the meeting had given him the willies; the little hollow could not be seen in field glasses from Gillem's Camp. To Meacham's frontier eye, the place signaled ambush. Now, with Toby

Riddle's concerns added to his own, he wondered whether an unexpected shoe was waiting to drop.[1]

· · ·

Kientpoos was no leader of soaring oratory, as Chief Joseph would be immortalized. Nor was he a dashing battlefield commander on the order of Crazy Horse or Geronimo. Indeed, in the Modocs' customary way of dividing leadership among civil, military, and religious spheres, Kientpoos was but a political headman, a practitioner of coalition building in a radically democratic society. His power was limited and conditional, dependent on voicing the consensus of the members of his band. That requirement was becoming increasingly tough to meet. Curley Headed Doctor, Hooker Jim, Ellen's Man, Black Jim, and several others wanted a war of apocalypse. The shaman's Ghost Dance and red-dyed, soldier-thwarting tule rope had proved invincible in January. Buoyed by the spirits arrayed on their side, the Modocs could rise up and crush the whites. And, to Hooker Jim, Curley Headed Doctor, and the other Tule Lake raiders, there was no choice between fighting to the death and surrendering to the gallows in Oregon.

Of course, Canby might spare them. He had made such an offer more than once. Yet everything, Kientpoos saw, depended on trusting Canby, the very leader who talked peace yet prepared war. The general would protect the raiders from the bad men in Oregon, he was promising, and find the Modocs a good home in a warm somewhere. All the Indians had to do was have faith in Canby and his airy offer. Based on what he was seeing all around him, Kientpoos refused to make that leap.

The military forces on the east were moving even closer to the Stronghold, breaking up their camp at Scorpion Point to settle near Hospital Rock, only two crow-fly miles away. The hostility explicit in choosing this site was unmistakable: from this very location Captain Bernard and his men had launched the eastern flank of the January 17 assault. The Whitehalls traveled easily over the lake between Gillem's Camp and Hospital Rock, well out of rifle range from the Stronghold, while signal stations sent messages back and forth in but minutes. Then the news that nearly a hundred Warm Springs scouts under Donald McKay were on their way south and would arrive soon at the Lava Beds stirred the Modocs up even more.

Kientpoos did see one possible way out, an idea he broached at the first meeting in the newly erected Peace Tent. Canby did not come this time, nor did Thomas, both of whom thought the proposed meeting a trap. Meacham and Fairchild, who were willing to trust the Modocs, went out. The Riddles came along to interpret. Kientpoos had brought both his wives—Rebecca, the elder, and Lizzy, the younger and his favorite—and seven or eight men.

Sitting on the ground, the headman confessed that he could talk freely with neither Canby nor Thomas present. Canby's military dress flustered the Modoc headman, and Thomas's status as a "Sunday doctor" scared him as well. "Now," the Modoc headman said to Meacham, "I can talk. I am not afraid. I know you and Fairchild. I know your hearts."

As was his wont, Kientpoos repeated the history leading up to the war. He wanted to make it clear yet again that he and his people had not started this fight. Kientpoos played to Meacham by laying particular blame on Odeneal. And this conflict could end so easily.

"Take away the soldiers, and the war will stop," Kientpoos said. "Give me a home on Lost river. I can take care of my people. I do not ask anybody to help me. We can make a living for ourselves. Let us have the same chance other men have. We do not want to ask an agent where we can go. We are *men*; we are not women."

Meacham shook his head. The settler killings made the Modocs' return impossible. "The blood would always come between you and the white men," Meacham said.

The Modoc headman mulled this answer. "I hear your words. I give up my home on Lost river," he announced. "Give me this lava bed for a home. I can live here; take away your soldiers, and we can settle everything. Nobody will ever want these rocks; give me a home here."

For the first time Kientpoos was trading the traditional Modoc home country on Lost River for the Lava Beds. Here, on badlands where no white man would want to live yet Indians had long sustained themselves, close to the place where the Modoc creator had formed the world from Tule Lake's mud, the Indians could make their home.

Meacham shook his head once more. Even though the Lava Beds

lay within California, the Oregonians would demand that the settler killers be hauled over the state line and tried for murder.

"Who will try them—white men or Indians?" Kientpoos asked.

"White men, of course," Meacham replied.

"Then," Kientpoos asked, "will you give up the men who killed the Indian women and children on Lost river, to be tried by the Modocs?"

"No," Meacham said, "because the Modoc law is dead; the white man's law rules the country now; only one law lives at a time."

"Will you try the men who fired on my people, on the east side of Lost river, by your own law?" he asked.

The very idea of bringing up Oliver Applegate and his vigilante Oregonians on the charge of murdering Indians was unimaginable. Meacham avoided a direct answer: "The white man's law rules the country,—the Indian law is dead."

"Oh, yes, I see," Kientpoos said, "the white man's laws are good for the white man, but they are made so as to leave the Indian out. No, my friend, I cannot give up the young men to be hung. I know they did wrong—their blood was bad when they saw the women and children dead. *They* did not begin; the white man began first." The solution was simple: "Take away the soldiers, and all the trouble will stop."

That, Meacham said, was impossible as long as the Modocs remained in the Lava Beds.

"I don't know any other country," Kientpoos said. "God gave me this country; he put my people here first. I was born here,—my father was born here; I want to live here; I do not want to leave the ground where I was born."

No, Meacham answered. The Modocs had to come out of the rocks and trust the beneficence of the United States government.

How, Kientpoos countered, could his people trust a government that had proven itself deceitful? "When you was at Fairchild's, you sent me word that no more preparations for war would be made by you, and that *I* must not go on preparing for war until this thing was settled. I have done nothing; I have seen your men passing through the country; I could have killed them; I did not; my men stayed in the rocks all the time; they have not killed anybody," he reminded Meacham.

"I have kept my promise,—*have you kept yours?* Your soldiers stole my horses, you did not give them up; you say 'you want peace'; why do you come with so many soldiers to make peace? I see your men coming every day with big guns; does *that* look like making peace?" Kientpoos stood and pointed across Tule Lake, toward the mouth of Lost River. He reminded Meacham and Fairchild how at that spot Ben Wright had slaughtered Modocs under a false flag of truce.

Meacham objected that Modocs killed many emigrants at Bloody Point. "Your people and mine were at war then," Kientpoos said. "We were not making peace." Meacham agreed that Wright did wrong. The Modoc remained unappeased: "*You* say it is wrong; but your *Government* did not say it was wrong." In fact, "Big Chief made him an Indian agent."

Kientpoos's passion rose further. "I am but one man. I am the voice of my people. Whatever their hearts are, that I talk. I want no more war. I want to be a man. You deny me the right of a white man. My skin is red; my heart is a white man's heart; but I am a *Modoc*. I am not afraid to die. When I die, my enemies will be under me. Your soldiers begun on me when I was asleep on Lost river. They drove us to these rocks, like a wounded deer," he exclaimed. "I want him [Canby] to take his soldiers away. I do not want to fight. I am a Modoc. I am not afraid to die. I can show him how a Modoc can die.

Meacham cautioned Kientpoos that the government would not back down. The only salvation for the Modocs lay in coming out of the Lava Beds and surrendering as prisoners of war. Kientpoos refused one last time.

"The talk lasted nearly seven hours," Meacham wrote in his memoir, "and was the only free, full talk with the Modocs during the existence of the Peace Commission."[2] He feared that things had reached the point where they had nowhere left to go but wrong.

• • •

In the parley postmortem at Gillem's Camp, the civilian peace commissioners agreed that Kientpoos's willingness to give up Lost River for the Lava Beds was a significant step forward. Canby dismissed their sense of progress, however: "The Modocs are now sensible they cannot live in peace on Lost river, and have abandoned their claim to it, but

Firing into a Continent

wish to be left in The Lava Beds. This means license to plunder and a stronghold to retreat to."[3] Instead, Canby took Kientpoos's willingness to surrender Lost River as a signal that he could split the Modocs along the peace-versus-war fault line. The general authorized Meacham and the commissioners to make an offer through a messenger: the army would protect any Indians who wanted to surrender against attack by other Indians who wanted to keep them against their will. Canby was hoping to divide Kientpoos, Scarface Charley, and as many Modocs as wished to come with them from Curley Headed Doctor, Hooker Jim, and the Hot Creek Modocs.

Toby Riddle was chosen messenger, and off she rode into the Lava Beds. Kientpoos refused to speak with his cousin privately, demanding that she address the whole community. Riddle spelled out the offer, and the Modocs voted. Only twelve men—Kientpoos and eleven supporters—voted to accept the peace offer. That left forty-odd who made it clear that any attempt to leave would mean death to those who tried. Kientpoos told Riddle to take his message back to Canby and the peace commissioners: "I am a *Modoc*, and I cannot, and will not, leave my people."

On her way out, Riddle stumbled onto the day's real news. Hiding behind a rock, Weium, aka Tame and husband to Wild Gal, got her attention and whispered, "Tell old man Meacham and all the men not to come to the council tent again—they get killed." Lest she give Weium fatally away, Riddle rode on as if nothing unusual had happened. By the time she returned to Gillem's Camp, the gravity of what she carried shocked her into silence. She refused to speak until Frank, her husband, listened privately to her tale. He went to Meacham with news of the threatened assassination. The chairman dutifully assembled Canby, Thomas, and Dyar and asked Riddle to tell the three what his wife had told him. Before Riddle would answer, he made the commissioners swear to keep the secret that Toby was the source of this information. Falling to his knees, Thomas made the most dramatic avowal of all: "I am a minister of the Gospel. I have my God to meet, and in the name of God I will not tell any secret that you may tell me."

Dyar and Meacham, the two men with the most experience in the

Indian Bureau, took the Modocs' threat at face value. Thomas, who knew nothing of Indians, thought the story ginned up to get the attention of Fox, Atwell, and other reporters desperate for a blood-and-thunder story in the midst of all this dull peace talk. Canby agreed with the minister. The Modocs "might talk such things, but they would not attempt it," he said.[4]

One the face of it, Canby was right. The general had nearly a thousand well-equipped riflemen, an artillery battery of three mountain howitzers and four Coehorn mortars, hundreds of horses and mules, wagons, tents, and the hay, oats, beans, bacon, and hardtack to feed animals and men for months. Against him were arrayed fifty-plus fighters who were indifferently armed and fed and encumbered by about a hundred women, children, and elderly. Such people might boast of wanting to kill the commissioners, but since they knew they had to be crushed in the end, Canby was convinced they would never make the attempt.

The general, though, was failing to think as the Modocs did. The Natives knew they were facing genocidal annihilation no matter what they did. Should they choose surrender and trust Canby to deliver on his trust-me promises of safety and subsistence, they would lose their ancestral homeland. Rooted as they were in that landscape, this solution might save their individual lives but it would finish them as a people. So would fighting. Even the fire-breathers among the Modocs knew they would lose a straight-up battle.

The solution to the Modoc dilemma was to land a blow so bold that it might fatally cripple the American enemy. It remains unclear who came up with the idea. Maybe Hooker Jim, maybe Curley Headed Doctor, maybe Shacknasty Jim, maybe the three of them egging each other on. In any case, the Modoc fighters who favored war hatched a vague plan to lure the unarmed commissioners, including Canby, to the Peace Tent and kill them all. Now Weium had let Toby Riddle in on the secret.

• • •

The day after Riddle rode in from the Stronghold with her ominous announcement, the two Charleys, Bogus and Boston, appeared in Gillem's Camp along with Shacknasty Jim. The three told Meacham and Canby that Kientpoos and four other Indians were waiting at the Peace Tent and wanted to talk. As a suspicious Meacham was telling Boston that the commission was unprepared to negotiate, an orderly handed Canby a note from the soldiers stationed on Signal Rock, a reddish outcrop up the bluff some fifty feet higher than Gillem's Camp. "Five Indians at the council tent, apparently unarmed," the paper read, "and about twenty others, with rifles, are in the rocks a few rods behind them." Canby passed the note to Meacham, who showed it to Dyar and Thomas. Meacham begged off politely, without tipping his hand that he was wise to the trap.

Thomas, though, could not let well enough alone. Before the Modocs left the army camp, he approached Bogus Charley and said, "What do you want to kill us for? We are your friends."

"Who told you that?" a stunned Bogus demanded.

Thomas hemmed, hawed, evaded. Bogus asked again and again, raising his voice to a shout until finally the minister caved and blurted out Toby Riddle's name. Bogus declared she was lying. "I thought she lied, Charley," a relieved Thomas said, "that is why I asked you."

Bogus hunted Riddle down and demanded that she tell him who had told her that a plot was afoot among the Modocs. She played dumb. While the three Modocs headed back to the Stronghold, Toby let husband Frank know what had just happened. The danger posed by Thomas's spilled beans was just sinking in when Boston Charley returned to Gillem's Camp to demand that Toby Riddle come to the Stronghold.

Meacham thought no great danger awaited her there. He was so sure she would come back unharmed that he lent her his overcoat and horse. He also gave her a derringer, just in case matters turned rough. Meacham alerted Canby, who was reassuring: should there be trouble, he would move his troops against the Modocs immediately. Somehow the general seemed to forget that more than three miles of broken ground lay between Gillem's Camp and the Stronghold and that no troops were in fact mobilized and ready to move out. Shoved forward by Meacham and Canby, a grim Toby mounted the loaner horse, hugged her ten-year-old son again and again, and mumbled something to her husband.

Just as she was ready to ride off toward the Stronghold, Thomas appeared. Frank Riddle exploded. "Thomas, you lied like a yellow dog last night when you promised my wife that you would not say anything about what she was to tell," he shouted. "[Captain] Jack has sent for her. You are the cause of it. I tell you this, Rev., if my wife ain't back here by sundown, I'll take my gun and shoot you in the right eye, you black-hearted son of a dog."

Thomas was stunned not by the breaking of his own promise but by Riddle's threat to a man of the cloth such as himself. "Brother Riddle," the minister demanded, "get down on your knees and pray to Almighty God for forgiveness."

"You living yellow dog," Riddle growled, "you might get down and pray the caps off your knees, then God would not forgive you for what you said last night."[5]

As Thomas slunk away, Toby trotted off on Meacham's horse. Frank climbed to a high point to watch his wife's progress across the Lava Beds through field glasses.

When she reached the Stronghold and dismounted, Modocs swarmed around her. Accusations flew. First she denied that she had said anything; the Indians were having none of it. Then she said a dream had come to her. The Modocs scoffed. Spirits—that was her third explanation, which fared no better than had denial or dream. With the Modocs threatening violence if she did not hand over the name of the insider informant, Riddle pointed in the direction of Gillem's Camp and snapped at her kin, "There are soldiers there; you touch me and they will fire on you, and not a Modoc will escape." Likely she knew help was much too far away, and she was bluffing for all she was worth. Riddle backed her threat with pure bravado. Smacking fist against chest with one hand and waving Meacham's derringer overhead with the other, she leapt atop a rock and shouted, "I am a Modoc woman; all my blood is Modoc; I did not dream it; the spirits did not tell me; one of your men told me. I won't tell you who it was. *Shoot me, if you dare!*"

Guns were leveled at Riddle, yet no Modoc fired. Riddle's defiant bravery may have saved her life. Or perhaps it was the half-dozen men—the closeted informer, Weium, among them—that Kientpoos and Scarface Charley dispatched to escort the headman's cousin back to Gillem's Camp. In either event, she returned unharmed. There she repeated a warning that by now seemed obvious: Go to the Peace Tent only if you are prepared to die.[6]

20

Pride and Prejudice in the Peace Tent

Well, so the matter stands at present, and that bright hope of
yesterday is a myth to-day, and may prove a frightful bugbear
tomorrow. There is no use trying to keep track of these negotiations.
One might as well follow a serpent's tail over the lava rocks.

—H. Wallace Atwell, "The Modoc War,"
Sacramento Record, April 16, 1873

The Reverend Doctor Eleazar Thomas was given to praying alone among the rocks around Gillem's Camp like Jesus in the wilderness. He was in deep conversation with his God when Boston Charley found him amid the sagebrush and the scoria. God had put a new fire in the Modoc people, Bogus assured the minister, and they were ashamed of their bad hearts. The Modocs wanted to surrender and make peace as soon as possible. All the peace commissioners had to do was come out, unarmed, to a final council with the Modocs and settle the details.

Joy filled Thomas at Bogus Charley's news. "God had done a wonderful work in the Modoc camp," he declared as he ran off to find Canby and Dyar.[1] Since Meacham was visiting the army camps on the eastern flank of the Stronghold, Thomas was acting Peace Commission chair for the day.

Canby took the minister's enthusiasm under advisement; he remained vaguely skeptical. Just to be sure, the general dispatched the Riddles to visit Kientpoos personally and carry to him a written message. This was a curious move, since both messengers and recipient were illiterate and could not read what Canby had written. The message, as Frank Riddle remembered it later, said that the general and the commissioners wanted to meet the Modocs the next day to talk peace and move them to a warmer climate. The Riddles did as they were told, translating the message from memory, handing the note to Kientpoos, and asking him to bring the paper with him to the meeting. The headman threw the note to the ground, declared he was no white man and no reader and needed no paper. In an effort to impress the Modoc chieftain, Canby had instead pissed him off royally.

Backed by a small group of armed men who held their silence, Kientpoos told the Riddles he was willing to meet the commissioners without weapons, but not at the Peace Tent. He preferred a site a mile closer to the Stronghold. And he assured the Riddles he was ready for peace. All Canby had to do was take the soldiers away. The Modocs would stay in the Lava Beds, and everything from then on would be peaceful.

As Kientpoos was talking, Frank Riddle scanned the Stronghold out of the corner of his eye. The Modocs had piled rocks into walls to make what he took to be fortified firing positions. And they had slaughtered and butchered several beeves and hung the thin-sliced meat to dry in sun and wind. It seemed odd to Riddle that Indians planning on prompt surrender would build fortifications and prepare several days' rations. He smelled a set-up.

Riddle told the commissioners so back at Gillem's Camp. "I thought," he said, "it was useless to try to make peace any longer."[2] Thomas, who already had a low opinion of Riddle as a blasphemer, would entertain none of the illiterate translator's suspicions. Canby was willing to meet the Indians unarmed, but the site closer to the Stronghold and invisible to the outpost on Signal Rock sounded dicey. The commissioners' response was to tell Kientpoos via Bogus Charley that an unarmed meeting was fine, but only at the Peace Tent the following day.

Thus did matters stand when Meacham returned in the evening. As Thomas informed him that God had worked his divine magic among the Modocs, Meacham shook his disbelieving head at the minister's blind faith. "God has not been in the Modoc camp this winter," the Oregon politician declared. "If we go we will not return alive."[3]

• • •

As the sun rose on Friday, April 11, events in the Modoc Stronghold revealed just how badly this Native society, developed over millennia in a demanding yet provident landscape, had broken down. In the traditional Modoc way, tribal affairs fell into three realms—civil, military, and religious—each with its own leader. This division recognized that activities necessary to each area demanded different skill sets. The fierceness of a war leader ill suited the coalition building central to a civil chief's role, for example. Then the crushing, twisting, and lopping of Modoc society that accompanied the emigrant invasion had conflated war and peace. Kientpoos, who fit into the tradition of Modoc civil leaders, had been saddled as well with responsibility for war. The Modocs who wanted to fight had to turn this born conciliator to their belligerent point of view.

With the Peace Tent meeting set for eleven the next morning, the Modocs needed a plan. Kientpoos had yet to agree to killing the commissioners. On his side were but a few allies: Scarface Charley, Weium, and several other fighters. The rest of the men voted to kill the commissioners and resume the war, preferring bullets to gallows. As Kientpoos was advocating surrender, Hooker Jim, Schonchin John, and others of the war party crowded around the chief. They draped a woman's shawl about his shoulders and forced a woman's woven-tule hat onto his head, then called him "a woman, a white-faced squaw." A shamed Kientpoos stood, tore off the shawl and hat, and, bending to majority sentiment as Modoc custom required, shouted, "I am a Modoc. I am your chief. It shall be done if it costs every drop of blood in my heart."

Now came the task of divvying up the killing. Kientpoos backed by Ellen's Man drew Canby. Schonchin John was given Meacham; Hooker Jim had his back. Thomas went to Boston Charley, whose second was Bogus Charley. Dyar was the target for Shacknasty Jim and Barncho. Gillem fell to Black Jim and Slolux.

With Frank Riddle the next on the list, Scarface Charley declared "the whole thing to be an outrage *unworthy* of the Modocs" and refused to have anything to do with it. In fact, he promised to defend both Riddles and avenge their deaths if need be.

Slolux and Barncho, the lowest-ranking members of the ambush team, were loaded up with three rifles apiece and told to hide close to the Peace Tent. Scarface Charley went with them, not to take part but to watch over the Riddles. Steamboat Frank joined him later, out of curiosity.[4]

The Modocs decided, too, to turn their single blow into a double whammy. Three men—variously identified as Curley Headed Doctor, Curley Headed Jack, Miller's Charley, Steamboat Frank, or someone nameless—would approach the army camp at Hospital Rock.[5] Their assignment was to lure Major Edwin Mason, the eastern outpost's commander, into the open and kill him. Those gunshots would signal the Indians in the Peace Tent that it was time to assault the peace commissioners.

• • •

Even as the Modocs' plans to heat this cold war back up were being made, Meacham rolled out of his tent on a clear, brisk early-spring morning and set to making breakfast. The enlisted man assigned to cook for the peace commissioners had deserted, and they were reduced to feeding themselves. Meacham cooked, Dyar washed, and Thomas opened his direct line to God to say grace.

As Meacham boiled coffee and baked biscuits, a thought occurred to him. Today—April 11—was Good Friday. On the Christian calendar this was the day when a scourged, thorn-crowned Jesus was paraded through Jerusalem to be nailed to a Roman cross. As good a Methodist as Meacham professed to be, this portent of violent death gave him no solace. His discomfort increased when the Riddles appeared.

Frank Riddle told the three breakfasting commissioners once again that they should stay away from the Peace Tent. The Modocs intended murder, he was sure. Toby Riddle took hold of Meacham and said, "Meacham, don't you go . . . for they might kill you today; they may kill all of you to-day." Meacham needed no convincing; he agreed there was danger. Dyar, too, sensed the peril. Thomas armored himself in blind faith. "Dr. Thomas, he came up," Frank Riddle said later, "and told me that I ought to put my trust in God; that God Almighty would not let any such body of men be hurt that was on as good a mission as that. I told him at the time that he might trust in God, but that I didn't trust any in them Indians."

Learning that Colonel Gillem was too sick to walk or ride to the

Peace Tent, Riddle asked all the commissioners, Canby included, to gather at Gillem's tent. Meacham, Dyar, and Thomas crowded inside, where the ill colonel lay on his cot. Canby remained outside, out of earshot, as if he somehow rose above what was going on inside.

"General Gillem," Riddle said, addressing the officer by his brevet rank, "these men are going out to hold council with them Indians today, and I don't believe it is safe. If there is anything happens to them, I don't want no blame laid on me hereafter, because I don't think it is safe for them to go, and after it is over I don't want anything laid on me."[6]

Gillem let out a big laugh and dismissed Riddle's concern, saying he would take care of the Indians in nothing flat if trouble broke out. He apparently forgot that he had done nothing to mobilize the troops except, as Canby had ordered, to have the soldiers at Signal Rock train their field glasses on the Peace Tent as soon as the commissioners left the camp.

Unconvinced by the spurious protection Gillem promised and certain that the Modocs meant harm, Riddle still felt duty-bound to go with the commissioners. Refusal would have brought him dishonor as a coward even in the event that he was right. A civilian, he could have simply walked away and taken Toby with him. Instead, he prepared to head out, with his wife at his side.

Once Riddle left Gillem's tent to make ready, Canby stepped inside the canvas. "I think there is no danger," he said, "although I have no more confidence in these Indians than you have; I think them capable of it; but they dare not do it; it is not to their interest."[7]

Thomas maintained that he was in the hands of God. He proposed to do his duty and leave the outcome to the wisdom of his Maker.

Meacham's only chance to save his own life lay in convincing the other commissioners not to go. If they did choose the Peace Tent, he would have to join them. Only if they refused could he do the same and retain his honor.

"I differ from you gentlemen; I think we ought to heed the warning," Meacham said. "If we do go, we must go armed; otherwise, we will be attacked. I am opposed to going any other way."

Dyar sided with Meacham. "We ought to go prepared for defence. We ought to heed the warning we have had," he said.

Canby remained dismissive, repeating his conviction that he had

Firing into a Continent

to honor the agreement to go unarmed and that the meager precaution of putting the signal station on alert lent the commissioners' adequate protection. Thomas sided with the general. "The agreement is to go unarmed; we must be faithful on our part to the compact, and leave it all in the hands of God," he said.[8]

Meacham came at the issue from another angle. Bring Fairchild along, he suggested, and let him be armed. The rancher was not a commissioner and under no sanction about weapons. He was a crack shot who knew every trick in the Modoc playbook.

Again Thomas would have none of it. Arming Fairchild would violate the compact with the Indians and somehow undermine the absolute faith in his God the minister wished to parade before Christians and heathens alike.

Meacham played his last card. "I made one further proposition," he said later, "that if, when we arrived on the ground, things looked dangerous, I would make them [the Modocs] any promise in the world rather than they should have my life or theirs [the commissioners']." Steele had used exactly this tactic to extract himself, Atwell, and the Riddles on his second, threatening visit to the Stronghold. Meacham figured it was worth laying the groundwork for this legerdemain should it be needed.

Canby and Thomas shook their heads yet again. "I will be a party to no deception," the Methodist minister said. "This matter is in the hands of God." Canby took a similarly righteous tone: "I have dealt with Indians for thirty years, and I have never deceived an Indian, and I will not consent to it—to any promise that cannot be fulfilled."[9]

Canby went to his tent to change into full dress uniform topped by high, black-felt hat festooned with gold cord. He fetched, too, a box of cigars and tucked it under his arm. Thomas vested himself in a new, light-gray, Scottish-tweed suit.

All the while Meacham was seeing that his sense of duty and honor had boxed him in. Wondering whether he was making mountains of slaughter out of molehills of anxiety, he asked Fairchild what he thought. Unsure, the rancher said, "Wait here a minute, and let me have another talk with Bogus; I think I can tell." He came back a few minutes later, whittling a stick as if he were simply whiling away the time. "I can't make out from Bogus what to think. I don't like the look of things; still he talks all right; maybe it's all on the square."

By the code of the time, Meacham had no choice but to go. He told Dyar that, although he himself was bound to participate in the meeting as the Peace Commission chairman, the Klamath Reservation agent was under no such obligation. Dyar said that if Meacham went, he would go too. Honor trumped self-preservation.

Like a soldier assigned to a suicide mission, Meacham counted his money, folded the bills, wrote a quick and formal note:

My dear Wife:

You may be a widow to-night; you shall not be a coward's wife. John A. Fairchild will forward my valuables and valise. The chances are all against us. I have done my best to prevent this meeting. I am in no wise to blame.

Yours to the end,

Alfred

P.S.—I give Fairchild six hundred and fifty dollars, currency, for you.

Dyar took the same precautions as Meacham, handing his possessions to Fairchild with instructions to send them to his wife if need be. Fairchild offered Meacham his revolver. The chairman refused to take it. And he made Fairchild swear that if he came out of the Lava Beds mutilated, the rancher would see that the corpse was buried promptly and not shipped like some macabre horror to his family in Salem. Fairchild agreed. Someone Meacham never named slipped a derringer into his pocket and said, "It's sure-fire—it's all right."[10] The small, short-barreled pistol held but one .41-caliber rimfire round—puny and low-velocity—yet at the across-the-poker-table range the gun was designed for, it could slow, stop, even kill. Meacham decided to keep the little gun in his pocket even though he knew Canby and Thomas would disapprove. Seeing what Meacham had done, Dyar ducked back into the tent to fetch his own compact, concealed weapon—one that had been given to him just the night before by Oliver Applegate.[11]

Meacham mounted Joe Lane, the spirited, sorrel stallion Fairchild had lent him. Dyar and Toby Riddle also swung up into the saddles

Firing into a Continent

of their horses. Frank Riddle preferred to walk. "I'm a-goin' a-foot; I don't want no horse to bother me," he said.[12]

Boston Charley hurried on ahead, as did Bogus Charley. Canby and Thomas, both on foot, were a couple of hundred yards into their mile-long walk when the others set out: Frank Riddle on foot, Toby Riddle, Meacham, and Dyar on horseback following the longer riding trail to the Peace Tent. The two lead walkers got there first, the others a few minutes behind. The sun was climbing toward midday.

• • •

The Indians had already piled sagebrush and set it alight to chase the chill. Canby handed out cigars; only Thomas, who never smoked, refused the tobacco. The Modocs acted cordial, friendly, welcoming, adding to Thomas's enthusiastic, eager mood. He missed the details that gave Meacham the willies the moment he arrived. The agreement was that Kientpoos would meet the commissioners with four companions, for a total of five Modocs. Instead, eight crowded close to the fire: Kientpoos, Schonchin John, Hooker Jim, Black Jim, Boston Charley, Bogus Charley, Shacknasty Jim, and Ellen's Man. The coats on some of the Indians bulged in a way that told Meacham they were carrying revolvers. Then there was that fire. The Modocs had built it on the far side of the Peace Tent, which screened the soldiers on Signal Rock from seeing the meeting site.

On the way out, Riddle, Dyar, and Meacham had talked about what they would do if the Modocs started shooting. Riddle and Dyar planned to take off running. The portly Meacham knew his legs would never carry him fast or far enough; he would need his mount, Joe Lane. Although the air was still nippy, Meacham took off his overcoat and folded it across the saddle horn. When Meacham dismounted, he snugged the bridle rein over the saddle horn, so he could remount Joe Lane and be off without untying. He was ready to move fast.

Puffing at the cigars Canby had passed around, Indians and Americans settled in around the fire. Kientpoos and Schonchin John sat opposite Canby and Meacham, with Thomas on Meacham's left. Then the Indians spotted a lone white man riding slowly across the plain nearby and objected loudly. Meacham sent Dyar out on horseback to tell the man—a civilian teamster hunting for stray horses—to head back to camp. When the Indian agent returned, he settled on Canby's right, close to the Modocs. Frank Riddle stood behind Meacham, and Toby Riddle sat herself down on a rock to Meacham's left.

Meacham began: "We have come here to-day to hear what you have to propose. You sent for us, and we are here to conclude the terms of peace, as your messengers of yesterday proposed."

The Riddles tag-teamed the translation. Frank turned Modoc into English; Toby, English into Modoc.

"We want no more war," Kientpoos replied. "We are tired, and our women and children are afraid of the soldiers. We want them taken away, and *then* we can make peace."

Meacham argued that the soldiers were in the Lava Beds to protect everybody, including Indians. Kientpoos had never bought this tired falsehood: "We do not want the soldiers here. They make our hearts afraid. Send them away, and we can make everything all right."

A restless Hooker Jim left the small circle and sidled up to Joe Lane. Glaring at Meacham, he lifted the horse's reins off the saddle horn and tied them to a sagebrush. Then he slid the overcoat off the saddle, slipped into it, buttoned top to bottom, and boasted in English, "Me old man Meacham now. Bogus, you think me look like old man Meacham?"

As if this hostile gesture meant nothing, the Peace Commission chairman played along. "Hooker Jim," he said, "you had better take my hat also." Meacham doffed his cover, revealing his bald head. Hooker waved off the gift, saying, "No," and adding in Modoc, "I will by-and-by. Don't hurry, old man."

Frank Riddle made a show of redoing the fastenings on the saddle of Toby's horse, which was standing behind the seated Thomas. Dyar, too, stood to take care of his horse. Both Riddle and Dyar were putting the animals between themselves and the Modocs. Feigning a yawn, Toby Riddle slid off her rock and stretched out on the ground, lying low.

Meacham turned to Canby and gave him a look, hoping that the general had detected the danger. The moment called for the escape stratagem Meacham had proposed earlier: promise the Modocs anything, then get out of there.

Instead, Canby stood and played the benevolent patriarch come from civilization to deliver the Indians from paganism, poverty, and savagery. "Toby," he ordered, "tell these people that the President of the United States sent the soldiers here to protect them as well as the white men. They are all friends of the Indians."

Next Canby told Toby to make the Modocs understand that he had moved a group of defeated Indians from an old home to a new and better life many years before. They did not like him at first, but he so impressed the exiled community that they made him a chief and named him "Friend of the Indian" and "The Tall Man." Years later he visited the transported Indians, many of whom came from great distances to see him again. Canby was sure the Modocs would have the same happy experience.

In point of fact, Canby was overselling his role in transporting the defeated Mikasukis from Florida to Oklahoma after the Second Seminole War. He returned to Oklahoma twelve years later on an inspection tour, yet his report mentioned nothing about the Mikasukis.[13] The general was either inflating or inventing.

When Canby sat down, Thomas dropped to his knees. "Toby, tell these people, for me, that I believe the *Great Spirit* put it into the heart of the President to send us here to make peace. We are all children of one Father. Our hearts are open to Him. He sees all we do. He knows all our hearts. We are all their friends," he said. "I know their hearts are all good. They [Canby, Meacham, and Dyar] are good men. We do not want any more bloodshed. We want to be friends of yours. God sees all we do. He will hold us all responsible for what we do."

Kientpoos walked away from the circle into the brush, saying he needed to relieve himself. Into his empty spot leapt Schonchin John. This old fighter flashed rage, demanded that the soldiers quit the Lava Beds and the Modocs get Hot Creek for their home. When Meacham said this was impossible, Schonchin turned on him and snapped, "*Take away your soldiers and give us Hot Creek, or quit talking. I am tired of talking. I talk no more.*"

Kientpoos had returned and was standing just back of Schonchin. To their rear Meacham caught sight of two young men, Barncho and Slolux, running toward the Peace Tent with rifles in their hands.

"Jack," Meacham demanded of Kientpoos, "what does that mean?"

The headman made no answer. He shouted a phrase in Modoc that Meacham did not understand, yet its tone told him it was a command. Kientpoos pulled a revolver from under his coat, cocked the weapon, and aimed. The heavy-caliber muzzle gaped but three or four feet from Canby's startled, disbelieving face. Kientpoos squeezed the trigger.[14]

21

Martyrs at Midday

The feeling in this city against the treacherous, murdering Modocs
is becoming more intense, and thousands of volunteers could be
obtained to go to the front to wipe out the entire band. . . .
[T]he treachery of the murderers is universally denounced
as an act meriting their immediate extermination.

—"Indian Treachery," *Daily Alta California*, April 14, 1873

The middle-aged Meacham failed to hear what Kientpoos's
younger ears were picking up: muzzle blasts echoing from Hospital Rock, the signal to assault the commissioners. Seconds before the
headman cocked his pistol and leveled the muzzle at Canby's face, the
attack on the eastern front was over.

Close to noon an army sentry spotted three Modocs approaching under a white flag. The suspicious sentry alerted officer of the day
Lieutenant William Sherwood of the Twenty-First Infantry. A young,
popular officer who had just returned from a tour of Europe and the
eastern United States, Sherwood was now serving in the first combat posting of what was expected to be a brilliant military career. He
ventured beyond the picket line to talk at shouting range with the
Indians, who said they wanted to talk to the big chief. Sherwood carried that message back to Major Mason, commanding officer of the
Twenty-First Infantry. Mason agreed to listen to what the Modocs had
to say, but he would venture no farther into the Lava Beds than the
picket post. Sherwood was leaving to relay that message to the waiting Indians when quartermaster Lieutenant William Boyle offered to
come along. Formerly an Indian agent on the Umatilla Reservation in
northeastern Oregon, Boyle spoke Chinook Jargon. The two young
officers headed out.

Still at shouting distance, the Modocs asked whether Boyle was the big chief. It disappointed them to learn he was only another messenger. The three refused to come in to the picket post in order to meet Mason. Instead, they invited Boyle and Sherwood to join them in the rocks. At that the two officers knew they were in trouble. They chatted with the three a bit longer as a bluff, then turned to hike back to Hospital Rock, eager to escape.

They had made but a few yards when the Modocs opened fire. Boyle shouted at Sherwood to split up, and they sprinted off in different directions. Two rounds hit the racing Sherwood, one shattering the left femur just below the hip and the other tearing through the left arm and severing the artery. The young lieutenant dropped, broken and bleeding. Boyle ran on, dodging among rocks, zigging and zagging through sagebrush. Alerted by the gunfire, sentries in the picket post opened fire on the Indians and drove them back toward the Stronghold. The sentries rushed out to find Boyle perched on a rock near the picket post, panting and, in his words, "very much excited."[1] They retrieved Sherwood where he had fallen and carried him back to camp. He would die of his injuries three days later.

Within minutes the signal team at Hospital Rock wigwagged a message to Signal Rock above Gillem's encampment that the eastern camp had been attacked. Lieutenant John Quincy Adams was on duty there along with his sergeant, following the orders to keep a close eye on the council tent. Adams scrawled a hasty note and gave it to the sergeant to take to Colonel Gillem. As the noncom raced down the bluff, Adams trained his field glasses on the Peace Tent. He spotted the tall form of General Canby stumble into the open and fall to the ground.

At that very moment Gillem was reading the note from Adams and realizing that the commissioners were in danger. Since many of the Modocs spoke English and would understand any shouted warning, the colonel fetched Dr. Thomas Cabaniss and asked him to carry a note to General Canby in the Peace Tent. He began writing, "General Canby—The Modocs have attacked Mason's pickets, wounding Lieutenant Boyle." Gillem had the wounded man's name wrong, but that hardly mattered. Then gunfire from the Peace Tent crackled in

Firing into a Continent

Gillem's ears. The colonel's pencil stopped, his message unfinished and now useless.[2]

Lieutenant Adams leaned out from the signal station and yelled into the camp, "They are firing on the commission!"[3]

· · ·

Edward Fox had wanted to go with the commissioners to the Peace Tent to report firsthand on what might be the last major event of the Modoc War. Since his own Stanley-meets-Livingston trek to the Stronghold, palaver had replaced the blood-and-thunder action that sold newspapers. Now, with the Indians saying they wanted peace and the commissioners so certain of a good outcome that they agreed to meet unarmed, Fox's journalistic nerve endings twitched at the prospect of this morning's confabulation. Then the peace commissioners refused to allow the newspaperman to go along. By way of payback Meacham liked making Fox's life difficult.

The *Herald's* man retreated to the tent he shared with Atwell and McKay, the two other journalists at Gillem's Camp. Fox opened a book. He was, he confessed, "rather sulky with the peace commissioners for refusing the press access to the talk."[4] Atwell was there, too, pencil to foolscap, writing background to what he hoped would be a dynamite report on the day's big doings.

A few moments after one o'clock the excited cry raised by Lieutenant Adams in the signal station was carried along the tented alleyways of Gillem's Camp: "They are firing on the peace commissioners! General Canby is killed!" Fox and Atwell bolted outside to have a look "just as the drum and bugle notes were calling the men to arms."[5] Reverting to his British army days, Fox buckled on a revolver. Then he found Colonel Gillem, who told the reporter that Modocs had fired on Mason's camp and the peace commissioners were in danger. Never a decisive officer, the sick Gillem had yet to make up his mind about what to do next. Minutes dragged past as officers and soldiers assembled, ready to move out. Finally, Gillem gave the order to advance toward the Peace Tent. Two batteries of artillerymen led the way in a skirmish line, reporters Fox and Atwell and civilian physician Cabaniss close behind, infantry and dismounted cavalry farther back. They double-timed through the bright, brisk afternoon.

On the way Fox spotted three Modocs running along the edge of Tule Lake back toward the Stronghold. Then he saw Leroy Dyar and Frank Riddle sprinting past.

Meacham was the first victim the advancing soldiers found. He was a sight: stripped to red-flannel long underwear, bleeding profusely from head, face, arm, and hand, blood already caking and crusting, his form as still as a dead man's. Closer to the Peace Tent lay Thomas, stripped to the waist, and a little farther on Canby, naked, both corpses bloody.

As the soldiers charged past the Peace Tent and set up a defensive line, Cabaniss performed triage. He knew within seconds that both Canby and Thomas had been dead since the signal station gave the alert. Meacham, though horribly wounded, lived still. He was slowly stirring, dazed, begging for water. Cabaniss put a canteen of brandy to Meacham's lips.

"*I can't drink brandy,*" Meacham protested. "I am a temperance man."

"Stop your nonsense. No time for temperance talk now," Cabaniss snapped. "Down with it! down with it!"[6]

As the alcohol did its work, Atwell sat down by Meacham and began the first interview with the one wounded survivor of the assault. The reporter wore no coat. He had taken it off to drape Canby's naked corpse. Seeing how inadequate this meager cover was on a big man like the general, Atwell sliced a strip of canvas from the now-useless Peace Tent and draped it over the corpse.[7] Then, ever the reporter, he pulled out notebook and pencil and sat down with Meacham.

Once the two bodies and Meacham were loaded onto stretchers, the soldiers fell back to Gillem's Camp. Toby Riddle came with them, leading her horse, weeping without cease, saying again and again, "Why would they not believe me?"[8]

Back in camp, Fox found Dyar, interviewed him about what he had seen, and drafted a report while a mounted courier waited to carry it to the telegraph office eighty miles away in Yreka. Atwell, armed with the information he had gleaned from the woozy, wounded, and tipsy Meacham, likewise went to work. He, too, had a rider at the ready.

Firing into a Continent

Each wanted to scoop the other and be the first to get the terrible story into print. Atwell won.

The *San Francisco Chronicle* devoted the whole front page to the story, under the banner headline "THE RED JUDAS." Atwell's story opened, "The peace negotiations with the Modoc Indians, which have occupied the attention of the country for the past two months, resulted today in the consummation of the most damnable plot that ever disgraced the Indian character."[9]

The *New York Herald* sounded much the same note. Below the headline "Massacre," Fox led with, "Peace policy and the Indian Bureau have accomplished the bitter end, and offered as martyrs to the cause the lives of Brig. Gen. E. R. S. Canby, commanding the District of the Columbia, and the Reverend Thomas of Petaluma, Calif., presiding elder of the Presbyterian Church."[10] He had the denomination wrong, but that hardly mattered.

The two stories sounded much the same; both reporters understood the implications of what had happened. Any pretense of negotiating peace with the Modocs had ended. President Grant's halfhearted Peace Policy had been dealt a fatal blow. A terrible vengeance loomed.

"The murder of General Canby has thrown a gloom over this camp," Fox reported, "and created a bitter feeling in the hearts of the men that will exact a bitter reckoning from these treacherous savages."[11]

• • •

As much as Fox and Atwell, and soon the rest of the nation, understood the import of the Good Friday killings, the facts of what had happened remained murky. It took days, even months to gather the differing eyewitness reports, from Americans and Modocs alike, before a trustworthy picture emerged from the fog that attends such events.

When Meacham spotted Barncho, Slolux, and their armloads of rifles headed toward the Peace Tent, Kientpoos pointed his revolver at Canby and squeezed the trigger. Hammer fell, cap burst, chamber misfired. Kientpoos cocked the pistol again to bring up a new cap and chamber, yet Canby sat where he was. He remained frozen in place until Kientpoos squeezed the trigger again. This time the revolver fired.

The slug crashed into Canby's face close to the left eye, plowed up through the skull, and lodged somewhere in his brain, a mortal injury that flattened the general. Still, he did not die where he lay. Canby picked himself up and took off running. In about forty yards, as the bullet's damage to Canby's brain was catching up with him, another slug—likely fired by Ellen's Man reaching over Kientpoos's shoulder—blew through the back of his head.[12] The general stumbled and fell among the rocks. There either Kientpoos or Ellen's Man drove a knife into the general's throat. With Canby now thoroughly dead, the two Modocs stripped off his dress uniform as spoils of war.

By this time, Boston Charley had drawn his weapon and shot Thomas in the left chest. Like some bizarre mirror image of what was happening with Canby, the wound through the heart took its lethal time. Thomas crumpled, holding himself up with his right hand, then rose and stumbled in much the same direction Canby had gone. Before he reached the fallen general, the minister collapsed. Another gunshot to the head finished him off. The two Charleys, Boston and Bogus, along with Steamboat Frank, helped themselves to the brand-new, gray-tweed suitcoat Thomas had put on for the occasion.

At the instant when Kientpoos's revolver misfired, Dyar had sprinted away. Hooker Jim pursued, firing at the racing Indian agent. "I heard someone after me, and had heard shooting," Dyar said later, "and balls whistling about me, and I supposed it was one of the Indians."[13] About 150 yards from the Peace Tent, Dyar turned, drew the derringer he was carrying, and pointed it at Hooker Jim. The Modoc about-faced and hightailed it back to the tent, well out of the underpowered handgun's range. Dyar pocketed the unfired weapon and ran on.

Frank Riddle hung at the scene just long enough to see the first shot shatter Canby's head. "I jumped up and ran then, and never stopped to look back any more," he said. "I saw General Canby fall over, and I expected he was killed, and I jumped and ran with all my might. I never looked back but once, and when I looked back Mr. Meacham was down and my woman was down, and there was an Indian standing over Mr. Meacham and another Indian standing over her, and some two or three coming up to Mr. Meacham."

Riddle went back to running. Shacknasty Jim, Barncho, and Ellen's

Firing into a Continent

Man took potshots, spattering the dust in front of him.[14] The three took care to miss, knowing that Scarface Charley was watching in the rocks and would kill any Modoc who killed a Riddle.

In the span of seconds between Riddle's jump and his furtive look back, Meacham had ducked death, then been struck down hard. As Kientpoos fired on Canby, Schonchin John drew a revolver with his right hand and a knife with his left. Unlike Canby, Meacham reacted fast. He ducked Schonchin's first shot at a range of only three or four feet, then bolted into the sagebrush as fast as a fat man could run, and took cover behind a rock. Schonchin followed and, from a distance of fifteen or sixteen feet, shot at Meacham peering over. The round ricocheted off the rock, hit Meacham between the eyes, and ranged down and out, away from his brain. Schonchin kept firing. One slug nearly severed Meacham's left forefinger, another traveled half the length of his right forearm and exited, a last bullet grazed his temple and cut away the top of the ear. Bleeding and concussed, Meacham passed out.[15]

It must have been at just this instant that Frank Riddle turned and saw Meacham and his wife down and Modocs standing over them. Slolux had struck Toby Riddle with his rifle and was preparing to hit her again as she tongue-lashed him for untying her horse to steal it. Kientpoos and Black Jim ordered Slolux to back off. Toby was kin. She deserved respect, and the horse was hers to keep.

The Modocs were gathering spoils from Meacham's unconscious form and running off with the stallion Joe Lane when Boston Charley decided that the bald white man's scalp, paltry pelt that it was, would add panache to his shot pouch. He drove a pocketknife into the fallen man's head and drew the dull blade back. The knife had traveled four or five inches along Meacham's skull when Boston Charley, afraid that the soldiers were coming faster than he could work, abandoned his trophy-taking and left Meacham where he lay.

• • •

Borne on a stretcher to the hospital tent in Gillem's Camp, Meacham looked like a man killed twice: carved, pierced, battered, bleeding. The two civilian surgeons working for the army on contract, Thomas Cabaniss and Bernard Semig, went to work on him. They stitched the long cut made by the would-be scalping knife, the furrow plowed by a slug along the side of Meacham's skull, and the glancing wound between the eyes. The physicians ran a probe along the wound tunnel that began in the right wrist and exited halfway up the forearm. Planning to amputate the badly mutilated left forefinger, the two physicians showed Meacham the line of cut the scalpel would follow through the palm.

"I can't hold still while you do that, without chloroform," Meacham said.

One of the doctors shook his head: "You have lost too much blood to take chloroform."

"Then let it stay until I am stronger," Meacham said.

The surgeon summoned the macabre humor of his profession: "The finger would not disfigure a corpse very much." He let Meacham have his way.

The military's physicians and senior officers were so sure of Meacham's imminent death that a courier had already been dispatched to summon his wife from their home in Salem, Oregon. Yet Meacham demonstrated that the human body, even one middle-aged and non-athletic, can be hard to kill. His sight returned as the wound between his eyes healed, and his strength gradually increased. He even kept his deformed left forefinger. The wound in his right wrist, however, severed nerves and left the hand virtually useless. Meacham never regained full use of it.[16]

Five days after the attempt on his life, Meacham felt recovered enough to write a short official summary of the attack. His letter was addressed to Interior Secretary Columbus Delano. Meacham wanted Delano to know that, injured though he was, he remained ready and willing to work as the situation required and draw his ten dollars a day, with continued deference to the military, of course: "We believe that complete subjugation by the military is the only method by which to deal with these Indians."[17]

Delano never answered Meacham. No doubt he was embarrassed that, after berating Meacham for being too quick to abandon hope for peace six weeks earlier, the negotiations had exacted such a terrible toll. Perhaps the interior secretary even knew that the good citizens of Yreka, upon hearing of the attack on the commissioners, had hanged him in effigy as chief enforcer of Grant's Peace Policy.[18]

Two days later a terse telegram from Edward Smith, newly appointed commissioner of Indian Affairs, arrived in Gillem's Camp. "Commission discontinued," it read.[19] Shot, slashed, and disabled, Meacham was now unemployed as well.

22

The War Goes Cosmic

Among the sculptured symbolisms that adorn the principal front
of the National Capitol, there is represented the fierce though
futile struggle of savage barbarians with the stronger and nobler
impersonation of civilization and progress. That prophecy in marble
finds its latest fulfillment in the treachery which sent the heroic
Canby and the devoted Thomas to their death—the Christian
Soldier and the Christian Minister. . . . Never were the Sword and the
Cross in more fitting juxtaposition.

—"The Modoc Victim," *Daily Alta California*, April 19, 1873

Over the first days of Meacham's hospitalization, banner headlines blared the killing of Canby and Thomas from newspaper
to newspaper, West Coast to East. These deaths on a battlefield few
Americans could even locate on a map shocked the news-reading public. A high and grisly bar had been hurdled in the Lava Beds: never
before and never again would an American general officer be killed
by Indians.[1]

Before he was shot down alongside Canby, Thomas was little known
outside the limited world of Protestant abolitionists and temperance
activists. Had he died in bed at his Petaluma home on Good Friday in
1873, Thomas's funeral might have drawn a couple hundred attendees.
The ambush in the Lava Beds raised his death from ordinary mortal-
ity to the passing of a hero.

Since Thomas was a member of San Francisco's Mount Moriah Lodge
of Free and Accepted Masons, the lodge master journeyed to Yreka to
receive the slain minister's embalmed and casketed corpse and attend
its transport back home. Six thousand people filed past Thomas's body

in San Francisco's Powell Street Methodist Episcopal Church, where he had once been pastor. The city's flags flew at half-mast as California governor Newton Booth and San Francisco mayor William Alvord paid their respects. The funeral was attended by the officers of General Schofield's staff and by six other generals and six colonels plus forty-five Christian ministers, one of whom came all the way from Chicago. Soon after the dead man was interred in Lone Mountain Cemetery, his son E. C. Thomas pronounced, "To few men, comparatively, is it given to die like a martyr."[2]

Canby, too, climbed far higher in death than in life. The brigadier at his most brilliant was a workmanlike military leader. In death, however, his star brightened the heavens like a passing comet.

First came General Order Number 3 from William D. Whipple, General Sherman's assistant adjutant general. The order stated that Canby was "endeavoring to mediate for the removal of the Modocs from their present rocky fastness of the northern border of California to a reservation where the tribe could be maintained and protected by the proper civil agents of the Government." The brigadier had been chosen for this benevolent task "by reason of his well-known patience and forbearance, his entire self-abnegation to the expressed wishes of his Government, and his large experience in dealing with the savage Indians of America."

Whipple was making this up. Canby got the job simply because the conflict had broken out within the boundaries of the military department he commanded. From that fiction, the assistant adjutant general's rhetoric grew even grander: "The record of his [Canby's] fame is resplendent with noble deeds well done, and no name on our Army Register stands fairer or higher for the personal qualities that command the universal respect, honor, affection, and love of his countrymen."[3]

Canby's heroic remains began a cross-country, month-long, funeral procession. The day after he was killed, the brigadier received final military honors, with the salutes and muffled drums of custom, at Gillem's Camp. The corpse was then transported, alongside Thomas's remains, to Yreka, where a crowd of citizens greeted the arriving ambulance and its military escort.[4] After lying in state at the Masonic temple in that mining town, a freshly embalmed Canby was placed in a zinc coffin inside a wooden box, packed in ice, and transported by stagecoach and special train to Portland. Following a private memorial at the family home that shielded his wife from crowds and media, Canby was borne through the city accompanied by an honor guard. Two enormous black horses draped in black and waving spectacular plumage drew the hearse as pallbearers walked beside. Numbered among them were top-ranking army officers of the Department of the Columbia as well as Oregon governor LaFayette Grover, District Court judge Matthew Deady, and Portland mayor Philip Wasserman. The body, wrapped in an American flag and wreathed in flowers, lay in state at the Portland Armory, where it was viewed by a steady flow of onlookers whose number nearly equaled the crowds brought out by Lincoln's assassination eight years earlier. The body was then shipped to San Francisco to lie in state for two days under half-mast flags and solemn military ceremonies. Ferried across the bay to Oakland, the coffin was placed on a flag-draped railcar supplied by the Central Pacific Railroad and drawn slowly across the country to Canby's home state of Indiana. The funeral at the First Baptist Church of Indianapolis was led by four officiating ministers—Baptist, Episcopal, Methodist, and Presbyterian—in a display of ecumenism unusual in this era of competitive denominationalism. Among the attendees were prominent military figures: General of the Army William T. Sherman; Philip Sheridan, Canby's commander in New Orleans during the Civil War; Irvin McDowell, Civil War general; and Lew Wallace, Civil War general, fellow Hoosier, and family friend who would go on to become governor of the New Mexico Territory, ambassador to the Ottoman Empire, and author of *Ben-Hur: A Tale of the Christ*. Following the church service, a long procession carried the casket to Crown Hill cemetery. There Canby was lowered into his grave.[5]

• • •

In the American mind of 1873, Canby and Thomas counted as much more than battlefield casualties. Edward Fox sensed this in an April 13 lead for the *New York Herald*: "Peace policy and the Indian Bureau have . . . offered as martyrs to the cause the lives of Brig. Gen. E. R. S. Canby . . . and the Reverend Thomas."[6] The key word was *martyr*, the same label Thomas's son claimed. The Modocs had, unwittingly, turned casualties into sacrificial victims and raised this local Indian war to the level of cosmic combat between good and evil.

When the fight began in November 1872, the struggle turned on whether indigenous Modocs or emigrant Americans would control the last contested bottomland along Lost River. As long as the conflict remained a fight over real estate, negotiations by the Peace Commission made political sense as a way of resolving the contest in the emigrants' favor with less bloodshed and expense than would a gunfight. And a successful Peace Commission worked toward the holy, Christian work of advancing civilization and liberating land from its Indigenous occupants.

When the Modocs shot Canby and Thomas, they put a violent halt to this process. They had done more than kill the military and spiritual leaders of their battlefield opponents. They had thwarted God's will.

Seeking to understand the rise of religious terrorism in our time, sociologist Mark Juergensmeyer coined the term "cosmic war" to describe a great conflict in which the struggles are part of a greater design, one sure to end in ultimate and eternal triumph. Juergensmeyer's former student, the writer and religion scholar Reza Aslan, borrowed the concept and popularized it. "A cosmic war . . . is a conflict in which God is believed to be directly involved on one side over the other . . . a ritual drama in which participants act out on earth a battle they believe is actually taking place in the heavens," Aslan writes. "It is, in other words, both a real physical struggle in this world and an imagined, moral encounter in the world beyond."[7]

A cosmic thread ran through the setting, goals, and strategies of all Indian wars, sometimes in the background, sometimes more to the fore. In the Modoc War, the killings of Canby and Thomas brought the cosmic front and center. Consider the journalistic arc that Edward Fox had traveled from February to April.

In his initial inquiry into the war's causes, Fox saw the Modocs as more wronged than wronging: "There is . . . little doubt that the Indians have been badly treated, and if the whites had kept faith with them, there would have been no disturbance at all." He kept this point of view even when he brazened his way into the Stronghold. "I feel satisfied that these Indians have been badly treated and forced into a war," he reported.[8]

Then, after Elijah Steele had the stuffing scared out of him on his second visit to the Stronghold, Fox's tone changed. He charged that the Peace Commission was "a stupendous humbug . . . or 'an expensive blunder.'" He saw renewed war against the Modocs as the best strategy. While Canby was moving his troops over Sheepy Ridge to Gillem's Camp to squeeze the Modocs, Fox wrote, "These tactics will, I am satisfied, have more effect upon Captain Jack and his band than all the moral suasion of the peace commission and the Indian Bureau combined."

Then came the Good Friday ambush. Fox declared Canby and Thomas martyrs and named the Modocs—the very people he had once cast as hounded and wronged—"one of the worst bands of Indians in the United States."[9]

Still, compared to some of his professional colleagues, the *New York Herald*'s reporter remained restrained. The San Francisco–based *Daily Alta California* argued that this cosmic struggle merited a grand, total, and final solution: "We regard the red men of California, Oregon and Nevada, and most of those of Arizona, as entirely irreclaimable, savage to the backbone, destined to misery, brutal savagism and extermination."[10]

And when the newspaper's editorial board learned that Henry Ward Beecher, brother to *Uncle Tom's Cabin* author Harriet Beecher Stowe, had requested that his congregation pray for the Modocs, it condemned the minister as "no fit representative of Christianity or humanity. . . . the great heart of the country throbs with sorrow for its dead, slain by treachery, and the blood of every patriot in the land is hot with a righteous indignation, with a holy rage, at the diabolical villainy of the Indian assassins. . . . We are sick unto nausea and disgust at this continued course of insincere sympathy with the detestible red savage. There is no sense, no intelligence, no Christianity in it."[11]

Harper's Weekly, the *People* magazine of its day, saw the Modocs' infernal nature revealed: "Once more the untamable fury of the savage blood has been illustrated in the murders of the Peace Commissioners, and like wild beasts granted a temporary opportunity of mischief, the Modocs, thoughtless of the consequences, threw themselves on their victims. They had probably no restraint over their fierce impulse of revenge. They were incapable of understanding that Canby and Thomas were their truest friends. They thirsted for their blood like tigers."[12]

Even the *New York Times*, which supported Grant's Peace Policy, saw the Modocs as evil: "Such an affair as this cannot be called an incident of war. It was murder, and should be treated as such.... Capt. Jack and the other miscreants engaged in this massacre should be taken alive, tried for their crime, and hanged."[13]

The Modocs' sole backer in all the roil over the Peace Tent attack came from a strange, and disreputable, source. The states of the defeated Confederacy remembered Canby's role in thwarting the Confederate invasion of New Mexico, his command of the Military Division of West Mississippi, and his civil government leadership during Reconstruction. The *Athens Northeast Georgian* applauded the general's violent death:

AN INDIAN MASSACRE
Captain Jack and Warriors Revenge the South
By Murdering One of Her Great Oppressors
*

Keep the Ball in Motion
Three Cheers for the Gallant Modocs[14]

• • •

The Applegates recognized that the killing of Canby and Thomas changed the political context. With Canby and Thomas venerated as martyrs and the war elevated to the cosmic plane, the Applegates' plan to rid the range of every last Modoc now had every chance of succeeding. Opposition to a violent final solution was bound to fade away as so much Quaker Indian-loving.

"Your letter came yesterday—same day got news of killing of Genl Canby and Thomas and wounding Meacham &c," Ivan Applegate wrote to brother Oliver; "we are all O.K. any how no man will dare more to hold up for 'Capt. Jack.'. . . Keep cool and quiet, and all will work out right yet."[15] Ivan grasped an important political point: now that the war had gone cosmic, no one outside the Stronghold dared argue that Canby and Thomas were ordinary wartime casualties.

Had they been there to comment, Canby and Thomas would have agreed. They saw the demise of the Modoc nation and the ethnic cleansing of their land as the inevitable working of God's plan, civilization's advance, and the nation's manifest destiny. The general and the minister imagined themselves as divinely chosen representatives of the superior, Christian civilization commanding the pagan primitives to accept annihilation. When Canby asserted that the Modocs dared not attack the peace commissioners, he was claiming the protection of civilization's inevitability and assuming, wrongly, that the Modocs saw matters in the same light. Thomas boasted that he placed himself in God's hands, trusting that the Almighty had to be on the side of a man who claimed the purest of hearts. In a cosmic conflict, God sides with the good guys.

Canby and Thomas's attitude toward Indians was paternalistic, in the word's literal meaning. They saw themselves as parents possessed of wisdom and right and the Modocs as children needing direction and salvation. The Natives had no choice but to bend to God's will and American civilization's progress.

Just before Kientpoos shot him, Canby spoke in this demeaning manner to the Modocs, according to Fox: "Nothing could have been kinder than his speech to these savages, and the kind old gentleman talked to them as if they had been his own children."[16] Jeff Riddle, Toby's son, recalled Thomas explaining to his mother the feelings he held for Indians: "We have got to deal with the Indian just the same as we have to with children. You see, Sister Tobey, we must treat them with kindness. . . . They will believe what we tell them."[17]

Canby and Thomas's refusal to heed Riddle's warnings that the Modocs planned to kill them arose from this same cosmic paternalism. It blinded them, too, to the Modocs' desperation. To believe Riddle and to see that the Modoc people were desperate to fend off their annihilation by any means necessary was to treat Indians as equals. That Canby, Thomas, and almost all of European America refused to do.

• • •

The pitting of good against evil in a cosmic war eliminated any rules of engagement tempered by ethics and morality. When a war goes cosmic, the only acceptable outcome is extermination of the infernal enemy. No tactic is too drastic, no weapon too vicious. A. Hamilton, a private citizen of New Brunswick, New Jersey, wrote to the Interior Department to propose gas made from sulfur as "the most sure means, of forcing the savages out of their lava holes."[18] This weapons-minded citizen saw no problem in using poison gas on Modoc women, children, and elderly as well as fighters.

Another bold idea came from R. M. Taylor of San Francisco. He wrote General Schofield three days after Thomas and Canby were killed and on the very day Lieutenant Sherwood died from his wounds: "I am a practical embalmer of the dead; and in the cause of science, and with a desire to gratify the curiosity of the people, I request a permit giving me the privilege of embalming and bringing to this city the bodies of the Modocs, Captain Jack, Schonchin, Boston Charley and Hoka Jim, in the event of their being executed or killed by the troops."

The *Daily Alta California*, which published the letter, understood its commercial potential: "If Mr. Taylor's request was granted, he would be very likely to succeed in accumulating a handsome fortune in a very short time. Who would refuse to give two bits to see the Modoc murderers of General Canby and Dr. Thomas?"[19]

General of the Army Sherman never took a stand on mustard gas or sideshow embalming. He did know, however, what he wanted done with, and to, the Modocs. He telegraphed Colonel Gillem, now interim commander in the Lava Beds: "Your dispatch of yesterday announcing the terrible loss to the country of Gen. Canby by the perfidy of the Modoc band of Indians has been shown to the President, who authorizes me to instruct you to make the attack so strong and persistent that their fate may be commensurate with their crime. You will be fully justified in their utter extermination."[20]

Sherman wanted to be sure that the senior officer he chose to succeed Canby was up to genocide. He had just the man in mind. This tough fellow had killed his own commander during the Civil War and demonstrated a further ruthlessness rare even among professional warriors. Sherman dictated a telegram to his choice. Ridding the Earth of Modocs was just the job for Colonel Jefferson C. Davis.[21]

23

Girding for Battle

Brig-Gen. Jeff. C. Davis killed Major-Gen. Nelson at the Galt House,
this morning. An altercation took place, when Nelson slapped
Davis in the face. Davis then drew a pistol and fired, killing
Nelson instantly. Intense excitement prevails.

—"A Deplorable Homicide," *New York Times*, September 29, 1862

A bantam with blazing blue eyes and an immense Van Dyke beard, Jefferson C. Davis carried a chip on his shoulder even before Jefferson F. Davis became the first and only president of the Confederate States of America and soldiers mocked him as General Reb— never to his face, of course. The hair-trigger temper may have come from his diminutive size, perhaps from prickliness over the lack of a West Point education. Davis came up through the volunteer ranks in the Mexican War, where he was nicknamed "The Little Sergeant," then received a commission in the Regular Army after the conflict ended and a hoped-for appointment to the military academy fell through.[1] Stationed at Fort Sumter for the opening battle of the Civil War, Davis quickly rose to brigadier general commanding volunteers from his home state of Indiana.

When Confederate forces invaded Kentucky, Davis was assigned to the defense of Louisville under General William Nelson. A naval officer for twenty-one years before the Civil War shifted him to the army, Nelson earned the nickname Bull for his immense size—six foot four, more than three hundred pounds—short temper, nasty manner, and foul mouth. Nelson was Davis on steroids. A native Kentuckian, he felt only disdain for people from Indiana, including Davis, all of whom he dismissed as white-trash emigrants from Appalachia. Nelson decided that Davis was shirking his assignment and ordered him to leave Louisville under arrest and report to Cincinnati for a new posting. Insulted, Davis appealed for help to Indiana governor Oliver P. Morton, then headed back to Kentucky.

Accompanied by Governor Morton, Davis confronted Nelson in the lobby of Louisville's fashionable Galt House hotel and demanded an apology. Nelson told Davis where he could get off, Davis flipped a piece of paper into Nelson's face, and the giant slapped the bantam twice upside the head. "This is not the last of it," Davis snapped at Nelson. The bantam stormed across the lobby, borrowed a revolver from a fellow officer, and challenged Nelson at the foot of the stairs. The general turned toward Davis and called him a coward. Before a crowd of witnesses, Davis fired.

The bullet tore through Nelson's aorta just above the heart. Despite the immediate attention of several surgeons, the plus-size general soon bled out. Placed under military arrest, Davis was released in but a few days owing to the intervention of Governor Morton, who was well connected in Republican circles in Washington, and Major General Carlos Buell. Both justified Davis's killing of Nelson as the only option for a man of honor, and they saw to it that no court-martial or civil trial was ever held.[2]

William Tecumseh Sherman, too, cut Davis slack. In fact, he helped Davis get his career back on track by appointing him to command the Fourteenth Corps during the March to the Sea. As Union columns slashed and burned their way across Georgia, thousands upon thousands of slaves from the razed plantations came with them. Major General Oliver O. Howard, commander of the right wing of Sherman's army, recalled seeing "throngs of escaping slaves . . . from the baby in arms to the old negro hobbling painfully along the line of march; negroes of all sizes, in all sorts of patched costumes, with carts and broken-down horses and mules to match." Young, able-bodied black men served as foragers and guides, and they formed an unarmed vanguard that cleared the road for the army. In return the army fed them. Not so the women, children, and old people, who clung to Union soldiers for protection against Confederate revenge and begged for food. In the sandy pine woods of the Georgia coast, provisions were becoming an issue for the soldiers, even more so for all those hungry camp followers. As Davis saw it, the former slaves' presence dragged on the Fourteenth Corps and exposed the troops to Major General Joseph Wheeler's Confederate cavalry, which was continually harassing the column's rear. Davis decided to address the problem as soon as an opportunity presented itself.

That chance came some twenty-five miles north of Savannah at Ebenezer Creek, a slow, dark flow of December-cold water too wide to leap and too deep to ford. Davis had his engineers float sections of pontoon bridge across the channel, then ordered the black road-clearers and all his troops, except a small rearguard, across to the far bank. The task of the rearguard was simple and clear: keep the refugees off the bridge.

"On the pretense that there was likely to be fighting in front, the negroes were told not to go upon the pontoon bridge until all the troops and wagons were over," explained Colonel Charles D. Kerr, who was stationed toward the rear. Once all the other troops had gained the far bank, the rearguard leveled rifles with fixed bayonets at the milling, black throng on the bank and backed onto the bridge. The engineers on the far bank winched the soldiers across. Hundreds, possibly thousands of women, children, and old people were left behind. They could hear the hoofbeats of Confederate cavalry bearing down on them, sabers drawn, Rebel yells rising.

Unarmed and helpless, the former slaves "raised their hands and implored from the corps commander the protection they had been promised," Kerr wrote, but "the prayer was in vain and, with cries of anguish and despair, men, women and children rushed by hundreds into the turbid stream and many were drowned before our eyes. . . . From what we learned afterwards of those who remained upon the land, their fate at the hands of Wheeler's troops was scarcely to be preferred."

A report on the incident written by an appalled Major James A. Connolly, one of Davis's subordinates, and sent to his Illinois congressman was leaked to the press, which turned the story into a torrent of bad publicity. Secretary of War Edwin Stanton steamed to Savannah to confront Sherman and demand an explanation. The general convinced the secretary that Davis's action at Ebenezer Creek was a military necessity that stripped the slowed column of its unsustainable human baggage. The point of the offensive in Georgia, Sherman made clear, was to cut the Confederacy in bleeding half and bring the rebellion to a halt. Shepherding slaves to safety was only an impediment to the campaign's military purpose.

Sherman never told Stanton that Davis's was the only column that abandoned its black camp followers. The other three let freed slaves continue to tag along, and they suffered no ill consequences. Davis's military necessity was unnecessary.

In the end, the Ebenezer Creek incident elicited not so much as an official reprimand. Sherman even recommended that Davis be promoted to the brevet rank of major general, and Ulysses S. Grant happily endorsed the recommendation. The Congress, though, ashamed by Ebenezer Creek, refused to confirm the promotion.[3]

Now, nine years later and looking for the right man to take over the Department of the Columbia and bring this cosmic Modoc war to its genocidal conclusion, Sherman remembered the kindred martial spirit he had seen in Davis. There was one problem. When Davis got the telegram informing him of his new command, he was back home in Indiana. The colonel had to get all the way to California. That was going to take a while.

...

Thus the matter of dealing the next blow against the Modocs dropped squarely into the lap of Colonel Gillem. "I have telegraphed Colonel Gillem to let the punishment of the Modocs be severe, as their treachery has merited, and hope to hear soon that he has made an end to them," General Schofield informed Sherman.[4]

A Tennessean who was a personal friend of Andrew Johnson, Lincoln's vice president and successor after the president's assassination, Gillem was a West Point graduate who made his way up the chain of command more by political connection than military sagacity. The Union wanted to place loyal southerners in positions of power as a way of demonstrating that not everyone below the Mason-Dixon Line was a loyal Confederate. Thus Gillem rose to command a division of Tennessee volunteers, spent combat time with the Marine Corps, and helped restore Tennessee to the Union and create its new state constitution. In an officer corps where advancement moved glacially, Gillem's rapid rise drew the envy and resentment of career officers who spent years waiting for promotion. It hardly helped that the colonel had a way of arrogantly dismissing his fellow officers.[5]

On the night before the Peace Tent attack, Gillem—ailing with some undiagnosed malady that would lead to his death two years later—was sitting inside his tent with General Canby, Majors Mason and Green, Captain Bernard, and Meacham.

Mason was less than sanguine about the prospect of attacking the Stronghold again in case peace talks broke down. "I think if we take them out with the *loss of one-third of the entire command, it is doing as well as I expect*," he said.

Green may have thought the number too big, but he agreed with Mason, in his usual colorful way. "I don't know," he said in his usually colorful way, "only we got licked on the 17th of January like ——."

Dismissing the two senior officers who had led the east and west jaws of the pincer in the First Battle of the Stronghold, Gillem—who knew the Lava Beds only through his field glasses—boasted, "Well, general, whenever you are through trying to make peace with those fellows, I think I can take them out of their stronghold with the loss of *half-a-dozen men.* . . . Oh, we may have some casualties in wounded men, of course; but I can take them out whenever you give the order."[6] A stunned silence followed Gillem's braggadocio.

Now, faced with the prospect of delivering on his boast only days after, Gillem found himself relying on the very officers he had insulted and the same battle plan Lieutenant Colonel Wheaton had used without success in January. In Gillem's professional opinion, the original strategy remained solid. Wheaton had been hampered by forces that were too small for the job and bad weather that nullified the mountain howitzers. The reinforcements Canby had ordered up gave Gillem more than three times as many Regular Army officers and soldiers as Wheaton had had. Besides the mountain howitzers, the artillery had added four 24-pound Coehorn mortars to lob explosive charges into the Stronghold's caves and trenches. Ammunition was plentiful, and hand grenades were in transit from the Benicia armory. The only missing element in the battle plan was the seventy-two Indian scouts that Donald McKay was bringing down from the Warm Springs Reservation, a mix of men from several Indigenous nations—mostly Wascos, Warm Springs, and Teninos, with one each Umatilla, Nez Perce, Snake, Simco, and (yes) Modoc.[7] Gillem, like Canby before him, wanted the Native fighters to take the brunt of Modoc rifle fire when the assault was launched. And if, God forbid, the Modocs should wiggle free, Indian scouts would be much better than soldiers at tracking the runaways over wild steppe and mountain.

While waiting for McKay's men, Gillem outlined the attack plan for his commanders. From his camp at Hospital Rock on the eastern flank, Mason would lead his infantry and the Warm Springs scouts toward the Stronghold, with the mountain howitzers in support. Counting the scouts, Mason had some three hundred men under arms. Among his officers were proven leaders: Captain Reuben Bernard, the veteran of the Apache wars and of the First Battle of the Stronghold; Captain James Jackson, who led the Lost River raid back in November; and Second Lieutenant Frazier Boutelle, whose duel with Scarface Charley had ignited the shooting war. Major Green, the impetuous officer who had braved Modoc fire to rouse his men with an obscenity-laced pep talk in the January battle, would direct the attack on the west. Besides some 375 soldiers under his command, Green also had the four Coehorn mortars, which would be lugged into firing position as the troops advanced. Captain Joel Trimble with his cavalry troop would stay behind to guard Gillem's Camp against any surprise Indian attack.

Late on Saturday, April 13, McKay rode into Hospital Rock at the head of the Warm Springs scouts. The last piece had been fitted to Gillem's puzzle. The order went out to be ready the next night to begin the assault to avenge Good Friday.

Firing into a Continent

"Tell your men," Gillem told his senior officers, "to remember Gen. Canby, Sherwood, and the flag."[8] God Himself, Gillem must have assumed, would see to appropriate punishment for the slaying of the Reverend Doctor Eleazar Thomas.

•••

When the sun rose on Easter Sunday morning, the Warm Springs scouts rose with it. Reservation Christians all, they sang hymns to celebrate this holy day and give themselves strength for the battle to come. The music and the words moved Meacham, who lay stitched, half-blind, partly paralyzed, and nearly bled out in a hospital tent. Recalling that morning, he wrote, "Blush now, will you not, you who prate so loudly of the superiority of white men! of his sense of right controlling his actions! Here are *red men*, who are but a few years removed from the savage life, *living* the '*new religion*'—Christians in real earnest, and shaming the hypocritical pretenders whose cant and whine make liberal-minded people turn away in disgust. You Christian Indian-hater, look at these red-skinned people, and learn a lesson in Christian honesty and moral courage!"[9]

In the Stronghold that same morning, Curley Headed Doctor was dancing. He had been dancing day and night since Friday, boosting the power that had already proved its worth, and he was joined in step and song by every Modoc moved to join in. The plan to strike the Americans suddenly and mortally had been a success. True, Dyar and Boyle escaped the surprise assault at the Peace Tent and Hospital Rock, yet Canby and Thomas died on the spot, and Meacham looked as good as dead. Two whole days had passed, yet no attack on the Modocs had come. It was as if the white soldiers were stalled, frightened, and cowed by the Natives' vigor, courage, and spirit.

Even as the shaman led the dance, Kientpoos, Scarface Charley, Schonchin John, Shacknasty Jim, and other war leaders continued preparing for the inevitable assault. Lead was melted and molded into bullets, powder distributed, every shooting position assigned, each rifle loaded. The Modocs knew the soldiers were coming even if the bluecoats were taking their sweet time about attacking. However confident the Modoc fighters felt that the Good Friday killings had dispirited the Americans, they knew to make ready. Sooner or later, hell was headed their way.

• • •

Listening through the canvas walls of the hospital tent, Meacham heard other singing later that Easter Sunday. After dark, the officers of Green's command gathered to trade jokes, banter, and drink just enough whiskey to buck up their courage for the coming fight. They sang a song both brave and sad:

> Then stand by your glasses steady,
> This world's a round of lies—
> Three cheers for the dead already,
> And hurrah for the next who dies—[10]

After midnight, the troops on both east and west moved forward, under orders to maintain strict silence for the sake of surprise. The weather had taken the army's side. "It was a beautiful and balmy night; not a breath of air was stirring, nor could the slightest sound . . . be heard," wrote Sergeant Maurice Fitzgerald, who was moving forward on the west. "There was no moonlight; but a star-bespangled sky afforded enough light to enable us to pick our footsteps over the jagged rocks."

Then some heavy-footed, half-sleepy soldier tripped against a rock, stumbled forward, and fired his rifle. Modoc sentries heard the .50-caliber blast and sang out an alarm that spread across the Lava Beds. The sound shivered Fitzgerald: "There burst forth from every crag, fissure, and cavern that same blood-curdling war signal, as if the rocky peninsula were alive with ten thousand fiendish redskins ready to bear down upon and annihilate us. The mouth of every Modoc sent forth that terrifying cry, every gloomy recess and cavern took it up, and from the bowels of the earth and the bosom of the placid lake, the echo kept reverberating until only a whisper of it came back to us from the naked bluffs beyond."[11]

Arrayed against Indians they saw as infernal enemies in this cosmic war, Fitzgerald and his fellow soldiers hurried forward. A surprise no longer, the Second Battle of the Stronghold had begun.

24

Half-Empty Victory

The history of westward expansion has ended up divided into two,
utterly separate stories: the sad and disheartening story of what
whites did to Indians, and the colorful and romantic
story of what whites did for themselves.

—Patricia Nelson Limerick, "Haunted America"

Edward Fox carried the heavy Springfield breechloader at a waist-high ready, felt the full cartridge box tug on his shoulder. He was ready to move out at the front of the skirmish line with Captain Marcus Miller's artillerymen, who this day would fight as infantry. Fox had crossed the line from embedded *New York Herald* reporter to warrior living a fantasy of cosmic Christian victory over treacherous heathens. Miller spread his men out at five-pace intervals and ordered them forward. As they moved past the flat where the Peace Tent had stood, they could hear the distant rattle of rifle fire to the east and see howitzer rounds burst bright over the Stronghold.

Charging up over a rise and silhouetting themselves against the sky, the soldiers took harassing fire from Modocs in well-fortified shooting positions about six hundred yards away. Miller found a route to the next rise hidden in a hollow. As the soldiers emerged and topped the low ridge beyond, fire from the Modocs in front heated up. Two or three Indian riflemen on the right poured in rounds as well. The artillerymen took cover.

Major Green arrived on the battle line to see how the advance was going—which, for a hard-charging officer like Green, was always too slow. Disdaining the cover of a large rock where Fox was sheltering, Green stood in the open, ordered the men forward, and remained exposed as he watched them advance. As in the First Battle of the Stronghold, Modoc after Modoc took long-range shots at Green. Once again, each and every round missed.

Green wanted the Modoc firing position ahead captured. He ordered First Lieutenant Peter Leary, Fourth Artillery, and First Lieutenant Charles Egan, Twelfth Infantry, to lead their two companies in the assault. "It was one of the most dashing charges of the day," Fox reported. "The officers led their men and cheered them on under a galling fire. In this charge Lieutenant Egan received a flesh wound in the thigh after making a brilliant rush with his company. A corporal of his company was killed in the same charge."

That corporal was Edward Drew, who took a round through the abdomen and died on the spot. Sergeant Herrman Gude was hit in the right leg, badly enough that the limb would later be amputated and buried in the low-walled, rectangular cemetery at Gillem's Camp. Gude's was the only severed body part to merit such reverence. Every other soldier who ended up within those four low walls lost his life to get there.[1]

As men dropped around him, Fox's fantasy lost its charm. "Up to this time I had been keeping up with the front," he wrote, "skirmishing in the hope of getting a shot at an Indian, but as the only intimation I received of their presence came from oral testimony of sundry bullets, I concluded the amusement and returned to Colonel Gillem's headquarters."[2]

From that position, some three hundred yards to the rear and beyond rifle range, Fox got a better view of the battle's progress. Things were going well enough for the army, but slowly, very slowly. Of the Modocs, the soldiers saw but little: an occasional puff of smoke from a concealed muzzle, a shadow flitting past a gap between distant boulders, a .50-caliber bullet splattering some eager enlistee's Irish, German, or redneck blood across the lava.

• • •

From his medical catbird seat as the most distinguished patient in the hospital tent at Gillem's Camp, Meacham watched the physicians and orderlies prepare. They laid out mattresses in rows, arranged dressings and instruments—amputation knives, bone saws, wound probes, artery clamps.[3] The physicians then divided themselves into medical teams.

Firing into a Continent

Bernard Semig, a civilian doctor under contract, was put in charge of the hospital at Gillem's Camp, and Assistant Surgeon Calvin DeWitt, a Regular Army physician, played the same role at the aptly named Hospital Rock. John Skinner and F. S. Stirling, both contract physicians, went into the field with Mason's force on the east. Assistant Surgeon Henry McElderry, the expedition's chief medical officer, along with civilian contract doctor Thomas Cabaniss took their field kits out to the battle line on the west to care for wounded from Green's command.[4]

The physicians on the west proved to be much busier than those on the east. Green pushed his men hard and kept them advancing into the Modocs' rifles. Mason moved his soldiers to within four hundred yards of the Stronghold—or so he claimed; seven hundred is more likely, according to Gillem's later, and bitter, report—and hunkered down under cover. Sitting even farther back and well out of rifle range, the mountain howitzers launched shells in the general direction of the Stronghold. Mason claimed that he made a vague attempt to move his left flank and close the circle as the battle plan projected. The Modocs in the outer defensive ring fell back. "I did not follow them as it was not part of *my plan* to expose *my men* unnecessarily," Mason explained.[5]

Green had no such compunction against exposing himself or his men. He leapfrogged one unit over another, letting each dig in and provide covering fire for the following unit's move forward. The Modocs held on until the incoming fire became too hot, then fell back to the next rifle position. Each time, Green ordered his men onward to capture the yielded ground. Now and again the Modocs found targets among the moving soldiers. Lance Corporal Edward Kilpeck was hit in the scalp, a minor if bloody and painful wound. Private Thomas Bernard was hit in the left shoulder, his clavicle fractured. Other rifle rounds struck Private Owen Dooley in the right forearm and Private Martin Connard in the right leg, tearing through flesh and muscle yet missing bone. Corporal Dennis Delaney took a round in the lower left leg that shattered the tibia at the knee.

Doctors Cabaniss and McElderry treated the wounded on the spot, then evacuated them on litters to physicians Semig and DeWitt in the hospital tent at Gillem's Camp. There Kilpeck's scalp was sutured, Bernard's broken clavicle strapped into place and the surrounding flesh bandaged, the wounds in Dooley and Connard packed with water dressings in the medical fashion of the time. Delaney's leg was beyond saving; it was amputated above the knee. If Delaney was lucky, he had not lost too much blood to rule out chloroform before Semig and DeWitt sliced down to the femur of the lower thigh with knives then sawed through the bone to part leg from body. Less lucky was Private Henry C. Harman, killed outright from a rifle round through the chest. Rifle slugs shattering heads ended the lives of bugler William Searles and Private Charles Johnson.[6]

Johnson's death site marked the day's farthest advance, to a small rise on the northwestern edge of the Stronghold. From this high ground, Modoc shooters had pinned down John Fairchild and his volunteers and Green's troops during the January battle. Now it was held by a small, charging contingent of the First Cavalry who drove the Modocs out of their firing positions. There Private Johnson made the mistake of rising up and peering out. Some Modoc rifleman was waiting. Johnson probably never heard the muzzle blast that carried much of his head away.

The first day's fighting had advanced the army only a little farther than it had gone in January. There were important differences this time, though. Gillem had a much larger force in position, and all his soldiers were professional fighters, not unreliable Oregon militiamen. In the First Battle of the Stronghold the men along the lakeshore were left without blankets or food as the sun fell. This time the soldiers carried rations and blankets. And they had gained a small strategic advantage: the high ground on the Stronghold's northwest corner. The soldiers could fetch water, but the Modocs were cut off from the lake, a loss that would soon prove critical.

The broken ground where the soldiers bedded down was covered with rocks that ranged in size from boulders to pebbles, all boasting blades and points. Attempting to sleep on this sharp, unyielding bed while wrapped only in a thin blanket was trying at best. All night long the Modocs probed and fired, and the soldiers shot back. The two sides were close enough to exchange curses. Between the rough

Firing into a Continent

ground, the off-and-on shooting, and the shouted profanities, no one got much sleep.[7]

The Coehorn mortars made it even harder to doze. At regular intervals of ten to fifteen minutes, one of the mortars launched a round. The muzzle erupted in a great gout of fire and black-powder smoke, then the shell arced high, whistling in crescendo until it fell back to Earth and detonated. It was easy, even comforting, for the soldiers dozing through the night to imagine destruction. Explosives fell amid the grottoes, ramparts, trenches, and caves of the Stronghold, filled them with fire and shrapnel, sheared Modoc flesh from bone, life from body. Old and young, men and women, combatant and bystander, perhaps the infant son Shacknasty Jim's wife, Anna, had birthed only a few weeks before: any and every Modoc was a target.

• • •

The Coehorn mortar was short and snub-nosed, cast from brass and mounted in a heavy wooden block that required a crew of four artillerymen to lug its 325 pounds into firing position. The mortar was fixed at a forty-five-degree angle, so its range of from twenty-five to twelve hundred yards depended on the amount of powder rammed into the barrel to launch the projectile. A Coehorn could fire a solid shot weighing 24 pounds or a hollow, 17-pound sphere stuffed with buckshot or explosives. To detonate the charge, the shot was fitted with a hollow wooden tube packed with powder that was lit just before firing. First came the thump of the propellant charge, then the shot arcing through the sky, its fuse spewing sparks as it rose and fell. And finally there was the blast, sometimes above the ground, where it scattered hot, jagged shrapnel, or after it hit and rolled.[8]

It must have been nerve-wracking to be a Modoc in the caves and hollows of the Stronghold that night and hear a shot plummet, crash, and explode again and again from sundown to sunup. Few Indians could have slept well through the night. Yet the mortars did direct damage but once, and that one time only because of malfunction.

When a shot failed to explode, Shacknasty Frank, Jim's brother, and another Modoc man—possibly Big Ike—attacked it with an ax to get at the much-need black powder within. That was a bad idea. The ax blow detonated the explosive, and the blast decapitated both men.[9]

•••

As the second day dawned bright and clear, Gillem ordered his forces to advance. Green was to move first, and his troops did as he expected, hopping and skipping from one large block of lava to another for cover. Then Gillem sent a heads-up dispatch to Mason: "We will endeavor to end the Modoc war today. Try and join Major Green's right [south of the Stronghold]. Push the Indians when Green attacks."[10] Gillem wanted to encircle the Modocs and push them toward Tule Lake. The colonel assumed that Mason was following Green's lead and moving forward. Then he received a message from Mason that Modocs were firing on his men from the flank and rear—almost certainly a delusion or a fabrication—and he could help Green only when the immediate predicament eased.

Captain Miller of the Fourth Artillery, commanding Green's right, moved ahead with his battery's seventeen men, became separated from the main force, and took hostile fire from the Modocs and friendly fire from the Warm Springs scouts. Miller and his men took cover in a shallow depression and lay low, scrambling to safety only after the sun went down. By then three of his men had been hit. Private Terence McManus had a bad wound in the upper left thigh that broke the femur; Private William Cunningham, a less severe flesh wound in the back; Sergeant Richard Morgan, a fatal round through the chest. McManus and Cunningham were carried back to Gillem's Camp on stretchers, and Morgan's body was left to be recovered later.

Meanwhile, Mason was explaining in a further message why his force could not connect with Green's: "It is absolutely impossible to connect our left with Green's right, we are separated by a deep chasm held by the Modocs, we cannot cross it without great loss of life."[11] Mason had made the same excuse during the First Battle of the Stronghold.

As the sun fell, Gillem could see only a small gain in the army's position: Mason's and Green's men had linked up along the Tule Lake shore north of the Stronghold. They were closer than ever before to

Firing into a Continent

the Modocs' citadel, and for the first time they had crossed the red tule rope Curley Headed Doctor laid out as spirit protection.

For the second night in a row, the officers and men of the Modoc Expedition bivouacked where they were, gnawing hardtack and wrapping themselves in blankets against the cold and the lava's many daggers. Through the dark hours the Coehorn mortars continued to launch loud fire.

● ● ●

Meanwhile, the Modocs were grappling with a crisis of faith. During and since the January battle, Curley Headed Doctor's Ghost Dance and red tule rope had held strong. Not a single Modoc died from gunfire, as he promised, nor did soldiers cross the rope. Now all that changed. Soldiers had stepped over the rope and were even now dozing only a couple of hundred yards from the center of the Stronghold. And at least two Modocs had been killed, the men beheaded by the hang-fire mortar shell. The spell had been broken. When a shaman's power fled, Modoc belief held, it stayed away forever after. Curley Headed Doctor had become the lamest of lame ducks.

To make matters worse, the Modocs were out of water and unable to break through to the lake. They knew their best chance to resupply lay among the lava-tube caves to the south. It is one of that terrane's many geological marvels that water fills these tubes during spring melt and refreezes in the cold earth, where it remains like an underground glacier even through summer heat. If the Modocs could make it to these caves, they might hide underground and live off the ice. And so they set out.

There were approximately 150 people, ranging in age from just a few weeks old to the stooped and gray. They packed clothes, blankets, and dried beef, then leashed dogs and haltered their few famished and bony horses. The entire band slipped out of the Stronghold before the waning gibbous moon rose a little after midnight. They walked south, silently, through the dark. To the Modocs' east the Warm Springs scouts bivouacked. On the west Captain Miller's battered Battery E had hunkered down for the night. The sentries posted on both sides saw nothing, heard nothing. The Modocs, this worn and weary band more refugee than combatant, slipped away undetected along the same path they had used to drive cattle into the natural corral west of the Stronghold, a relatively smooth, downhill route between two long tongues of lava.[12]

Not all the Modocs abandoned the Stronghold on the night of April 17. Three, maybe four people, either elderly or injured and unable to endure a rough walk through the night, remained behind. And a small unit of young, unmarried men kept on fighting through the dark, lest the army hear nothing but silence and realize that the Modocs had escaped.

To inflate their ruse, the Modoc skeleton force built a fire in the open, where the artillerymen could easily spot it. Sure enough, the mortar battery used the blaze as a target. As Fox, himself taken in by the tactic, reported, "On one occasion a shell burst close to one of their fires and made them so mad that one of the party got up and made a speech in tolerably good English, calling the soldiers all the names his limited knowledge of the language commanded. Although they were few, it would be hard to excel them in vulgarity and profanity. Our men answered back."[13] The Modocs furthered the deception by advancing on the mortars and firing, only to retreat when the artillerymen shot back. The Indians did not need to die for bravery. They only needed to convince the army that they were many and resolute.

As the escaping Modocs headed south, some ten or eleven men headed by Hooker Jim broke off from the main column. They looped west and then north, in the direction of Gillem's Camp. Hooker Jim had a little surprise in mind.

• • •

Henry McElderry had decided to visit the field hospital at Hospital Rock and move four horses for stretcher bearing to that facility. Since the army now held the entire lakeshore, McElderry chose to forgo the Whitehalls and ride along the lake from the one camp to the other. At 7 a.m. on the morning of the battle's third day, he and his companions set out, all mounted. Ahead of McElderry rode a group of three:

Firing into a Continent

an unnamed enlisted man; H. C. Tickner, a civilian packer and team-ster serving as guide; and reporter H. Wallace Atwell. Riding with McElderry was Fox, who was again brandishing a Springfield breech-loader. At a distance behind Fox and McElderry and leading the four packhorses rode Eugene Hovey, a twenty-one-year-old teamster from Yreka, and another civilian named Watson.

Around the bay of the lake about a thousand yards from Hospital Rock, Fox saw the enlisted man ahead jump off his horse in a hurry and dive into the sagebrush. A few second later, Tickner and Atwell likewise came off their mounts and fled for cover.

McElderry turned to Fox and said, "They must be firing this way," just as four or five slugs whizzed past. Fox and McElderry dismounted. McElderry led his horse toward a ridge; Fox hesitated. "I stood for a minute, but a couple more bullets cured me of hesitation, and letting go my horse, [I] started on a run to get behind the cluster of rocks we had just left." Once behind cover, Fox gave in to what he called his "mur-derous intentions." He "crept up behind these rocks in order to get a shot at the red devils who had caused all this commotion, but just as I was slipping a cartridge into the breech, two fresh leaden messengers—one so unpleasantly close it made my left ear tingle—changed my tac-tics, so that I made a flank movement, left my rear open to the fire of the enemy, and rejoined the doctor after a brilliant dash of some two hundred yards. Some officers who had been watching my evolutions with the aid of a powerful glass afterwards acknowledged that I had made the most brilliant retreat of the day."

The doctor and the reporter made it to Hospital Rock without fur-ther incident. There they learned that a slug had torn Atwell's boot open and bruised his foot badly. The hobbled reporter took a White-hall back to Gillem's Camp, stretching out in the stern sheets to com-pose his dispatch from this eventful day.

Much worse befell the two civilian teamsters who had been follow-ing Fox and McElderry. Hooker Jim's commando ambushed them, missing Watson, who escaped at a dead run toward Hospital Rock, but killing Hovey outright, then made off with the four horses. The ambushers turned Hovey's corpse into a calling card of Modoc contempt. Fox saw the body a few hours later: "His entire scalp had been taken off and his stomach slashed through with a knife, making a fearful gash from which the entrails were protruding."[14]

By the end of this day, more acts of egregious cruelty would be added to the scales of atrocity.

• • •

Through the third morning the artillery barrage continued, from both the mortar battery and the mountain howitzers. The foot soldiers remained holed up behind rock and sagebrush, letting the artillery do its standoff assault. Around 10 a.m. Modocs in the Stronghold fired in one flurry after another, then fell silent. Green began to think that the Modocs had evacuated. As time passed, Mason and Gillem came to the same conclusion.

The howitzers and mortars ceased firing to allow the soldiers to advance, and they did so, hesitantly. The quiet, the lack of incoming fire, emboldened the troopers. They ran farther ahead at each increment, stood taller as they moved up. Finally a small squad disappeared into the Modoc rocks and emerged standing on a high point. At that signal, the scattered, hiding soldiers gathered in ranks and walked boldly into the Stronghold.

They entered along a passageway where lay the severed head of one of the men who had been killed by the hang-fire mortar. It was, Sergeant Fitzgerald remembered, "as black as the darkest native of the Congo. Passing troopers generally saluted it with a passing kick." The head bounced from rock to rock with the wet thunk of thrown meat. Finally some soldier picked it up. The other loose head was retrieved as well.

Fitzgerald was watching as a lieutenant, whom he left unnamed, encountered an elderly Modoc woman and said, "Is there anyone here who will put that old hag out of the way?" A private stepped forward, said, "'I'll fix her Lieutenant,' . . . placed his carbine to her head and blew out her brains."[15]

That was only the first killing of defenseless Indians. "The soldiers and Warm Springs scouts were soon scattered all through the rocks, and occasional shots tolled the death knell of some wounded Modocs that were pulled out of holes in the rocks, where they had been left when the main body retreated," Fox wrote.[16] This reporter who had raised cosmic howls over Canby and Thomas scarcely batted a journalistic eye at killing wounded and aged Natives, all of them left nameless.

With the Stronghold secure, Gillem ordered a skirmish line to probe to the south. Within minutes the soldiers came under fire from a group of Indians a hundred yards ahead, most likely Hooker Jim's commando come back from the Hospital Rock ambush earlier that morning. The soldiers took cover and returned fire, and soon the Modocs slipped away.

This was the final firefight of what would come to be called the Three-Day Battle, April 15–17, 1873. Gillem's report said that "during this advance . . . the Indians opened a sharp fire on us wounding (not seriously) Private Nolan, company G First Cavalry, which was the only casualty in Major Mason's Command during the three days fighting except Warm Spring 'Bob' slightly wounded in the leg."[17] In the tally of the battle's wounded and dead, even friendly Indians counted only as afterthoughts.

• • •

Colonel Gillem had to be of conflicted mind. Counting Nolan and the scout Bob, the military's losses in the official medical tally came to six dead and fifteen wounded, well below the First Battle of the Stronghold's toll of ten dead and twenty-two wounded. And where the army had had to retreat badly beaten in the January battle, Gillem had driven the Modocs out of the Stronghold. Even though the *Army and Navy Journal* would report that sixteen Modoc men had been killed and one woman captured during the Three-Day Battle, the more likely death toll among the Indians, apart from the three or four old people killed in the capture of the Stronghold, was two or three.[18] As small as the Modoc community was, it could ill afford these losses.

The capture of the Stronghold changed the nature of the Modoc War as well. Beforehand, Gillem always knew where the Indians were. Now he had to locate their hideout and figure out how to obliterate them. This was a different kind of fight, one more akin to the ride-and-fight Indian wars on the Great Plains. Gillem ordered cavalry scouting parties to ride circuits around the Lava Beds to locate the Modocs. And to ensure that the Indians did not slip back into the Stronghold, he had Mason's force occupy it. Gillem pulled the rest of the troops back to the camp at the foot of Sheepy Ridge.

Some of the returning soldiers were carrying the severed heads retrieved from the Stronghold as trophies. They wanted to know whether they had taken out somebody important.

25

Scalps and Skulls

The Medical Officers of the Army have collected a much larger series
of American skulls than have ever before been available for study.
The collection embraces many ancient crania from caves and tumuli,
from Greenland and Alaska, to Florida and Arizona, and specimens
from the majority of the existing tribes of Indians.

—Surgeon General J. K. Barnes to Honorable John Coburn,
January 18, 1873

The soldiers brought their battered trophies to young Jeff Riddle,
ten-year-old son of Frank and Toby. The bluecoats were sure
they had killed Modoc fighters of importance, and they asked the boy
to verify the heads' original owners. Jeff identified one as Shacknasty
Frank. The other was a man he had seen, but his name Jeff did not know.

One soldier disliked this answer, since it deflated his claim to dead-
Modoc fame. "I guess you do not know these heads," he said. "I'll tell
you which Indians these heads belonged to. One is Scarface Charley's
head and the other belonged to Bogus Charley."

Jeff knew better, and he told the pushy glory-hound of a soldier so.
Just then the bluecoat remembered Jeff was half-Modoc. Through a
dark scowl he said, "It's a pity that you are not in Capt. Jack's camp right
now. I wish you was there so I could draw a bead on you and let drive."

Young Jeff felt mannish enough to snap back, "I'm here in Mr. Gillem's
camp. I do not see why you cannot draw a bead on me here and let drive."

The soldier shut his mouth when Frank and Toby appeared and confirmed their son's identification of the dead men. The soldier hardly
cared. He knew that what this Modoc woman, her Indian-loving white
husband, and their mixed-blood spawn said counted for nothing. What
mattered was the story he, the white man, chose to tell. He dubbed

the heads Scarface Charley and Bogus Charley even though both men were, in fact, very much alive. He and his messmates kicked the heads around, shouting at each hard boot, "Hello you black demon. How do you like this?"[1]

One of the heads was booted about, Meacham reported, "until a surgeon interferes, and saves it from further indignities by sending it to the camp, where the face was carefully skinned off, and 'put to pickle' in alcohol."[2]

The surgeon was most likely Henry McElderry, who planned to add the head to a fast-growing collection of Native skulls funded by the federal government. The sawbones was less saving an Indian body part from atrocity than following orders to turn it into a specimen.

•••

The Field Museum, the American Museum of Natural History, the Smithsonian Institution, and many other smaller museums founded in the 1800s eagerly collected all manner of Indian artifacts for study and display, including bones and burial goods. The Army Medical Museum, founded in Washington, DC, in 1862, was singularly devoted to skulls.

In 1868, George Alexander Otis, then assistant surgeon general of the United States Army, circulated an order among military physicians requiring their service in the museum's effort to build its collection of crania. Already a year old, the collection had 143 skulls representing a dozen or more tribes, as well as a few specimens of "doubtful or mixed breeds. . . . The chief purpose had in view in forming this collection," Alexander explained, "is to aid in the progress of anthropological science by obtaining measurements of a large number of skulls of aboriginal races of North America." Military medical officers in Indian country were in good position to collect skulls for the museum. As many specimens as possible were needed: "It is chiefly desired to procure sufficiently large series of adult crania of the principal Indian tribes to furnish accurate average estimates. Medical Officers will enhance the value of their contributions by transmitting with the specimens the fullest attainable memoranda, specifying the locality where the skulls were derived, the presumed age and sex."[3]

The army's medical officers responded enthusiastically. Part of the collection, which had swelled to a thousand skulls by the time of the Modoc War, came from ancient burial sites, such as the mounds of the eastern United States, others from tribal cemeteries captured during military operations. Plagues and epidemics were helpful, since, in addition to killing Indians in droves, widespread disease tore apart their societies and made it difficult for survivors to protect the dead against grave robbers. And then there were executions and battles. Medical officers enjoyed easy access to all these opportunities. They also had the surgical skills to dissect away the soft tissues of the face, scalp, and upper neck and prepare the head for boiling or steeping in lime to leave only the unfleshed bone the Army Medical Museum sought.

The official reason for collecting Indian skulls was comparative study of racial differences. This putatively scientific work produced an unsurprising result. In 1870, Otis, now with the Army Medical Museum, after studying the "osteological peculiarities" of the skulls collected to date, announced that America's Native peoples "must be assigned a lower position in the human scale than has been believed heretofore."[4] Lewis Henry Morgan, a pioneering physical anthropologist, said that American Indians "have the skulls and brains of barbarians, and must grow toward civilization."[5] In this way, the putative science of the time supported exterminating Native nations and segregating the survivors on reservations.

The Army Medical Museum owned 2,206 skulls by 1898, when the collection was turned over to the Smithsonian Institution. The collection had fallen into disuse. No good science, other than spurious evidence supporting genocide, ever came out of it. And it marked the United States as the only national government ever to collect human skulls as an official enterprise.[6]

In Gillem's Camp, Henry McElderry was rescuing that battered, soccer-ball head from one kind of indignity and subjecting it to another. Even Meacham, who considered himself a friend of Indians, saw McElderry's treatment as appropriate. In a cosmic and genocidal war, collecting enemy skulls for study and display becomes pseudoscience that supports the triumph of good over evil. McElderry would get yet another chance to turn Modocs into specimens in the war's last grisly act.

Meanwhile, Sergeant G. W. Lee of the First Cavalry scalped the head dubbed Scarface Charley. He had someone he wanted to show that trophy to.

• • •

That someone was William Simpson, an accomplished reporter and illustrator from Great Britain. When he appeared in the Lava Beds soon after the Second Battle of the Stronghold, Simpson became the first and only international newsman to cover an American Indian war.[7] And, but for a last-minute decision, he would have been the first reporter to die in one.

Forty-nine years old and well known in his home country, Simpson was a longtime war correspondent who had worked the Crimean War, the Sepoy Rebellion in India, the British invasion of Abyssinia, and the Franco-Prussian War. He not only reported but also, in this age before photography became easily portable, illustrated his stories with drawings and watercolors.[8]

The Modoc War fell into Simpson's newshound lap. He had left England on assignment from the *Illustrated London News* and the *Daily News* to cover the wedding celebration of the Chinese emperor. On his way back to England the long way around, he arrived in San Francisco. There he heard about the Lava Beds conflict and headed north.

When that enthusiastic sergeant presented Scarface Charley's putative scalp, Simpson demonstrated his professional skepticism. He sketched with pen and ink and captioned the drawing as "Scalp of Scaur-faced Charley, Modoc Chief, taken by Sarg. G. W. Lee, 1st Cav., K troop, third days fighting—Many believe to be Scaurfaced Charlie's Scalp, but others say that is either Charlie Miller or Steamboat Frank's."[9]

Believe, gentle reader, at your peril, Simpson was saying. Yet he would soon show himself as capable as that soldier of self-serving invention.

• • •

When Simpson arrived in Gillem's Camp, the first man he met surprised him by speaking with an English accent. Fellow countryman Edward Fox then introduced Simpson to the officers of the Modoc Expedition, who welcomed the illustrator warmly. "One reason for this cordial reception," Simpson realized, "was the feeling that the public did not understand the locality, and that blame was attached to them for being held at bay by so small a number of rude savages. 'Now,' they said, 'the public will see pictures of the place, and be able to understand what we have had to fight against.'"[10]

The Lava Beds' tactical difficulty impressed Simpson, who knew battlefields and fortifications. The Modocs' tenacity awed him as well: "The last engagement before my arrival continued three days. About forty Modocs against six hundred, they fought all that time like perfect devils." The Indians further displayed their inborn nature by ambushing Canby and Thomas: "That crime put them beyond the pale of mercy, and extermination like vermin was decreed against them."[11]

Simpson took an up-close look at Kientpoos's cave, which he found most unappetizing: "Bones, some of them picked; others with pickings still left; horns of cattle; hoofs; skins, with the hair on; hides and pieces of deer-skin, from which they made moccasins. Fish in a putrid state, and fish-bones were in shelves of the rock; pieces of fat, and dark, questionable lumps lay about which were said to be meat."

The illustrator took this scene not as evidence of the Modocs' desperate straits but as proof of their savagery: "The much-talked-of cave where Captain Jack and his family lived in the Lava-beds . . . indicates the primitive condition of civilization reached by the Indian tribes of this region, who seem to be very little in advance of the ancient cave-people."[12]

Simpson's drawing of Kientpoos's cave shows trash strewn about and the horned skull of a slaughtered steer filling a corner, its eyeholes blank and threatening. A naked toddler crowds close to a fire where three dark-clad women talk with two rifle-toting men. Another man, his weapon on his shoulder, stands near the entrance. The overall feeling is troglodytic.

Memory must have faltered between Simpson's visit to the cave and his drawing. The space he depicted was far too big. The actual cave is surprisingly small, more pit with overhang than a deep cavern. Simpson was drawing a place imagined, not real.

This injection of imagination holds true of almost all of Simpson's illustrations. Consider his drawing of a dead bluecoat being scalped.

The Modoc wears the buckskin leggings, breechcloth, and feathered headband of a Plains Indian.[13] In fact, the Modocs dressed in the dungarees and calico of sodbusters, not buckskin and feathers.

Then there is his depiction of Kientpoos shooting Canby. The artist shows the uniformed brigadier too young and athletically trim, standing tall, leaning back, and holding out his hand as if to stop the bullet Kientpoos is sending his way. Dyar is already mounted on his horse; in fact, he abandoned the animal and ran like a rabbit. Thomas and Meacham are impossible to tell apart. Frank Riddle does indeed look like Frank Riddle; Simpson met him in Gillem's Camp and knew his appearance. Yet he shows Frank down on one knee at his wife's side and raising a brave hand to protect her. In fact, Riddle took off running the second Kientpoos drew his pistol. Toby he left to fend for herself.

Simpson would have met her, too, yet Toby's face is all wrong, almost African. Kientpoos, too, has the same look. The illustrator transformed his Modocs into creatures of low race who carried within them something of night and cave.[14]

•••

Simpson's fellow countryman was disappointed that, with the Modocs on the run, a dramatic and climactic confrontation of arms was most unlikely. "I am tolerably well satisfied that they will not stand together in a body and will have to be exterminated by ones and twos," Fox wrote in his very last dispatch from Gillem's Camp.[15]

Simpson lacked Fox's willingness to carry a weapon, but he did have an affinity for common soldiers and a willingness to show life in the ranks.[16] Captain Evan Thomas and First Lieutenant Thomas Wright were preparing to lead a patrol to locate the escaped Modocs and set up an artillery observation post. They asked Simpson whether he wanted to come along.

He was giving the offer hard thought when he and Fox learned that, at the same early-morning hour when the patrol was due to set out, a large, heavily armed cavalry force would be heading to Yreka to meet Colonel Jefferson C. Davis and escort the new commander back to the Lava Beds. Simpson and Fox looked at one another and realized this was their chance to exit the war zone safely. The two Britishers decided to leave.

Early next morning, the cavalrymen and the reporters paused to let their horses breathe after the climb up Sheepy Ridge. Simpson spotted the Thomas-Wright patrol far below; the polished steel of their rifles glinted in the sun, a sight both beautiful and portentous.[17] "Had I not been leaving," he wrote, "I should most certainly have gone out with the scouting party. . . . I look upon this as one of the narrowest escapes of my life."[18]

26

Into the Volcanic Valley of Death

Yea, though I walk through the valley of the shadow of death, I will
fear no evil: for thou art with me.

—Psalm 23:4

The glistening patrol Simpson was watching on his final gaze across the Lava Beds was the latest attempt to plug a gap in military intelligence: Where were the Modocs hiding out? Already Colonel Gillem had dispatched Donald McKay and his scouts to find them. In the far southern reaches of the Lava Beds, they caught two Modoc men, but, without questioning the captives, the overeager Warm Springs slit their throats and lifted their scalps.[1] All the while, cavalry patrols continued to circle the Lava Beds, finding no sign that the Modocs had broken out. Clearly, the Indians were holed up somewhere between the Stronghold and the first uphills of the Medicine Lake highland, a jumbled reach of grottoes, hollows, and caves.

Meanwhile, the Modocs kept making their belligerent presence known. They laid an ambush for a mule train hauling supplies between Hospital Rock and the army-occupied Stronghold. The first volley killed one man—an Irish private, John Walsh—and badly wounded another Irishman, Morris Darcy. Driven off by the pack train's escort, the Indians sniped at the Hospital Rock signal station and launched several long-range rounds at Gillem's Camp, punching a bullet hole through a tent. The Modocs scattered when a single mortar round dropped some fifty yards in front of them. Watched by the signal stations on Sheepy Ridge and Hospital Rock, a dozen or so fighters then made their way down to the lake, took long drinks, and washed in the cold, springtime water. The Modocs' motivation was as much defiance as hygiene. It took almost two hours to organize a patrol to pursue the Indians, who had slipped off single file to the south, clean and well watered, by the time the soldiers arrived.[2]

Since the warming weather continued to melt the snow in the high country, chances increased daily that the Modocs would slip out of the Lava Beds into the mountains. Mule deer were following the retreating snow up into the wooded slopes. If the Modocs escaped the lava plains, they would enjoy both food and cover. Gillem wanted to wipe the Modocs out before they could escape and scatter into small bands the army would have to hunt down one by one.

The Warm Springs scouts felt certain that the Modocs were hiding in a lava flow about four miles south of the Stronghold, just east of a lone hill the soldiers dubbed Sand Butte.[3] Major Green got an idea. He wanted a patrol to assess the difficulty of moving the mortar battery to the butte's summit to rain fire on the Modocs. Gillem liked Green's idea; he had to get something going before Colonel Davis arrived. Gillem chose his best young officers to lead the patrol.[4]

Captain Evan Thomas, commander of Battery A, Fourth Artillery, was the son of Lorenzo Thomas, who retired as adjutant general of the army and was himself a decorated Civil War veteran. First Lieutenant Thomas Wright, who led Company E, Twelfth Infantry, had a prominent army father as well: Brigadier General George Wright, who died on his way to take over command of the Department of the Columbia eight years earlier. Young Wright, too, was a Civil War veteran. First Lieutenant Albion Howe, Battery K, Fourth Artillery, was the third son of a military father assigned to the patrol. His father was Colonel A. P. Howe, also with the Fourth Artillery, and he had fought in the Civil War battles of Cold Harbor and Petersburg. For First Lieutenant George Harris, Battery K, Fourth Artillery, the Modoc Expedition was his first taste of war. Also new to war was First Lieutenant Arthur Cranston, Battery M, Fourth Artillery.[5]

Green gave Captain Thomas explicit instructions: he was to avoid picking a fight. This patrol was a reconnaissance in strength, Green made clear, not an offer of battle.[6]

The column leaving Gillem's Camp in the early morning of April 26 looked impressive. With about seventy officers and men, whose ranks would swell to more than eighty after McKay and a dozen Warm Springs scouts met them at noon near Sand Butte, the patrol far outnumbered the Modoc fighters. At the front of the column marched the infantry under Lieutenant Wright and Captain Thomas leading two batteries of artillerymen, who had traded howitzers and mortars for Springfield rifles and Spencer carbines. Alongside Thomas and Wright walked H. C. Tickner, a local guide who knew the area well from laying out a wagon road across it years before. Following the artillerymen were contract physician Bernard Semig and Louis Webber, a civilian packer whose two assistants led a train of four mules loaded with stretchers, medical supplies, food, and extra ammunition. Corporal Charles Pentz served as signalman carrying the standard sixteen-foot hickory staff broken into four-foot sections and a four-foot-square red-on-white signal flag.[7] The rear was brought up by an infantry sergeant and three privates charged with ensuring that no Modocs could attack through the back door.

As the patrol headed toward Sand Butte, the infantry spread out in a loose skirmish line to right and left. This was a standard tactic for crossing hostile ground on foot, this spreading-out along the fringes of the line of march to surprise ambushers and prevent the enemy from sneaking into close range.[8]

The route the Thomas-Wright patrol followed posed little difficulty. It headed south by southeast from Gillem's Camp over an eroded lava flow that ran gently uphill through sagebrush and the occasional juniper tree. Thomas and Wright took the route water would, finding the low ground and avoiding the rough-lava ridges to both east and west. Wright kept calling Thomas's attention to caves or crevices that could hide Modoc fighters, cursing the Indians for bringing him to such a "son of a bitch" of a country. The skirmishers and flankers found walking on the rough lava of the ridges difficult, and they kept drifting down toward the main column. They knew full well the Modocs lurked somewhere nearby, and they clung to the imagined safety of numbers away from the hard walking on the broken high ground.[9]

The Modocs knew the soldiers were there. This large-scale patrol in full daylight, with all its metallic clatter, was no secret. Since the patrol's skirmishers were leaving the ridges open, the Modocs paralleled the line of march yet stayed out of sight, shadowing the moving column. And Kientpoos and Scarface Charley, who were leading the Modoc force,

Firing into a Continent

could not believe their good fortune when Thomas chose the hollow at the base of Sand Butte to halt, eat lunch, and await the arrival of McKay and his scouts. Confident in his invincibility, lulled by the midday quiet, the captain stationed no guards. Soldiers stacked their rifles, broke open packs, and fetched out hardtack and cold bacon. Some pulled off their boots to dry socks and air feet. As Thomas's men ate, rested, and tended to the health of their walking parts, the Modocs edged ever closer.[10]

• • •

To see today what at noon on April 26, 1873, was about to become a killing field, drive south from Gillem's Camp on the main road through Lava Beds National Monument, then pull off a little more than four miles along into the small parking area on the east side of the road. A paved trail winds toward Black Crater, a spatter cone that spewed thick, pasty lava only three thousand years ago and remains raw, rough rock. Beyond this point the pavement ends. A dirt trail continues on, smooth and easy to follow, as it descends to a thick volcanic lip. A rock wall signals the end of the path. About a mile and a half ahead, Sand Butte rises some two hundred feet above the lay of the uneven land now known as the Thomas-Wright Battlefield. You will better appreciate the place, and what happened here, if you go beyond the rock wall. Just hike a little south, to your right, skirt the wall's end, and pick your way downhill. Watch where you put your feet; rattlesnakes cling to shade.

The hollow where the Thomas-Wright patrol took its lunch break is the lowest piece of ground for a half-mile in three directions. Except to the north, the bearing from which the patrol had come, the land rises all around. On the east is Sand Butte itself, with one long ridge tailing north and another looping around to the south and connecting with the overlook ridge. Below the overlook lie a few small ridges and an open meadow.

As officers and soldiers lounged, ate, and smoked, the Modocs slipped into position. The group led by Kientpoos and Scarface Charley bellied up into a small stand of mountain mahogany trees on the north face of Sand Butte. Two other squads moved into position on the east, one a little to the north of Kientpoos and Scarface Charley, another to the south. On the west more Modocs crawled onto the top of the overlook ridge.

By all accounts the Indians numbered but twenty-five to thirty men, yet their firing positions lay on high ground above the patrol. If soldiers tried to escape west or east, they ran right into the muzzles of Modoc riflemen. If they went south, they had to dash up a stiff slope under crossfire from both flanks. The only way out lay to the north, along the very route the patrol had come, still under Indian guns for at least the first quarter-mile.[11]

As his men finished lunch, Thomas ordered three soldiers to take a picket position on a ridge a short distance away. Then Thomas, Semig, Tickner, Pentz, and the signalman's assistant started up the butte. Thomas wanted to wigwag the patrol's position back to Gillem's Camp. They were perhaps halfway up when the Modocs, realizing they were about to be spotted, fired at the three pickets.

In the following seconds, as Pentz wigwagged that the patrol had run into Indians, all the Modocs in their surrounding positions opened up. Round after round poured into the hollow, a sudden, crashing chaos descending upon the unprepared soldiers. Fifty-caliber slugs cracked the air, sang off the lava, thwonked into flesh, blood, and bone.[12] Picnic spot became death zone.

• • •

Around noon the first distant cracks of gunfire reached Gillem's Camp, four and a half miles away. The Springfield rifles' blasts carried far, muffled and distorted yet unmistakable. The signalmen up the bluff reported puffs of smoke as well, and they decoded Pentz's abbreviated message. Alerted, Green climbed to the signal station to keep watch. He was not worried, not yet. A firefight had broken out, but, given the numbers, he was sure that any firefight was certain to tip to the army's favor in no time.

About 1:30 the first few runaways emerged from the sagebrush, shouting that Thomas's command was being pounded in a crossfire. These men were so panicked, Green said, that "very little reliance was placed on their report." Not until a winded but even-minded Pentz appeared did Green get a straight story.

The signalman had had quite an afternoon so far. In the opening seconds of the attack, Thomas stood in the open and told Pentz what

Firing into a Continent

to signal until he realized that the red-on-white flag waving on its sixteen-foot staff was drawing intense fire. Thomas ordered Pentz to get himself and his flag to the rear. The signalman ran through a storm of bullets, his flag in one hand and an old Remington revolver in the other, until he found Wright, who told him to get rid of the flag. The signalman managed an offhand joke: "What am I supposed to do with it? Eat it?" Before he got an answer, Pentz watched a panicked Lieutenant Howe throw himself at Wright's feet and implore him, "Oh! Save me! Save me!" Seeing an officer in such a state so demoralized the enlisted men nearby that they broke and ran toward Gillem's Camp. Still under orders to get to the rear, Pentz took off as well, his waving flag drawing the fire of every Modoc in range. He threw himself down on his back, tore the flag off the staff, and folded it inside his shirt. Pentz jumped up and ran on until he was out of range of the Modoc barrage. There he came upon eleven soldiers escaping in a panicked bunch. Pentz wanted to stand his ground and wait for a relief column, and he threatened to shoot any man who kept on running. All but two or three of the eleven called Pentz's bluff and took off. Seeing that he was beaten, Pentz followed.

He told Green that "it was the most demoralized affair that I ever saw in my life." Asked how he got out, Pentz said, "I told him wherever I went with my signal flag they would order me away. Both officers and men . . . kept away from me as if I had the Cholera."[13]

The usually dilatory Gillem had to act. He ordered Green to gather all the men he could—about sixty-five, as it turned out—and head toward Sand Butte. Pentz volunteered to serve as guide and left with Green. Gillem had Mason dispatch yet another unit from his camp at the Stronghold. Given their late start, the two contingents arrived below Sand Butte only as dark was falling. They were joined by the small detachment of Warm Springs scouts who had hunkered down during the firefight, claiming that the ambushed soldiers were shooting at them instead of Modocs. Rather than blunder around in the dark and stumble into yet another ambush, Green had his men build low rock walls for protection and bed down for the night. Rescue would have to wait until morning.

Around midnight a handful of soldiers from the Thomas patrol stumbled into Green's camp and spilled a hurried, horrid tale. All but two of these arrivals were wounded. The two able-bodied men said they could guide rescuers to where some officers and men lay badly wounded yet alive. Green pointed the walking wounded toward Mason's camp at the Stronghold and assigned a few Warm Springs scouts to guide them. Then he took the two men up on their offer to locate the wounded. The dark night and rough terrain soon confused the guides, however. The major again called the search off till morning. He and his men heaped rock walls in their new position and bedded down on the cold, stony ground.[14]

Little did they know that one small clump of dead and wounded lay just 150 yards away in a small hollow. The survivors heard distant voices and the clatter of piled rocks. Frightened and weak, they thought they were listening to Modocs. All night, in pain from wounds and desperate for food and water, they lay suffering and silent, in fear of what terror dawn could bring.[15]

• • •

Alone and on their own, Privates Francis Rolla and William McCoy, Fourth Artillery, and Private William Benham, Twelfth Infantry, staggered toward Gillem's Camp. All three were badly shot up. Rolla had been hit in the left leg, McCoy in the right buttock and testicles. Benham was wounded the worst: bone-breaking wounds in both arms and the left foot, plus a soft-tissue wound in the back. McCoy, who had to be hurting horribly, somehow carried and hauled Benham along. After the three wounded men crawled into camp early the next day, they told reporter H. Wallace Atwell how, lying in a shallow hole with eleven others and no cover against the Modoc rifle fire, they had seen Lieutenant Wright die. Already wounded in the hip, the young officer buried his watch and said, "They shan't get this," then rose up with his revolver blazing. In seconds rifle slugs tore through Wright's groin, right wrist, and chest. He slumped and died.[16]

Green's rescue party was at that very moment seeing for itself what Rolla and McCoy were telling Atwell. As the sun rose, Sergeant August Beck staggered in among the little rock forts, shot through the mouth and unable to talk. Green's men fanned out, weapons at the ready. Private Charles Hardin discovered the first dead man, then followed a bloody trail for three hundred yards and came upon Malachy Clinton, his legs smashed yet still alive.[17]

Such sights struck a chord of horror even for hardened, professional soldiers. Lieutenant Boutelle called it "the most heartbreaking sight it has been my fate to behold. . . . The sight of dead men was not new to me. In my service during the Civil War I had seen them by the acre, but the sight of the poor fellows lying under the sagebrush dead or dying and known to have been uselessly slaughtered was simply revolting."[18]

Captain Trimble, another cavalry officer of long battlefield experience, was shaken, too, by what daylight revealed. The dead and the wounded were "found, presenting different forms of anguish and distortion, some in the position of desperate defense, others prostrate in figures of dire helplessness, and quite a number yet alive, but in the agony of painful wounds."[19]

Boutelle was with the group that found the patrol's commander, Captain Thomas, along with Howe, Harris, Semig, and a number of enlisted men. Thomas had bled out from a torn femoral artery. Howe died from a rifle ball through the head. Harris and Semig were alive, though badly wounded. All the enlisted men were likewise either dead or wounded. Wright's body was discovered close by, along with two dead enlisted men.[20] Although the search continued all day, no sign was found of Lieutenant Cranston or any soldiers who might have been with him. Green and the other officers came to suspect that Cranston, too, was dead. It would, however, be almost two weeks before the bodies of the young officer and the five men he led on a futile charge were found.

As the rescuers piled the dead and gathered the wounded, they realized that they had left two necessities behind. One was water. Except for what the soldiers carried in their canteens, the closest source lay in Tule Lake, five miles away. And, despite the certainty that there would be wounded to care for, Gillem failed to send a medical officer with the rescue column.

Sometime in the late afternoon Henry McElderry, summoned from Gillem's Camp by wigwag, appeared at Sand Butte. He had already had a long day. The pack train the surgeon was leading got lost and then encountered a stretch of rough lava the mules refused to cross. Drafting a soldier and a friendly Indian to carry the load on their backs and leaving three men behind to tend the balky mules, McElderry took off cross-country with a small supply of "dressings, stimulants, water and a hand litter." Facing almost twenty wounded men needing trauma care, McElderry could do no more than apply first aid.[21]

The arrival of such paltry medical help did little to end the horror. "The pleadings of some suffering from peritonitis, the result of intestinal wounds, were dreadful and continuous. When it ceased, we knew what had occurred," Boutelle wrote. "They were dead."

For all the suffering surrounding him, Boutelle managed a bit of banter with Semig. He asked the shot-up doctor how he felt. "I am all right," Semig answered, "but I am so damned dirty." Boutelle questioned whether he was hit hard. "My shoulder here is busted and my heel down there is all split to hell," Semig said. Boutelle checked the wounds and told Semig that "he was as good as three-quarters of a man at least, that his shoulder was not dangerous, though serious, and that with the loss of a few inches of his leg, he would be able to go on all right."

Semig was having none of this false cheer; he knew more than enough to dread amputation. "Boutelle," he said, "do you think I'm a damned fool? I'm a doctor."[22]

The doctor did live, less that destroyed left foot. His right arm remained partially paralyzed for the rest of his days.

The young Lieutenant Harris had been hit dangerously deep in the upper back. McElderry extracted the rifle slug before loading Harris onto a stretcher. There were others so badly wounded they needed stretchers as well, nine in all, and seven or eight others who could walk. Green waited until dark to start back, concerned that the Modocs would sense vulnerability and attack. Indians had indeed appeared on the ridge tops, just out of rifle range, to keep watch. About seven o'clock the column set off. The Warm Springs scouts led, navigating toward a beacon fire in the signal station above Gillem's Camp. Six men carried each stretcher, with the unencumbered soldiers shouldering their weapons. For both able-bodied and wounded, this would be the longest night of their lives.[23]

Just keeping the men together as they carried the wounded over broken ground was a challenge. "The darkness had now become so intense that each man had constantly to tap the shoulder of his comrade in front in order to keep the direction and avoid being left entirely behind," Trimble remembered. As the bearers tired, they halted more and more often to catch breath and ease muscles. They had slept little the night before and worked all day with the dead and the wounded. Now they had to hike, weighed down and clumsy, across ground that tripped them up and shredded boots and feet. Rain had blown up, too, and a chilling breeze. Around midnight the bad weather worsened. Rain in torrents froze into sleet, then snow, and the breeze blustered into wind. Trimble wrote that "with short notice all were soon drenched and shivering in our thinly covered pelts." He knew that, as bad as he felt, the wounded were worse off: "Our movements were slow, the head of the column frequently halting, and those at the stretchers calling often for relief, as the poor sufferers had to be lifted over high rocks and across gulches. They were jarred and shaken terribly and frequently had to be adjusted in position. Not a sound was heard except those made by the fall and shifting of the great black boulders, as they were displaced to clear the trail, and the occasional groans from the wounded."

When a pair of loosed pack mules took a fright and set to braying wildly, Modoc riflemen fired two or three rounds in the general direction of the column. The soldiers went into a squat, close to the ground, anxious that the attack they feared was but minutes away. When no further shots came, they stood and resumed their cold, tired march. The Indians were not attacking, only warning the soldiers away from their camp hidden in the lava flow to the east. There women, children, and elders crowded into hollows and grottoes against the same snow and freezing wind.

At first light Trimble figured he and the column were only midway through the four and a half miles between Sand Butte and Gillem's Camp. "Now was the extent of the great lava-bed disclosed . . . the row of black lava buttes towering grimly in the distance, resembling huge red ovens gone out of business," he wrote. "Aided by the storm in the air and our own abject feelings, amidst this chaos of nature one could almost discover in imagination a resemblance to a scene in the drama of the 'Inferno,' substituting the misery of cold for the torture of heat. There were only lacking the little black Modocs to represent the demons."[24]

Not until 8 a.m. on April 28, two full days after the ambush and thirteen hours since the rescue column had departed the battlefield, did its officers and soldiers stumble into Gillem's Camp. The rescuers were nearly as bad off as the wounded. "Such looking faces as the dawn revealed are seldom seen," Boutelle said. "Eyes seemed to have receded a half inch and around all were dark circles. Several times I heard one man say to another, 'I wonder if I look as you do!'" The feeling they shared was one of "utter demoralization."[25]

That mood only deepened over the following days as the grim toll of Sand Butte became clear. Once Cranston and the five enlisted men with him were found, Harris and Benham died of their wounds, and the body of the civilian packer Webber was discovered, the dead numbered twenty.[26] Among them were every Regular Army officer on the patrol; only the civilian contract physician Semig, who held the equivalent of officer rank, lived, much the worse for wear. Seventeen men survived their wounds, although most of them were too badly hurt to return to duty. The number of dead in two hours of fighting on April 26 exceeded the fatal carnage from four days of battle for the Stronghold. As if to heighten the loss, the Modocs did all this damage without taking a single casualty.[27]

In the aftermath of Sand Butte, rank-and-file soldiers gave their headquarters a new name: Gillem's Graveyard.

About thirty soldiers, all enlisted men, plus the civilian guide H. C. Tickner and the two muleskinners came out of the battle unscathed. They had survived in the worst possible way from the army's point of view: turning tail and scampering away as fast as they could go.

• • •

When he arrived at the Lava Beds on the evening of May 2, Colonel Jefferson C. Davis, the new District of the Columbia commander, took stock of the situation and reported to General Schofield's headquarters: "The troops are in very good health, being well located, well fed and clothed but owing to the heavy losses they have sustained in their recent conflicts with the Indians and the little successes gained by them there is a very perceptible feeling of despondency pervading the entire command."

Because all the Regular Army officers on the patrol were either dead or dying, Davis admitted that he still had only a partial picture of the Sand Butte debacle. Still, he gave the officers a bye, including Gillem and Green. The military objective of the reconnaissance was worthy, he said, and the size of the patrol sufficient to accomplish it. Davis faulted Thomas for not pushing his skirmish line onto the ridges. Still, poor tactics did not explain the disaster. The root cause of the Thomas-Wright massacre, Davis insisted, was a failure of backbone in the ranks.

Thomas's tactical failure "would have been quickly and easily remedied had the men, as a few did, stood by the officers and obeyed orders—this they did not do," wrote Davis. "The result was conspicuous cowardice on the part of the men who ran away and conspicuous bravery and death on the part of the officers and men who did. The lesson taught by this affair is, that a great many of the enlisted men here are utterly unfit for Indian fighting of this kind, being only cowardly beef eaters." Davis's solution was to drill these sad sacks hard and force them to fight. "I shall take such steps while here as I think will ensure this training," he promised.[28]

Davis refused to admit that the army had been out-officered. Scarface Charley and Kientpoos had exploited Thomas's every error. The young officer succumbed to the common military hubris that the patrol's superior force would strike fear in Indian hearts. He thought he could march his men within rifle range of the Modocs' hideout and so intimidate them that he had little need for flankers and skirmishers and less for noontime guards. Thomas had grown cockily overconfident. The Modocs made him pay.

Still, there was a character issue, though not the one Davis cited. Enlisted men signed on for a roof over their heads, three gut-twisting vegetable-free meals a day, and a measly thirteen dollars a month in greenbacks as base pay. In return they got to wear leftover Civil War uniforms and share their one thin blanket with a buddy called a "bunky." Morale was nearly nonexistent. It hardly helped that most Regular

Army officers saw themselves as a class above the enlisted men: separate, superior, entitled to absolute obedience. Green made it clear to the rescue column he was interested only in the bodies of officers. When a search party returned with the corpses of enlisted men, Green was unimpressed: "Several dead bodies were found, and brought in, but not those more particularly looked for"—namely, the officers.[29]

Of such stuff, then, were the some sixty-five enlisted men at Sand Butte. Trapped in an ambush brought on by incompetent officers whose sense of honor compelled them to fight to the death, many men in the ranks made the rational calculation: running away sure beat getting killed.

•••

The character issue on the Modoc side of the battle line differed. The Indians were fighting for survival. Dispossessed of their home country over almost three genocidal decades, the Modocs of Lost River were locked in a struggle as existential as it was desperate.

By the time of the Battle of Sand Butte, the Modocs under Kientpoos had been living in the open for five months, sleeping on rocks, shivering and freezing in rain and snow. They had little more than the clothes they wore when they abandoned the Stronghold. For water they now depended on ice in lava tubes. Food was the last of the dried beef they had slaughtered and prepared before the Second Battle of the Stronghold. Only the dogs and horses were thinner than they.

And, even in a culture that valued fighters and fighting, the struggle was wearing them out. Something of the ferocity that the Modocs had brought early to the fight was draining away. As bad as the Battle of Sand Butte went for the army, the Indians could have made it worse. When the shooting ceased, the Modocs declined to hunt down and kill the wounded, and they left at least some of the dead soldiers' weapons on the field.[30] Indeed, as the Modocs told Meacham later, when Scarface Charley had had his fill of slaughter, he called out in English in his booming bass, *"All you fellows that aint dead yet had better go home. We don't want to kill you all in one day."*[31]

At the moment of their greatest triumph, the Modocs were hitting bottom.

Firing into a Continent

FIG. 1. Before the Modoc War, Kientpoos often visited the mining town of Yreka, where this studio portrait was taken by T. N. Wood in 1864. Courtesy Braun Research Library Collection, Autry Museum, Los Angeles; P. 482.

FIG. 2. John Fairchild employed Hot Creek cowboys on his ranch, developing a cooperative relationship with the Modocs that ended abruptly when the cavalry raided Lost River. Fairchild (*far right*) with three of the men who once worked his cattle, horses, and mules (*from left*): Shacknasty Jim, Hooker Jim, and Steamboat Frank. Photographic portraits of the Modoc Indians of the Modoc War, courtesy California Historical Society, PC 006_07.

FIG. 3. Jesse Applegate, the Oregon pioneer who stirred the pot that led to war, was so sensitive about his appearance that he refused any and all photographs. This drawing was made from memory by a nephew decades after Applegate's death. Courtesy Oregon Historical Society, bb007055.

FIG. 4. Brigadier General Edward Richard Sprigg Canby in a portrait taken between 1860 and 1870. Canby's killing on Good Friday 1873 transformed this plodding, by-the-book commander into a cosmic martyr for the advance of white civilization. Courtesy Library of Congress, Prints & Photographs Division, Civil War Photographs, LC-B813-6326 A.

FIG. 5. William Simpson's illustration of Kientpoos about to shoot General Canby—which ran in *Harper's Weekly* on June 28, 1873, only days before the war crimes trial began at Fort Klamath—drew more from popular imagination of how such a scene must have played out than from factual, on-the-ground research. Courtesy National Park Service, LABE 5789.

FIG. 6. Toby and Frank Riddle—she a Modoc and cousin to Kientpoos, he an emigrant from Kentucky—served as interpreters and go-betweens during the siege of the Lava Beds and as witnesses for the prosecution at the Fort Klamath war crimes trial. This stereoscopic image was taken by famed San Francisco photographer Edward (later Eadweard) Muybridge in Gillem's Camp in early May 1873. Courtesy Rosenstock Collection, Autry Library, Autry Museum, Los Angeles; 90.253.1830.

FIG. 7. Scarface Charley in a portrait taken by Louis Heller soon after the Modoc surrender in June 1873. Respected by both Indians and whites, this Modoc combat leader choreographed the ambush at Sand Butte, effectively obliterating an army patrol three times the size of his own force. Photographic portraits of Modoc Indians of the Modoc War, courtesy California Historical Society, PC 006_02.

FIG. 8. Colonel Jefferson C. Davis in a portrait taken between 1860 and 1870. A fierce bantam who got away with killing his commanding officer and abandoning escaped slaves to Confederate cavalry, Davis put his mark on the closing act of the Modoc War and the Fort Klamath war crimes trial. Courtesy Library of Congress, Prints & Photographs Division, Civil War Photographs, LC-B813-6345.

FIG. 9. The women in Kientpoos's life (*from left*): second wife, Lizzie, sister Princess Mary, daughter Rosie, and first wife, Rebecca. Photographed by Louis Heller after their surrender in June 1873. Photographic portraits of Modoc Indians of the Modoc War, courtesy California Historical Society, PC 006_03.

FIG. 10. After surrendering, Schonchin John (*left*) and Kientpoos were shorn of their long hair and shackled together, an indignity that Louis Heller captured in this image. Photographic portraits of Modoc Indians of the Modoc War, courtesy California Historical Society, PC 006_05.

FIG. 11. The Modoc Touring Company assembled by Alfred B. Meacham in hopes of lecture-circuit profit from the Modoc War's notoriety (*from left*): Shacknasty Jim, Steamboat Frank, Frank and Toby Riddle with son Jeff at their feet, and Scarface Charley. Courtesy Denver Public Library, Western History Collection, x-32143.

PART 4

Things Fall Apart

Turning and turning in the widening gyre
The falcon cannot hear the falconer;
Things fall apart; the centre cannot hold.

—William Butler Yeats, "The Second Coming"

27

The Center Cannot Hold

I can see him [the packer H. C. Tickner] yet, standing on the packs,
shouting, and waving his hat, as we charged past him. I afterward
asked him why he had not gotten behind the packs, instead of
so exposing himself. He told me that he had to see it; that it was
the prettiest thing he had ever seen, and he would
not have missed it to save his life.

—Charles B. Hardin to William S. Brown, March 15, 1928

As newsprint reports of the Sand Butte debacle spread across
the country through the early weeks of May, the Modoc victory required explanation. Various theories made the rounds. Among
the most curious was the idea that the Modocs were something other
than your typical Natives. Stories circulated that they had received
a dose of Caucasian genes from Spanish explorers way back when.
And no less a local authority than Oliver Applegate believed that the
Modocs had sprung from Aztecs who followed waterfowl north from
Mexico and settled around the lakes.[1] This evidence-free explanation
made the Modocs the degenerate remnant of city-building and human-
sacrificing ancestors, explaining both their strategic skill—degraded,
of course—and their barbarity. Even more fanciful was a fiction from
Kentucky, reported in the *New York Times*, that made Kientpoos the
son of a Frankfort, Kentucky, native Captain Jack Chambers, who had
journeyed to California before the gold rush and bedded the comely
daughter of the Modoc head chief. The admixture of gentile southern
blood and sexy, savage stock explained Kientpoos's military acumen.[2]

The *Daily Alta California* argued that the matchup of civilized soldiers who were not sharpshooters against savages who were and who

knew, too, the lay of the land was patently unfair. The Modoc War required army leaders who went into combat without concern for the hobbling niceties of civilized warfare.[3]

Taking much the same editorial position and wanting to get closer to the action of a war the whole country was now watching, the *San Francisco Chronicle* dispatched twenty-three-year-old staff writer William Bunker north. The *New York Times*, which had been relying on arms-length rewriting of other reporters' stories by veteran Oregon newsman S. A. Clarke, sent him to the Lava Beds to report in person.

At the Manhattan offices of the *New York Herald*, James Gordon Bennett Jr. had to be kicking himself. The country's leading paper had missed its chance at firsthand reporting when, in a stroke of reverse genius, Edward Fox had left Gillem's Camp only hours before Sand Butte and was now taking R&R in Yreka. The little mining town boasted its own brewery, a decent hotel, a dining room or two with a civilized menu, and painted women of negotiable virtue. Fox agreed to stay in Yreka for a couple of weeks more before heading back to New York, but he was not about to return to the Lava Beds. In Fox's place, Bennett turned to someone already on the scene: H. Wallace Atwell.

Atwell lacked Fox's polished writing, clever wit, and natural storytelling talent. Yet where the diplomatic Fox tended to buy the official version of events and their conventional explanations, Atwell was a skeptic, a curmudgeonly reporter who took pleasure in discomfiting the comfortable. Like his namesake in the Book of Job, Atwell's byline persona Bill Dadd the Scribe resisted received wisdom and refused to bend a knee to authority, no matter its military rank.[4]

• • •

Even as the newspapers buzzed, Major General John M. Schofield, commander of the army's Division of the Pacific, told the newly arrived Colonel Davis to avoid any "more fruitless sacrifices of our troops," since "we seem to be acting somewhat in the dark."[5] Schofield was already boosting the number of troops at Davis's disposal. Two more companies of the Fourth Artillery arrived at the Lava Beds in the days following Sand Butte. One had been issued horses in Redding on their way north from San Francisco and told they would be fighting with

Things Fall Apart

sabers and Spencers instead of howitzers and mortars. And since practically every other soldier in the West was already committed, the War Department ordered the Fourth Infantry Regiment in Arkansas to head toward California. Although these foot soldiers never made it—second thoughts from on high stopped them in Omaha—Davis's force on the ground was edging up toward the thousand-man command Lieutenant Colonel Wheaton had requested after his shellacking in the First Battle for the Stronghold.[6]

Davis himself issued most orders, making Colonel Gillem redundant. Before the month was out, Davis banished Gillem to his garrison back in Benicia, summoned Wheaton from exile at lonely, distant Fort Warner, and restored the lieutenant colonel to his old job as commander of the District of the Lakes.[7]

All the while, Davis drilled his troops mercilessly to instill military discipline. Yet he relied for his first strategic move not on motivating his soldiers but on the local savvy of two Modoc women.

Artina Chockus, the Hot Creek who had served as a go-between with the Peace Commission, and One-Eyed Dixie, another Hot Creek living on John Fairchild's ranch, set off into the area around Sand Butte. The women had to know they were risking their lives, trusting that the insurgent Modocs would respect their communal connection and do them no harm. Unarmed, they disappeared into the lava.

The pair returned two days later, exhausted from walking hard miles and sleeping rough. Their exertions brought significant news. The Modocs' water source was exhausted, and they had moved on. Exactly where they had gone, Chockus and Dixie were unsure. The two women had also found where Lieutenant Cranston and the five men with him lay dead. Davis did not fully trust the report, however; Chockus and Dixie were Modocs and women, after all. Just to be sure, he sent Donald McKay at the head of a patrol of Warm Springs scouts to double-check. McKay found the dead men right where the women had told him they would be.

A large, well-armed, and extremely wary contingent of soldiers went out to collect the dead. The corpses were so putrid after thirteen days in the spring sun and the ongoing attentions of coyotes and ravens that the soldiers were forced to forgo transporting them back to Gillem's Camp. Instead, they dug shallow graves in the thin soil, planted wooden markers, and buried the cadavers on the spot, glad to be rid of the awful, clinging stench that could shoot the vomit right out of a man.

Meanwhile, the Modocs reappeared to ambush a train of four wagons near Scorpion Point, close to the Tule Lake shoreline. As soon as the raiding party opened fire and wounded three soldiers, the cavalry escort turned tail and ran. The Modocs rooted through the abandoned wagons, took what they wanted, and cut the horses loose. There is a story, possibly apocryphal, that the Indians helped themselves to two barrels of whiskey and were soon riotously drunk. If so, they retained sense enough to vacate the premises before Lieutenant Frazier Boutelle led his cavalry squadron to a belated rescue: Indians gone, horses running loose in cut traces, and wagons burning.[8]

Davis fretted that this ambush evidenced again how his men turned tail at the first shot from a Modoc rifle. What he could not know was that this attack arose from Modoc desperation about water. Soon after Sand Butte, Kientpoos led his people east to an ice cave close to Juniper Butte. The thirsty Modocs used the cave's supply up in only three days and had to move again, this time some four miles south, to yet another ice cave. It was a guard of fighters sent out to protect the moving Modocs' flank that happened upon the wagons and chased off the escort.[9]

Had Davis known what the Modocs were up to, he would have realized that he had them on the ropes. That discovery would have to wait until he determined where the Indians were.

•••

The officer Davis chose to lead the search for the missing Modocs was new to Indian fighting. A West Point graduate and Civil War veteran, Captain Henry C. Hasbrouck commanded Battery B, Fourth Artillery, the unit that had traded howitzers and limbers for Spencers and saddles. Two troops of the First Cavalry, headed by Captain James Jackson—who had led the Lost River raid—and Lieutenant John Kyle, were also assigned to the patrol, as was a detachment of Warm

Things Fall Apart

Springs scouts under McKay. Since the best bet was that the Modocs had headed southeast, away from the army camps and toward the Pit River, the plan was to ride down the east side of the Lava Beds to find the Indians and prevent them from escaping.

On the morning of May 9, soldiers, scouts, and civilian packer Tickner saddled up and headed south. Their route headed across playas of pumice gravel and sandy soil dotted with sagebrush and junipers, country that favored mounted troops over Indians on foot. After a full day's ride without encountering any sign of the missing Modocs, the soldiers and scouts stopped for the night at Sorass Lake. The place was aptly named; it lay a long, bottom-beating ride from Gillem's Camp, and what meager water it offered was gut-scouring alkali. Still, Hasbrouck had been counting on that alkali water to replenish the patrol's supplies. When the lakebed proved dry, and even shallow wells dug into the surrounding marsh yielded nothing drinkable, the captain politely renamed the site Dry Lake. Hasbrouck had cavalry troops and scouts set up camp on the west side of the lakebed, and he sent the mounted artillery about a mile south to bivouac among the ponderosa pines on the lower slopes of Timber Mountain. The soldiers spread out for the night. Each man put his saddle blanket down for a mattress, pillowed on saddle and greatcoat, and pulled a single blanket over himself against the night chill.

North of the cavalry camp some two hundred yards, a line of lava hummocks ran west to east. Another two hundred yards beyond, a stony bluff rose about thirty feet above the dry lakebed. Aware that unseen Modocs had likely been watching his men and that the high ground would give the Indians good firing positions, Hasbrouck stationed night guards on the bluff. He posted others to keep an eye on the horses and mules turned out to graze.

In their silent way the Modocs slipped around the sentries in the dark and took firing positions, some on the bluff and some among the hummocks farther on, as dawn crept over the hilly horizon. They heard the bugler sound reveille, noticed that the sleeping soldiers barely stirred. As soon as they could see what they were shooting at, the Modocs opened up.

The volley stampeded horses and mules, which crashed through the camp, neighing and braying. Sleeping soldiers, groggy and disoriented, rolled out of their blankets, trying to make sense of all this racket of guns and animals. Hasbrouck sent Lieutenant Boutelle to fetch the artillerymen from their camp to the south, ordered Lieutenant Kyle and part of his cavalry troop to catch the loose and frightened horses. Some soldiers rolled behind their saddles as incoming rounds showered gravel over them. The Sand Butte horror flashed through their minds with every rifle slug zinging past.[10]

"The situation was becoming serious," wrote Charles B. Hardin, then a cavalry private. "The men were milling like frightened animals. It began to look like the prelude of a stampede."

A cool Hasbrouck ordered Jackson to advance on the Modocs from the right with his troopers, and Moss and his cavalrymen to do the same on the left. In the next moment, amid all the smoke and clatter of the gunfight, the men in the ranks almost became the cowardly beef-eaters Davis had called them. At the command to charge they wavered between disbelief and fear, going nowhere.

It fell to Thomas Kelley, a quartermaster sergeant, to turn the tide. He shouted, "Goddamn it, let's charge." Amazingly, Kelley's Irish-inflected curse did the trick. "With loud cheers that would drown the best efforts of any band of Indians, the charge was on," Hardin remembered, "the two troops all mixed up and charging without order. It was a real foot race, with every man going as he liked it. Men were falling fast: some were shot, and others hit with gravel, only thinking they were shot. Nothing could stop that charge."[11]

When the oncoming soldiers reached the hummocks, the Indians fell back, heading toward a lava flow almost five miles away. By this time Lieutenant Kyle and his men had snagged some of the panicked horses, and the Warm Springs scouts had mounted up. The scouts split into two bands and rode to the right and the left of the escaping Indians, hoping to cut them off. The gunfight continued on the run, armed hounds and hares. One Modoc fell wounded, and his fellow fighters dragged him along until he died and they abandoned the body. All the surviving Modocs made it into the lava before soldiers or scouts caught them up.

Things Fall Apart

On the way back, some scout looped a rope around the dead Modoc's neck and dragged the cadaver to camp. By the time rider and horse reached Sorass Lake, the corpse was twisted and torn. Someone who knew, probably Tickner, identified the dead fighter as Ellen's Man, Kientpoos's backup at the Peace Tent on Good Friday. Left in the sun and the open, the discarded body became food for ravens and coyotes.[12]

•••

On the scorecard of dead and wounded, the Modocs appeared to come out well ahead at Sorass Lake. Ellen's Man was their only casualty. The Warm Springs suffered two killed, Wassanukka and Lebasten, while Yonowtus received an arm-fracturing bullet wound. Among the soldiers, James J. Totten and Adolphus Fischer died on the battlefield. Shot through the leg by a bullet that severed the artery in the back of the knee, Patrick McGrath should have bled out and succumbed on the spot. John Skinner, the civilian contract surgeon accompanying the patrol, stanched the flow as rifle slugs flew around him and his patients. A temporarily patched-up McGrath did make it back to Gillem's Camp, where the leg was amputated. Despite Skinner's bravery under fire, McGrath died two weeks later, likely of sepsis. Among the six remaining wounded, James Reeves was hurt the worst. A badly fractured right arm was amputated; Reeves survived.[13]

Yet the blood-and-bone calculus of war allowed the army of the Modoc Expedition, which comprised nearly a thousand men, to shake off such death and damage as trivial. The Modocs, who had no more than fifty armed men in total, had lost a fiery fighter in Ellen's Man. And he was a Hot Creek Modoc, a communal identity that soon proved significant. To make matters worse for the fast-retreating Modocs, they abandoned several ponies, a pile of blankets, bags of gunpowder and lead, and dozens of rifle cartridges. Hasbrouck awarded the haul to the Warm Springs scouts as booty.

The captain considered his next move. Pursuing the Modocs into the lava flow he knew to be stupid, and he had eight wounded soldiers and scouts to attend to, with a mere twenty gallons of water on hand. Hasbrouck reserved that meager supply for the wounded and had them hauled in wagons back to camp with an escort under Boute-lle. The rest of the command rode north to Tule Lake, the closest reliable water. By the time they reached it, they were one thirsty band of bloodied brothers.[14]

• • •

For Davis, the Battle of Sorass Lake turned on morale: "The troops have had, all things considered, a very square fight, and whipped the Modocs for the first time." The soldiers had withstood a surprise attack, charged into the Modocs' teeth, and driven them into retreat. The colonel who loved nothing so much as fighting adored the way his men had fought muzzle to muzzle and redeemed themselves.[15]

The Modocs realized they had hit a wall at Sorass. They were poorly fed, short of water, and drained from roughing it for months. Now they had lost one of their most stalwart fighters. The Indians were losing hope as well, and their community was unraveling.

Shacknasty Jim—Ellen Man's cousin—Hooker Jim, Bogus Charley, and Steamboat Frank, all Hot Creeks, accused Kientpoos of putting the Hot Creeks front and center at Sorass Lake to protect his own Lost River people. This hidden agenda had cost the life of Ellen's Man, they argued, and the Hot Creeks wanted nothing more to do with the headman who had cooked up this fruitless attack. Exercising the long-standing right of Modoc fighters to leave a war party when they chose, the four Hot Creek leaders gathered their families and broke away. Another nine men joined them, including Hooker Jim, his father-in-law, Curley Headed Doctor, and Weium. Unless he wanted a gun-fight, Kientpoos could do nothing to stop them. Before the attack at Sorass Lake, the headman had summoned spirit power to protect the Modocs against rifle bullets, purportedly with a purloined military chronometer. Ellen's Man's death proved that Kientpoos's power was a failure. His medicine had fled, never to return.[16]

Almost one-third of the fighting men and one-half of the total Modoc community trudged away to the northwest, in the direction of Hot Creek. A diminished Kientpoos and the people loyal to him struck out six miles due west of Sorass Lake. They planned to decide their next move from the summit of Big Sandy Butte.

···

Entrenched at the base of this high ground two days later, Captain Hasbrouck thought he could end the war with a little help from Major Edwin Mason. The two commanders had more than two hundred men pitted against a depleted Modoc force under Kientpoos of no more than thirty fighters. What made the contest close was the terrain. Big Sand Butte rises steeply some 350 feet above the surrounding country and, but for a few scattered junipers, offers no cover from base to summit. Modocs firing down on soldiers slogging uphill in the open could take a terrible toll. Since it was already late in the afternoon and the soldiers were tired from marching some fifteen miles from Tule Lake, Mason and Hasbrouck camped for the night with the Modocs between them. The next day Mason and Hasbrouck developed a plan of attack and scheduled the assault for the following morning.

That night, in an escape as disciplined as their silent exit from the Stronghold a month earlier, the seventy-odd Modocs descended the butte without being detected. They slipped across the surrounding flatland into the cracks and crevices of a black-lava flow to the north and west.

As the sun came up on the morning the attack was to begin, Mason recognized what Kientpoos had pulled off. A commander so cautious that he preferred doing nothing to doing the least little bit, Mason conferred with Hasbrouck to draw up yet another plan of attack for the following day. That same afternoon, a Warm Springs scout told Hasbrouck it looked as if the Modocs had pulled their slip-away-undetected move yet again and escaped the lava flow. The only way to find out whether the Modocs were still there was to send a out small detachment as a probe. First Lieutenant J. B. Hazelton of the Fourth Artillery offered to lead the patrol, and he enlisted twenty-six volunteers, a sign that morale had improved. The patrol went out and came back, not a shot fired. The Modocs had gone undetected yet again.[17]

The escaping Indians were heading for a spot north and east toward Willow Creek on the east side of Clear Lake, a good place to lie low and hide out. Kientpoos and the Modocs with him would never quite get there.

Mason and Hasbrouck had to be chagrined and frustrated. They had had Kientpoos and what they thought to be every Modoc fighter clamped in a pincer between them. Then the Indians vanished. Mason and his companies marched back the way they had come, toward Tule Lake. Hasbrouck rode out to find where the Indians had gone. Soon he and his men came across what they took to be the tracks of the escaping Indians following an old wagon road to the north and west. They did not realize that this was the spoor not of Kientpoos and his people, who were trudging toward Clear Lake, but of the Hot Creeks, who had already made their way to the neighborhood of the Fairchild and Van Bremer ranches south of Lower Klamath Lake.

The mounted artillerymen rode on along the wagon road. Serendipity was about to work in Hasbrouck's favor.[18]

• • •

With the Modocs on the run, Davis's basic tactic was to keep his units in the field and ready for action.[19] Even as Hasbrouck was moving north and west from Big Sand Butte, Captain David Perry with his squadron from the First Cavalry was scouting the ridges west of Tule Lake, looking for Modocs. Hasbrouck's mounted artillery and Perry's yellowlegs encountered one another near the Antelope Springs watering hole. The next day, the two captains joined forces and swept the valley south of the Van Bremer ranch.

Perry's men, dismounted, took the east side of the valley. Hasbrouck's, all dismounted except the cavalry squadron under Jackson and the Warm Springs scouts, searched on the west. When Hasbrouck hit the fresh, clear trail left by the Hot Creeks crossing the valley and heading uphill, he and his men followed it. The Modocs hiding on the slope fired down on their pursuers. The shooting brought the scouts and Jackson's cavalry at a run, and Hasbrouck ordered them to charge up the ridge and pursue the Modocs. For some eight miles the yellowlegs and their Indian allies chased the fugitives, capturing five women, five children, a bundle of blankets, and a few jaded horses, They also shot down three women, purportedly by mistake. Jackson claimed to have killed two Modoc men as well. In fact, all the Hot Creek men got away.

Convinced that Kientpoos was close, Hasbrouck, Perry, and their men spent the next two days scouring the surrounding hills, valleys, and creeks and coming up empty. While the soldiers were beating the brush, John Fairchild, Artina Chockus, and One-Eyed Dixie chatted up the newly captured Modoc women at the Van Bremer ranch. The women told their Modoc cousins and the white rancher that the men were willing to surrender, intelligence Fairchild passed on to Hasbrouck. Deciding to take a chance, the captain sent one of the captured women out with Chockus and Dixie to tell the Modoc men that if they came in and surrendered unconditionally, hostilities would cease. Hasbrouck let Davis know what was happening, and the colonel set out for Lower Klamath Lake to receive the surrender. The Hot Creek Modocs sent the women back with a return message to Hasbrouck: they would come in only if Fairchild himself led them. The rancher took his life in his hands once again and agreed. He rode out of his ranch and up the mountain early the next morning.[20]

Fairchild returned a little before sunset, the Hot Creek Modocs with him. Bunker had his notebook out and his pencil ready to record the scene.

"At six o'clock in the afternoon of May 20th," Bunker wrote, "the Cottonwoods [Hot Creeks] wound around a hill near the camp in motley procession, and came at a funeral pace to a bench of greensward in front of headquarters." The Modocs' speed was slowed by the emotional weight of this surrender, after so many months of siege and fight, and by the physical toll the struggle had taken. The Indians were "filthy, ragged, and generally repulsive." The women smeared pine tar on their faces in mourning, and they were dressed in tattered calico or the patched-together remnants of blankets. The men wore uniforms stripped from dead or wounded soldiers to replace their own worn-out clothing. The children were naked or nearly so. Modoc horses looked to be all "mane, tail, foretop, and fetlock" on "mere skeletons."[21]

Like Bunker, H. Wallace Atwell was struck by the worn, torn state of the surrendering Hot Creeks. Yet, despite their desperation, they had not forgotten their fighter's heritage. Each Hot Creek man carrying a weapon approached Davis and laid his rifle in the dust at the colonel's feet. "When they laid down their guns, the stoutest could hardly withhold their tears," Atwell reported. Each fighter called out his own name, a gesture of pride, and shook Davis's hand. Now the commander knew he was holding Shacknasty Jim, Steamboat Frank, Bogus Charley, Weium, Hooker Jim, and Curley Headed Doctor, as well as nine other men and adolescents. The colonel told the Indians he would give them a camp for the night and feed them. He warned them, too, that any Indian trying to escape would be shot.[22]

As the prisoners broke their long fast on army rations and bedded down in the falling dark, the mood among the military rose into elation. The Hot Creeks' surrender brought the end of this war into sight. There remained but one hawser-sized loose end to tie up.

28

Hounds and Scouts

The pursuit from this time on . . . partook more of a
chase after wild beasts than war.

—Colonel Davis to Major General Schofield, November 1, 1873

As the Hot Creeks surrendered, Davis realized the obvious: his seventy-odd prisoners did not include Kientpoos and the fighters still with him. It concerned Davis that "this band of the marauders were still at large . . . enjoying an Indian's luxuries in the settlements outside of reservations"—meaning robbery, rape, and murder. Somehow it never occurred to him that Kientpoos and his people just wanted to lie lower than lizards on a hot day and hope everything would pass them by.

The Hot Creeks were unsure which direction Kientpoos and his people had gone after the spat between Hot Creek and Lost River Modocs. Some of them thought south and east, toward the Pit River; others guessed more east and a bit north, onto the high lava plateau between Clear and Goose Lakes called the Devil's Garden.

Davis's strategy for finding Kientpoos—putting Modocs on the trail of Modocs—was not his own idea, the colonel reported; no, it came from the Indians themselves. "I determined to accept the offered services of a Modoc captive; one who, up to the time of their separation, was known to be in the confidence of his chief, and could lead us to the hiding place of the band," Davis reported. Although he did not name the captive, Davis's description fit Hooker Jim: "He was an unmitigated cutthroat, and for this reason I was loath to make any use of him that would compromise his well-earned claims to the halter." Since Hooker Jim had long been identified as the leader of the band that killed the Tule Lake settlers, and since A. B. Meacham and Leroy

Dyar placed him among the attackers at the Peace Tent, Hooker Jim was likely to be stood up on the gallows right next to Kientpoos. Still, if this Modoc could be put to good use in running down the last fugitive Indians, the ever-ruthless Davis was willing to accept his help.

Hooker Jim proposed bringing eight of his fellow Hot Creeks with him, practically all the men in the band. He wanted a strong bodyguard should pursuit turn into gunfight. Davis shook his head. Hooker Jim could bring only three men along: Shacknasty Jim, Bogus Charley, and Steamboat Frank. And as for the deal, Davis kept the upper hand, promising nothing. The four had to hope that running their former leader to ground would induce Davis to cut them slack down the line. "Believing the end justified the means, I set them out, thoroughly armed for the service," he boasted.[1]

• • •

During the Seminole wars in Florida, about thirty years earlier, Zachary Taylor's army faced a challenge much like what Davis was up against. The Indians disappeared into the swamps, which they knew in every detail of waterway, current, and vegetation, and regular soldiers proved worthless at finding them. Himself a slave owner, Taylor won approval from the War Department for a tactic that raised protesting howls from abolitionists: import slave-hunting bloodhounds from Cuba to run Seminoles to ground. The dogs were tried for a time and dropped, though less because of politics than tactical failure. Bloodhounds simply could not find the Seminoles, who knew a thing or two about covering tracks and scents in their swamp world.[2]

Davis understood that his Modoc collaborators were much more than hunters with good noses. The four Hot Creeks knew their quarry's language, habits, quirks, strengths, weaknesses, and favored haunts. And, by turning some members of the Modoc nation against others, Davis was proving the cosmic righteousness of the American conquest and shattering the Indians' community, exterminating them culturally as well as physically. He was advancing genocide without shooting.

Davis did ensure that the four Modoc scouts could shoot, however. He equipped them with Springfield rifles and what William Bunker of the *San Francisco Chronicle* described as "a prodigal supply of car-

Things Fall Apart

tridges."[3] And Davis was so sure of the soundness of his strategy and the loyalty of these four enemies turned allies that he was willing to trust his life to them.

The colonel ordered all mounted detachments, both cavalry and artillerymen on horse, to gather at an encampment on the narrow neck of the peninsula that in those days reached into Tule Lake from its southeastern corner. That site sat athwart the route to the Pit River, and it was close as well to Clear Lake and the Devil's Garden. Whichever way Kientpoos had gone, the cavalry could get there quickly from this outpost, which was coming to be known as Boyle's Camp. Davis set off to ride from Fairchild's ranch across the Lava Beds to join the forces gathered at Boyle's Camp. Besides himself and five soldiers, Fairchild, Bunker, and the four newly enlisted Modoc scouts rode along.

Bunker was none too comfortable with the company he was keeping on this overnight trek. The Modocs' looks alone shook him up. "Huka [Hooker Jim] . . . had the characteristic popularly ascribed to the singed cat, in that he was smarter than his appearance indicated." The taciturn Shacknasty Jim was tiny, barely five feet tall; Steamboat Frank and Bogus Charley, at five foot ten, towered over him. Bogus was willowy and agile, while the bulky Steamboat "smiled with the whites of his eyes. It always made my flesh crawl to look at Steamboat."

It bothered Bunker even more that the Modocs were well armed. "It was difficult for me to realize that the four savages, who rode just in the advance, had been divested of their hostile intent, and transformed into peaceful, plodding scouts in the space of twenty-four hours." As he rode, Bunker thought about what he would do if the Indians started shooting. He resolved to ride off at the fastest speed he could extract from his mount—to summon help, of course.

After camping on top of Sheepy Ridge, Davis and his escort of Americans and Modocs descended toward the Lava Beds first thing next morning. Often leading their horses over the rough and broken terrain, the Modocs led the way, on the lookout for ambush. Bunker saw just how attuned the scouts were to their world of lava and sagebrush. "If one scout halted for a moment, his companions followed suit. The passing of signals was unnecessary." Only about a mile beyond the base of the ridge, close to the spot where Canby and Thomas had been killed, all four Indians slipped off their horses, left the animals browsing among the sagebrush, and wriggled on their bellies through grooves in the lava. They came back to announce they had found an Indian fire, but it was two days old and nothing to worry about. A little farther on, Hooker Jim signaled everybody down at some small movement in the distance. He sent them on once he realized he had spotted nothing more dangerous than stray cattle.

Past the Stronghold the riders strung out single-file, and the Modocs along with Fairchild passed out of Bunker's sight. A loud rifle shot was followed by a shout, then more shots and yells that raised the hair on the reporter's neck. Bunker, Davis, and the soldiers dismounted and moved ahead on foot. The colonel was "cool and perfectly calm. As the firing increased, his face was illumed with smiles, and his actions betokened supreme delight. . . . [H]e looked on the fight, whatever the result might be, as a pleasant feature." Weapons cocked, Davis, Bunker, and the soldiers rounded a point to find the scouts shooting at ducks on the lake and yelling in triumph at each kill. Hitting a duck with a rifle is no small feat, and the Modocs "had already bagged a goodly number." These Indians could shoot.

After reaching Boyle's Camp, the ever-confident Davis told a greatly relieved Bunker why he had ridden across the Lava Beds with the Modocs. The move was strategy, not bravado. The colonel wanted to convince the four Modocs "that he reposed confidence in them and had not the slightest fear of treachery."[4]

•••

Their bellies full of roast duck, mounted on good horses cut from Fairchild's huge herd, and cradling Springfield rifles with full cartridge boxes, the Modoc scouts rode out of Boyle's Camp early the next morning. Of the various retreats to which Kientpoos and his remnant band might have headed, the four scouts thought Willow Creek canyon the most likely. It offered clean water, game, fish, edible roots, and caves for shelter and hiding. And, although the surrounding country was open enough for mounted travel by cavalry, the narrow canyon itself threw up many a hurdle for horses. Banking on their hunch, the Hot Creek Modocs headed toward Willow Creek.

Davis gave their judgment enough credence that he and a large detachment of cavalry decamped to Jesse Applegate's ranch, which lay an easy half-day's ride from Willow Creek. It would not do to allow Kientpoos to take revenge on the upstanding Oregonian who had fanned this war into a blaze and planned to profit from the Modocs' defeat and removal.

Even as Davis and the cavalry were on the move to Applegate's, the four Modoc scouts encountered Kientpoos's camp guards four miles from Willow Creek. Guards and scouts, all armed, rode together to within a mile of Kientpoos's campsite. The headman came out to meet them and ordered the four Hot Creeks to surrender their rifles. The scouts refused, kept their weapons close. Men loyal to Kientpoos formed a line opposite the Hot Creeks; it was twenty-four to four, every man armed.

Bogus Charley announced that the Hot Creeks had been well treated since they surrendered, good reason for the other Modocs to follow the four back and give themselves up. Kientpoos informed the Hot Creeks that he would never surrender. He preferred dying with a gun in his hands to being hanged from a military gallows. He had heard the last of this surrender talk and wanted no more of it, not from them, not from anyone. Kientpoos would allow the scouts to go back to the Americans if they wished, but should they return, he swore to shoot them down.

It had to be particularly galling to the Modoc chieftain to hear the four scouts talk of surrender. Hooker Jim led the party that killed the Tule Lake settlers, and he fought vehemently against Kientpoos, Scarface Charley, and others who wanted to negotiate a truce with Canby and the Peace Commission. Hooker Jim, Bogus Charley, and Shacknasty Jim had all helped plan and execute the Good Friday attack at the Peace Tent. If Kientpoos kept on fighting, he was a dead man; if he surrendered, he was a dead man. The certainty of his death in either case was due in no small measure to the machinations of the four who now told him to surrender. Kientpoos turned away, fuming at his inescapable fate.

Scarface Charley and some of the other Modoc men stepped in and said they would talk anyway. They told the four they were tired of fighting, tired of being hounded like animals, tired of being afraid for their lives, tired of being hungry, tired of being tired. They wanted to know when the soldiers were coming, whether the four would lead the cavalry to Willow Creek. Bogus was coy; the soldiers would come no matter who led them, he said.

In the end, nothing was settled. The four rode off, back toward Clear Lake, and the twenty-four retreated into Willow Creek canyon. They all had to know the shooting was almost over.

•••

When Davis received the four scouts' report at the well-garrisoned Applegate ranch, he ordered his men to move out the next morning to entrap the last Modocs. They organized into three squadrons, each with a Modoc guide or two and a detachment of Warm Springs scouts. Captain Hasbrouck with Hooker Jim took the north side of the canyon; Major John Green and Steamboat Frank, the south; Fairchild, the canyon floor with Shacknasty Jim and Bogus Charley.

The three squadrons found the Modocs where the scouts had left them. In short order, negotiations with the insurgents began, led by Boston Charley on one side and by Fairchild and the Modoc scouts on the other. Boston Charley laid his rifle down in front of Fairchild. As Boston was telling the rancher that the Indians wanted to come in, Steamboat Frank on the canyon rim turned his horse. The hammer on his Springfield snagged in the brush and snapped. At the rifle's thunderous blast the Modocs took off running. Boston was himself heading into the canyon to let them know all was well when overeager soldiers in Hasbrouck's squadron, ignorant of what had happened, seized him. By the time the error was discovered and Boston Charley freed to finish his errand, most of the Lost River Modocs were long gone. Staying behind were only seven women, including Princess Mary, Kientpoos's sister, and several children. All were gathered up and sent back to Applegate's as prisoners.[5]

The next day the Modoc scouts found fresh tracks angling north from Willow Creek toward Langell Valley. Fairchild, some Warm Springs and Modoc scouts, assorted cavalrymen, reporter H. Wallace Atwell, and physician Thomas Cabaniss followed. They spotted three Modoc men ahead walking toward then disappearing into a canyon on the east

Things Fall Apart

side of the valley. Kientpoos himself fired several shots, all wide of the mark, to keep the pursuers at bay, then Scarface Charley emerged to talk with Cabaniss. The doctor went with Charley into the canyon to parley directly with Kientpoos. The headman said he would surrender, but not until the next morning, for the hour was late, the women tired, and everyone hungry. Cabaniss talked the cavalrymen into withdrawing to a ranch five miles away to show good faith, then returned with a load of hardtack for the Modocs. In a display of trust, the doctor spent the night with the Indians.[6]

As Cabaniss slept, Kientpoos and his family slipped away. Next morning, however, the other Modocs came in to surrender to the cavalry, Scarface Charley in the lead. His face unspeakably sad, he laid his weapon down. Next up was Schonchin John, who gave up his repeating rifle with a look of mistrust and sorrow. Another dozen men likewise handed their weapons over. They and their families were herded under guard to a campsite along Lost River. Next morning the captive Modocs—fourteen men, ten women, and nine children—were sent in the company of sixteen soldiers, one junior officer, and Fairchild to the Applegate ranch.[7]

Now the end of the war was as close as catching Kientpoos. A squadron of cavalry led by Captain Joel Trimble and guided by Warm Springs scouts, Fairchild, Bogus Charley, and Charles Putnam, a nephew of Jesse Applegate, found the headman's trail leading back toward the same stretch of Willow Creek the Modocs had abandoned only three days before. As the pursuers neared the hideout, they divided into two, one group heading north of the creek, the other south. Soon the scouts, Bogus Charley, and Putnam flushed Humpy Joe, Kientpoos's hunchback brother and one of the last two fighters in the headman's shrunken following. Joe let them know that Kientpoos was hiding nearby. Seeing that the end was near, he led the pursuers down to a cave. When his brother called out, Kientpoos boldly stepped out onto a shelf of rock.

There are two stories—one true, the other false—about just who received the Modoc headman's surrender. Atwell, going on what Putnam saw, reported that Kientpoos gave up to Car-pi-o-in and We-na-shet, two of the Warm Springs scouts, who then conducted their captive to Trimble, who took him into custody.[8] Of course, it would not really do to have this notorious Native rebel surrender to other Indians. The official story soon became that Trimble confronted the chief in person and received his rifle in surrender.[9]

Either way, the time was the afternoon of June 1, 1873, and the place the verdant, stream-singing canyon of Willow Creek. Then and there the armed struggle of the Modoc War whimpered its last.

• • •

Over the following hours, dignity in surrender struggled with subjection in defeat. Each won for a time.

Kientpoos changed into clean clothes for the ride to Applegate's, and his younger wife, Lizzy, the one whose soft eyes had bedazzled Edward Fox, pulled a clean muslin dress over her soiled calico. Then Kientpoos, his two wives, his little daughter, Rosie, plus Humpy Joe and one other man and their families mounted up behind Warm Springs scouts to ride double back to Applegate's. All the while Kientpoos remained stoic and silent. Only when he passed by Fairchild did he make any sign. The headman bowed to the rancher, both men as laconic as ever.

The Warm Springs scouts sang their triumph song as they entered the Applegate compound and passed in front of Davis. Their chant swelling, the scouts strung out in a line and handed their prisoners over.

Davis could not abide the least pride in the chief he now held fast. He ordered leg shackles made up and directed a detachment of soldiers to chain Kientpoos and Schonchin John together. Scarface Charley translated the orders from English to Modoc for the two, who protested hugely against an indignity they saw as unnecessary. Kientpoos and Schonchin John said they had surrendered in good faith and would make no attempt to escape. Davis had none of it. "It was really an affecting scene to witness the grief with which they submitted to have the shackles placed on them," wrote S. A. Clarke, "but when they saw that their fate was inexorable, they made no complaint or resistance, though they keenly felt the indignity."[10]

Shackles were only the beginning of Davis's plan to grind down the Modocs' last reserve of pride. He had other cold, hard lessons he wanted to teach not only the Modocs but every other Native on the Pacific coast who contemplated resistance.

Things Fall Apart

29

Hang 'em High

The entire band of lately hostile Modocs is now grouped, rather inartistically too, under a long walled tent, which holds them all, because Indians do not require a very great amount of space for their comfort.

—"The Modocs," *New York Times*, June 18, 1873

Davis rode back to Boyle's Camp with his escort of cavalrymen and Warm Springs scouts on horseback and the Modoc prisoners crowded into a wagon. Soldiers and scouts in the camp shouldered each other aside to get a look at Kientpoos, this chief who had kept them in the field, poorly fed, shot at, and sleeping on stony ground for months on end. Kientpoos had anticipated the gawking. He wrapped himself in a blanket and stayed hidden as the Indians were herded into a prison tent under strong guard.[1]

Davis ordered the Hot Creek Modocs held at the Fairchild and Van Bremer ranches to be brought down to Boyle's Camp as well. When Oregon volunteers operating on their side of the state line took the surrender of yet another dozen Modocs from Kientpoos's faction still on the run, Davis had them transported to Boyle's as well. All the Indian prisoners were packed tight into a single prison tent.

The colonel's solution to the overcrowding issue was to hang any number of Modoc men as soon as possible. He wanted to do it right, so he had his men build a proper gallows. And, to demonstrate his quest for justice, Davis invited Louisa Boddy and her daughter, Katherine Schira, to Boyle's Camp. The two Australian immigrants had lost the men in their families to vengeful Modocs in the aftermath of the Lost River raid, and Davis wanted them to point out the killers and so justify this prompt, summary execution.

To date, the record of the two women in identifying the Modoc raiders had been a total flop. The dozen Modocs taken by Oregon volunteers included Black Jim, who was named in practically every account of the Tule Lake killings. Asked to pick out any of the killers they recognized among the captives, Boddy and Schira had no idea who any of them were, including Black Jim.[2]

Now Davis wanted to give Boddy and Schira another chance to identify the killers. The two women were sitting in a tent with reporter Atwell, when Davis sent Hooker Jim and Shacknasty Jim inside. Whether they recognized Hooker Jim or not, the two women accused him of murder. Boddy was drawing a pistol from her valise and trying to cock it when Atwell dashed outside and called to Davis. The officer burst into the tent in time to wrest the handgun from Boddy and confiscate a second concealed pistol. Schira carried yet another gun and a knife, and she too was disarmed.[3]

Vengeance itself did not bother Davis. It was just that he wanted it to be the one to deliver it, not two immigrant women with those funny Aussie accents.[4]

•••

On the very day the headman surrendered, Davis telegraphed the Military Division of the Pacific trumpeting the capture of Kientpoos—"I am happy to announce the termination of the Modoc difficulties."[5] His superiors, John M. Schofield and William T. Sherman, sent back their appreciation for Davis's success and their first take on what should be done next. Even as the generals forwarded Davis's dispatches to the War Department for review, they were of the opinion that any "disposition . . . of the prisoners according to law and Justice" required that "the name 'Modoc' should cease."[6] Justice equaled genocide, and the law could help, a strategy Sherman spelled out to Secretary of War Belknap. He requested that Belknap persuade President Grant to sanction his order that the Modocs be imprisoned until a military tribunal could decide their fate. The best solution, in Sherman's eyes, was to try Kientpoos and the other murderers of Canby and Thomas by court-martial, turn the killers of the Tule Lake settlers over to the State of Oregon, and scatter the remnant Modocs among conquered tribes farther east. "Thus the tribe of Modocs would disappear," the general concluded.[7]

Privately, Sherman wished that Davis had acted much sooner and eliminated the Modoc problem Indian by Indian. "Davis should have killed every Modoc before taking him [Kientpoos]. Then there would have been no complications," Sherman complained.[8]

Belknap sent Sherman's request on to President Grant, who in turn forwarded it to Attorney General George H. Williams. Williams put the Modocs on the top of his to-do list.

Meanwhile, Davis considered the message from Sherman and Schofield as a green light. Ever since he took command, the colonel "thought that captives taken in the future should be executed on the spot, as the surest and speediest method of settling the Modoc problem." Now that all the insurgents were in his hands, Davis saw no reason to do anything other than what he had originally planned. He disagreed with his superiors that the Modocs who killed settlers along Tule Lake after the Lost River raid should be turned over to the state authorities in Jackson County for trial.[9] A civilian trial would be wasted effort; Indians were too stupid to get the point. They "do not recognize the jurisdiction of civil or military courts because they are incapable of understanding their working. . . . [I]f convicted and sentenced to death, [they] could not be made to understand that justice figured into the matter at all." Since a trial would instill no object lesson upon people so backward and savage, why go to the trouble and expense? In addition, the delay caused by a drawn-out trial would be unmerciful to the Modocs, an ironically compassionate Davis argued: "The Indians are cooped up in tents—men, women, and children, guilty and innocent alike, fearing a massacre all the time. They must remain in this condition of suspense for months." Surely the better course, Davis argued, was to bring this Modoc business to a close. Having "procured lumber, chains, ropes, and tackle, and all the paraphernalia of execution," Davis chose sunset on Friday, June 6, as the time of reckoning.[10]

The colonel never made clear just whom he planned to hang. He gave the number of condemned as eight or ten, a curious imprecision in this matter of life and death. Since the four Modoc scouts had been invaluable in capturing Kientpoos, Davis felt that honor required him to exempt them from execution.[11] Since that left only forty-some Modoc men, Davis was planning to hang about a quarter of them.

On June 5, with the gallows nearly ready, Davis received an urgent telegram from Washington. It ordered him to do nothing with the Modoc prisoners until Attorney General Williams could decide the proper legal procedure. Eyes shining, beard bristling, Davis flew into a tantrum. He screamed at a bystander that if he had any way other than soldiering to make a living, he would resign on the spot.[12]

Davis answered Washington in a telegram burning with brusque rage. The colonel was certain that his status as commander of the Department of the Columbia gave him the authority to "execute a band of outlaws, murders and robbers. Your dispatch indicates long delay. . . . Delay will destroy any moral effect which their prompt execution would have upon other tribes as also the inspiring effect upon the troops."[13]

Still spewing fury, Davis stormed toward the tent where the Modocs were imprisoned. He wanted to visit upon Kientpoos and his henchmen the charges he was planning to read to them on the gallows at sunset the next day. The colonel's shouted words bristled with the historical righteousness of a westering America. Citing the inflated frontier count of three hundred settler killings by Modocs, Davis faulted the government for overlooking this blood-dipped history and offering the Indians a reservation. Instead of showing gratitude, the Modocs "strewed the shores of Tule Lake with the slain victims of your bloody band." Yet the government still offered to negotiate for peace. Decoying the unarmed peace commissioners into ambush was the last straw: "These acts have placed you and your band outside the rules of civilized warfare." The only appropriate punishment for this history of blood and terror was hanging.[14]

Davis tromped back to his tent. How Kientpoos and the other Modocs reacted went unreported. Likely they felt relief, at least for the time. Likely, too, they knew their fate was only postponed. The next day showed that vengeance was just awaiting its chance.

• • •

Rumor carried the story throughout southern Oregon that Colonel Davis himself had thwarted the two Australian settler women from avenging the loss of their men on Hooker Jim and Shacknasty Jim. Soon Oregonians learned as well that higher-ups in Washington had stopped Davis from hanging the Modoc leaders. This delay in making the Modocs pay the full price of justice meant they might escape their fate. Some Oregonians decided that should never happen.

The day after the Modocs were spared the gallows, James Fairchild, John's brother, loaded a wagon with four Modoc men: Tee-He Jack, Little John, Pony, and Mooch, plus their families, seventeen people in all. Two of the men were old and feeble. A third, Little John, was laid up with a gunshot wound in the thigh and a fracture of the same leg below the knee.[15] The Fairchild brothers, with the help of Shacknasty Jim and Bogus Charley, had brought these harmless Modocs in from their camp near Bogus Creek. Now, as Davis had ordered, the Fairchilds and the Hot Creek duo were taking the Indians to Boyle's Camp to join the rest of their people. John Fairchild, Shacknasty Jim, and Bogus Charley rode ahead, while James Fairchild came along behind in the wagon with the Modocs. In time over the rough road, the two groups separated too far for the one to see or hear the other.

When James Fairchild and his wagon reached the Lost River ford at Natural Bridge, on the Oregon side of the state line and close to the campsite of a state militia company led by Joseph Hyzer, a handful of volunteers stopped him. Who, they wanted to know, was he carrying? Hot Creeks, Fairchild answered, but for the wounded Little John, and none wanted for any crime. Apparently satisfied, the volunteers rode off. Something about the militiamen, though, disturbed and unsettled Fairchild as he drove on. His gut feeling proved right. At the place on Tule Lake known as Adams Point, two hooded men on horseback stopped the wagon, pointed rifles at Fairchild, and called him an "old white-headed" son of a bitch. One of them ordered him down.

"By what authority?" Fairchild demanded.

"By mine," the masked man said. "I am going to kill the Indians and you, too."

The vigilante unhitched the mules, and Fairchild, still holding the reins, had to jump. He was pleading for the Indians, as were the women and children. The Modoc men stayed silent and stoic.

Little John fell first, his brains blown out. The rifle blast frightened the mules into a run, dragging Fairchild behind them, even as the hooded riders emptied their weapons into the wagon. In seconds, the three other Modoc men were dead or bleeding out, and Little John's wife had been badly wounded in the shoulder.

The gunfire attracted a patrol of mounted artillerymen, who rode in to see the two shooters galloping away. The soldiers protected the wagon while Fairchild and a teamster riding with the patrol transported the wounded Modoc woman and her two children to Boyle's Camp. It took them till 2 a.m. to get there. After sunrise new mule teams were sent to bring in the shot-up wagon and its surviving occupants.[16]

On that sparsely populated frontier, every settler knew every other settler. Still, Fairchild claimed that he did not recognize the men who stopped his wagon. Perhaps they were from some other part of Oregon, and he had no idea who they were. Or perhaps he knew that if he identified them, he too would stop a bullet the next time he crossed the state line. In either case, the killers surely came from among the ranks of the Oregon volunteers.

Atwell felt no qualms about accusing the militiamen of the crime. And he fully understood the moral implications of the murders. "This is on a stripe of all the cowardly acts which have heretofore provoked Indian wars. Cowardly, brutal acts have marked the frontier history, and Oregon has had her full share of these stains on a people's honor," he wrote. Granted, the Modocs killed Tule Lake settlers as well as Canby and Thomas. Still, "I question if either case equals in atrocity and cold-blooded cowardice the massacre of these defenseless prisoners."[17]

Hyzer denied that his men were involved. Oliver Applegate, who was leading another militia company nearby and surely knew something, remained strategically silent.[18]

Oregon Indian Affairs superintendent T. B. Odeneal later requested that Leroy Dyar, once of the Peace Commission and still Indian agent at the Klamath Reservation, bring in the killers. A target at the Peace Tent on Good Friday, Dyar gave not a fig for taking down any Oregonian who killed Modocs. He had an excuse: the passage of time made the task impossible. The militiamen who were the obvious suspects were now "scattered all over Jackson Co. so that it will require much time and money to work the case up." Dyar suggested that a private detective be hired; he had too much work to do to be pulled away.[19] Odeneal let the matter drop.

So did Davis, who made it clear that he lacked legal authority over the Oregon volunteers.[20] The issue mattered so little to him that when he wrote his summary report of the Modoc War he failed even to mention the Adams Point atrocity.[21] This colonel who had abandoned freed slaves to attack by Confederate cavalry was not the least concerned over the slaughter of four unarmed Modocs by vigilante Oregonians.

Finding the killers, in fact, would have required no more investigation than asking around. Some two weeks after the Adams Point killings, a onetime Oregon volunteer named March admitted that Hyzer's men had pulled the triggers and killed the four Modoc men. Even though the story was published in the *Yreka Journal*, nothing came of the public revelation.[22] The Oregon militiamen got away with murder.

• • •

Boyle's Camp was too primitive and remote, even by frontier standards, to host any semblance of a trial. Davis needed to move the prisoners to Fort Klamath, about seventy miles north, and hold them there. He dispatched Captain Jackson and his cavalrymen to return to their home base and make preparations. Davis, the other officers and men of the Modoc Expedition, and the prisoners waited at Boyle's Camp for word that Fort Klamath was ready.

When it came, the Modocs were loaded into big freight wagons drawn by several pairs of mules. Never designed to carry humans, the wagons were packed solid with bodies. The Modocs numbered in the vicinity of 160: about 45 men, shackled one to another, some 55 women, and more than 60 children.[23] Since the murders at Adam's Point made it clear that the locals were none too friendly, a large armed escort comprising one battalion and two companies of infantry as well as a mounted artillery battery went along. The wagons, their human cargo, and the guards rolled out of Boyle's Camp and headed north along the eastern shore of Tule Lake, aiming for the Lost River ford at Natural Bridge as their first night's stop.

The Modocs were quiet at first. Then, early in the day's rough journey, as the wagons clattered and shook up a slope, the men rose in one body, murmuring among themselves, and looked back. The guards clutched rifles close, thumbed hammers, wondered whether the Modocs were planning something. The wagons crested the small hill and started down. The Indian men sat, fell silent, pulled blankets around themselves. They had risen to look back at the Lava Beds, taking this last chance to see that wild and beautiful and lost place, the center of the earth from which they were being torn loose.[24]

The next morning the army had one less Modoc to worry about. Curley Headed Jack somehow slipped off by himself, drew a stolen revolver, and shot himself in the head. He had told his mother that he preferred dying from a bullet to twisting on a noose. The soldiers buried the young Modoc on the spot, without ceremony, and herded the rest of the Indians into the wagons to continue the journey to Fort Klamath.[25]

To hold the Modocs, Jackson and his cavalry troop had built a stockade about 250 yards west of the fort's main quad and the same distance north of the garrison's garden. The structure measured 100 by 150 feet. Twelve-foot ponderosa logs were sunk three feet deep on end, so that the palisades were too high to vault over and too deep to tunnel under. An interior fence traversed the stockade and divided it into two sections, one twice the size of the other. Into the smaller section the Hot Creek Modocs, including the four men who had helped capture Kientpoos, were herded. The larger section became the new home of Kientpoos's more numerous Lost River band. Tarpaulins were stretched here and there to provide shelter against sun and rain. Twenty-four soldiers were assigned to stand guard around the clock, four at each of the two doors into the stockade, the remainder on raised platforms in the structure's corners.[26]

The eleven highest-value prisoners, all shackled in pairs, were confined in the guardhouse on the south side of the fort's main quad, across from the officers' quarters and south of the cavalry barracks. It was a small, whitewashed building, only thirty by forty feet, its windows high and barred. Little light entered the shadowy interior, which was divided into one large and two small cells. One of those cells housed Kientpoos and Schonchin John; the other held Barncho, Slolux, Black Jim, and Boston Charley. The large cell contained the rest: Curley

Things Fall Apart

Headed Doctor and his adult son, Dave, plus One-Eyed Mose, Ike, and Pete. At all times a half-dozen infantrymen stood guard outside.[27]

The guardhouse was a jail, the stockade a concentration camp. Each of the Modoc men, women, and children confined within its new-cut palings had to make do with a little less than thirty-five square feet of space, the equivalent of a five-by-seven room, for everything from sleeping and cooking to latrine duty. In that tight space, with its mingled smells of bodies, food, old clothes, and ripening sewage, the once-proud Modocs awaited their next humiliation.

30

Varnishing Vengeance

The trial of the Modocs is closed, and dispatches from San Francisco
say that the evidence was very complete against the accused and
that there is very little doubt of the finding. . . . In point of fact the
military trial was hardly more than a form . . . to impress upon the
redskins . . . that justice was to be dealt out to them.
—*New York Times* editorial, July 12, 1873

Even before the Modocs were freighted north, the federal government and the army were determining how they could try whom for what. Both entities produced a legal opinion: Attorney General Williams for the government, and Major H. P. Curtis, judge advocate in the army's District of California, for the military. The two lawyers laid the legal foundation for what would be the first and only trial of American Indians for war crimes.

When Colonel Davis wanted to hang the captured Modocs summarily, he was relying on an Indian-war tradition dating into the seventeenth century. Victorious whites simply dispatched defeated Indians when, where, and how they chose to. In the mid-nineteenth century this strategy shifted. When Cayuse Indians killed Marcus and Narcissa Whitman in 1849 at their mission near modern Walla Walla, Washington, five putative ringleaders were tried for murder by the territorial government and hanged. In 1858, the governor of the Washington Territory, Isaac Stevens, had the Nisqually leader Leschi brought up on a murder charge for killing a militiaman in battle and sent to the gallows. And in 1871 the Kiowa chiefs Satanta and Big Tree were tried in Texas on state murder charges for killings during raids on wagon trains.[1]

The federal government and the army could have simply turned the men who killed the Tule Lake settlers over to the Oregon courts and surrendered the men who shot Canby and the Thomas to California for trial.[2] This wash-the-hands solution posed major problems, however. The inability of the Boddy women to identify the Modocs who had killed their husbands underscored the difficulty of prosecuting the Tule Lake raiders for murder: even the best witnesses were very bad. And the killing of the two peace commissioners, the one a popular general officer and the other a martyr to Christian naïveté, were cosmic outrages far too stunning to be booted to state courts. With the federal government and the army wanting this one for themselves, they had to build a case for some crime other than murder.

Williams's and Curtis's opinions were dated the same day—June 7, 1873—and shared considerable legal ground. Both agreed that the proper tribunal for the case against the Modoc was a military commission, not a court-martial. Courts-martial held jurisdiction over violations of written statutes governing the armed forces. Military commissions could judge violations against the common, unwritten law of war. Since no statute applied to the killing of negotiators during a truce, this trial belonged to a military commission.

The military commission was still a relatively new channel for military law, having arisen only during the Mexican War. It came into its own during the Civil War, when 4,271 trials took place, and Reconstruction, with another 1,435 specifically authorized under the Reconstruction Act.[3]

The military commission had also been used to deal with Indians: 392 men who surrendered to end the 1862 United States–Dakota War in Minnesota. The proceedings were conducted before five officers, first in a tent and later in the kitchen of a fur trader's cabin, and usually lasted but a few minutes apiece. Evidence was sparse, defense nonexistent, attention to procedure perfunctory. In the end, 303 Dakotas were condemned to hang. Conviction came not only for killing Americans directly but also for being in the vicinity of attacks that killed settlers or soldiers. The purpose of the military commission was, in the words of the campaign's commander, to "strike terror into all the Indians on the continent and save hundreds perhaps thousands of valuable [i.e., white] lives."[4] Too weak to exterminate the Dakotas in battle, the military would settle for hangings by the acre as the best genocidal alternative.

As commander in chief, President Abraham Lincoln had to sign off on the death warrants. Concerned that executing more than three hundred Dakotas made the United States look as brutal as the Indians were said to be, yet aware that commuting all the sentences could unleash a lynch mob, Lincoln spent an agonizing month reviewing the commission's findings. In the end he signed off on the executions of only thirty-nine men convicted of killing Americans in what he viewed as "massacres."[5] The others had fought "battles" against soldiers. They were spared, as was one condemned man whose death sentence was lifted only hours before the hanging.

Lincoln's decision had more to do with political optics than with law. The gunfights that sent thirty-eight Dakotas to the gallows in Mankato, Minnesota, on December 26, 1862, for the largest mass hanging in American history should have fallen under the normal immunity against prosecution granted to soldiers in wartime.[6] By the time the Modoc War broke out eleven years later, the government and the army had learned to steer around this major legal pitfall.

A former senator from Oregon, a core member of the radical wing of the Republican Party, and an author of the Reconstruction Act with its authorization of post–Civil War military commissions, Attorney General Williams knew what he had to do. He began by making it clear that this Modoc business had been a war, not simply an insurrection. Williams argued that since "Indians have been recognized as independent communities for treaty-making purposes, and as they frequently carry on organized and protracted wars, they may properly . . . be held subject to those rules of warfare which make . . . perfidy like that in question punishable by military authority." In the same way that "it cannot be pretended that a United States soldier is guilty of murder if he kills a public enemy in battle," Modoc fighters were immune from prosecution for battlefield killing. Violation of the laws of war, however, was another matter altogether, one properly within the jurisdiction of a military commission.[7] Such had been the justification in the war crimes trials of Henry Wirz, the commandant of the brutal Andersonville prison camp, and the Lincoln assassins.[8]

Judge Advocate Curtis furthered Williams's argument: "That these hostile Indians were and are a distinct people and therefore capable of carrying on legal and legitimate war with the U.S. seems to me to be open to no doubt." Citing U.S. Supreme Court opinions dating back to *Johnson v. M'Intosh*, Curtis borrowed the phrase "domestic dependent nations" from Chief Justice John Marshall to describe the Natives' status. And, since Indian nations could make treaties with the federal government, they were capable of making war as well.

It made no difference that the Modocs in the Lava Beds represented only a portion of their nation. If anything, the failure of peaceable Natives to intervene with their war-making cousins "might be in strictness considered a breach of duty, justifying war upon the whole tribe. That the U.S. Government sees fit to waive it's [*sic*] right to call the entire nation to account, cannot, in my judgment, detract from it's right to enforce all the laws of war upon those of the nation who actually took arms against it's peace."

Williams and Curtis came to essentially the same conclusion. The attorney general stated that "a military commission may be appointed to try such of the Modoc Indians now in custody as are charged with offenses against the recognized laws of war." Curtis added another consideration. Punishing the Modocs would send a strong message to any other frontier Indians looking to follow in their war-making, atrocity-committing footsteps. This went beyond revenge to provide what he saw as "protective retribution" against cosmic evil.[9]

•••

When General Schofield forwarded the legal opinions to Colonel Davis, he reminded his subordinate that the same rules applied to military commissions as to courts-martial. Schofield was reinforcing military legal practice that had been in effect since the Civil War.[10] Those rules, Davis knew full well, were spelled out in the *Field Manual of Courts-Martial*, compiled by Henry Coppée in 1863.

When the manual worked to his advantage, Davis followed it. When it gave the Modocs a break, he ignored it.

The colonel's disregard began with his own role. Article of War 65 provided that a senior officer who accused an inferior officer of wrongdoing could not himself convene a court-martial to try the inferior.

Since prejudgment was inherent in such a situation, and since the senior officer would be the first to review the commission's findings, the inferior would be left unprotected against bias.[11] Because Davis was not bringing charges against his own inferior officers, he did not violate the technical letter of Article 65 in convening and naming a military commission to try the Modocs. But he had served as the field commander against the Indians after Canby's death and shown prejudgment in spades by preparing to hang the Modoc leaders summarily, undercutting the spirit of a provision designed to ensure the military commission's impartiality.[12]

Davis appointed officers who shared his dim view of the Modocs.[13] The ranking officer and president of the military commission was Lieutenant Colonel Washington L. Elliott. Elliott himself had not campaigned against the Modocs, but five troops of his First Cavalry regiment fought front and center. The other appointees were all directly involved in the war. Captain John Mendenhall, Fourth Artillery, had been in the field since just after the Battle of Sand Butte. So had Captain Hasbrouck, Fourth Artillery, who led the fight at Sorass Lake and helped bring in the Hot Creek band. Second Lieutenant George W. Kingsbury, Twelfth Infantry, owed his company command to the Modocs, which he assumed after First Lieutenant Thomas Wright was killed at Sand Butte. Captain Robert Pollock, Twenty-First Infantry, served as the Modoc Expedition's quartermaster throughout the conflict. All had either served directly under Canby or joined what had been his command while the memory of his killing still stung. Even among military commissions, which tended to include members with more interest in the outcome than civilian courts would allow, the Fort Klamath five stand out as unabashedly biased.

If Davis had had his way, that commission would have also been unabashedly ambitious. The colonel's instructions directed Judge Advocate Curtis to try every Modoc male on every possible accusation, even those based only on rumor. Davis's broad sweep was, however, blunted by presidential order. President Grant told Secretary of War Belknap that Curtis should only bring charges related to the three men killed on Good Friday: Canby, Thomas, and Sherwood. The rest of the Modocs were to be held as prisoners of war.[14]

Things Fall Apart

Curtis soon found that he had to drop any hope of prosecuting the Modocs who killed Sherwood; they could not be reliably identified. Instead, he focused on the Peace Tent. Identities were undisputed, and the prosecutor could call as witnesses several of the Modocs who had taken part in the killings and then turned on Kientpoos. Curtis granted them immunity from prosecution "to teach these savages that treachery to their tribe . . . will meet with its sure reward."[15]

Justice was hardly the sole object of this trial, Curtis was saying. The military commission served the political purpose of breaking the bonds that held Indians to their ancestral culture and territory and turning them into self-interested individuals who might someday become real Americans. If that happened, Canby and Thomas did not die in vain: the Modocs, as a people and a culture, would be rubbed out.

• • •

Word of the pending trial at Fort Klamath made its way to Elijah Steele in Yreka. As author of the unratified 1864 treaty that cost him his job as Indian agent, longtime adviser of Kientpoos and his people, and former negotiator for peace in the Lava Beds, attorney Steele knew the Modocs needed a good lawyer. He was aware, too, that his status as an object of hate and scorn in Oregon made travel over the state line ill advised. Still, Steele had a good attorney in mind. E. J. Lewis, who lived in the Sacramento Valley hamlet of Tehama, was a sharp dresser, an eloquent advocate, and a crack criminal defender whom he met while both men served as state legislators in Sacramento.[16] Lewis accepted Steele's invitation to take the Modocs' case and headed north.

Lewis was still on the road when the military commission convened on July 1. Major Curtis, who had just arrived from San Francisco, told the other officers he needed time to prepare his case. He polished the charges, and on July 5 at 10 a.m. the military commission met for its second official day.

A barracks mess hall had been fashioned into a temporary court-room by finishing the interior with rough boards and splashing it with whitewash. In the middle sat a table with chairs to accommodate the commissioners. The five officers wore brand-new full-dress uniforms sparkling with braid, buttons, ribbons, epaulets, and medals. Their swords lay on the table. Facing them at another table sat Judge Advocate Curtis, decked out in the spit and polish of his rank and role. Beside him was E. S. Belden, the court reporter, and behind them the two interpreters, Frank and Toby Riddle. Yet another table, which ran perpendicular to the military commission and the judge advocate, was taken up with newspaper reporters, among them Atwell of the *Sacramento Record* and the *New York Herald* and Clarke of the *New York Times*. Spectators, who included the Modoc scouts and certain unnamed ladies, sat at both ends of the room.

The six Modoc defendants were consigned to a bench off to the side. Dressed in the same worn-out workingman's denims and cast-off army pants, threadbare shirts, and scuffed work boots they had fought in, the Indians looked like bums, bindlestiffs, and hobos. Kientpoos and Schonchin John were shackled together, as were Boston Charley and Black Jim. The two youngest defendants, Barncho and Slolux, were left unchained. They often sat on the floor, finding it more comfortable than the backless bench. Now and again Barncho and Slolux stretched out on the boards and fell asleep. Unlike their young helpers, Kientpoos and Schonchin John paid close attention to what was happening. The chief often puffed a pipe as he listened, now and again leaning against Boston Charley, likely because of pain from an inflamed hip.[17]

Shackling prisoners was discouraged by the *Field Manual of Courts-Martial* as prejudicial. So were armed guards, who marched the prisoners from the guardhouse to the temporary courtroom and kept watch, bayonets fixed on rifles. Once again, the Fort Klamath military commission ignored standard court-martial procedure.

Before Curtis read his charges, various niceties were observed. The first called for proclaiming Colonel Davis's order creating the commission and naming its five members. Curtis then asked the six Modocs whether they objected to any of the commission members. According to the trial transcript, once the request was translated from English to Modoc, "they severally replied in the negative."[18]

Had the Modocs known the *Field Manual of Courts-Martial*, they would have realized that a defendant could justly challenge any member who "has been injured by the accused and may therefore cherish a desire for revenge." Again according to the manual, Curtis should have let the Modocs know their rights. It was up to him to ensure that the accused's "rights are not infringed, and that he is not permitted to do anything ignorantly, to his own detriment." Instead, the judge advocate allowed the Modocs' ignorance of trial procedure to work against them, again and again.[19]

Curtis swore in the officers of the military commission, and Elliott swore in Curtis. Then there was the matter of the interpreters, Frank and Toby Riddle. Employed at the handsome rate of ten dollars a day, they were sworn to "the faithful performance of their duty in the interpretation of the evidence and proceedings." The commission's shorthand reporter, E. S. Belden, took his oath as well.

Next Curtis asked the prisoners "if they desired to introduce counsel; to which they severally replied in the negative . . . they had been unable to procure any." Apparently, no one had told the Modocs that attorney Lewis was somewhere in transit between Tehama and Fort Klamath.

The next step in the day's ritual entailed arraigning the prisoners on two charges, each with two specifications. The first charge was that the six Modocs had committed murder in violation of the laws of war—one specification for killing Canby, another for Thomas. The second charge was assault with intent to commit murder, also in violation of the laws of war. One specification centered on the attack on A. B. Meacham. The second concerned the shots taken at Dyar as he sprinted away from the Peace Tent. The charges ran long and ornate:

CHARGE I. "Murder in violation of the laws of war."

Specification I. "In this, that they, Indians called and commonly known as Captain Jack, Schonchis, Boston Charley, Black Jim, Barncho, *alias* One-Eyed Jim, and Slolock, *alias* Cok, members of a certain band of Indians known as the Modocs, which band, including the prisoners above named, was, at the time and place hereinafter alleged, engaged in open and flagrant war with the United States, under the command of said Captain Jack, did, as representatives of said Modoc band, meet, under a flag of truce and suspension of hostilities, Brig. Gen. E. R. S. Canby, U.S.A., commanding the Department of the Columbia, and certain peace commissioners on the part of the said United States, namely Eleazur Thomas, A. B. Meacham, and L. S. Dyer, citizens of the United States, all representing the Government of the United States, for the agreed and professed purpose of discussing and arranging terms upon which hostilities existing between the United States and said band should cease, and did thereupon, in wanton violation of said flag of truce, and treacherously disregarding the obligations imposed by said truce under the laws of war, willfully, feloniously, and of malice aforethought, kill and murder said Brigadier-General Canby.[20]

It fell to Frank and Toby Riddle to translate this charge and specification—with its spidery syntax, abundant adjectives and adverbs, and latinate words—into Modoc. English was Toby's second language, and Modoc was Frank's. Both were illiterate and uneducated. One wonders whether the two understood the legal concepts embodied in the charge. And it would have been nothing short of miraculous if the Modoc language, which never before had had to wrap its linguistic arms around an alien legal code, contained words to convey those concepts. The defendants could only listen and nod and wonder at what they were hearing.

• • •

Frank Riddle was not only one-half of the translation team; he was also the first prosecution witness. Curtis had to know how unusual and compromising such a dual role was, particularly since Toby Riddle was cousin to Kientpoos and Black Jim, making Frank their in-law. That obvious conflict of interest caused the judge advocate no hesitation, however.

The shovel-bearded, short-spoken Riddle was uncharacteristically chatty on the stand. In answering Curtis's questions, he identified the Modocs at the Peace Tent and the role each played. Kientpoos was the chief, Schonchin John a "sergeant," Black Jim a "watchman," Boston Charley "nothing more than a high private," and Barncho and Slolux "not anything." Curtis asked Riddle whether he had been present when Canby and Thomas were killed. Riddle had. He said he considered the situation dangerous and had told the commissioners of his fears. In fact, he thought talking further with Kientpoos and the Modocs was stupid: "I said, 'I think the best way to make peace with them is to give them a good licking, and then make peace.'" The Modocs were preparing for war: fortifying the Stronghold and drying beef, signs Canby chose to ignore. After placing Kientpoos, Schonchin John, and the two Charleys, Boston and Bogus, at the Peace Tent and recounting how he saw Kientpoos pull a revolver and fire the first round into Canby's head, Riddle said, "I jumped up and ran then, and never stopped to look back any more. . . . [T]hey were firing, and I did not turn around to look to see who it was. I thought it was warm times there."

Curtis turned to the Modoc defendants and "asked the prisoners severally if they desired to cross-examine the witness, to which they replied in the negative."[21] Since Frank Riddle was on the stand, Toby Riddle must have done the translating. One wonders how "cross-examine" came out in Modoc and what it could possibly have meant, first to her in English and then, in the Modoc words she chose, to the prisoners.

Second in the prosecution's witness lineup came Toby herself, furthering the trial's confusion. Curtis put factual questions to her, and she responded with factual answers. She had seen Schonchin John firing at Meacham, Boston Charley shooting Thomas, Hooker Jim chasing and shooting at her husband, and Shacknasty Jim, Barncho, and the now-deceased Ellen's Man pursing her husband. Slolux, who with Barncho had run up carrying loaded rifles, had knocked her to the ground. She expected violence that day and had seen Kientpoos shoot Canby at a range of no more than five feet. Again, the six Modocs made no cross-examination.[22]

The third witness was Leroy Dyar, the Klamath Reservation agent who replaced Jesse Applegate on the Peace Commission. Curtis worked Dyar for various facts about Good Friday, extracting one after another in a back-and-forth as slow and painful as nineteenth-century dental work. The Indian agent became talkative only when he addressed his reluctance to take part in the meeting. He went, Dyar testified, because "I thought that if I didn't go, and there was trouble, I would be blamed, perhaps considered a coward."

The Indians yet again had no questions.[23] They could have asked Dyar about the derringer he was carrying and whether a flag of truce was actually flying at the Peace Tent, as the charges alleged. But the Indians did not. They had no idea that such inquiry would have worked to their advantage in a complex legal game they had never before played.

On this note the first day of testimony and the second day of the trial ended.

...

When the military commission reconvened on Monday morning, Dyar again took the stand to clear up confusion about the Council Grove Treaty. Shacknasty Jim, Steamboat Frank, Bogus Charley, Hooker Jim, and Weium then offered various small points of fact.

Curtis asked Hooker Jim whether he was a friend of Kientpoos, who was called Captain Jack throughout the trial. "I have been a friend of Captain Jack," Hooker answered, "but I don't know what he got mad at me for."

"Do you like Captain Jack now or dislike him?"

"I don't like him very well now."

Hooker Jim, who most of all the Modocs had insisted that the Peace Commission be attacked, lied baldly when Curtis asked him how he knew the commissioners were to be killed. "Captain Jack and Schonchis [Schonchin John]—I heard them talking about it," he answered. "At Captain Jack's house."[24]

In cross-examination, the Modoc prisoners could have pushed Hooker Jim to the wall as a leader of the Hot Creek faction that shamed Kientpoos into going along with the attack. They could have asked him, too, about the deal he made with Davis in hope of saving his own neck. Yet again they had no questions.

Most of the day focused on gathering Meacham's testimony. The onetime peace commissioner cut quite a figure in the witness chair: right hand useless, left hand maimed, head and face displaying the livid scars of the Good Friday attack. Milking Meacham's star quality, Curtis questioned him at length. Although the loquacious Meacham was unwontedly to the point, he testified for hours on how the fatal gathering had come to pass and what happened when literal hell broke loose. He made it clear that he had protested the meeting because of repeated warnings from the Riddles, yet "as chairman of this commission, my honor compelled me to go." He gave, too, a dramatic recount-

Things Fall Apart

ing of Schonchin John's attack on him and what he had seen of the assaults on Thomas and Dyar before he passed out.

Although Meacham testified that neither Canby nor Thomas was armed, he failed to mention that he and Dyar carried concealed weapons. The Modocs could have asked about that in cross-examination, had they known to. They did not know, nor did they ask.[25]

•••

The following morning Curtis called his final two witnesses. First Lieutenant H. R. Anderson, who was acting adjutant general on Canby's staff, offered up details on the general's command, the position of various military units, and the course of the war overall. He did testify that in the days before the final, fatal meeting Canby had brought his forces nearly to the edge of the Stronghold. The Modoc prisoners again passed on cross-examination. And they let army medical officer Henry McElderry go without further questioning after he testified, unsurprisingly, that Canby and Thomas died of gunshot wounds.

Now it was the defense's turn. Lacking any experience with the American court system, the Modocs had no idea what was in or out. The traditional Modoc system for adjudicating disputes lacked a formal legal code, and wrongful death was seen as a matter of revenge and compensation between the perpetrator and the victim's family. Unschooled in American rules of evidence, Kientpoos saw the Good Friday killings in a different, wider context than the events of April 11, 1873.[26]

First he hoped to advance the idea that the Modocs were not the only ones responsible, that this war blamed on his people was also the work of the Klamaths. Kientpoos's lead witness was Scarface Charley. The command the headman put to him was, "Tell about Link-River Jack coming and giving us powder and stuff." Scarface launched into a looping story about getting ammunition from the Modocs' neighbors to the north.

Knowing that Charley's testimony was irrelevant, Curtis waived cross-examination. Likewise, the narrative Kientpoos was following interested the military commissioners little. They asked Charley where he was when the firing broke out on Good Friday—near the lake, about a half-mile away, he told them—and which Indians took part in the Peace Tent ambush. Then they let him go.

Kientpoos called Dave, Curley Headed Doctor's son, who told about Allen David, the Klamath chief, advising the Modocs to keep fighting and about under-the-table help from other Klamaths. Then One-Eyed Mose testified to getting percussion caps from Link River One Eye, another Klamath. Neither Curtis nor the members of the military commission cared to ask a single question.

Kientpoos changed tack. He called no further witnesses, and the other five prisoners told the court they, too, had no witnesses. Then Kientpoos addressed the commission on his own behalf.

The flaw to this proceeding, he argued, was that the commission's members had no idea what sort of good neighbor he had been before the war. "You men here don't know what I have been heretofore; I never accused any white man of being mean and bad; I always thought them my friends," he said. "No white man can say that I ever objected to their coming to live in my country; I always told them to come and live there, and that I was willing to give them homes there."

Kientpoos spoke the truth. He had long been accommodating to ranchers Fairchild and Dorris and to the settlers in the Lost River country.

Then this trial by an alien law that had its noose around his neck overwhelmed Kientpoos. "I hardly know how to talk here," he confessed. "I don't know how white people talk in such a place as this; but I will do the best I can."

"Talk exactly as if you were at home, in a council," Curtis said. It was the one and only time the judge advocate advised a defendant on how to proceed in this foreign setting. His confidence restored, Kientpoos did as he had done throughout the peace negotiations: he turned to the war's beginning, to argue that this mess was not of his or his people's making.

"I didn't know anything about the war—when it was going to commence," he said. "Major [the captain's brevet rank] Jackson came down there and commenced on me while I was asleep," referring to the dawn timing of the Lost River raid. "It scared me when Major Jackson came and got there just at daylight, and made me jump out of my bed without a shirt or anything else on. . . . I thought, then, why were they mad with me. . . . I went into my tent then and sat down, and they commenced shooting."

When the firefight was over and the Modocs fled to the Lava Beds, Hooker Jim's settler-killing rampage around Tule Lake created an even worse bind. "I didn't know anything of any settlers being killed until Hooker Jim came with his band and told me," Kientpoos testified. "Then I thought that, after hearing that those white people had been killed, . . . the whites would all be mad at me."

The chief tried to talk his way out of this mess. "I do not deny telling Fairchilds, or anybody else, that I wanted to talk good talk," he explained. "I always wanted to talk good talk. I wanted to quit fighting. My people were all afraid to leave the cave." And Kientpoos feared for his own life.

"This old Indian man told me . . . that that day Meacham, General Canby, Dr. Thomas, and Dyer were going to murder us if we came at the council. All of my people heard this old man tell us so," Kientpoos said. "And then there was another squaw came from Fairchilds and told me that Meacham and the peace commissioners had a pile of wood built up, and were going to burn me on this pile of wood."

If Kientpoos wanted to imply that he shot Canby in self-defense, he left the connection unmade. Rather, he lamented his lack of command: "I wanted to talk and make peace and live right; but my men would not listen to me." The Americans had the wrong man in chains and on trial. "Hooker Jim was one that agitated the fighting," Kientpoos accused. "Hooker Jim is the one that always wanted to fight, and commenced killing and murdering. When I would get to talking they would tell me to hush . . . that I was nothing more than an old squaw."

Exhausted from explaining himself and his history, Kientpoos asked to stop where he was then pick up the following morning. The military commission agreed.[27]

Schonchin John, the next defense witness, gave a roundabout account of the Lost River raid. He was out hunting ducks when distant muzzle blasts told him something was wrong. By the time he got back to the village, his own house was aflame and all the surviving Modocs were on the run. Schonchin himself took off into the mountains to find his scattered family. He saw Hooker Jim, but did not go with him on his Tule Lake raid. Then he encountered the shaman.

"I met Curly-Headed Doctor down in the settlement where the

whites were living, after he had killed the settlers," Schonchin John said. "I talked to them, and told them not to do it; but they would not listen to me. I went down toward the east end of Tule Lake and saw two white men. I have no more to say."[28]

The judge advocate asked the four remaining Modocs whether they wished to offer a defense. When they declined, the military commission adjourned.

• • •

Sometime late on this fourth day of the trial, attorney Lewis arrived at Fort Klamath, weary, dusty, and bone-rattled. He must have been surprised when he entered the long, thin makeshift courtroom and realized that the proceeding had been rolling along without him.

Lieutenant Colonel Elliott was under no obligation to accept Lewis as defense counsel; at the time defense was a privilege, not a right.[29] Admitting Lewis at this late stage in the proceeding would mean restarting the trial and hearing again the three days of testimony to date, with the further slowdown that Lewis's cross-examination would surely cause. That prospect appealed little to the five officers on the military commission. They said no, a decision of so little import that the trial's official transcript omits it.

Atwell did note this event, however. It was one of several over the past few days that were troubling him more and more.

• • •

If Lewis lingered at Fort Klamath and took in the trial's last day, he would have heard Kientpoos pick up where he had left off. The four Modoc scouts were in this thing over their heads, the chief argued, because they were the ones who advocated killing the commissioners and then pulled the triggers. They even told Kientpoos that Thomas and others were packing pistols and intended to kill the Modocs.

"Hooker Jim, he said that he wanted to kill Meacham, and we must do it," Kientpoos said. "That is all I have got to say."

Curtis began his rebuttal of the defense curiously: "I did not intend to say a single word in reference to the evidence, nor do I intend to now." Curtis judged the case so ironclad he saw no reason to waste breath. Still, he had to address one vexing issue: "But Captain Jack has cast some imputations upon the military and moral character of Major Jackson, which it seems to me to be my duty to do away with if I can."

The six Modocs were on trial for murdering Canby and Thomas and attempting to kill Meacham and Dyar. The Lost River raid that Jackson led was irrelevant. Yet Curtis would not let it lie that Kientpoos had testified that the raid lacked provocation or justification. As he rebutted Kientpoos's claim, Curtis became his own witness.

"It is a perfectly well-known fact that there is a treaty existing between the United States and the Modocs, by which the Modocs are obliged to remain upon the Yainox reservation," Curtis began. He introduced the order of November 28, 1872, that sent Jackson and his cavalry troop to Lost River as evidence that the raid was lawful enforcement of the Council Grove Treaty against off-reservation Modocs.

Kientpoos knew nothing of the Tule Lake settler killings, Curtis said—making this point even though those particular killings had nothing to do with the charges before the military commission. "I have investigated the matter somewhat since I have been here," the judge advocate asserted, "and I do not believe he was concerned in them or knew of them in advance.... I acquit Captain Jack of that. But when he accuses Captain Jackson of having acted in an unmilitary manner, by opening fire upon him in his bed, and killing his women without notice, I deem it my duty, in vindication of Major Jackson's character, to submit to this commission the official report made by Major Jackson himself."

With that, Curtis finished. "I submit the case without further remark," he concluded.[30]

It was still early, only eleven o'clock in the morning of July 9, 1873.

• • •

Trials, both civil and military, in the 1870s did not provide the protections for defendants taken for granted in the early twenty-first century. Yet, even by the standards of the time, the Fort Klamath military commission was a mess. Had the commission accepted Lewis as defense counsel and restarted the trial, the newly arrived attorney would have had a great deal to challenge.

Each Modoc on trial was being held responsible for the crimes every other defendant was accused of committing. Curtis had made it clear in his original memo on the military commission that all the Modocs at the Peace Tent were equally guilty of every crime committed there. "The escape from death of Dr. Meacham," he wrote, "does not I think diminish in any degree, the responsibility of the Indian designated to kill him, for the murder of General Canby and Dr. Thomas. They are all equally answerable for the results of the conspiracy."[31]

This all-for-one-and-one-for-all approach created an injustice. Witness after witness testified that Kientpoos had shot Canby, Boston Charley killed Thomas, and Schonchin John launched the assault on Meacham. Yet, in the case of Black Jim, only Shacknasty Jim testified that he saw him shooting at Meacham. Barncho and Slolux, the unshackled pair who often slept on the courtroom floor, brought up the extra rifles from their hiding place in the rocks as the firing broke out. Slolux struck Toby Riddle with a rifle butt and knocked her down; that was the end of his involvement. Barncho chased Frank Riddle, according to Shacknasty Jim. Riddle himself was running so fast and hard he had no idea who was on his tail. No evidence linked Black Jim, Barncho, and Slolux to the killings of Canby and Thomas, and Lewis could have impugned Shacknasty Jim's testimony as perjury to save his own neck.

Lewis had even more to work with. The formal charges used the phrase "flag of truce" to describe the setting at the Peace Tent. In fact, no flag of truce was flying. And, although the judge advocate took the truce for granted throughout the trial, a lawyer as sharp as Lewis could have readily argued that it had already been broken, by Canby himself. When a cavalry patrol seized some three dozen Modoc horses during the armistice, Kientpoos protested mightily through his sister, Princess Mary, yet Canby refused to return the animals. Meacham took Kientpoos's side and argued that holding onto the horses violated the truce. Still, Canby did not budge. Rather, he continued to whittle the armistice down in his own favor. In the days leading up to the April 11 meeting, Canby moved his forces to less than two miles from the Stronghold, a deployment Kientpoos saw as another violation. He protested again to Meacham, again to no avail. And the headman knew full well that there were nearly twice as many soldiers as there had been when the armistice was struck, and that Coehorn mortars had been added to the artillery. It hardly helped the Americans' case that the Modocs were not the only ones who came to April 11 meeting armed: Meacham and Dyar were carrying concealed weapons.

The Modocs had endured a cruel baptism in artful armistice with Ben Wright twenty-one years earlier. That Oregon Indian killer flew the white flag as a subterfuge to draw the Modocs in, then he and his men shot down some fifty of them. A good argument could have been made that any Modoc with a brain in his head knew from Wright's treachery and Canby's cavalier treatment of the cease-fire that truce meant what Americans wanted it to mean, and always to their advantage.

Lewis could have created the scenario that the armistice was already broken, Canby was preparing a final assault, and the Modocs were attacking preemptively, making Canby and Thomas the initial casualties of resumed hostilities. In the absence of this argument, Canby and Thomas remained innocent, chivalrous victims of Indian treachery, and their deaths became cosmic war crimes justifying genocide.

The defense counsel might have also asserted that the common law of war was far less common than the prosecution assumed. Indeed, Williams's memo to President Grant admitted that "all the laws and customs of civilized warfare may not be applicable to an armed conflict with the Indian tribes upon our western frontier."[32] The European armies after which the United States military fashioned itself fought each other according to customs and rules that differed markedly from the way Indians gave battle.

Before American emigration, Modoc wars amounted to quick raids that lasted no more than three days total. Battles were brief, one or two hours long, and seriously bloody; fighting ended when one side fled the battlefield.[33] Soon after the war was over, Steamboat Frank told Major Charles Throckmorton of the Fourth Artillery that the American mode of warfare seemed bizarre to the Modocs: "White man fight one day, two days, three days; one week, two weeks, maybe three weeks or a month; Indian fight one day and want to quit." After the trial, Boston Charley explained just why the Modocs had killed the two peace commissioners: "The young warriors thought that Canby, Thomas, Meacham, and Gillem were powerful men and that the deaths of these Tyees [leaders] would avoid all further troubles."[34] If the Modocs had lost their war chief on a raid, they were likely to pack up and go home. On April 11 they were hoping the army would have the good sense to follow Modoc custom once Canby was dead. With Americans and Indians fighting on different ethical planets, it is hardly surprising that the army did not get the message the Modocs were sending. So much for a common law of war.

As for atrocities, the military committed them, too. The Lost River raid killed a baby in its mother's arms, a six-year-old child, and one or two women, possibly more. When the army captured the Stronghold after the Modocs escaped in the night, victorious soldiers shot down the old, unarmed, and wounded Indians who stayed behind. Then there were the severed heads soldiers kicked around like soccer balls and carted back to Gillem's Camp as trophies. No officer or soldier was ever so much as reprimanded for these outrages.

The purpose of the Fort Klamath military commission was to brush a thin varnish of law over the conquest, dispossession, and extermination of a Native people. Despite the improper collective guilt, the nonexistent flag of truce, the broken armistice, and the biased application of an uncommon law of war, the narrative of the era demanded that the Modocs pay, and dearly.

• • •

The trial transcript fails to say whether the military commission cleared the courtroom and huddled together at their long table or whether the officers retired to some private space to deliberate. It also fails to mention how long they took. One suspects that the process consumed minutes at most. And the outcome came as no surprise: Kientpoos, Schonchin John, Black Jim, Boston Charley, Barncho, and Slolux were found guilty of every specification on both charges. The sentence passed on each Modoc defendant was the same: "to be hanged by the neck until he be dead."[35]

Not that the military commission could tell anybody about the decision, at least not right away.

Things Fall Apart

31

Still Small Voices Swell

And, behold, the Lord passed by, and a great and strong wind rent
the mountains, and brake in pieces the rocks before the Lord; but the
Lord was not in the wind: and after the wind an earthquake; but the
Lord was not in the earthquake: And after the earthquake a fire; but
the Lord was not in the fire: and after the fire a still small voice.

—1 Kings 19:11–12

Procedure required that military commissioners keep the trial's verdict to themselves until transcript and sentence had been reviewed and approved by the senior officer who ordered the commission. That would take a while. When the commission adjourned, Colonel Davis was far from post office or telegraph. In the afterglow of victory over the Modocs, Davis decided to return to his Portland headquarters the long way around. Riding at the head of a column of troops who had come to the Lava Beds from Fort Vancouver, Davis made a grand tour through the Indian country of eastern Oregon and Washington to impress the Natives with the victorious might of the United States Army. Since it would be two or three weeks before Davis arrived in Portland, Judge Advocate Curtis dropped the transcript into the mail on his way back to San Francisco.[1]

It was in Portland when Davis arrived there. He signed off promptly: "The proceedings and findings in the above cases of . . . Modoc Indian prisoners, are approved and the sentences are confirmed."[2] The formal language hid what must have been his deep pleasure at putting the noose around those six stiff, Native necks.

The buck on this trial, however, did not stop with Davis. President Grant reserved to himself final approval of the Modoc trial and the sentences. He wanted the last word. And he would have it, more than once.

• • •

H. Wallace Atwell was undergoing a change of heart. When the last rebellious Modocs were rounded up in late May and early June, the *New York Herald* and *Sacramento Record* reporter demanded the prompt hanging of the Canby and Thomas killers as a lesson for any and every insolent Indian. Then, reporting the Fort Klamath military commission in July gave Atwell another view of the Modoc matter. The proceeding went all too pat and fast, as if the trial were just something to be gotten through on an expedited way to the gallows. He was aware that Curtis was required to act as the Modocs' counsel,[3] yet the judge advocate offered the Indians no legal advice. It bothered Atwell even more that, for reasons of its own convenience, the military commission refused to admit E. J. Lewis as defense counsel.

Atwell threw in with attorney Steele, rancher Fairchild, and Siskiyou County sheriff William H. Morgan to make a modest proposal to Interior Secretary Columbus Delano. The four argued that most of the Modocs in the Fort Klamath stockade were guilty of "no charges . . . except open warfare with the United States. . . . [A]ll of these Indians are useful farm hands, capable of and fully competent intellectually to trade for and take care of themselves . . . they have expressed a desire to make their own living and be no burden to the government." Naming Scarface Charley, Miller's Charley, Bogus Charley, Shacknasty Jim, Hooker Jim, and Steamboat Frank, the four white men asked that these Indians be allowed to go to work on a large Yreka farm owned by John Burgess, former sheriff of Siskiyou County.[4]

Atwell also composed his own letter to Delano as well, one that challenged the military commission's obvious bias. "We know that these prisoners were tried without counsel," he pointed out, "and before their counsel was aware that the day of the trial had been named." The Riddles' work as translators left the reporter unimpressed: "The general belief is that the Interpreter is unworthy of credence. We know he [Frank Riddle] is illiterate, can neither read nor write, can not translate the idioms of our tongue, can not even understand good english. We know the squaw with whom he cohabits [Toby Riddle] has shielded her relatives in her Interpreting." The Modoc six were owed "a full and fair investigation of the causes leading to that sad affair for which they were tried." And Atwell knew where this investigation would lead, "because this war was brought about by designing men for selfish purposes. And we will show gross mismanagement and treachery by those whose positions should have been a guarantee of fair dealing." The reporter proposed that a commission of three respected men who lived somewhere other than the Pacific coast be appointed to investigate. "I can not, in common with thousands, avoid the feeling that a great wrong has been committed and should be investigated for the honor of our Government which is supposed to protect the weak," Atwell concluded.[5]

Atwell, Steele, Fairchild, and Morgan had an ally in high political places. Representative John K. Luttrell, a Democrat, represented California's Third Congressional District, which included the Lava Beds, Yreka, and Luttrell's own large ranch in Fort Jones. In the last month of the war, Luttrell visited the battlefield. From his camp in the Lava Beds, Luttrell dashed off a letter of hurried, dashed, haphazardly capitalized phrases to Delano.

"I have spent several days in the Lava beds and the Country adjacent thereto—I have investigated as far as I could—the causes of the War between the whites and Modoc Indians—and from a careful investigation—I can arrive at but one conclusion—viz—that the War was caused by the wrongful acts of bad white men," the congressman wrote. The hungry Modocs on the Klamath Reservation had to slaughter horses for food, and when they ran out of animals, they returned to Lost River. "The land is valuable," Luttrell continued, "Land speculators—desired it—and sought to have the Indians removed." So they chose to fight.

Luttrell was all for hanging the killers of Canby, Thomas, and the Tule Lake settlers. Still, "humanity and justice demand an investigation of the war and its causes from its first inception. . . . [T]here never was a time since the organization of our Government, that there was as much corruption and swindling—not only of the Government, and people, but the Indians as is to day being practiced on Indian Reservations *on this Coast.*" Although Luttrell was pointing in the direction of the Applegates, he named no names. He said only that "Justice demands that if any particular individual or individuals—are guilty of inciting the Modocs to war—that he or they should be punished."[6]

When Luttrell heard nothing back from Delano, he sent off another letter, this to the members of the Fort Klamath military commission, offering to help investigate the causes of the war. Ever the politician, he appealed to the army's interests in the struggle between the War and Interior Departments about jurisdiction over Indians: "If the Military must do the fighting—I think it is about time to remove all dishonest agents and speculators from the reservations—and let the Military department take charge of the Indian Department."[7]

• • •

The congressman, Atwell, and the good men of Yreka were not alone. A tide of opinion opposing the unannounced but certain hanging of the Modoc six was rising. Enough time had passed since the Canby and Thomas killings for public sentiment to cool. As the *New York Times* editorialized, "The fate of the Modoc murderers has become a matter of comparative indifference to the public. It is, indeed, doubtful whether their execution will not excite among a certain class a kind of mild sympathy."[8] The *Times* was sensing the strengthening political pulse of those segments of the American public that, like Luttrell and Atwell, believed the Modocs had been wronged.

A committee formed by New York City's Cooper Institute prepared a statement, or memorial, to be presented to President Grant on the issue. It was written by John Beeson, a former Oregonian who had taken an unorthodox view of the Rogue River wars of the 1850s by blaming settlers, not Indians. "Your memorialist respectfully represents that he is in possession of important facts relitive to the Modock war," Beeson wrote. "The conduct of the whites, and . . . the failure of the government to fulfill its treaty obligations" were the real cause of the war, and "therefore, the trial and punishment of the Indians are a farce and a *tradigy*, the truthful history of which are posterity will blush to read."

Things Fall Apart

Beeson cited Luttrell's letter to Delano, then picked up where the congressman left off. Look into the Modoc War only from the Lost River raid on, he argued, and the Indians come off as the bad guys. But if you push the historical frame back, a different picture emerges. "When Monopolists dispossess Indians of their land, or when swindlers defraud them of annueties and in consequence they become restless and dissattisfied, it [is] forthwith proclaimed that they are preparing for war, and instead of investigation and redress, chastizement and addetional outrage is the general rule."[9]

In a vein similar to Beeson's, the American Indian Aid Association took to the pages of the *New York Star* to announce the organization's ambitious plan to disseminate materials proving the injustice visited upon Native Americans, beginning with the Modocs. The association saw the trial as a farce created by Colonel Davis to ignore the war's original causes and hang the Modocs. Indeed, they believed that any execution resulting from a trial organized by Davis was itself murder, and everyone who participated an accomplice.[10]

The association put the public record of the Fort Klamath military commission before four anonymous, practicing jurists and asked their opinion on key legal issues. The four were in unanimous agreement that Davis's demonstrated bias rendered him incompetent to organize a military trial against the Modocs. Likewise, three of the four held that Davis's subordinate officers were also incompetent to make up the military court. The legal experts were of mixed opinion as to whether the military's own flagrant misuse of truce and armistice, including Ben Wright's 1852 ambush of Modocs under a false flag, gave the Indians the right to play the same deceptive game. The final question was whether jurisdiction rightly fell to a military court. All four said no: "The civil court of the United States is the only court having lawful jurisdiction."

To remedy these many legal flaws, the association proposed a radical solution: "We demand that all of the survivors of those engaged in the slaughter of Modocs under [Ben] Wright and [John] Ross, in 1852, and also those who attacked Captain Jack's villages and murdered his people in December last be immediately arrested and placed in chains with Captain Jack, until both parties have a fair trial"[11]—an idea as bold as it was improbable.

· · ·

All the contentious while, the army kept plodding through procedure. Once Davis signed off on transcript and sentence, the entire pile of paper was forwarded to the army's Bureau of Military Justice. Given the significance of the case, the judge advocate general himself, Joseph Holt, took on the review.

Holt was a political animal, a man who never ran for office yet served at high levels of government for almost two decades, including as secretary of war under President James Buchanan. During the Civil War he joined the Union army as a colonel, was named judge advocate general by President Abraham Lincoln soon after, and rose to the rank of brigadier general.

Holt knew military commissions firsthand. In the wake of Lincoln's assassination, Holt served as chief prosecutor in the military commission that tried eight Confederate sympathizers for conspiring to assassinate the president. Four were sentenced to prison and four to the gallows, among them the first women executed by the federal government. Rumors that Holt had suppressed exculpatory evidence that would have saved the condemned conspirators from hanging so stung him that he published an apologia for his professional conduct.[12] Reviewing the Modoc trial, the judge advocate general must have experienced déjà vu as he read of plots, conspiracies, and assassinations. Holt's report was as much a justification of his own prosecutorial past as a review of the Fort Klamath trial.

Small things impressed Holt favorably, such as the presence of interpreters: "It may here be stated that . . . T. F. Riddle (a citizen) and his wife (an Indian) were sworn as interpreters, and that through them, the testimony, as well as the material proceedings, appear to have been duly communicated to the accused and, as it would seem, to their full understanding and comprehension." Holt lacked all knowledge of the Modoc language, and the transcript used only English. His judgment on this count was uninformed guesswork.

Holt summarized the prosecution testimony, which showed that

Things Fall Apart

the accused Modocs had shot Canby and Thomas and assaulted Meacham and Dyar. "The testimony introduced on the part of the defense, though admitted without objection, was wholly irrelevant," he wrote. This wasted effort, and what it evidenced of the Modocs' grasp of procedure in the alien setting of a courtroom, bothered Holt not at all.

He noted that no flag of truce was flying at the Peace Tent, as stated in the charges, and steered around this flaw: "The term, . . . a 'flag of truce,' was evidently intended to press the fact that there was a subsisting *truce* between the parties. The obligation of such a truce is, indeed, no less sacred, and its violation no less criminal, whether or not a flag, its usual symbol, is actually employed."

Nor was Holt put out that the Modocs lacked an attorney: "The accused were not supplied with counsel, but there appears no reason to believe that, on this account, their rights were any less guarded upon the trial." The interpreters—"one of whom was an Indian"—made the proceedings intelligible to the defendants, and "nothing in the record" indicated that "such defense as they had deemed themselves to have was not fully brought out."

In the end, Holt argued himself into a place where the politics of genocide and cosmic war trumped law. Truth be told, the Fort Klamath military commission was fatally flawed: convened by a biased senior officer, composed of officers who had fought the defendants on the battlefield, and carried out in a hasty manner that denied counsel to defendants tried for their lives in a language they did not speak and in a setting they had never before faced. Yet behind the commission stood General of the Army Sherman, who had plucked Davis from obscurity and given him a chance to redeem a long-stymied career. Overturning Davis's approval of the military commission, Holt had to know, would repudiate not only Davis's judgment but also Sherman's, not the most politic course for an army insider. And the judge advocate general knew from published reports that Sherman wanted the Modocs broken into dust and scattered to the four winds. President Grant, too, had a stake in the outcome. He had to appear much tougher than his misnamed Peace Policy. Political optics required the gallows.

Behind Sherman and Grant stood the mythology of the time, according to which an innocent, Christian America was fated to exterminate "heathen savages" and advance the inevitable progress of civilization. It mattered not that Canby had violated the truce, boxed the Modocs in, and left them no exit but his trust-me tactic. Nor did it make any difference that Thomas was convinced that God had his back. Self-serving truces and blind faith were, in the belief system of the day, signs of righteousness and strength, not hubris and stupidity. And, as the Modocs were discovering, woe to those Natives who saw through the fakery and fought back.

Holt argued himself to the inevitable: "It is the conclusion, therefore, of this Bureau that a full and just trial had been had." Hanging was the fitting punishment for the "treacherous and dastardly assassination of unarmed men, engaged in the peaceful discharge of a high public duty to which they had brought the purest motives and the most humane intentions of the Christian and the patriot."[13]

He forwarded his favorable judgment and the transcript itself to the War Department for transmittal to the White House. Ten days later, Grant approved the sentences and ordered the army to carry them out. The very next day, Belknap calendared the hangings. The Modocs would dance their last at Fort Klamath in a little over six weeks, on Friday, October 3.[14]

Still, the final small voice had yet to speak.

• • •

The Philadelphia-based Universal Peace Union, headed by the aptly surnamed Alfred H. Love, was less given to taking no for an answer than those who saw the Modoc issue in the secular time frame of electoral politics. Quakers had been at this work since the denomination's founding, and they knew that in the faith-based struggle for justice you had to keep on keeping on. Universal Peace Union's leadership testified to this long-standing commitment. The organization's vice president, Lucretia Mott, was an ordained Quaker minister who had spent decades leading the struggle for women's and minority rights.

Displaying its religious pedigree, the Universal Peace Union appealed to higher laws and powers in a letter to President Grant and Secretary Delano: "Were pure Peace Principals [*sic*] applied in the case of the Modocs it would show the civilized worlds that there is in the soul of man a far mightier and more enduring power than any of the nations of the earth have yet brought into use." The Modocs could not be tried fairly, because "few of the citizens or soldiers on the Pacific coast are in such a frame of mind as to dispassionately prosecute it; and in case of conviction there will be haste and unfeeling executions, which we most earnestly desire to prevent."[15]

When neither Grant nor Delano changed course, Love, Mott, and their allies cranked it up with yet another letter. This one offered that, if the government scattered the Modocs into a diaspora, persons of the peaceful persuasion on the East Coast could be found to take the Indians in and to educate and civilize them.[16]

In the silence following that second appeal, Love heard rumors that the Modocs had been condemned. Again he took up his pen "in the confident hope that our Gov. will so manage the matter that their lives shall be saved."[17] Delano did not answer.

Despite declining health, Mott had yet to lose the fire that had driven her Quaker soul into one struggle after another to stop war, oppression, slavery, and discrimination for a half-century. She owed something to Indians for showing her how women could run their own lives. Years earlier, the Philadelphia meeting of Quakers to which Mott belonged had befriended the Senecas, one of the Six Nations known to Americans as the Iroquois, helped them defeat the machinations of land speculators, and set up a school and model farm. During the summer of 1848 she spent a month living among the Senecas as men and women alike debated reorganization of their government. Fresh off this practical lesson in feminist political power, Mott headed to Seneca Falls to helped lead the world's first convention on women's rights.[18]

When Mott learned that Grant had approved execution of the Modocs and that the mass hanging had been set for early October, she was appalled. And when she heard that Grant was visiting financier and railroad magnate Jay Cooke at his mansion not far from her own country house, her eighty-year-old soul was newly energized. Small as she was, she knew better than to remain still. She resolved to drop in unannounced at Cooke's, confront the president, and argue the Modocs' cause to him in person.

Mott's cheek flustered her son-in-law Edward M. Davis, who had been an active abolitionist but was taken aback by such forwardness. He explained the situation to her in Quaker English: "Mother, thee has no invitation, thee has not announced thy desire, etiquette demands thee to send first, and see if it will be agreeable and convenient."

Mott gave not a fig for courtesy or custom. "My spirit says go and it will not wait for etiquette," she demanded. "My visit is urgent! Harness the horse!"

Grant received the uninvited Mott, and he listened to her. Passing blame in the way that is a political stock in trade, the president explained that he was being goaded to hang the Modocs. Still, leaning close as if speaking to her alone, he whispered, "Madam, they shall not all be executed."[19]

Mott must have left the president's presence and Cook's mansion pleased. And Grant would keep his word to her, even if he gave that promise a last, sadistic twist.

32

Strangled Necks, Severed Heads

I saw strands of the rope with which Jack was hanged, and the locks
of his hair . . . sold [for] as high as five dollars apiece.

—"Second Dispatch: After the Hanging," *San Francisco
Daily Morning Call*, October 5, 1873

Displaying prosecutor's remorse, Curtis created an opening
through which the president could slip his promise of mercy
and still send a message of retribution to America's Indians. Ten days
after Grant had approved the Modoc death sentences, Curtis wrote
to General Schofield, his commanding officer in San Francisco, about
nagging concerns over whether justice had indeed been done. Not that
the judge advocate had anything good to say for Kientpoos, Schonchin John, Boston Charley, and Black Jim. Rather, he was thinking of
Barncho and Slolux.

"Barncho appeared to me to be of a low order of intelligence, and to
have imperfectly understood the purpose of the trial, or the danger in
which he stood," the judge advocate wrote. "Sloluck is quite young in
years; is apparently extremely ignorant and obtuse; and, to all appearances, stands in mental capacity little above the level of the brute."

The duo's behavior in the courtroom had added to Curtis's suspicions. Slolux sat on the floor most of the time, buried his head in his
arms, ignored everything going on around him, and slept through much
of the trial. Barncho was barely more attentive, displaying "a degree of
stolid indifference so surprising as to compel a doubt of his comprehension of what was taking place."

Curtis was convinced that the four other defendants had knowingly
conspired to commit terrible crimes that deserved equally terrible punishment. But when it came to the two young ones, his certainty wavered.

"I cannot, however, avoid the feeling that Barncho and Sloluck knew little of all this," he concluded, "and that they obeyed the order of their chief in the same spirit with which an enlisted man obeys the orders of his officer; but with far less intelligence, and with little conception of the atrocity of the deed which they were required to take part in."[1]

Schofield thought enough of Curtis's second thoughts to pass his letter on to the Adjutant General's Office in Washington, DC. From there it moved up to Judge Advocate General Holt, who sent it up yet again, to Grant. The president saw how he could both make an object lesson of the Modoc prisoners and fulfill his whispered promise to Lucretia Mott. On September 10 he signed an executive order commuting the death sentences for Barncho and Slolux to life imprisonment at Alcatraz.[2]

Grant spiced his measured mercy with gratuitous cruelty, however. He ordered Edward D. Townsend, General Sherman's adjutant general, to make sure that Schofield and every officer down the chain of command understood that no one was to tell Barncho and Slolux they were spared the noose before the morning of the hanging. Until that fateful day, the two young Modocs were to believe that they, too, were destined to die.[3]

• • •

In front of the Fort Klamath guardhouse, soldiers set to digging graves. True to Grant's order, there were six of them. The Modoc prisoners could see the man-sized pits when they were led out, shackles glinting in the sunshine and clanking at each step, for a fresh bit of air. Army carpenters had been given orders to build six rude coffins as well. No one told the Modocs anything, but they could guess.

There was construction activity, too, in an open meadow off to the south, where the gallows was being framed. Built of dressed pine logs one foot in diameter, it was a massive structure, with a thirty-foot crossbeam set on seventeen-foot uprights, capacious enough to accommodate six nooses and the weight of six contorting bodies. The trap spanned four feet, and it was held in place by a single rope. Cutting it would cause the trap to open and the noosed Modocs to drop. The gallows was tall enough that everyone witnessing the execution,

Things Fall Apart

including the Modocs confined in the stockade to the south, would have a clear view of drop and death.[4]

Lieutenant Colonel Wheaton let the condemned Modocs, in chains and surrounded by soldiers, leave the guardhouse to visit families and friends in the stockade. The shackled Kientpoos shuffled in with his companions; all were weak and weary from confinement. Scarface Charley saw the chief coming. He fetched an empty wooden crate and set it on end to serve as a seat for the chief. Lizzy, Kientpoos's younger wife, spread a shawl over the box to cushion the chief's hip, sore with neuralgia. She squatted to one side, and Rebecca, the older wife, to the other. Only then did Rosie, Kientpoos's daughter, spot her father. The four-year-old ran to him, squealing and laughing. The chief gathered her tiny being into his arms, set her on his lap. The little one fidgeted and wiggled in pleasure as her father smoothed her black hair with one hand and held her body close to his chest with the other. Kientpoos said nothing; his face displayed no emotion.

Other Modocs gathered round their leader in a silent circle. Kientpoos shook hands with one and all. An old man filled and lit a pipe, puffed its smoke strong, placed the stem in Kientpoos's mouth. Between the tobacco and his daughter's caress, the chief's face took on an unusual calm. When the pipe was finished, the guard signaled to Kientpoos that the end of his visit had come. All the while, neither chief nor wives nor bystanders spoke a word.

Kientpoos handed Rosie back to Lizzy and shuffled off in the center of the cordon with fellow prisoners and the guards. As he walked away, Princess Mary, his sister, shrieked, and little Rosie cried. Some of the women scooped mud from a puddle and blackened their faces below the eyes in the Modoc sign of mourning. From their mouths came a terrible keening.[5]

• • •

As the nooses were being strung onto the finished gallows, H. S. Shaw, city editor of the *San Francisco Chronicle*, toured the guardhouse in the company of Second Lieutenant Anderson, the officer of the day, and the physician Thomas Cabaniss. With Shaw was a cross-country traveler he had met in San Francisco and accompanied north: Leonard

Case Jr., the Cleveland, Ohio, philanthropist whose generous endowment would later attach his surname to Case Western Reserve University. Both Shaw and Case had been cautioned by Wheaton not to let it slip when the Modocs were to be hanged.[6] The lieutenant colonel was saving that surprise for later.

The sergeant of the guard unlocked the padlock securing the first door. Shaw, Anderson, Cabaniss, and Case stepped inside.

"A strange scene challenged the eye and a stronger odor attacked the nose," Shaw reported. Open latrine buckets and bodies months from a bath would do that. Eight Indians were packed into the cell, leaving "hardly room to enter without treading on them." The day was hot, yet the Modocs had wrapped themselves in blankets and sat on the floor, knee to chin, leaning against the wall. As their names were ticked off, Case made a list and sketched the tiny room in his diary: Long Jim, Barncho, Slolux, Curley Headed Doctor's unnamed brother, Black Jim, Schonchin John's son Peter, Boston Charley, Ike. Boston Charley and Black Jim were manacled together, as were Barncho and Slolux.

"Boston Charley seemed to feel his imprisonment the most," Shaw noted. The Modoc asked Cabaniss, whom he knew from the old days, to return later and visit with him, then slumped onto the floor in a gloomy lump.

A smaller, darker, narrower cell held Kientpoos and Schonchin John. A gray blanket covered the sleeping chief from head to foot as he lay on the floor, feet toward the cell door. Schonchin, also stretched out on the floor, rested on his elbow and held his head in his hand. Both men wore ankle shackles. Anderson woke Kientpoos, and the chief stood to offer a clammy hand to the visitors. He said nothing, only looked each man deeply in the face. Schonchin remained on the floor, unmoving.

Cabaniss explained to Shaw that Kientpoos was suffering from neuralgia in his hip and an arm fractured years before. The chief was eating but little; he looked weak. The doctor planned to return later with opium for his pain.

The last cell held Curley Headed Doctor, Dave, and One-Eyed Mose, the latter two chained together. Curley Headed Doctor "was the most cheerful Indian met. A fat smile spread over his face, and he appeared

Things Fall Apart

to really enjoy the intrusion, shaking hands with much enthusiasm," Shaw wrote.[7]

Shaw and Case did more than take careful notes of what they saw; they also collected souvenirs from the Modocs at Fort Klamath. Shaw bought a ring from Shacknasty Jim for $1.50. Case picked up a ring from Hooker Jim and a cap from Scarface Charley, and his secretary, Henry Abbey, acquired a necklace from Shacknasty Jim and a cap from Princess Mary. Case must have had a playful side, as did Princess Mary. He showed her his gold teeth, and she answered with a display of her strong, all-natural chompers.[8]

• • •

The day after Case and Princess Mary compared dentition, Wheaton arrived at the guardhouse about eleven in the morning. Trailing him were the Reverend Charles Huquemborg, the Episcopal priest who served as Fort Klamath chaplain; Oliver Applegate, the Indian Bureau's commissary at Yainax; and Dave Hill, a Klamath Indian interpreter. Case came along too, his diary open and pencil ready, as did reporters Shaw and Atwell. All the Modocs imprisoned in the guardhouse were assembled in the main room, the one the guards used, its space tightly packed, the air ominous.

Huquemborg took Kientpoos's hand in his, then the hand of each of the other Modocs in turn. He told the Indians that Jesus had come from heaven for them as well as for whites and that they had to accept him as their savior lest God send them to a frightening place after death for the evil they had done. All the while, Applegate translated into Chinook Jargon, and Hill translated yet again into Klamath-Modoc.[9]

Wheaton told the minister to inform the six Modocs what they had already guessed: they were to hang the next day. The seven who would survive were led back to their cells. The condemned men remained.

Wheaton asked whether any of them wished to speak. Several stirred, but no one said anything, not at first. Kientpoos looked ready to talk more than once, but each time he only swallowed and said nothing. To break the heavy silence, Wheaton asked the chief what he had hoped to gain from killing Canby and Thomas.

"I was always for peace," Kientpoos said through Hill's and Applegate's translations. His young men and the soldiers just kept on killing: "they made my heart sick." As for the hanging, it surprised Kientpoos. "After I had surrendered and was taken to the Fort, I had no idea of being punished for what I thought was right. I thought to come and live in peace on Klamath Lake."

Wheaton promised Kientpoos that his family would be cared for and that he would be permitted to see his wives and child him one more time. The chief asked Wheaton whether he might be allowed to live. No, the colonel made clear; "the President's order will be carried out."

"I want the Great Chief at Washington to know there have been lies to him about Jack," Kientpoos said. "I have always been friendly to white people. Perhaps if the Great Chief come here he might change his opinion."

Wheaton told Kientpoos that the chief's death was of no import to Grant: "Tell Captain Jack that the Great Chief has millions of people. He cannot see them all nor do everything." He advised Kientpoos to abandon hope and attend to Huquemborg's message about getting right with God.

Ever the negotiator, Kientpoos agreed. "I know what the Chaplain told us was good," he said. "He gave us good advice and we want to follow it, but to follow it we should have more time."

Bemused, Wheaton promised Kientpoos that he could talk with Bogus Charley and Hooker Jim if he wished and that his family would be sent to him.

The long-silent Slolux spoke up. "I was arrested and ironed through misrepresentation," he said. "I was here in the guardhouse when my child died yesterday. I felt bad. I wished to be among the mourners." Slolux should not have had to endure such pain, for he was an innocent man. Showing that he had paid much closer attention to the military trial than he seemed to, Slolux blamed his unjust predicament on Toby Riddle.[10]

Barncho, too, laid claim to innocence. Wheaton would have none of it. The two had brought rifles to the Peace Tent, he said, and that was enough to send them to the gallows. He knew full well that Barn-

Things Fall Apart

cho and Slolux were but hours from having their sentences commuted, yet he continued Grant's cruel fiction.[11]

Black Jim was stoic. "My heart tells me I am a good man and a strong man," he began. "I am afraid of nothing. If I am guilty, and the laws and the evidence decide that I must die, I am willing to die. I am not afraid."

Boston Charley, too, played tough guy: "During the whole war, it seemed to me that I had two hearts, one indian and one white heart. I am a boy, yet you all know very well of what I am guilty. Although I am only a boy, I feel that I am a man. When I look at the others, I see only women. When I die and go to the other world, I dont want them to go with me. I realize that I am the only man in this room to day," he boasted. "I am all man, not half woman."[12]

Schonchin John, too, had last words. "The Great Spirit, who looks from above, will see Schonchin in chains, but He knows that his heart is good, and says, 'You die; you become one of my people.' I will now try to believe that the President is doing according to the will of the Great Spirit in condemning me to die. You may all look at me and see that I am firm and resolute." He hoped that his four children would be well cared for and argued that the Hot Creek scouts were the ones who should be hanged. And he knew the right American to blame. "I look back to the history of the Modoc war, and I can see Odeneal at the bottom of all the trouble," he said. "I think that Odeneal is responsible for the murder of Canby, for the blood in the Lava Beds, and the chains on my feet. . . . My heart tells me that I should not die,—that you do me a great wrong in taking my life. War is a terrible thing. All must suffer—the best horses, the best cattle, and the best men. I can now only say, *let Schonchin die!*"[13]

Huquemborg offered up a prayer and broke into tears. As he and the rest of Wheaton's entourage filed out of the guardhouse, the families of the condemned were let in. The women's voices rose into far-reaching, anguished howls.[14]

•••

Although the Fort Klamath military trial had drawn only passing editorial interest as a done deal without drama, the hanging promised such great copy that it called for on-the-ground reporting. The *San Francisco*

Chronicle's Shaw was but one of the prominent journalists on hand. Fox of the *New York Herald* had returned, daring again the eleven-day journey from New York City. Atwell was reporting for the *Sacramento Record* and the *Yreka Journal*, and Alex McKay for the *Yreka Union*. These newspapermen competed in a loose alliance against the Western Union telegraph monopoly and its Associated Press alliance in the person of William Turner of the *San Francisco Call-Bulletin*. The race to get the first account of the hanging into print was on.

Fox and Shaw set up a relay of three riders and nine horses—a one-shot Pony Express lite—to cover the ninety miles from Fort Klamath to the telegraph office in Jacksonville, Oregon, with the copy in their saddlebags. They had a backup plan as well: pigeons. Shaw had borrowed the birds when he passed through Yreka on the way to Fort Klamath. Although the pigeons were not trained to carry messages, Shaw assumed they would fly away home when released. Turner was also aiming for Jacksonville, but by a different route over an old Indian trail cleared at the *Call-Bulletin*'s expense to save his riders fifteen miles of hard travel. Ever a minority of one, Atwell set up his own string of horses and riders to carry the Modocs-drop-to-their-deaths story from Fort Klamath to Ashland.[15]

The good people of southern Oregon were coming, too, their wagons clogging the roads from Ashland, Jacksonville, and up and down the valley of the Rogue River. One school in Ashland had been granted "a week's holiday, so as to enable the preceptor and pupils to come here and gloat over the ghastly scene."[16]

This hanging had national significance as well, signaled not only by the presence of East Coast newspapers but also by distinguished guests from centers of power across the continent. Case and Abbey of Cleveland were joined by three prominent yet unnamed businessmen from Pittsburgh who had come to watch the execution of Indigenous fighters who dared resist America's destined march to the sea.[17]

• • •

Hanging kills in more ways than one. In the old days—before 1866—the hangman snugged a noose around the condemned's neck and simply kicked away stool or ladder under the feet, hoisted the soon-to-die into the air, or whipped the horse on which the condemned was sitting. Typically, someone hanged this way died of strangulation from a crushed trachea compounded by pinching the jugular veins shut. Air could no longer enter the lungs and bloodstream even as blood unable to flow out of the head swelled the brain like an overfilled water balloon. Over the ten to twenty agonizing, muscle-twitching, and convulsing minutes it took for the condemned to die, red dots called petechiae blotched the face and the whites of the eyes as capillaries burst and leaked. The lips turned blue from lack of oxygen, and saliva drooled from the mouth. Sometimes the tongue swelled, protruded like a panting hound's, and turned brown or black.[18]

In 1866, Samuel Haughton, an Irish academic physician and Unitarian divine, published a scientific paper that codified a new, arguably more humane method of hanging.[19] The idea was to drop the condemned four to six feet, so that the noose jerked hard and sharp against the neck and hyperextended the spine. The second vertebra fractured and separated from the third vertebra, crushing or severing the spinal cord and the arteries in the spinal column. Unconsciousness and death followed soon, sometimes within seconds, from this classic hangman's fracture.

Standard-drop hanging, as Haughton's method became known, spread quickly through the English-speaking world. If the hanging went according to plan, the standard drop killed without blackening the face, pushing the tongue out between the lips, or leaving the condemned twitching, kicking, and convulsing for long minutes. This new method was hardly idiot-proof, however. If the drop was too short for the individual's height or weight, the spine did not break and all the horrors of slow strangulation were revisited. The rope might also be too long, in which case the jerk ripped the head off the neck and body, showering spectators in the hot, bloody spray of the torn carotid arteries. As much as hangmen tried to calculate the perfect drop, finding that just-right-Goldilocks spot amounted to guesswork.

A modern forensic study of hanging showed that executions on the gallows more often went wrong than right. In fewer than one case out of five did the condemned die swiftly and cleanly from a hangman's fracture. Four times out of five, death came from some combination of spinal damage, asphyxia, and strangulation.[20]

No matter which of the various lethalities of hanging propelled the condemned from life into death, the passing often loosened the sphincters. Urine and feces poured from the corpse in a hot river of stink.

Modoc fighters practiced the warrior's disdain for death, loved to taunt soldiers shooting at them, and showed no fear of dying from a bullet. Yet they despised hanging. Since the breath of the hanged man could not escape into the atmosphere to be drawn in by new beings, they believed, the spirit stayed trapped within, lost to the continuing round of life and death. The indignity of dying trussed, suspended, and dripping waste became eternal.[21]

The officers and soldiers at Fort Klamath had little practice at standard-drop hanging. They wanted the execution to go cleanly no doubt, so that it would redound well upon their professionalism and dispassion. Perhaps the American spectators and newspaper correspondents hoped for a swift, humane end to the Native rebels. Or perhaps they wished for something grisly to draw out the drama and make the Modocs' execution an edifying spectacle. In the end, both soldiers and spectators got something of what they wanted.

•••

The night before the hanging, Wheaton let the reporters and distinguished guests in on a little secret: Grant had commuted Barncho's and Slolux's death sentences to life imprisonment on Alcatraz. True to his orders, he kept the news from the two lucky Modocs until the very day of the execution. At 8 a.m. on the sunshiny morning of October 3, 1873, Shaw and Fox went along to the guardhouse to watch as the news was announced. At that moment, the other four Modocs knew they were irretrievably doomed.[22]

A little over an hour later, a column of soldiers marched to the guardhouse and loaded the condemned men into a wagon—Boston Charley and Black Jim to the front, Schonchin John and Kientpoos to the rear. They were dressed in the same ragged, dirty pants and shirts that had clothed them throughout the war. A bareheaded Kientpoos, who was so weak he had to be helped in, wrapped a blanket around himself. Boston Charley, wearing a military cap reputed to have been taken from an officer killed at Sand Butte, eyed the gallows and the coffins beneath it as the column and the wagon made the short commute to the execution site.[23]

At least two thousand people had gathered to watch. Several hundred Klamath Indians, no doubt ordered to attend by Indian agent Dyar, had taken positions behind the assembled officers and soldiers of Fort Klamath, who formed three sides of a rectangle enclosing the gallows. White Oregonians lined up much as the Indians did, in a semicircle behind the troops. Some stood on the ground and craned to watch; others sat on horses or stood in wagon beds. Louisa Boddy, the Tule Lake widow, and her family were seated in a wagon in a privileged position between the Twelfth Infantry and Troop B of the First Cavalry, close to the inner square of witnesses. That area contained as well Lieutenant Colonel Wheaton, several junior officers, the reporters, medical officer Henry McElderry, Cabaniss, Case, Abbey, and the three anonymous Pittsburgh businessmen. Six empty coffins were lined up under the gallows. In the structure's shadow a few dogs belonging to soldiers at the fort took refuge from the warming sun.

The wagon from the guardhouse drew to a halt at the rear of the gallows. Black Jim and Boston Charley climbed up to the platform first; Schonchin John and Kientpoos came behind. The four sat down on the platform to be pinioned around the arms and legs—"with merciless pulls" in Case's telling.[24] Just before 10 a.m., Oliver Applegate and Dave Hill told the four in Modoc that what they were about to hear concerned the execution. Second Lieutenant Kingsbury, Fort Klamath's adjutant, called the soldiers to attention, then read the English-language execution order and another governing the movement of troops that day. Barncho and Slolux were marched to the front of the gallows, and Kingsbury read the order commuting their death sentences to life imprisonment on Alcatraz. Then it was Reverend Huquemborg's turn. He recited the Episcopal service for the dead, which meant nothing to the Modocs, in English, which only Boston Charley understood well. A noncommissioned officer offered the Modocs water in a dipper. Black Jim and Boston Charley drank; Schonchin John and Kientpoos refused. Four enlisted men each slipped a noose over a condemned Modoc's head. When Kientpoos's hair got in the way of a snug fit, the soldier trimmed his locks to give the rope better purchase. The enlisted men then pulled worn-out army haversacks, of the sort soldiers used to carry ammunition into battle, over the heads of the condemned. These makeshift hoods saved spectators from witnessing the fearsome color change and blood spots on the face or the swollen, protruding tongue that would accompany strangulation. The Modocs were told to stand, and did, without protest or struggle. The Fort Klamath quartermaster, who was positioned in the front of the gallows, pulled a handkerchief from his pocket and, with a pause and a flourish, let it fall. As the white cloth touched the ground at 10:15 sharp, a corporal swung a hatchet and sliced the rope holding the trap. The four Modocs dropped.

At that instant the hundreds of Klamaths gasped as one person, and the Modocs keened. All the gathered captives, their mourning-blackened faces pressed to chinks and gaps among the pales of the stockade, sang out as the condemned fell. Perhaps the four could hear that grieving chorus through the terrible split seconds of their drop.

The ropes jerked taut, and the Modocs snapped hard against the nooses. All four spun round one way several times, then several times the other. The army had gotten it half right. Kientpoos and Boston Charley nary moved nor twitched. Schonchin John and Black Jim shuddered and convulsed, drew their legs up again and again, twisted and turned and struggled against the noose. It took them long, hard minutes to quiet and die. For a half-hour the four hung from the cross-beam, just to make sure, then enlisted men cut them down.[25]

• • •

No sooner were the Indians pronounced dead than the assembled reporters penciled the last line in their copy and entrusted it to the three competing horse-and-rider relays. The courier for the *San Francisco Daily Morning Call* and the Associated Press made it to Jacksonville in the late afternoon, twenty minutes ahead of the *New York Herald* and *San Francisco Chronicle* rider. Even though the *Call* won the horse race, the *Herald* got the scoop, both because it was a morning paper on the East Coast and because Fox had filed a preliminary story marked "more to come" that was already typeset. Atwell was jinxed. One of his riders got drunk on the trail, fell out of the saddle, and lost his horse. His copy arrived six hours later than the competition's. Still, even Atwell fared better than the pigeons Shaw and Fox let fly as Plan B. One of the birds circled the fort and then headed south, never to be seen again. The other promptly lost its message and, as if it knew the mission aborted, landed in a ponderosa only a hundred yards from the gallows. There the bird perched and eyed the crowd.[26]

· · ·

There would come a time when spectators at lynchings had their pictures taken with the corpses as mementoes of the spectacle. On October 3, 1873, such a photographic possibility was still a long technological way off. Instead, the soldiers provided, and the spectators purchased, souvenirs of the dead. The hank of hair that had been cut from Kientpoos's head was auctioned off to the highest bidder, the money going into a fund to be shared among Fort Klamath's officers. Case secured some of Kientpoos's shorn hair and noose for an unstated sum. Kingsbury appropriated sections of the hemp for himself and later displayed them on cards detailing their historic provenance. Even Cabaniss, although a friend of the Modocs, got caught up in the frenzy. He claimed the nooses on which Kientpoos and Schonchin John died and later presented them to fellow Yreka physician F. G. Hearn, a well-known collector of all things Indian. Some spectators pulled pieces and parts off the gallows. One later fashioned his wooden memento into a gavel to bring order to meetings of the Oregon department of the Grand Army of the Republic. There was even a report that an unnamed someone offered Lieutenant Colonel Wheaton $10,000 for Kientpoos's body. The straight-arrow senior officer turned it down.[27] Wheaton knew it a less-than-smart career move to get in the way of the ghoulish booty the United States government was expecting.

Once the hubbub was over, soldiers loaded the corpses into the new coffins and carried them to McElderry, who was waiting in a nearby tent out of view. A battlefield surgeon practiced in swift amputation, McElderry severed the heads and then had the soldiers return the decapitated corpses to the coffins, nail them shut, and carry them out for burial in the graves close to the guardhouse. No prayers were said, no headstones raised. Canby and Thomas had drawn elaborate funerals and granite monuments; the four Modocs were dumped into the ground to be forgotten.

A little more than three weeks later, the surgeon forwarded a barrel with the skinned, defleshed, and preserved heads to Washington for inclusion in the collection of Indian crania at the Army Medical Museum. McElderry sent a letter along with the barrel to identify "the heads of four Modoc Indians, Capt. Jack, Schonchis, Boston Charley and Black Jim." The label on the barrel listed the contents as "specimens of natural history." The barrel was unpacked on arrival at the museum, and each skull numbered. Kientpoos became 1018, Schonchin John, 1019, Boston Charley, 1020, and Black Jim, 1021.[28]

33

Exile and Showbiz

We, as Indian people, were not intended to survive.

—Linda Hogan, *The Woman Who Watches Over the World*

Even as McElderry shipped out the skulls of the four executed Modocs, the remainder of the Lost River people were likewise headed east, into the exile that General Sherman and President Grant hoped would wipe out their very name. The State of Oregon had not wanted the Modocs to leave Fort Klamath at all, at least not until a state court could try and hang the men charged with murdering the Tule Lake settlers. No sooner were the four dead men cut down from the gallows than Sheriff McKenzie of Jackson County presented Lieutenant Colonel Wheaton with writs of habeas corpus demanding that Scarface Charley, Hooker Jim, Curley Headed Doctor, Long Jim, One-Eyed Mose, Humphrey, Little Charley, Boston Charley, Dave, and Little Jim be surrendered. Colonel Davis responded by making it clear that the "prisoners are captives of the General Government, charged with crimes committed in violation of the laws of war. The *Attorney General* has decided that the prisoners are only triable by the Military Courts of the United States."[1] He was telling Oregon to bug off.

With that last bit of legal business concluded, the military loaded the Modocs into twenty-one wagons, placed them under the command of Captain Hasbrouck, and dispatched them into exile nine days after the hanging. Hasbrouck had the men from his own battery of artillery plus a company from the Twelfth Infantry to serve as guards. Progress from the fort to the railhead at Redding was plodding, at an average of only a little more than twenty miles a day. When the Indians reached Redding, practically the whole town turned out to see the people who had caught the nation's attention for months and embarrassed the army time and again. Whatever the locals were expecting, the real-life Modocs did not measure up. They were "anything but attractive in appearance. A more filthy, insignificant band of Indians could not be imagined," one newspaper reported. "All the Modocs looked as though they had lain out all winter under an ash heap."[2] The journalist who wrote that line saw the Modocs' condition as evidence of their purported savagery, not the concentration-camp conditions of the Fort Klamath stockade. Once the Californians' curiosity was satisfied and their racial preconception validated, the Modocs boarded the train south to the Sacramento junction. There Slolux, Barncho, and their guards were to move to another train bound for San Francisco. The two Modoc convicts spared from the gallows would be taken to Alcatraz to serve life sentences, while the soldiers returned to their home base at the Presidio. The rest of the Modocs—153 by the army's count[3]—remained where they were, on a train bound east to Fort David A. Russell, just west of Cheyenne, Wyoming.

• • •

Atwell and a cub reporter serving as his assistant were waiting to meet the Modocs. The correspondent saw the Indians' passage through Sacramento as a chance to add an epilogue to this months-long tale of conflict and conquest.

As the train wheezed into the junction, Atwell approached. Windows flew open, and soldiers' heads and unshaven faces stuck out. The men in blue called out to him, excited to see this burly, hard-boiled curmudgeon who had reported the war since the first week of February. He shook hands and climbed into the prison cars, his assistant jotting away as he disappeared inside.

It was late October, when the weather in the Sacramento Valley turns nippy, yet the second-class cars holding the Modocs were warm, the air purer, in Atwell's judgment, than one might expect in such crammed accommodations. All the Indians wore cast-off settlers' duds, but for woven-tule skullcaps on most of the women and children. And the prisoners were mostly women and children, infants and old people among them, about three-quarters of the Natives headed toward exile in a place they had never heard of. Some had fashioned little beds of blankets on the hard benches and stretched out; others sat bolt-upright. The men, shackled singly or in pairs, wrapped themselves in blankets. They knew Atwell, yet refused to stand or to speak.

"Over all there seemed to hang a cloud of gloom, and almost perfect silence reigned in the cars, not even the children breaking the painful stillness," Atwell's journalistic understudy reported. "Curiosity had no place in countenance or action. A settled resignation to a hard fate seemed to be written upon every face."

Practically all those faces were painted in the black of Modoc mourning. These Indians had lost family members on the gallows, and now they had been uprooted from the lakes, mountains, and juniper steppes that defined their heritage, community, and religion. They had good reason to grieve.

Atwell found Lizzy, Kientpoos's younger and favorite wife and now his widow: "She has sad and pretty eyes, swollen with weeping. She barely nodded in response to greeting, and the tears began to flow at once." Rebecca, the older wife, held Rosie, her daughter and Kientpoos's only child, and refused to so much as look up. On the floor near her lay Princess Mary, Kientpoos's sister. Wrapped head to toe in a blanket, she had spoken not a word since her brother's drop on the Fort Klamath gallows.

Nearby sat Black Jim's widow, her two now-fatherless children, and a pair of Schonchin John's sons. They too said nothing. Atwell tried complimenting the young woman on how well she had dressed her smaller child. That ploy drew no response.

Atwell did finally get some conversation going with the Modoc men who could speak English. He asked Scarface Charley about this journey into exile: "Well, Charley, are the boys satisfied to go?"

"Yes, very well," he answered. This man, who was "tall, slender, and closely knit . . . with keen, sharp eyes," asked Atwell whether he knew Captain Hasbrouck, who commanded the guard detail. "You good heart to him?"

"Certainly."

"Well, tell him I had nothing to eat since yesterday—hungry."

A soldier told Atwell that Scarface had made the mistake of wolfing down his share of the rations when they were handed out the day before. "You know savages," the military man seemed to be saying. "Indians never plan ahead."

Atwell next found Steamboat Frank, Bogus Charley, Hooker Jim, and Weium with his wife, Wild Gal, a couple he knew from his first overnight stay in the Stronghold with Elijah Steele. The pretty young woman, noted for her "beautiful teeth and small hands," was arrayed in pink calico. Weium took pride in her as "the handsomest wife in the band."

The Modocs wanted to convince Atwell that everything on this long haul to God-knows-where was just fine. Bogus Charley said, "I got good heart all the time; Frank too."

"I know that, boys; you were led wrong," Atwell replied. Kientpoos and Schonchin could take the blame; they were dead.

Bogus Charley said, "I could tell you my heart—all good now. You remember old man Steele and you in Captain Jack cave."

"I do that."

"Good," Charley continued. "Wee-um and I stay outside all night. Our heart good, we keep Modocs off you, eh?" He was reminding Atwell just how dangerous that night of the second visit had been.

"Yes, Charley, that's true," the reporter agreed.

After joking with Frank, Charley, and Weium—Hooker kept to himself and would not talk—Atwell asked Bogus Charley how he liked the railroad cars. "First time me see cars me feel good," the Modoc said, "but . . . it makes sick heart go 'way off from lakes, 'way off."

When the Indians found out that one young officer among the guards, a Lieutenant Smith, had been to the Modocs' destination at Fort Russell, Steamboat Frank asked him, "Good place?"

Smith hesitated before saying, "Well, yes," without conviction.

Frank, Charley, and Weium slumped into silence. They had had little to look forward to; now they had even less.

Shacknasty Jim asked Atwell whether he was afraid on the last day of the Three-Day Battle in April, when he was caught in an ambush on the way to Hospital Rock. A rifle slug sliced Atwell's shoe open and stung his foot like an oblique hammer blow. Had the reporter been afraid? Of course not, Atwell answered; newspapermen don't do fear.

By then Barncho, Slolux, and their guards had been moved and a fresh locomotive coupled onto the Modocs' train. Atwell and his assistant off-boarded. They stood and watched as one train headed west toward San Francisco, the other east toward Wyoming.

For Atwell the Modoc War was now over.[4] For the Modocs its last engagement had only just begun.

$$\bullet\ \bullet\ \bullet$$

More than two weeks of bumpy, dusty travel in tightly packed wagons and second-class passenger cars had passed by the time the Indians reached Cheyenne and Fort Russell. There Hasbrouck and the Indians discovered that this was but a way station. General Philip H. Sheridan, who headed the Military Division of the Missouri, had decided that Fort Russell was too close to both town and mountains to hold the exiles securely. He wanted them taken more than two hundred miles farther, to Fort McPherson in Nebraska, an isolated fort that offered better hunting. The train carrying the Modocs pushed on. At a depot near the modern town of North Platte, Nebraska, the Modocs were offloaded, herded into wagons, and carted to Brady's Island in the middle of the Platte River. There, furnished with tents and stoves, the 153 hungry, travel-weary Modocs made camp. Captain Hasbrouck took a receipt for the Indians from a colonel of the Third Cavalry and headed back west with his men.[5]

The Modocs had had only a few days to settle into their new home on the prairie when the army once again herded them together, shackled the men, and packed them onto cattle cars coupled to a train to Kansas City. From there the Modocs were borne south to Fort Scott and then on to the railhead at Baxter Springs, on the Kansas-Oklahoma state line. The Indians arrived on a dreary Sunday, November 16, 1873, more than a month after their departure from Fort Klamath. A ragtag settlement devoted to providing the for-profit pleasures cowboys coming off cattle drives from Texas craved, Baxter Springs offered little for exiled Indians. The women, children, and elderly were put up in the town's Hyland Hotel while the able-bodied men were hauled in wagons six miles farther to a reservation across the state line known as Quapaw Agency. Winter was fast approaching, the Modocs needed shelter, and their men were put to work building it. In but a week, these

onetime fighters, cowboys, and hunters working with three white carpenters erected a temporary barracks-like building, complete with a
large stove, from scrap lumber at the low price of $524.40—less than
$10,500 in today's money. This rude and rough group home was situ-
ated only two hundred yards from the Quapaw Agency headquarters
so that Hiram W. Jones could keep a close eye on his new charges of
bad reputation. Once construction was complete, the Modoc women,
children, and elders came from Baxter Springs to join their men. Worn,
tired, hungry, and miserably clothed, the Modocs from the Lava Beds
settled in as best they could.

• • •

The federal government was more concerned with sending the Modocs
into exile than in ensuring their welfare once they arrived. No money
had been allocated to buy the Shawnee land the Modocs were living
on or to provide them food, clothing, and farm tools. The American
Indian Aid Association came up with a charitable grant of less than
$100, far too little to care for the Indians' immediate needs. Mean-
while, the men hunted and fished to feed their families. Not until
more than a year had passed did $15,000 in federal money earmarked
for the Modocs reach Quapaw.

Despite the government's yawning disregard, the Modocs tried mightily to make Quapaw work. While the women sewed clothes to replace
the torn rags they had been wearing since the Fort Klamath stockade,
the men learned and applied carpentry and farming skills. Within two
years they built twenty log houses, most with two rooms, planted and
harvested fifty acres of corn, cut trees and split seventeen thousand
rails, and fenced 160 of their 200 plowed acres. The Modocs sold cut
timber and Indian beadwork in nearby towns for cash money. The
men and boys continued to fish and hunt to supplement their families' diets, and they worked on farms and in settlements to boost their
incomes. By one assessment, the Modocs did more with less land than
any other tribe on the Quapaw Agency.

At the same time, the Modocs were undergoing a religious conver-
sion. Stung by defeat, many in the tribe converted to Quakerism, the
Christian denomination most devoted to peace. Quapaw was a Quaker

agency, and Hiram Jones was himself a Friend. Some years later, Steamboat Frank—by then known as Frank Modoc—left Quapaw to attend seminary in Maine. He became the first full-blooded American Indian registered as a minister in the Society of Friends.[6]

• • •

One major player in the Modoc story realized that opportunity lay not in what the exiled Modocs were becoming but in what they had been. Nostalgia for the "vanishing Indian" was all the rage, and A. B. Meacham wanted to capitalize.

Out of a regular job since the Good Friday attack, Meacham had been trying to piece together a living on the lecture circuit. Yet all by himself, even with his visible scars and paralyzed hand, a self-proclaimed pro-Indian do-gooder such as he was no big draw. On the very eve of the Fort Klamath hangings, Meacham lectured about the Modoc War in San Francisco's Mercantile Library Hall to an audience both disappointingly small and disappointed. Meacham was a flop. "His elocution was very defective, the delivery bad, and two thirds of the audience could not understand one word that was uttered," the *San Francisco Chronicle* reported. "The sounds emanating from an adjoining dance hall did not tend to remedy this defect."[7]

The former peace commissioner continued to mine the past in writing *Wigwam and War-path*, a memoir of his many years of dealings with Indians across Oregon. As humane men of letters concerned over the Indian cause pronounced the book worthy in the *New York Times'* flattering review,[8] Meacham saw a way to spin his self-interest into altruism: "I determined to make an opportunity for the red-men of the West to speak for themselves"—under his guidance of course. Bearing various humanitarian endorsements of his plan to take Indians on a lecture tour, Meacham arrived in the nation's capital to pitch the idea.

Edward Smith, commissioner of Indian Affairs, favored Meacham's plan. Interior Secretary Delano was less sanguine, and President Grant downright disliked the notion of putting Indians onstage to make money. In the end, convinced of Meacham's benevolent intentions, Grant relented, and the necessary permit was granted, with conditions. Meacham would pick up all expenses, and he was to ensure that no Indian got anywhere near beer or whiskey. A lifelong teetotaler, Meacham had no trouble with the abstinence pledge. Money would prove to be another matter.

Securing the help of the Modocs was key to his plan. And so, just one day shy of the first anniversary of the Modocs' arrival in Oklahoma, Meacham showed up at Quapaw on a recruiting trip.

Steamboat Frank, Bogus Charley, Shacknasty Jim, and Hooker Jim were outside playing croquet. Bogus Charley was dressed in a style Meacham called half Quaker and half Spanish: broad-brimmed hat, high-heeled boots with red laces and tassels, and matching red sash about the waist. All the Modocs in the vicinity gathered to behold this Lazarus of the Lava Beds and to hear his enlistment pitch. Shacknasty Jim, Steamboat Frank, and Scarface Charley liked it. They agreed to head out on the road with him, hoping to make some money.

In the new year of 1875 Meacham gave his traveling show a trial run in Sacramento before the Oklahoma Modocs joined in. He brought along five Oregon Indians, Oliver Applegate, and the Riddles—Frank, Toby, and Jeff. To boost the Indian flavor of the enterprise, Meacham billed Jeff by his Indian name, Charka.

Toby Riddle also had an original Modoc name, possibly Dus-wha-re-le.[9] This was not the name Meacham chose to use. Rather, he dubbed her Winema, a moniker lifted from "The Tale of the Tall Alcalde," an overwrought narrative poem by Joaquin Miller set loosely in northeastern California. Miller's rhymed and metered tale tells of a gorgeous Native maiden named Winnema who falls in love with a white man, the alcalde of the title, and rescues him from prison after a decisive battle between her people and the invading whites. Besmirched by betraying her doomed race and offering her body to the jailer to free the alcalde, Winnema kills herself with a dagger after demanding that her body be burned upon a funeral pyre, much like Dido in the *Aeneid*.[10]

Meacham did more than alter Miller's spelling and appropriate the name Winema for Toby Riddle. He was making the Modoc woman into a heroine on the mythic order of Pocahontas, the Indian maiden who purportedly rescued Jamestown colonial leader John Smith from summary execution by her father. To buttress the mythic status of Winema as Pocahontas the savior, Meacham invented an elaborate backstory.

In *Wigwam and War-path*, Meacham referred to Toby as Toby—or Tobey, in his often-variable spelling. She entered the narrative when Meacham confronted Kientpoos on Lost River in December 1869 in the effort to move him and his people onto the reservation. Toby, who was Kientpoos's cousin, and her husband, Frank, served as interpreters. The book's drawings depict the two of them in the clothes and hairstyles of American settlers.

As Meacham planned his speaking tour and wrote the publicity pamphlet that would grow into *Wi-ne-ma (the Woman Chief) and Her People*, he built out a new fiction. The woman was of royal birth, Meacham claimed, although he likely knew full well that the radically democratic Modocs had no hereditary nobility. Her father dubbed her Kaitch-ko-na Wi-ne-ma, which Meacham claimed meant "little woman chief," when this wonder-child rescued a canoe full of children from the Link River rapids. Meacham depicted her hunting grizzles, absorbing ancient wisdom from elders, leading Modocs on a revenge raid against Pit River Indians, and pining for civilization after learning of the "higher life of the white man" from a lost, starving emigrant she nursed back to health.[11] The book's woodcut frontispiece shows Winema in the imagined dress of an Indian princess, from royal crown to fringed moccasins. Her marriage to Kentuckian Frank Riddle became a strategic move away from her doomed Native people and toward the exalted and inexorable white race.

Winema achieved her mythic apotheosis in saving Meacham from death at the Peace Tent. This story, too, was Meacham's latter-day invention, one that swelled from telling to telling.

When Meacham appeared as a witness before the Fort Klamath military commission, he testified under oath that during the attack he passed out after a pistol round hit him in the head. He came to, he said, only when the rescue party appeared some time later. Never did Meacham testify that Toby Riddle intervened during the attack on him, nor did Toby make any such claim in her sworn testimony.

Meacham's account changed by the time he was speaking to that disappointing crowd in San Francisco three months later. He passed out and was being scalped when, he said, "Toby Riddle, womanlike, came to his rescue, and, failing in all else, clapped her hands and called out, 'Soldiers!'"[12]

Toby Riddle had told Atwell, on the day after the Peace Tent killings, that she called out, "Don't do that—the soldiers are coming," then Boston Charley stopped scalping Meacham and ran off.[13] So far, so factual. Meacham, though, kept inflating the story. In *Wigwam and War-path*, Toby slammed into Boston Charley as he was slicing into Meacham's scalp and bowled him over. Charley rose, threatened her with his pistol, then went back to scalping. Only then did Riddle call out that the soldiers were coming and scare away the murderous Modocs.[14]

Wi-ne-ma and Her People goes further. Now Riddle runs from one of Meacham's Modoc assailants to another, turning their pistols aside as each tries to deliver the final, fatal shot. She attacks Boston Charley as he is scalping Meacham, only to be flattened by a vicious pistol whip to the head. Somehow she still finds the energy to call out that the soldiers are coming. Riddle is wiping the blood from Meacham's savaged face when the soldiers appear. It made for a stirring tale.[15]

Yet Fox and Atwell, who went to the Peace Tent with the rescue party soon after the assault, failed to mention Toby's presence anywhere in the wounded Meacham's vicinity.[16] Maurice Fitzgerald, one of the soldiers rushing toward the Peace Tent, wrote later that he saw Toby running away close on the heels of Leroy Dyar, who took off at the first shot.[17] It is beyond unlikely that all three witnesses failed to notice the Modoc woman tending to the wounded commissioner. Meacham invented the story that Toby had wrestled with the Modoc attackers, stopped Boston Charley halfway through the scalping, and cared for Meacham until help arrived.[18]

And Meacham's show-business strategy worked. Adding Indians and casting Riddle as Pocahontas reincarnate boosted his show's appeal. "His apostrophe to Toby as she took her life in her hands and . . . several times tore herself from husband and son, to serve the pale-faces was on a scale grandly eloquent," reported a review in the *Sacramento Record*. "Mr. Meacham is a natural orator. His words are rapid, and seem to crowd to his lips from a heart full to overcrowding with his subject, and more than earnest in advocacy of humanity in the treatment of Indians."[19]

A pleased Meacham and his associates took the train from Sacramento to St. Joseph, Missouri, where Scarface Charley, Steamboat Frank, and Shacknasty Jim joined them. Meacham met, too, James Redpath, the Boston-based owner of the Lyceum Bureau, then the country's leading lecture agency. Redpath had booked Meacham's company on a tour across Missouri, Indiana, Kentucky, the District of Columbia, Pennsylvania, and New Jersey. New York City was the final destination.

Meacham and Redpath duded the Modocs up in the fringed buckskins and face paint of Plains Indians, yet the earnest retelling of the Modoc story roused but meager interest across the Midwest and the East. Newspaper after newspaper wrote good reviews of Meacham and his entourage; however, ticket receipts fell short of expenses. Meacham's money-making plan was going into the hole, and he was on the hook.

Meacham tried to claw back with a choreographed display of Shacknasty Jim's dead-eye skill with bow and arrow. Huffy that receipts were so low, Jim refused to join the show and instead took a seat in the audience. Meacham had to apologize to the crowd that, without Jim, he could not present the planned display of Modoc archery. The audience clapped hands and stamped feet to demand that this renowned archer strut his stuff. The stratagem worked. Jim had Oliver Applegate hold the pine-board target in his hand at the front of the stage while the other Modocs shot from the center of the main aisle, a far longer distance than usual. Indian after Indian hit the target in or near the bull's-eye, bristling the board with shafts and fletchings. Jim came close to eye the target, spotted a small opening among the arrows at the very center, walked almost to the back wall of the auditorium, snapped around with bow drawn, and instantly released the arrow. It hit the clear spot precisely, to great applause.

Yet even such Buffalo Bill–ish showmanship fell short for reasons outside Meacham's control. Although the Gilded Age would bring the United States unprecedented economic growth, the 1870s started badly. With the country reeling under the financial slowdown, rising unemployment, and business failures brought on by the Panic of 1873—a global economic collapse that qualified as the worst ever until the Great Depression of the 1930s—Indian shows were a hard sell to people short of cash. By early April 1875, Meacham found himself several hundred dollars in debt and unable to continue the tour.

Philanthropist Peter Cooper offered Meacham the use of the Cooper Union Foundation Building—an imposing, landmark Italianate brownstone in Lower Manhattan made famous by an Abraham Lincoln speech in the run-up to the 1860 presidential election—for a grand show, including live music, to showcase the Modocs. The hope was that this New York City extravaganza would cover the loss and allow everyone in the lecture company to buy a train ticket home. Again, though, expenses consumed receipts. Meacham was back under water and up against a hotel proprietor who would not let the Indians leave until the bill was settled. Finally, a number of generous benefactors stepped in and bailed Meacham out. The onetime peace commissioner, his former translators, and the Modocs packed up and headed home.[20]

•••

After returning to Salem, Oregon, Meacham continued speaking about the Modoc War and Indian matters on tours throughout the East and Midwest. He launched *The Council Fire*, a periodical that addressed Indian affairs, and moved the magazine and his family to Washington, DC, where he could better wield influence on Native matters. At the request of Interior Secretary Carl Schurz, Meacham went west again to work with the Ute Indians, a mission that nearly got him hanged by a lynch mob inflamed by land speculators who—in echoes of Jesse Carr and Jesse Applegate—wanted the Utes cleared out of Colorado's Uncompahgre Valley. By the time Meacham returned to Washington, his health had deteriorated badly. In early 1882 he suffered a stroke at his writing table and died a few hours later. Meacham was fifty-six.[21]

After Meacham's speaking tour, the Riddles went back to the Klamath Reservation, where they hunted, fished, and raised livestock. In his son's estimation, Frank Riddle always made money, then always lost it.[22] Fortunately for the family, Toby was awarded a federal pension of twenty-five dollars a month for her Modoc War service as the result of a bill sponsored by Binger Hermann, a Republican member of the House of Representatives from Roseburg, Oregon. Hermann used Meacham's transformation of the Modoc translator into Pocahontas to justify the pension. His bill lauded the woman it called Winemah Riddle for "prov[ing] herself to be the friend of the white man at the risk of her own life . . . running from one [attacker] to another" as she sought to save Meacham.[23] The pension sustained the family until Frank died in 1906 and Toby in 1920.

Steamboat Frank, Scarface Charley, and Shacknasty Jim went back to Quapaw with no more money in their pockets than when they left months earlier. Things were going poorly in Oklahoma. Despite the willingness of the exiled Modocs to work hard and adopt the ways and religion of their conquerors, death stalked Quapaw. Exile killed far more Modocs than did rifles and mortars in the Lava Beds.

Of the 153 people who had arrived in Indian Territory in 1873, only 99 were still alive six years later. One of the first to die was Rosie, Kientpoos's daughter and his one direct descendant, who succumbed only six months after reaching Oklahoma. Hooker Jim died in 1879, Bogus Charley the next year, and Shacknasty Jim the year after that. All were in their thirties. Steamboat Frank lived until 1886, passing away from lung disease at the Quaker seminary in Portland, Maine. Three years later, George Denny—the former Slolux, who had spent five years at Alcatraz before being released and transported to Quapaw—died. Denny's prison partner, Barncho, had met his end on the Rock in San Francisco Bay. Of the principal players in the Modoc War on the Indian side, Princess Mary, sister to Kientpoos, was the longest-lived, dying at Quapaw in 1906. A photo of her late in life shows a proud, strong, still-beautiful woman who, despite her sixty-plus years and the trauma she had suffered, radiated great personal power.[24]

These individual deaths figured into an overall pattern of decline among the Oklahoma Modocs. Their numbers fell to ninety-one in 1886 and eighty-eight in 1889. With some of the Modocs selling their reservation allotments after the Dawes Act of 1887 and moving away, and with many of the rest dying, the Oklahoma population numbered but fifty in 1899.[25] The conditions of life for the exiled Modocs were killing them off.

Uprooting the Natives from their land worked deep spiritual harm, which exacerbated depression and despair. Anthropologist Jeremiah

Curtin, who visited Oklahoma to learn Modoc myths, wrote, "Exile for the Modocs was a crushing sorrow. When I saw them, in 1884, they were still mourning over their changed condition, and for the Klamath country—the country Kumush [Gmukamps] created and gave to them."[26] The change in climate, from the high, dry semidesert of northeastern California to the lowland humidity of eastern Oklahoma, did them no good as well. Diseases such as tuberculosis and pneumonia were endemic. Most important, the Modocs remained the victims of the same corruption by Indian agents that helped precipitate the Lost River gunfight. In Oklahoma it created murderous public-health conditions.

A premise of President Grant's Peace Policy was that Indian agents from religious backgrounds would resist profiteering and manage reservations in an honest and fair way. Quapaw should have been among the most favored reservations, since Quakers ran the place. In fact, Hiram Jones and his family proved yet again that good people in bad systems behave badly. Jones hired his own relatives at inflated salaries, restricted Indian trade to a single store that was owned by his wife's first cousin and charged exorbitant prices, purchased old equipment at the price of new from relatives, shorted the Indians on food, and failed to provide medical services that had been budgeted.[27]

Bogus Charley gave a sworn account to a government inspector: "Agent Jones never came near us to see us when we were sick. . . . He has only been to our camps twice in the past year. We have found it hard work to get medicine from him. I have been to him and told him my people are sick, my people are going to die and he told me, 'I've got no medicine for you.' He said he was sorry he had got no money for us; the Government didn't allow any money for us." The flour Jones supplied was all bran and shorts, and the beef was good only if the Modocs slaughtered and butchered the steers themselves. Otherwise, he fed the Modocs "bad meat. It was rotten and old bull."[28]

In 1879, as complaints about Quapaw swelled, the government replaced Jones and appointed physicians to serve the agency. The harm, though, had already been done. Between malnutrition, exposure to disease in an alien climate, the long-term lack of even minimal medical care, deaths far outpaced births. The Oklahoma Modocs were disappearing.

General William Tecumseh Sherman had wanted the tribe exterminated. Without firing a shot and with the Interior Department footing the bill, the general saw his wish fulfilled.

34

Requiem

Who will find peace with the lands? The future of mankind lies
waiting for those who will come to understand their lives and take up
their responsibilities to all living things. Who will listen to the trees,
the animals and birds, the voices of the places of the land? As the
long-forgotten peoples of the respective continents rise and
begin to reclaim their ancient heritage, they will discover the
meaning of the lands of their ancestors. That is when the invaders
of the North American continent will finally discover that
for this land, God is red.

—Vine Deloria Jr., *God Is Red*

The exiled Modoc who held most fiercely to the old ways was
Curley Headed Doctor. The shaman who had once kept the
United States Army at bay with Ghost Dance and red tule rope refused
to give up his familiarity with the ancient animal spirits for the conqueror's Christianity.

As he grew old and weak and readied himself to walk on in 1890,
Curley Headed Doctor predicted the circumstances of his death. The
doves that were his spirit birds and that Modoc belief held to be the
chief mourners among the animals would come in great flocks, he
prophesied. "Don't kill these birds or you may suffer," he warned family and friends. "They have come to bid me farewell. As soon as I die
the spirits leaving me will cause the greatest storm you have ever seen."
And the shaman demanded that his body be burned, in the old way,
and offered to the air, not deposited in a wooden box and dropped
into a slit in the Earth like some Quaker.

It happened the way Curley Headed Doctor foretold. On the shaman's last day, sky-filling flocks of doves appeared to perch, bob, and

coo near the dying man. When the end came and Curley Headed Doctor walked on, a storm bigger than anything the Oklahoma Modocs had ever seen blew up out of the prairie and engulfed Quapaw.

Once the rain passed, the Modocs burned Curley Headed Doctor's body as he had demanded. The pyre under the corpse was kindled, fire seized wood and flesh, and enormous flames of many colors leapt high. It was a funeral spectacle unlike any the people at Quapaw could remember. They knew then, as we know now, that something ancient, something powerful, something rooted deep in this continent, was leaving the American earth.[1]

Epilogue

When Frazier Boutelle and Scarface Charley dueled along Lost River on the cold, soaked morning of November 29, 1872, their lives entwined in rough parallel for the next eleven months. Both played continuing parts in the war: Charley as battle leader on the Modoc side, Boutelle as junior cavalry officer on the American. The two resided at Fort Klamath, Boutelle outside the stockade and Charley inside, during the war crimes trial and public hanging of Kientpoos and three other Modocs. Thereafter their fates separated, with the Modoc exiled to Oklahoma and the cavalryman remaining at Fort Klamath for the time being.

Boutelle's military career stretched almost a half-century longer. Breveted first lieutenant for his bravery at Lost River, Boutelle went on to win a medal in the war against Chief Joseph and the Nez Perce. After promotion to captain, he became acting superintendent of Yellowstone Park, enacting policies that foreshadowed Teddy Roosevelt's conservationism, from protecting bison to stocking depleted streams and lakes with trout. Boutelle later led the Washington State National Guard, left military service for a time, then rejoined the army as a recruiter, becoming the oldest serving officer of his time. He died at home in Seattle in 1924 at the age of eighty-four.[1]

Scarface Charley succeeded the executed Kientpoos as chief of the Lost River Modocs. He lost that post when he failed to clamp down on gambling, a long-standing custom that Indian agent Hiram Jones wanted to stamp out. After touring with A. B. Meacham's lecture circuit through the eastern United States, Scarface Charley returned to the poverty and graft of the Oklahoma reservation. This talented and widely respected leader died there in 1896, at the age of only forty-five.[2]

Charley had been in his grave for thirteen years when the federal government finally relented on Modoc exile. A 1909 law allowed the Oklahoma Modocs to return to Oregon from Quapaw.

To this day a small Modoc reservation remains in northeastern Oklahoma, near the town of Miami. As for the Klamath Reservation to which some of the exiled Modocs returned, it no longer exists. The reservation's 880,000 acres, which included the largest stand of ponderosa pines on Native American lands, were removed from Indian ownership by the 1954 Klamath Termination Act despite the clear opposition of the reservation's Native residents. The federal government planned to sell the former reservation lands to private timber companies. Only one tract was purchased, however, and the remainder became part of the Winema National Forest—administered by the United States Forest Service, generally to the benefit of those same timber interests.

A decades-long struggle to restore federal recognition succeeded finally in the 1986 Klamath Indian Tribe Restoration Act. This law returned no reservation lands to the Klamath Tribes (Klamaths, Modocs, and Yahooskin Paiutes),[3] but they did regain control of the water. After an adjudication process that took thirty years, the Klamath Tribes won the most senior water rights in the upper Klamath Basin.[4]

Land and water lie still at the heart of the matter, just as they did in the time of Kientpoos and the Lost River Modocs.

• • •

Joel Trimble, a cavalry captain during the Modoc War, came to realize that the conflict had nothing to do with avenging wronged innocence, enforcing a treaty, or bringing war criminals to justice. The purpose of the hostilities was rather to "drive a couple of hundred miserable aborigines from a desolate natural shelter in the wilderness, that a few thriving cattle-men might ranch their wild steers in a scope of isolated country, the dimensions of some reasonable-sized counties."[5]

With the Lost River Modocs exiled to Oklahoma, Jesse Applegate, the Oregon pioneer and surveyor, and Jesse Carr, the California land speculator, set out to finalize their grand plan for a cattle barony on what had been Modoc land. They realized that whoever controlled the water in this semi-arid steppe country also controlled the land. Applegate surveyed and mapped water sources, and Carr used his wealth and skill at backroom bribery to gain control of the most strategic parcels. Through hired stand-ins filing homestead and swampland claims, Carr acquired land parcel by parcel by parcel, first surrounding Clear Lake, then moving closer to Tule Lake, and had fences erected to enclose the land within.[6]

The barrier on the Clear Lake ranch ran for forty-five miles. Much of it consisted of local volcanic stone, five feet wide at the base and four feet tall, with barbed wire strung along the top. The strenuous labor of erecting the fence was supplied by Swedish, Chinese, and Chilean workmen imported from San Francisco. The barrier was so formidable, and the Asian workers so exotic, that it came to be known as the China Wall.

Carr treated public lands inside the walls and fences as if they were his own, even though federal law forbade the practice in 1885. Doubling down on his illegal practice, Carr had his Tule Lake holdings enclosed. Now the 150,000 acres he controlled included almost 85,000 acres of public land.

A special federal agent issued a notice-to-remove order to Carr to pull down the China Wall and the Tule Lake fence. When Carr did nothing, the agent had him indicted. Carr's lawyers got the trial postponed. Then the agent was replaced by a man who declared the matter not worth pursuing. Somebody, it appears, had been bribed, a dark art at which Carr excelled.

This dirty deal held through the turn of the century, when a crew headed by a United States marshal knocked down sections of the China Wall. An undaunted Carr continued his scheme, buying up more Tule Lake homesteads. The only thing that stopped him, blind but still avaricious, was sudden death in 1903 at age eighty-nine.[7]

•••

Jesse Applegate fared far less well than his erstwhile partner. The cattle baron used Applegate to his own ends, then cut the Oregon pioneer loose. Applegate took the loss hard.

Of a melancholy turn of mind, he became a reservoir of despair. Invited to speak to a gathering of the Oregon Pioneer Association as a standout representative of the territory's early days, Applegate refused.

Addressing a leader of the association, he disparaged the popular notion that the early settlers came west for grand and glorious reasons: "So far from being proud of the years I have been in this country, I am ashamed to confess the insufficient motives upon which I acted."[8] He concluded that his life, deemed illustrious by his peers and contemporaries, added up to little: "For me, my speculations have been loss, my philanthropy has been an injury to those in whose favor it was exerted, and my ambition has been fed on disappointment."[9]

After his wife died, Applegate lost what little money and land he had, suffered from insomnia broken by nightmares that morphed into delusions, and took to demented wandering. His family had him committed, first to an asylum in Linkville, then to one in Salem. In the last winter of his life he was released to the care of his son Alexander. He died in Alexander's house on April 22, 1888, at the age of seventy-seven.[10]

• • •

Even while the two Jesses were scheming to gain control of the headwaters of Lost River, other settlers were working to corral its flow downstream. From the late 1860s through the turn of the century, various landowners dug irrigation channels to bring water to dry land.[11] Private irrigation schemes rested on shaky economics, however, and one after another went bust. The federal government stepped in.

The Reclamation Act of 1902, which created the United States Bureau of Reclamation, aimed to recharge emigration to the West by boosting the water supply. What became known as the Klamath Project grew into a grand scheme to reroute and repurpose the lands and waters of the Klamath Basin. As Marc Reisner writes in *Cadillac Desert*, "Remote, wild, half-forgotten, the Klamath was a perfect example of how God had left the perfection and completion of California to the Bureau of Reclamation."[12] By the time the bureau finished its work, Tule Lake shrank from 100,000-plus watery acres to no more than 15,000 acres today.

In the process Lost River began to die. No longer is this the wild flow that sustained the Modocs with its water, fish, and game. In the words of a scientific report, Lost River these days "can best be characterized as an irrigation water conveyance, rather than a river. Flows are completely regulated, it has been channelized in one . . . reach, its riparian habitats and adjacent wetlands are highly modified, and it receives significant discharges from agricultural drains and sewage effluent."[13]

In the end and in our time, Lost River has been lost all over again.

NOTES

Prologue

1. Biographical detail from Northwest Digital Archives, "Guide to the Frazier Augustus Boutelle Papers 1869–1933," http://nwda.orbiscascade.org/ark:/80444/xv43100 .

2. Johnson, "Frazier Augustus Boutelle," 52.

3. See C. James, *Modoc*, 55, for the Modoc name.

4. Boutelle, "Major Boutelle's Account," 264–71.

1. Bad to Worse

1. "Statement of Mr. Henry Miller," undated, Fisher Papers, 1:169–71. The online version of this documentary source features consecutively numbered pages divided into eleven volumes. To simplify locating the original document, the volume number precedes the page number.

2. Murray, *The Modocs*, 83.

3. Since Klamath-Modoc was not a written language in the early 1870s, the spelling of the headman's name varies from source to source: Kientpoos, Keintpoos, and Kintpuash are the most common, with the variants including Kienteepoos, Keentpuash, Kiuntpuas, Kintpuas, Kintpoos, Keintpoos, Keintpoess, and Pientposes.

4. Murray, *The Modocs*, 56–59.

5. Walker to Odeneal, July 6, 1872, Fisher Papers, 11:1696–97.

6. Odeneal to Walker, December 23, 1872, Fisher Papers, 3:434–46.

7. Wheaton to Assistant Adjutant General, November 14, 1872, Fisher Papers, 2:288–89; Adams to Commanding Officer, November 14, 1872, Fisher Papers, 2:290–91; Canby to Adjutant General, December 3, 1872, Fisher Papers, 3:335.

8. Boutelle, "Major Boutelle's Account," 265; Orders No. 93, November 28, 1872, Fisher Papers, 2:299–300.

9. Jackson, "The First Blow," 261.

10. Dillon, *Burnt-Out Fires*, 95–96.

11. O. Applegate, "The Battle on the East Side," undated, Fisher Papers, 2:304–5.

12. Odeneal, "Report Pertaining to the Removal of the Modoc Indians," December 23, 1872, Fisher Papers, 3:440.

13. Odeneal, *The Modoc War*, 55.

14. Boutelle, "Major Boutelle's Account," 270.

15. O. Applegate, "The Battle on the East Side," 305.

16. Boutelle, "Major Boutelle's Account," 266.

17. O. Applegate, "The Battle on the East Side," Fisher Papers, 2:306.

18. Murray, *The Modocs*, 82–84.

19. Boutelle, "Major Boutelle's Account," 267.

20. I. D. Applegate, "The Initial Shot," 276–77.

21. Jackson, "The First Blow," 262–63.

22. Riddle, *Indian History*, 46–48, reports that an old woman, abandoned by her family in the tumult of the gunfight, died in the flames. Hooker Jim later told a reporter that the woman was already dead when the soldiers set fire to the houses; "The Modocs," *Sacramento Record*, July 8, 1873.

23. Boutelle, "Major Boutelle's Account," 268.

24. O. Applegate, "The Battle on the East Side," Fisher Papers, 2:307.

25. "The Modoc Troubles," *New York Times*, December 27, 1872. Hooker Jim later corroborated this account of a wounded mother and dead infant; "The Modocs," *Sacramento Record*, July 8, 1873.

26. O. Applegate, "The Battle on the East Side," Fisher Papers, 2:305–7.

27. Dillon, *Burnt-Out Fires*, 132; "From the Front—History of the Modoc War," *Daily Alta California*, December 12, 1872.

28. Riddle, *Indian History*, 47.

29. "The Modocs," *Sacramento Record*, July 8, 1873; Murray, *The Modocs*, 91; C. James, *Modoc*, 63.

30. Bill Miller, "Run for the Hills—the Boddy Killings," *Mail Tribune*, August 4, 2013; "Thrilling Account . . . By the Wife of One of the Victims," *San Francisco Chronicle*, January 8, 1873.

31. Jackson to Green, December 2, 1872, Fisher Papers, 2:328; author's e-mail correspondence with Ryan Bartholomew, Klamath County Historical Society, September 23–25, 2013.

32. O. Applegate, "The Battle on the East Side," Fisher Papers, 2:309.

2. Stone and Story

1. Jesse Applegate, "The Modoc Lava Bed," *New York Times*, February 24, 1873.

2. Donnelly-Nolan, "Geology of Medicine Lake Volcano."

3. Waters, "Captain Jack's Stronghold."

4. Deur, *In the Footprints of Gmukamps*, 158–60, 165–79.

5. This version of the Modoc creation story comes from the kiosk at Petroglyph Point in Lava Beds National Monument.

6. Zdanowicz, Zielinski, and Germani, "Mount Mazama Eruption," 621–24. The date these scientists give falls with the range of 5827 BCE and 5527 BCE, with 5677 BCE the midpoint.

7. "Mount Mazama and Crater Lake: Growth and Destruction of a Cascade Volcano," U.S. Geological Survey, August 2002, Fact Sheet 092-02, Online Version 1.0, http://pubs.usgs.gov/fs/2002/fs092-02/fs092-02.pdf.

8. Howe, *Ancient Modocs*, 1–5.

9. "Indian Perceptions of Crater Lake."

10. Deur, "A Most Sacred Place."

11. Deur, *In the Footsteps of Gmukamps*, 185–87; Ray, *Primitive Pragmatists*, 77–81; Haynal, "The Influence of Sacred Rock Cairns"; Curtin, *Myths of the Modocs*, 7–10.

12. Howe, *Ancient Modocs*, 19–35, argues that the site he excavated, called Nightfire Island on Sheepy Creek close to Lower Klamath Lake, has been continuously occupied longer than any other site in the western United States and calls this the Cradle Culture. Corroboration comes from research on Oregon's Paisley Caves, located about 150 miles from the Tule Lake Basin, that points to human occupation of that area as early as 12,500 BCE. See Curry, "Pre-Clovis Breakthrough," and Jenkins et al., "Clovis Age Western Stemmed Projectile Points."

13. Dicken and Dicken, *Ancient Lake Modoc*, iv.

14. Howe, *Ancient Modocs*, 68–69.

15. Howe, *Ancient Modocs*, 19–59.

16. Deur, *In the Footprints of Gmukamps*, 157; Ray, *Primitive Pragmatists*, 204, and map 2, 207; David, "The Landscape of Klamath Basin Rock Art," 9–10.

17. Ray, *Primitive Pragmatists*, 146–54.

18. Deur, "'A Caretaker Responsibility.'"

19. Ray, *Primitive Pragmatists*, 180–200.

3. Running the Pagans Out

1. Boutelle, "Major Boutelle's Account," 268.

2. Jackson, "The First Blow," 257.

3. Lönnberg, "The Digger Stereotype in California"; Heizer, *They Were Only Diggers*, xiv–xv.

4. *Dum Diversas*, translation at http://unamsanctamcatholicam.blogspot.com/2011/02/dum-diversas-english-translation.html.

5. Newcomb, *Pagans in the Promised Land*, 39–50. For the original documents, see Davenport, *European Treaties*, 13–20, 20–26.

6. Echo-Hawk, *In the Courts of the Conqueror*, 17–19.

7. Newcomb, *Pagans in the Promised Land*, 53.

8. Quoted from *The Danger of Apostasy* (1679) in Drinnon, *Facing West*, xxv.

9. Quoted in Berkhofer, *The White Man's Indian*, 136–38.

10. Echo-Hawk, *In the Courts of the Conqueror*, 59–62.

11. Kades, "The Dark Side of Efficiency," 1081–93; Echo-Hawk, *In the Courts of the Conqueror*, 62–76; Newcomb, *Pagans in the Promised Land*, 72–87. See also Robertson, *Conquest by Law*, for an in-depth treatment of the background and legacy of *Johnson v. M'Intosh*.

12. *Johnson v. M'Intosh*, 573–74, 596. The relationship to land has to do not only with law but also the core of culture. As Deloria, *God Is Red*, 70, observes: "The basic divergence of viewpoints between American Indians and the rest of American society must be seen . . . in the conception of land, and the choice appears to be between conceiving of land as either a subject or an object." Deloria quotes from Albert Camus's *The Rebel*: "When the Church dissipated its Mediterranean heritage, it placed the emphasis on his-

tory to the detriment of nature, caused the Gothic to triumph over the romance, and . . . has made increasing claims to temporal power and historical dynamism. When nature ceases to be an object of contemplation, it can be nothing more than material for an action that aims at transforming it."

13. Johnson v. M'Intosh, 590.

4. Death Squads, Sex Slaves

1. *Report of Governor Grover*, 4–5.

2. Davies, *Ogden's Snake Country Journal*, xv. See also Cline, *Peter Skene Ogden*, 48, 69.

3. Langston, *Where Land and Water Meet*, 18–20.

4. Davies, *Ogden's Snake Country Journal*, 14. This note, like all citations from primary sources of the time, follows their original spelling and usage even when it runs against contemporary practice.

5. Davies, *Ogden's Snake Country Journal*, 7.

6. Davies, *Ogden's Snake Country Journal*, 12.

7. Davies, *Ogden's Snake Country Journal*, 23.

8. Davies, *Ogden's Snake Country Journal*, 118.

9. LaLande, *First over the Siskiyous*, 7–23, 118.

10. Cothran, "*Lúgsh* and *Laláki*."

11. DeVoto, *Year of Decision*, 371–76.

12. Turner, *Years of Harvest*, 35–42.

13. L. Applegate, "Notes and Reminiscences," 15.

14. Kluger, *Seizing Destiny*, 400–431.

15. Sides, *Blood and Thunder*, 85–88. Frémont had been in the Klamath country three years earlier as well; see Frémont, *Narrative*, 122–24.

16. Deur, *In the Footsteps of Gmukamps*, 161–62.

17. Dicken and Dicken, *Ancient Lake Modoc*, 1–9; L. Applegate, "Notes and Reminiscences," 24.

18. L. Applegate, "Notes and Reminiscences," 24–45.

19. Ridge, *Westward Journeys*, xxxvi.

20. R. Powers and Leiker, "Cholera among the Plains Indians"; Turner, *Years of Harvest*, 46; Boyd, *The Coming of the Spirit of Pestilence*, 145–64, describes a widespread measles epidemic in 1847; S. Powers, *Tribes of California*, 536, claims smallpox hit the Modocs that year, but historical epidemiologist Boyd dates the widespread outbreak of this disease later, to 1853; S. Powers, *Tribes of California*, 256; C. James, *Modoc*, 276–78.

21. Quoted in Robbins, *Landscapes of Promise*, 4.

22. Dunbar-Ortiz, *An Indigenous Peoples' History*, 6.

23. Lemkin, *Axis Rule in Occupied Europe*, 79.

24. Lemkin, *Axis Rule in Occupied Europe*, 80.

25. McDonnell and Moses, "Raphael Lemkin."

26. United Nations General Assembly Resolution 260 (III) of 9 December 1948.

27. Deur, *In the Footprints of Gmukamps*, 284, quotes an unpublished 1853 journal by Martha Ann Tuttle McClain on this tactic.

28. Murray, *The Modocs*, 18; Riddle, *Indian History*, 27.

29. Dillon, *Burnt-Out Fires*, 50; W. Thompson, *Reminiscences*, 77.

30. W. Thompson, *Reminiscences*, 78–79.

31. "Governor's Message," *Sacramento Transcript*, January 10, 1851.

32. Lindsay, *Murder State*; Madley, "California and Oregon's Modoc Indians," 97–98. See also Heizer, *They Were Only Diggers*, especially 23–57, on the extent of vigilante genocide in California's Indian "wars" of the 1850s.

33. Madley, *American Genocide*, 178: "As in some other genocides, war provided the context and the smokescreen for intentional mass murder. Thus, many have used California Indian resistance to camouflage the genocide with martial rhetoric."

34. Wright to Samuel Clark[e], March 9, 1888, in "Miscellaneous Ben Wright Information."

35. Thrapp, *Dictionary of Frontier Biography*, 3:1601; Wells, *History of Siskiyou County*, 126; Fisher, "Ben Wright," 3

36. Quoted in C. James, *Modoc*, 25–26; Wells, *History of Siskiyou County*, 129–30.

37. Wells, *History of Siskiyou County*, 23–126; Wells, "The Modocs in 1851."

38. Riddle, *Indian History*, 15–23.

39. Victor, "Knight of the Frontier."

40. "Verified Statement of W. T. Kershaw," 41–43.

41. Ross, "Narrative of an Indian Fighter," 25–26.

42. *Annual Report of the Commissioner of Indian Affairs, 1863*, 57–58.

43. "The Testimony of Another Eyewitness," *San Francisco Chronicle*, May 6, 1873.

44. C. James, *Modoc*, 4, gives thirty; the eyewitness Kershaw reports forty; Riddle, *Indian History*, 28–30, more or less agrees, citing only five survivors among a group of about fifty; Fisher and Doerr, "Outline of Events," set the number at eighty; W. Thompson, *Reminiscences*, 83, boosts the body count to ninety, based on a conversation he reported with Frank Riddle, Jeff Riddle's father. The disparity between the father's and son's numbers makes one doubt Thompson's accuracy, always a safe assumption.

45. Dillon, *Burnt-Out Fires*, 54.

46. Wells, *History of Siskiyou County*, 141–44; Madley, "California and Oregon's Modoc Indians," 110.

47. Evans, *History of the Pacific Northwest*, 449; Bancroft, *History of Oregon*, 391–94; Parrish, "Anecdotes," 81–83.

48. Victor, "Knight of the Frontier," 162.

49. Fagan, *History of Benton County*, 204; W. S. Brown, *California Northeast*, 25–31.

50. *Annual Report of the Commissioner of Indian Affairs, 1863*, 56–60.

51. Meacham, *Wigwam and War-path*, 299; W. Thompson, *Reminiscences*, 76–77.

52. Slotkin, *Regeneration through Violence*, especially 102–28 and 442–56.

53. Limerick, *Legacy of Conquest*, 37–41.

54. Hurtado, *Indian Survival*, 171–92.

55. See Smith, *Conquest*, 7–33.

56. Madley, "California and Oregon's Modoc Indians," 95, 117, and 119.

57. Meacham, *Wigwam and War-path*, 297.

5. The Peace That Wasn't

1. Steele to his unnamed brother, May 26, 1873, U.S. House of Representatives, *Official Copies of Correspondence*, 303–4; C. James, *Modoc*, 29.

2. Steele to Dole, March 2, 1864, in "The Modoc War: The 1864 Treaties."

3. Steele to Dole, March 2, 1864, in "The Modoc War: The 1864 Treaties." See also Murray, *The Modocs*, 36–37, and Dillon, *Burnt-Out Fires*, 57–59. Cothran offers the best analysis of the background to the treaty and the reasons for its failure in Washington in "The Valentine's Day Treaty," *New York Times*, February 14, 2014.

4. Mix to Huntington, June 22, 1864, in "The Modoc War: The 1864 Treaties."

5. Quoted in Dillon, *Burnt-Out Fires*, 64.

6. Huntington to Dole, *Annual Report of the Commissioner of Indian Affairs, 1865*, 101–5.

7. "Letter from the Acting Secretary," January 16, 1873, Fisher Papers, 11:1735.

8. *Statutes at Large*, 707–13; *Annual Report of the Commissioner of Indian Affairs, 1872*, 65; Deur, *In the Footsteps of Gmukamps*, 149–52.

9. *Annual Report of the Commissioner of Indian Affairs, 1867*, 91–93.

10. *Annual Report of the Commissioner of Indian Affairs, 1868*, 123–24.

11. *Annual Report of the Commissioner of Indian Affairs, 1868*, 123–24; Dillon, *Burnt-Out Fires*, 59–69; Murray, *The Modocs*, 38–42.

12. I. Applegate to Odeneal, May 8, 1872, Fisher Papers, 11:1691.

13. Meacham, *Wigwam and War-path*, 4.

14. Meacham, *Wigwam and War-path*, 12–13.

15. Meacham, *Wigwam and War-path*, 19.

16. Meacham, *Wigwam and War-path*, 22–23.

17. Meacham, *Wigwam and War-path*, 306–32.

18. *Annual Report of the Commissioner of Indian Affairs, 1870*, 54.

19. I. Applegate to Odeneal, May 8, 1872, Fisher Papers, 11:1691.

20. *Annual Report of the Commissioner of Indian Affairs, 1871*, 305–6.

6. Bacon of Three Hundred Hogs

1. Ridge, *Westward Journeys*, 3.

2. Baker, "Experience, Personality and Memory," 234–37.

3. W. H. Brown, *This Was a Man*, 9.

4. J. Applegate, "A Day with the Cow Column."

5. J. A. Applegate, "Recollections," in Ridge, *Westward Journeys*, 95–105. Jesse Applegate Applegate was Lindsay Applegate's son and Jesse Applegate's nephew.

6. W. H. Brown, *This Was a Man*, 22, 32.

7. W. H. Brown, *This Was a Man*, 25–27; LaLande, "'Dixie' of the Pacific Northwest," 50–52.

8. W. H. Brown, *This Was a Man*, 29

9. Baker, "Experience, Personality and Memory," 247–49.

10. S. Applegate, *Skookum*, 163.

11. Johnston, "Two Jesses," 5–21.

12. Baker, "Experience, Personality and Memory," 249.

13. "Wonderful Career of a 90 Year Old Cattle King," *San Francisco Call*, July 19, 1903.

14. Gates, *Land and Law in California*, 131–32.

15. "Wonderful Career of a 90 Year Old Cattle King," *San Francisco Call*, July 19, 1903.

16. Charles B. Hardin to William S. Brown, October 13, 1933. From a collection of letters by Modoc War veteran Hardin donated by the Brown family to Lava Beds National Monument in 1991. Hereinafter referred to as "Hardin Letters."

17. J. Applegate to Meacham, July 27, 1871, Fisher Papers, 1:40–45.

18. Jackson to Acting Assistant Adjutant General, August 29, 1871, Fisher Papers, 1:61–63.

19. W. L. Clarke, Enclosure No. 2, Fisher Papers, 1:99.

20. Petition to Governor Grover, January 29, 1872, Hagen, "Modoc War Official Correspondence," 71–72.

21. J. Applegate to Meacham, February 1, 1872, Fisher Papers, 1:128–32.

22. Petition to Meacham and Canby, January 25, 1872, Fisher Papers, 1:103–6.

23. Meacham to Canby, February 18, 1872, Fisher Papers, 1:131–34.

24. Odeneal, *The Modoc War*, 22–27; O. Applegate to Brother, May 15, 1872, Fisher Papers, 231; I. Applegate to Odeneal, May 16, 1872, Fisher Papers, 11:1693–95.

25. Odeneal to Walker, June 17, 1872, Fisher Papers, 2:248–51.

26. Walker to Odeneal, July 6, 1872, Fisher Papers, 11:1696–97.

27. Green to Assistant Adjutant General, October 5, 1872, Fisher Papers, 2:276–80.

7. Rancher to the Rescue

1. Rollin A. Fairchild, "Reminiscences"; C. James, *Modoc*, 67–68.

2. "Biography of John Fairchild," in Riddle, *Indian History*, 236–39.

3. De Tocqueville, *Democracy in America*, 374–75.

4. S. Powers, Fairchild biographical sketch.

5. Etter, "Effect of the California Gold Rush."

6. "Traveling in Modoc Land," *New York Times*, July 7, 1873.

7. C. James, *Modoc*, 55.

8. Quinn, *Hell with the Fire Out*, 62.

9. Green to Fairchild, December 4, 1872, Fisher Papers, 3:350–51.

10. McConnell to Caziaro, December 5, 1872, Fisher Papers, 3:356–57; Dyar to O. Applegate, December 20, 1873, Fisher Papers, 10:1672–73. See also Murray, *The Modocs*, 97–99, and C. James, *Modoc*, 98–99.

8. Glove and Fist

1. Caziaro to Officer, September 10, 1872, Fisher Papers, 2:271–72. Caziaro served as Canby's assistant adjutant general.

2. Wheaton to Assistant Adjutant General, November 14, 1872, Fisher Papers, 2:288–89.

3. Wheaton to Odeneal, November 29, 1872, Fisher Papers, 2:302–3.

4. Adams to Commanding Officer, December 1, 1872, Fisher Papers, 2:321–22.

5. Grover to Canby, December 2, 1872, Fisher Papers, 2:331–32.

6. Canby to Grover, December 3, 1872, Fisher Papers, 3:340–41.

7. Green to Canby, December 3, 1872, Fisher Papers, 2:333–34.

8. Quoted in Gwynne, *Empire of the Summer Moon*, 220.

9. Kelman, *A Misplaced Massacre*, 8–18, 22–29.

10. Coward, *Newspaper Indian*, 113–19.

11. Quoted in Fritz, "The Making of Grant's 'Peace Policy,'" 430.

12. Fritz, "The Making of Grant's 'Peace Policy,'" 431–32; Prucha, *Great Father*, 1:481–539.

13. "The Modoc War," *New York Times*, December 22, 1872.

14. Canby to Assistant Adjutant General, District of the Pacific, January 15, 1873, Fisher Papers, 4:516–18.

9. Modoc Steak for Breakfast

1. Ross to Grover, December 3, 1872, Fisher Papers, 3:337.

2. Wheaton to Canby, December 5, 1872, Fisher Papers, 3:359–60.

3. J. M. Schofield to Adjutant General, December 3, 1872, Fisher Papers, 3:353.

4. Wheaton to Bernard, December 3, 1872, Fisher Papers, 3:338–39.

5. E. N. Thompson, *Modoc War*, 168.

6. Pollock to Green, December 29, 1872, Fisher Papers, 3:467.

7. Pollock to Wheaton, December 17, 1872, Fisher Papers, 3:412–13.

8. Rickey, *Forty Miles a Day*, 99.

9. Wheaton to Canby, December 26, 1872, Fisher Papers, 3:456.

10. Rickey, *Forty Miles a Day*, especially 17–18, 34–35, 57–58, 97, 116–17, 128, and 143; Utley, *Frontier Regulars*, chapter 2.

11. Boyle, *Personal Observations*, 18.

12. Trimble, "The Kind of Country They Marched Over," 280–83.

13. Rickey, *Forty Miles a Day*, 128.

14. Adjutant E. D. Foudray to Adjutant General W. A. Owen, January 1, 1873, Fisher Papers, 3:477.

15. Wheaton to Canby, December 26, 1872, Fisher Papers, 3:457.

16. Murray, *The Modocs*, 107–8; "The Modoc War," *San Francisco Chronicle*, December 31, 1872.

17. "War's Wrinkled Front," December 11, 1872, and "The Indian War," December 12, 1872, *San Francisco Chronicle*.

18. Dillon, *Burnt-Out Fires*, 166–67.

19. Wheaton to Canby, December 26, 1872, Fisher Papers, 3:456.

20. O. Applegate, "The Last Conflict between the Races," 31–32, Applegate Papers.

21. Wheaton, General Field Order No. 1, December 20, 1872, Fisher Papers, 3:421.

22. Wheaton to Canby, January 15, 1873, in U.S. House of Representatives, *Official Copies of Correspondence*, 49–50.

23. Wheaton, General Field Order No. 3, January 12, 1873, Fisher Papers, 3:503.

24. Hardin, Letters, June 11, 1931.

25. W. Thompson, *Reminiscences*, 97.

26. Meacham, *Wigwam and War-path*, 386.

10. A Look Inside

1. Spier, *Prophet Dance*, 5–29.

2. La Barre, *Ghost Dance*, 227.

3. Nash, "The Place of Religious Revivalism," 415–16.

4. Deur, *In the Footsteps of Gmukamps*, 203.

5. Mooney, *Ghost-Dance Religion*, 1054.

6. Nash, "The Place of Religious Revivalism," 389–92.

7. Quoted in Solnit, *River of Shadows*, 108–9.

8. Nash, "The Place of Religious Revivalism," 393–95; C. James, *Modoc*, 73–75; Murray, *The Modocs*, 117–18.

9. E. N. Thompson, *Modoc War*, 29.

10. Waters, "Captain Jack's Stronghold," 156 and map.

11. First Fog of War

1. Meacham, *Wigwam and War-path*, 403.

2. Dillon, *Burnt-Out Fires*, 172.

3. "Later Particulars of the Fight with the Modocs," *Yreka Journal*, January 29, 1873.

4. O. Applegate to Ross, February 28, 1873, Fisher Papers, 4:664–67; Boyle, *Personal Observations*, 24–25.

5. Murray, *The Modocs*, 120–21; E. N. Thompson, *Modoc War*, 41.

6. "The Modocs," *New York Herald*, February 16, 1873.

7. W. Thompson, *Reminiscences*, 101; Murray, *The Modocs*, 124; C. James, *Modoc*, 82–83.

8. W. Thompson, *Reminiscences*, 104–5.

9. Murray, *The Modocs*, 126.

10. Bernard, report to Samuel Buck, adjutant general of Department of the Pacific, January 26, 1873, Fisher Papers, 4:589.

12. Celebration and Postmortem

1. Bernard to Buck, January 26, 1873, Fisher Papers, 4:589.

2. Meacham, *Wigwam and War-path*, 408–10.

3. Canby to Lieutenant E. W. Stone, January 20, 1873, Fisher Papers, 4:531.

4. Wheaton to Canby, January 19, 1873, Fisher Papers, 4:525–26.

5. O. Applegate to I. Applegate, January 13, 1873, Fisher Papers, 4:508.

6. O. Applegate to Ross, February 2, 1873, Fisher Papers, 4:661–68.

7. "Captain Kelly: Assessment of the Modoc Threat," *San Francisco Daily Examiner*, February 4, 1873; Coward and Campbell, *Greenwood Library*, 117.

8. Meacham, *Wigwam and War-path*, 411–12.

9. "Later Particulars of the Fight with the Modocs," *Yreka Journal*, January 29, 1873.

10. Arlington National Cemetery website, http://www.arlingtoncemetery.net/rfbernard.htm.

11. Bernard to Green, January 19, 1873, U.S. House of Representatives, *Official Copies of Correspondence*, 62–63.

12. C. James, *Modoc*, 87.

13. Bernard to Buck, January 26, 1873, Fisher Papers, 4:586–92. U.S. House of Representatives, *Official Copies of Correspondence*, includes Bernard's preliminary report of January 19 but not this longer meditation.

14. H. Clay Wood to Canby, February 14, 1873, Hagen, "Modoc War Official Correspondence," 628, forwarding Bernard's "most sensible and convincing letter . . . upon the Modoc question and situation. . . . [I] would like you to see it, before your final decision and action regarding the Modocs. It favors peace." Wood later recorded Chief Joseph's well-known "I will fight no more forever" speech during the Nez Perce campaign.

15. Wheaton to Canby, January 31, 1873, Fisher Papers, 4:651.

16. Canby to Gillem, January 29, 1873, Fisher Papers, 4:623–28.

13. Give Peace a Chance

1. "The Modoc War," *New York Times*, January 25, 1873.

2. Quoted in C. James, *Modoc*, 88.

3. Meacham, *Wigwam and War-path*, 419–21.

4. Sherman to Canby, January 30, 1873, U.S. House of Representatives, *Official Copies of Correspondence*, 64.

5. Canby to Sherman, January 30, 1873, U.S. House of Representatives, *Official Copies of Correspondence*, 64.

6. Sherman to Canby, January 31, 1873, U.S. House of Representatives, *Official Copies of Correspondence*, 65.

7. Delano to Acting Commissioner, January 31, 1873, Fisher Papers, 4:645–46.

8. *Oregonian*, February 28, 1873, quoted in Murray, *The Modocs*, 138.

9. Meacham, *Wigwam and War-path*, 421; Delano to Canby, February 5, 1873, Fisher Papers, 4:686.

10. J. Applegate to H. R. Clum, February 19, 1873, Fisher Papers, 5:777.

11. "The Modoc Blunder," *New York Herald*, March 26, 1873.

12. Clum to Meacham, February 5, 1873, Fisher Papers, 5:705.

13. Meacham, *Wigwam and War-path*, 413–14.

14. Wheaton to Assistant Adjutant General, February 5, 1873, Fisher Papers, 5:697–700.

14. The News That Fits

1. Coward, *Newspaper Indian*, 99–102; O'Connor, *Scandalous Mr. Bennett*, 16.

2. Knight, *Following the Indian Wars*, 108–9.

3. O'Connor, *Scandalous Mr. Bennett*, 52–64, 83; Seitz, *The Bennetts*, 264.

4. Coward, *Newspaper Indian*, 20, 38–39.

5. "The Modoc War," *New York Herald*, February 21, 1873.

6. "The Modoc Reds," *New York Herald*, March 8, 1873.

7. "Captain Jack's Band," *New York Herald*, February 27, 1873.

8. Copeland, *Greenwood Library*, 112–13; Knight, *Following the Indian Wars*, 106–10; Bill Dadd the Scribe, *Trans-Continental Railroad Guide*.

15. Reporter Dens with Lions

1. "The Modoc Murderers," *New York Herald*, February 17, 1873; Grover to Peace Commission, February 10, 1873, Fisher Papers, 5:750–53.

2. O. Applegate to L. Applegate, February 20, 1873, Fisher Papers, 789–90; O. Applegate to L. Applegate, February 26, 1873, Fisher Papers, 5:827–28.

3. "No Peace Yet," *New York Herald*, March 6, 1873.

4. "The Modoc Reds," *New York Herald*, March 8, 1873.

5. "Modoc War," *Daily Alta California*, February 17, 1873.

6. "Modoc War," *Daily Alta California*, February 19, 1873.

7. O. Applegate to L. Applegate, February 26, 1873, Fisher Papers, 5:827.

8. Canby to Colonel J. C. Kelton, assistant adjutant general, February 17, 1873, Fisher Papers, 5:772.

9. "The Modoc Reds," *New York Herald*, March 8, 1873.

10. "Rob Roy Mac-Modoc," *New York Herald*, March 17, 1873.

11. "The Modoc Reds," *New York Herald*, March 8, 1873.

12. Canby to Rosborough, February 24, 1873, Fisher Papers, 5:809–10.

13. "The Modoc Reds," *New York Herald*, March 8, 1873.

14. "Rob Roy Mac-Modoc," *New York Herald*, March 17, 1873.

15. "The Modoc Muddle," *New York Herald*, February 28, 1873.

16. "Rob Roy Mac-Modoc," *New York Herald*, March 17, 1873.

17. "The Modoc Muddle," *New York Herald*, February 28, 1873.

18. Quoted in Cothran, "Marketplaces of Remembering," 59.

16. Talking for Peace

1. Odeneal, *The Modoc War*, 50–56.

2. Canby to Sherman, March 2, 1873, Fisher Papers, 5:832.

3. Steele to his unnamed brother, May 26, 1873, U.S. House of Representatives, *Official Copies of Correspondence*, 308.

4. Meacham, *Wigwam and War-path*, 316–20, turned this tale of commerce into a romantic courtship.

5. Hurtado, *Indian Survival*, 186, 191–92.

6. O. Applegate, "Death of Frank Riddle," *Klamath Falls Express*, March 12, 1906, reprinted in Riddle, *Indian History*, 221–23.

7. Meacham, *Wigwam and War-path*, 428, italics in original.

8. "Letter from the Modoc War," *Sacramento Record*, March 8, 1873.

9. Meacham, *Wigwam and War-path*, 429, italics in original.

10. "The Modoc War," *Sacramento Record*, March 12, 1873; Fox, *New York Herald*, March 5, 1873, Cozzens, *Eyewitnesses*, 215–16 (Cozzens includes no original headlines in his collection). Meacham wrote (*Wigwam and War-path*, 429) that Frank Riddle would have nothing to do with this second mission, but let Toby go instead, trusting that Kientpoos would protect her as his cousin. Either Meacham had a faulty memory or he made this up. As will be seen later in this narrative, Meacham created various fictions to bathe Toby Riddle in heroic light.

11. "The Modoc War," *Sacramento Record*, March 12, 1873, from March 4 dispatch.

12. "The Modoc War," *Sacramento Record*, March 12, 1873, from March 5 dispatch.

13. Meacham to Clum, March 8, 1873, Fisher Papers, 6:875–76; "The Modoc Blunder," *New York Herald*, March 26, 1873.

14. "Capt. Jack Relents," *San Francisco Chronicle*, March 9, 1873.

15. Later in life, still penniless and now divorced, Blair resided on the Klamath Reservation. This sketchy picture emerges from census data for 1870, 1880, and 1890. Charles Blair of Linkville was made even more of a knave by the marked contrast with the other Charles Blair on the scene: a Siskiyou County cattleman who worked for Fairchild as ranch foreman. The good Charles Blair was a seasoned stock hand in his early thirties, worth some $1,500, and a native of Vermont.

16. Quoted in O. Applegate, "The Last Conflict between the Races," 9, Applegate Papers; Compton, "Kill the Chief," 175, cites a penciled note dated November 29, 1870, from the Oliver Applegate collection at the University of Oregon; Clarke to State of Oregon, January 3, 1872, Fisher Papers, 1:99.

17. J. Applegate to Clum, February 26, 1873, Fisher Papers, 5:821–22.

18. E. L. Applegate to I. and O. Applegate, March 7, 1873, Fisher Papers, 6:872.

19. Paullin, "A Half Century of Naval Administration," 1230–32; "Bogart's Case" and "Bogart in Court," *Daily Alta California*, March 23, 1873; "Pacific Coast Items," *Sacramento Daily Union*, December 25, 1873.

20. J. Applegate to Clum, March 9, 1873, Fisher Papers, 6:881–82.

21. Meacham to Delano, March 4, 1873, Fisher Papers, 5:842.

17. The Warrior Takes Command

1. Delano to Meacham, March 5, 1873, Fisher Papers, 5:848.

2. "No More of Peace," *San Francisco Chronicle*, March 12, 1873; Meacham, *Wigwam and War-path*, 433.

3. Sherman to Canby, March 14, 1873, Fisher Papers, 6:911; Delano to Meacham, March 13, 1873, Fisher Papers, 6:904; Delano to Odeneal, March 11, 1873, Fisher Papers, 5:885; Odeneal to Delano, March 12, 1873, Fisher Papers, 6:891.

4. O. P. Fitzgerald, *California Sketches*, 134–43; Delano to Meacham, March 18, 1873, Fisher Papers, 6:927; Sargent to Delano, March 18, 1873, Fisher Papers, 6:929.

5. Delano to Belknap, March 22, 1873, Fisher Papers, 6:953; Sherman to Canby, March 24, 1873, Fisher Papers, 6:982.

6. Heyman, *Prudent Soldier*, 47.

7. Heyman, *Prudent Soldier*, 59.

8. Heyman, *Prudent Soldier*, 117.

9. Enslavement of Indians, mostly Navahos, was a long-standing social ill in New Mexico that worsened during and after the Civil War. Canby, like most other Anglos in the territory, turned a blind eye to the practice and took advantage of it. See Reséndez, *The Other Slavery*, 266–94.

10. Heyman, *Prudent Soldier*, 117–36.

11. Heyman, *Prudent Soldier*, 144, 145, 150.

12. Sides, *Blood and Thunder*, 286–306; Heyman, *Prudent Soldier*, 137–87.

13. Message brought by Mary, March 6, 1873, Fisher Papers, 6:1015–18.

14. Canby to Sherman, March 7, 1873, Fisher Papers, 5:869.

15. Sherman to Canby, March 13, 1873, Fisher Papers, 5:896.

16. Message brought by Mary, March 6, 1873, Fisher Papers, 6:1017.

18. Squeeze Play

1. *New York Times*, June 10, 1873.

2. Quoted in Heyman, *Prudent Soldier*, 373–74.

3. Steele, U.S. House of Representatives, *Official Copies of Correspondence*, 307.

4. Canby to Sherman, January 30, 1873, Fisher Papers, 4:633; E. N. Thompson, *Modoc War*, 168; Canby to Wood, March 21, 1873, Fisher Papers, 6:942; Kelton to Canby, February 19, 1873, Fisher Papers, 5:782; Canby to Stone, January 30, 1873, Fisher Papers, 4:629; E. W. Stone to Assistant Adjutant General, January 31, 1873, Fisher Papers, 4:649.

5. "The Modoc Blunder," *New York Herald*, March 26, 1873.

6. Meacham, *Wigwam and War-path*, 437.

7. Meacham, *Wigwam and War-path*, 433.

8. Canby to Sherman, March 22, 1873, Fisher Papers, 6:947–48.

9. E. N. Thompson, *Modoc War*, 57.

10. On Cabaniss, see Cozzens, *Eyewitnesses*, 733n24.

11. Fox, *New York Herald*, April 7, 1873, Cozzens, *Eyewitnesses*, 229–33.

12. Canby to Gillem, March 22, 1873, Fisher Papers, 6:955–56, italics in original.

13. Canby to W. D. Whipple, assistant adjutant general, March 24, 1873, Fisher Papers, 6:1000–1001.

19. A Homeland to Be Named Later

1. Meacham, *Wigwam and War-path*, 440–42.

2. Meacham, *Wigwam and War-path*, 443–52, italics in original.

3. Canby to Whipple, April 7, 1873, Fisher Papers, 7:1044–45.

4. Riddle, *Indian History*, 77–79; Meacham, *Wigwam and War-path*, 452–53.

5. Riddle, *Indian History*, 81–83.

6. Meacham, *Wigwam and War-path*, 455–56. Meacham gave a different version of the Stronghold exchange, though to much the same effect, in *Wi-ne-ma*, 49–50.

20. Pride and Prejudice

1. Meacham, *Wigwam and War-path*, 462–63.

2. W. L. Elliott and H. P. Curtis, "Proceedings of a Military Commission at Fort Klamath," U.S. House of Representatives, *Official Copies of Correspondence*, 138–39.

3. Meacham, *Wi-ne-ma*, 52–53, and *Wigwam and War-path*, 463–64.

4. Meacham, *Wigwam and War-path*, 464–66, and *Wi-ne-ma*, 56.

5. Meacham named Curley Headed Doctor, Curley (Headed) Jack, and an anonymous someone he called "a Cumbatwas," one of the Modoc bands, in *Wigwam and War-path*, 466. Boyle, *Personal Observations*, 35–36, one of the assailants' targets, saw three

Modocs and named one of them Steamboat Frank, an impossibility since that Modoc was at the Peace Tent. Hathaway, Landrum, and Quinn hold that there were but two eastern ambushers, Curley Headed Jack and Miller's Charley; see Benterou et al., "The Fields of Battle Tour," 23.

6. Elliott and Curtis, "Proceedings," 139–40.

7. Elliott and Curtis, "Proceedings," 161.

8. Meacham, *Wigwam and War-path*, 468–69.

9. Elliott and Curtis, "Proceedings," 162.

10. Rollin Fairchild, born to John Fairchild seventeen years later, said the gun was his father's in "Reminiscences."

11. O. Applegate, "The Last Conflict between the Races," 37–38, Applegate Papers.

12. Meacham, *Wigwam and War-path*, 469–76.

13. See Heyman, *Prudent Soldier*, 85–92, for details on this 1853 tour.

14. Heyman, *Prudent Soldier*, 484–91, italics in original.

21. Martyrs at Midday

1. Boyle, *Personal Observations*, 36–37.

2. Fox, *New York Herald*, May 5, 1873, Cozzens, *Eyewitnesses*, 243.

3. Trimble, "The Killing of the Commissioners," 289.

4. "Massacre," *New York Herald*, April 13, 1873.

5. "The Death of Canby," *New York Herald*, May 5, 1873.

6. Meacham, *Wigwam and War-path*, 503–4.

7. "Base Treachery," *Sacramento Record*, April 14, 1873.

8. Fox, *New York Herald*, May 5, 1873, Cozzens, *Eyewitnesses*, 242.

9. *San Francisco Chronicle*, April 13, 1873, quoted in Knight, *Following the Indian Wars*, 143–44.

10. "Massacre," *New York Herald*, April 13, 1873.

11. "Massacre," *New York Herald*, April 13, 1873.

12. "The Modocs—Hooka Jim Interviewed by Our Special Correspondent," *Sacramento Record*, July 8, 1873. Also, Howard, Field Notes, October 29, 1928, reports that, according to Peter Schonchin, Ellen's Man shot Canby after Kientpoos's revolver misfired. Since no other eyewitness saw it this way, and since fifty-five years had passed by the time an elderly Schonchin spoke to Howard, it is likely that Ellen's Man fired the second round, as Hooker Jim told Atwell.

13. Elliott and Curtis, "Proceedings," 152.

14. Elliott and Curtis, "Proceedings," 142–43.

15. Elliott and Curtis, "Proceedings," 165–66.

16. Meacham, *Wigwam and War-path*, 508–9.

17. Meacham to Delano, April 16, 1873, Fisher Papers, 1062–63.

18. "Excitement in Yreka," *San Francisco Chronicle*, April 14, 1873.

19. Smith to Dyar, April 18,1873, U.S. House of Representatives, *Official Copies of Correspondence*, 288.

22. The War Goes Cosmic

1. While George Armstrong Custer of the Seventh Cavalry was often addressed as general, that was only his brevet rank. He was at the time of his death a lieutenant colonel in the Regular Army.

2. "The Modoc Victim: Obsequies of the Late Rev. Dr. Thomas," *Daily Alta California*, April 19, 1873; E. C. Thomas quoted in Dillon, *Burnt-Out Fires*, 249.

3. Whipple, General Order No. 3, April 14, 1873, U.S. House of Representatives, *Official Copies of Correspondence*, 77–78.

4. "Secretary Delano Hung in Effigy," *Sacramento Record*, April 14, 1873.

5. "The Late Gen. Canby," *New York Times*, May 3, 1873; Heyman, *Prudent Soldier*, 380–83; Cothran, "Marketplaces of Remembering," 65–66.

6. "Massacre," *New York Herald*, April 13, 1873.

7. Juergensmeyer, *Terror in the Mind of God*, especially 145–63, and "Performance Violence"; Aslan, *How to Win a Cosmic War*, 5–6.

8. "Captain Jack's Band," *New York Herald*, February 27, 1873; "In the Modoc Camp," *New York Herald*, February 28, 1873; "The Modoc Peacemakers," *New York Herald*, March 1, 1873.

9. "The Modoc Blunder," *New York Herald*, March 26, 1873; "The Lava Beds," *New York Herald*, April 7, 1873; "The Death of Canby," *New York Herald*, May 5, 1873.

10. "The Dogs of War Let Loose," *Daily Alta California*, April 14, 1873.

11. "The Eternal Savage," *Daily Alta California*, April 24, 1873.

12. "The Modocs," *Harper's Weekly*, May 3, 1873, 364.

13. "The Modoc Murders," *New York Times*, April 13, 1873.

14. Quoted in Heyman, *Prudent Soldier*, 378.

15. I. Applegate to O. Applegate, April 13, 1873, Fisher Papers, 7:1059.

16. "The Death of Canby," *New York Herald*, May 5, 1873

17. Riddle, *Indian History*, 83n1.

18. A. Hamilton to Secretary of the Interior, April 17, 1873, Fisher Papers, 7:1067.

19. "An Embalmer's Speculation," *Daily Alta California*, April 16, 1873.

20. Sherman to Gillem, April 12, 1873, reprinted in "The Modoc War," *New York Times*, April 15, 1873.

21. Townsend to J. C. Davis, April 14, 1873, U.S. House of Representatives, *Official Copies of Correspondence*, 78.

23. Girding for Battle

1. Hughes and Whitney, *Jefferson Davis in Blue*, 6–21.

2. Hughes and Whitney, *Jefferson Davis in Blue*, 100–126; "General Jeff C. Davis Dead," *New York Times*, December 2, 1879.

3. Churchill, "Betrayal at Ebenezer Creek"; Hughes and Whitney, *Jefferson Davis in Blue*, 304–14.

4. Schofield to Sherman, April 12, 1873, U.S. House of Representatives, *Official Copies of Correspondence*, 76.

5. Murray, *The Modocs*, 130; Cullum, "Alvan C. Gillem," 443–49.

6. Meacham, *Wigwam and War-path*, 457–58, italics in original.

7. Caziaro to Canby, April 4, 1873, Fisher Papers, 7:1032.

8. Pentz, "Modoc War Journal," 9.

9. Meacham, *Wigwam and War-path*, 517, italics in original.

10. Meacham, *Wigwam and War-path*, 519.

11. M. Fitzgerald, "The Modoc War," 125–26.

24. Half-Empty Victory

1. Benterou et al., "The Fields of Battle Tour," 24.

2. "Retribution," *New York Herald*, April 19, 1873.

3. Meacham, *Wigwam and War-path*, 523.

4. "Retribution," *New York Herald*, April 19, 1873.

5. Gillem to Assistant Adjutant General, June 1, 1874, Fisher Papers, 10:1524–66, quotation on 1540.

6. Phillips, "List of Wounded," June 13, 1873, Fisher Papers, 7:1172–85.

7. M. Fitzgerald, "The Modoc War," 128–29.

8. Benterou et al., "The Fields of Battle Tour," 29–30.

9. Riddle, *Indian History*, 110.

10. Gillem to Assistant Adjutant General, June 1, 1874, Fisher Papers, 10:1543.

11. Gillem to Assistant Adjutant General, June 1, 1874, Fisher Papers, 10:1545.

12. Waters, "Captain Jack's Stronghold," 156, 158.

13. "The Lava Bed Battle," *New York Herald*, May 7, 1873.

14. Pentz, "Modoc War Journal," 18–20; "The Lava Bed Battle," *New York Herald*, May 7, 1873.

15. M. Fitzgerald, "The Modoc War," 129–30. Cozzens identified the unnamed lieutenant who ordered the old woman shot as George R. Bacon, who was as the company officer of Fitzgerald's cavalry troop.

16. "The Lava Bed Battle," *New York Herald*, May 7, 1873.

17. Gillem to Assistant Adjutant General, June 1, 1874, Fisher Papers, 10:1546–47.

18. *Army and Navy Journal* cited by E. N. Thompson, *Modoc War*, 75; Riddle, *Indian History*, 110–11, puts the death toll on the capture of the Stronghold as one man maimed from the January battle plus four old people, one of them the mother of the maimed man; Boyle, *Personal Observations*, 44–45, set the number of old people at two women and one man, and the number of dead fighters at three, including the two beheaded by the hangfire mortar shell; Simpson, *Meeting the Sun*, 376–77, says four bodies were found plus one wounded man and two old women; Meacham, *Wigwam and War-path*, 541, places only one old man in the Stronghold at the time of its capture.

25. Scalps and Skulls

1. Riddle, *Indian History*, 102–7.

2. Meacham, *Wigwam and War-path*, 541.

3. Quoted in Bieder, *Brief Historical Survey*, 36–37.

4. Quoted in Bieder, *Brief Historical Survey*, 39–40.

5. Quoted in Bieder, *Brief Historical Survey*, 50.

6. United States Army Medical Museum, Anatomical Section, "Records"; Juzda, "Skulls, Science, and the Spoils of War."

7. Knight, *Following the Indian Wars*, xvi.

8. Harrington, "The First True War Artist."

9. Simpson, *Meeting the Sun*, facing p. 364.

10. Simpson, *Meeting the Sun*, 371.

11. Simpson, *Meeting the Sun*, 373.

12. Simpson, *Meeting the Sun*, 380.

13. Simpson, *Meeting the Sun*, 298.

14. "The Modocs—Murder of General Canby," *Harper's Weekly*, June 28, 1873, 548; Simpson, *Meeting the Sun*, facing p. 356.

15. "The Modocs," *New York Herald*, April 29, 1873.

16. Lipscomb, "William Simpson." Lipscomb is Simpson's great-grandson.

17. Simpson, *Meeting the Sun*, 381.

18. Lipscomb, "William Simpson."

26. Volcanic Valley of Death

1. M. Fitzgerald, "The Modoc War," 131.

2. McElderry, "List of Wounded," Fisher Papers, 7:1093–96; Pentz, "Modoc War Journal," 27–32; Boyle, *Personal Observations*, 47–48.

3. Boyle, *Personal Observations*, 50.

4. Green to Assistant Adjutant General, June 22, 1873, Fisher Papers, 9:1374.

5. Murray, *The Modocs*, 224; E. N. Thompson, *Modoc War*, 83.

6. Green to Assistant Adjutant General, Fisher Papers, 9:1374.

7. Raines, *Getting the Message Through*, 13–16.

8. Murray, *The Modocs*, 226; E. N. Thompson, *Modoc War*, 83.

9. Gillem to Assistant Adjutant General, June 1, 1874, Fisher Papers, 10:1551–52; Pentz, "Modoc War Journal," 35–52.

10. Murray, *The Modocs*, 226–28.

11. E. N. Thompson, *Modoc War*, map 7.

12. Green to Assistant Adjutant General, June 1, 1874, Fisher Papers, 10:1552–53.

13. Pentz, "Modoc War Journal," 35–52.

14. Green to Assistant Adjutant General, June 22, 1873, Fisher Papers, 9:1375–76.

15. Boutelle, "The Disaster to Thomas' Command," 307.

16. "Particulars of the Reconnoissance and Ambuscade," *Daily Alta California*, April 30, 1873.

17. Hardin, Letters, February 1 and December 19, 1929. In the 1930s Sand Butte was renamed for Hardin, who careered in the army after the Modoc War and retired as an officer; see Hardin, Letters, February 26, 1934.

18. Boutelle, "The Disaster to Thomas' Command," 307, 309.

19. Trimble, "Carrying a Stretcher," 314.

20. Pentz, "Modoc War Journal," 35–52; Hardin, Letters, December 19, 1929.

21. McElderry to Green, June 30, 1873, Fisher Papers, 9:1420–21; Pentz, "Modoc War Journal," 35–52.

22. Boutelle, "The Disaster to Thomas' Command," 309–10.

23. Trimble, "Carrying a Stretcher," 310.

24. Trimble, "Carrying a Stretcher," 315–17.

25. Boutelle, "The Disaster to Thomas' Command," 311.

26. These numbers and the details on specific injuries are taken from Henry McElderry, "List of Wounded in Major Thomas' Command," October 5, 1873, and H. J. Phillips, "List of the Wounded in the Troops Operating against the Modoc Indians," June 13, 1873, Fisher Papers, 7:1108–15 and 7:1172–85.

27. Riddle (*Indian History*, 113–19) told of the killing at Sand Butte of the Modoc Kankush, or Little Ike, by a badly wounded soldier named Jim Ross, who died later in the Gillem Camp hospital after losing all four limbs to amputation. It is a vivid tale, and wrong. Riddle, who worked from memory some forty years after the war he had witnessed as a ten-year-old, confused something with something else. Kan-kush was photographed very much alive by Louis Heller in early June, almost six weeks after Sand Butte, and no report of military casualties from the Modoc War lists a Jim Ross. The closest is James Rose; this private in the Fourth Artillery died on the Sand Butte battlefield.

28. Davis to Assistant Adjutant General, Division of the Pacific, May 4, 1873, Fisher Papers, 7:1151–53.

29. Green to Assistant Adjutant General, District of the Lakes, May 4, 1873, Fisher Papers, 9:1376.

30. M. P. Miller to W. H. Winters, June 22, 1873, Fisher Papers, 9:1392.

31. Meacham, *Wigwam and War-path*, 572, italics in original.

27. The Center Cannot Hold

1. W. S. Brown, *California Northeast*, 43–44; Dillon, *Burnt-Out Fires*, 48.

2. "General Notes," *New York Times*, May 28, 1873.

3. "The Last Massacre," *Daily Alta California*, April 30, 1873.

4. "The Modoc Misery," *New York Herald*, June 2, 1873.

5. Schofield to Davis, April 30, 1873, Fisher Papers, 1127.

6. Hamont, "The Modoc Indian War," 267; Schofield to Davis, May 2, 1873, Fisher Papers, 3:1141; Schofield to Davis, May 6, 1873, Fisher Papers, 3:1157.

7. Wheaton to Assistant Adjutant General, May 11, 1873, Fisher Papers, 8:1186–87; Summer, Special Orders No. 59a, May 21, 1873, Fisher Papers, 8:1212–13.

8. Davis to Assistant Adjutant General, May 8, 1873, Fisher Papers, 7:1164; "The Modoc Misery," *New York Herald*, June 2, 1873; Howard, Field Notes, September 5, 1924, gives Peter Schonchin as the source.

9. Howard, Field Notes, October 29, 1928, again from Peter Schonchin.

10. Hasbrouck, "The Last Fight," 321–22.

11. Hardin, "'Gosh Dash It, Let's Charge,'" 277–79. As the title indicates, Hardin cleaned up the profane reality of an Irish sergeant's outburst under deadly fire to suit the sensibilities of his audience.

12. Hardin, Letters, July 3, 1935; Pentz, "Modoc War Journal," 58. According to Howard, Field Notes, September 5, 1924, Peter Schonchin said that Ellen's Man, with Canby's watch and $350 in gold coin still in his pockets, was cremated. Howard claimed later that the treasure remained to be discovered; see letter to Gudde, October 2, 1957, in Field Notes.

13. "Medal of Honor to Maj. John O. Skinner" (Skinner received the honor, forty-two years after the fact, for rescuing a wounded soldier under fire and getting him to safety during the First Battle of the Stronghold); Phillips, "List of the Wounded," Fisher Papers, 7:1182–84.

14. Hasbrouck, "The Last Fight," 321–22.

15. Davis to Schofield, November 1, 1873, U.S. House of Representatives, *Official Copies of Correspondence*, 109.

16. Ray, *Primitive Pragmatists*, 134–45; Bunker, "In the Lava Beds," 161; "Capt. Hasbrouck's Brilliant Pursuit and Fight," *New York Times*, May 23, 1873.

17. Hasbrouck, "The Last Fight," 322–23. Hardin (Letters, March 16, 1934) gives a different account. He maintains that he was part of an unauthorized patrol that spotted diversionary fires set by the Modocs, slipped into the lava, and discovered the Indians gone.

18. Mason to Acting Assistant Adjutant General, June 10, 1873, Fisher Papers, 8:1296–98.

19. Davis to Schofield, November 1, 1873, U.S. House of Representatives, *Official Copies of Correspondence*, 109.

20. Hasbrouck, "The Last Fight," 323–25.

21. Bunker, "In the Lava Beds," 162.

22. "The Modoc Misery," *New York Herald*, June 2, 1873. The tale that Hooker Jim hid in the brush until the other Hot Creeks surrendered, then appeared to hand his rifle over to Davis is fiction, although it is given in Murray, *The Modocs*, 261, and Dillon, *Burnt-Out Fires*, 291, who likely took it from W. Thompson, *Reminiscences*, 120–21. Atwell and Bunker recounted no such incident, simply listing Hooker Jim among the Hot Creek men. Had such an unusual drama unfolded before their eyes, surely these two newshounds would have reported it.

28. Hounds and Scouts

1. Davis to Schofield, November 1, 1873, U.S. House of Representatives, *Official Copies of Correspondence*, 110.

2. Campbell, "The Seminoles."

3. Bunker, "In the Lava Beds," 163.

4. Bunker, "In the Lava Beds," 165–66.

5. "Capt. Jack: Details of the Movements Resulting in His Capture—His Stoicism," *New York Times*, June 17, 1873.

6. "Ending the Modoc War," *New York Herald*, June 16, 1873.

7. "Capt. Jack. Details of the Movements Resulting in His Capture—His Stoicism," *New York Times*, June 17, 1873; Davis to Assistant Adjutant General, June 1, 1873, Fisher Papers, 8:1249.

8. "The Modocs," *New York Herald*, June 23, 1873. Photographer Louis Heller later took a portrait of McKay and two unnamed Warm Springs scouts (plate 17 in Peter Palmquist, "Imagemakers of the Modoc War") identified by the caption as "Jack's capturers." The image was signed off by Colonel Davis, although it is unclear whether he approved the caption. Two Modoc War enlisted men, Hardin (Letters, December 26, 1930) and Pentz ("Modoc War Journal," 73), also attributed the capture to Warm Springs scouts. Trimble wrote three chapters about the war for Brady, *Northwestern Fights and Fighters*, and in none of them did he say he took Kientpoos's surrender. Long after the fact, McKay tried to claim credit for the capture and the $10,000 reward he maintained Canby promised for the feat; see Clark and Clark, *Daring Donald McKay*, xii, 108. That was but one of many tall tales McKay spun.

9. "Capt. Jack. Details of the Movements Resulting in His Capture—His Stoicism," *New York Times*, June 17, 1873; Davis to Schofield, November 1, 1873, U.S. House of Representatives, *Official Copies of Correspondence*, 111, does not name Trimble, reporting that Kientpoos surrendered to "troopers" and "said his 'legs had given out.'"

10. "Capt. Jack Caught: End of the Modoc War," *New York Times*, June 3, 1873; "Capt. Jack: Details of the Movements Resulting in His Capture—His Stoicism," *New York Times*, June 17, 1873.

29. Hang 'em High

1. Dillon, *Burnt-Out Fires*, 302–3.

2. W. Thompson, *Reminiscences*, 126.

3. "The Modocs," *New York Herald*, June 23, 1873.

4. W. Thompson, *Reminiscences*, 128.

5. Davis to Wood, June 1, 1873, Fisher Papers, 8:1250.

6. Sherman and Schofield to Davis, June 3, 1873, Fisher Papers, 8:1255.

7. Sherman to Belknap, June 3, 1873, U.S. House of Representatives, *Official Copies of Correspondence*, 84–85.

8. Sherman to Sheridan, June 5, 1873, quoted in Hughes and Whitney, *Jefferson Davis in Blue*, 412, and Utley, *Frontier Regulars*, 205.

9. Grover to Belknap, June 4, 1873, U.S. House of Representatives, *Official Copies of Correspondence*, 87.

10. Davis, "Observations on the Modoc War," 280–82.

11. Davis to Wood, June 5, 1873, Fisher Papers, 8:1259.

12. Schofield to Sherman, June 5, 1873, U.S. House of Representatives, *Official Copies of Correspondence*, 86; W. Thompson, *Reminiscences*, 127.

13. Davis to H. Clay Wood, June 5, 1873, Fisher Papers, 8:1260.

14. Davis, "Observations on the Modoc War," 282.

15. C. James, *Modoc*, 151; E. P. Curtis to Secretary of the Interior, June 19, 1873, Fisher Papers, 8:1345.

16. "Modoc Indians Murdered," June 9, 1873, Fisher Papers, 8:1306–9.

17. "The Modocs," *New York Herald*, June 23, 1873, Cozzens, *Eyewitnesses*, 295.

18. Hardin, Letters, October 14, 1932.

19. Dyar to Odeneal, June 18, 1873, Fisher Papers, 8:1335–36.

20. Davis made this arrangement clear: "Oregon Volunteers were in the field and were occupying the country along the border for the protection of the citizens of the State. They never reported to me for duty and I assumed no Command over them." Davis to Adjutant General of the Army, September 11, 1873, Fisher Papers, 8:1224–25.

21. Davis to Schofield, November 1, 1873, U.S. House of Representatives, *Official Copies of Correspondence*, 105–13.

22. Foster, "Imperfect Justice," 274, cites the *Yreka Journal*, June 18, 1873.

23. The exact number of Modoc prisoners hauled north is slippery. The first detailed census at Fort Klamath dates to October 5, over three months later, and gives a total of 161, yet this accounting does not jibe with the number of Indians later executed, imprisoned, or sent into exile. See Hasbrouck to Breck, November 5, 1873, U.S. House of Representatives, *Official Copies of Correspondence*, 102, and "List of Modoc Prisoners of War," October 5, 1873, Fisher Papers, 10:1632–39.

24. Quinn, *Hell with the Fire Out*, 181.

25. Riddle, *Indian History*, 156–58.

26. Landrum, *Guardhouse*, map II; Boutelle to Green, June 11, 1873, Fisher Papers, 8:1316–17.

27. Landrum, *Guardhouse*, 65; Murray, *The Modocs*, 283.

30. Varnishing Vengeance

1. Herbert, "Explaining the Sioux Military Commission of 1862," 754–57; Lansing, *Juggernaut*; Kluger, *Bitter Waters of Medicine Creek*; Chomsky, "The United States–Dakota War Trials," 81.

2. Siskiyou County, in fact, issued an arrest warrant for the Modoc leaders on murder charges shortly after they were captured. Nothing came of it. See "Object Lessons: Captain Jack Arrest Warrant," *Herald and News*, July 18, 2014.

3. Glazier, "Precedents Lost"; Witt, *Lincoln's Code*, 330–35.

4. Sibley quoted in Herbert, "Explaining the Sioux Military Commission of 1862," 773. For a complete history of the Dakota War, see Berg, *38 Nooses*.

5. Herbert, "Explaining the Sioux Military Commission of 1862," 771–83.

6. Chomsky, "The United States–Dakota War Trials," 71–86.

7. Williams's argument was cited in John Yoo's infamous memo to the George W. Bush administration justifying the torture of suspected terrorists. See Cothran, *Remembering the Modoc War*, 76–78.

8. Witt, *Lincoln's Code*, 334–35.

9. Williams to the President, June 7, 1873, U.S. House of Representatives, *Official Copies of Correspondence*, 88–90; Curtis to Schofield, June 7, 1873, Fisher Papers, 8:1263–74.

10. Schofield to Davis, June 9, 1873, Fisher Papers, 8:1303; Glazier, "Precedents Lost."

11. Chomsky, "The United States–Dakota War Trials," 56–57.

12. The "spirit" of Article 65 became an issue in a second round of Dakota War trials, where the commanding field office brought charges against Indians he had fought; see Chomsky, "The United States–Dakota War Trials," 42–43.

13. Davis, Special Field Orders No. 1, June 30, 1873, Fisher Papers, 9:1408–9.

14. Davis to Curtis, June 30, 1873, Fisher Papers, 9:1425–26.; Townsend to Schofield, June 30, 1873, Fisher Papers, 9:1428.

15. Curtis to J. C. Kelton, July 8, 1873, U.S. House of Representatives, *Official Copies of Correspondence*, 93.

16. California Genealogy, http://www.rootsweb.ancestry.com/~cagha/biographies /state/senate1878.txt, August 20, 2016; Bancroft, *History of California*, 328.

17. "The Modoc Trials," *New York Times*, July 23, 1873; Meacham, *Wigwam and War-path*, 607–8.

18. Elliott and Curtis, "Proceedings," 134. The trial transcript is reprinted in Landrum, *Guardhouse*, 84–135.

19. Foster, "Imperfect Justice," 258–60. Curtis's duty to stand as counsel for the Modocs was no secret; see "The Modocs—Trial at Fort Klamath," *Sacramento Record*, July 12, 1873.

20. Elliott and Curtis, "Proceedings," 134. Dyar's name was misspelled as Dyer.

21. Elliott and Curtis, "Proceedings," 136–44.

22. Elliott and Curtis, "Proceedings," 144–47.

23. Elliott and Curtis, "Proceedings," 147–53.

24. Elliott and Curtis, "Proceedings," 154–57.

25. Elliott and Curtis, "Proceedings," 157–66.

26. Ray, *Primitive Pragmatists*, 10–11. See Torres and Milun, "Translating Yonnondio," 645–47, on differing systems of narrative and evidence in a courtroom setting. Jacoby, *Shadows at Dawn*, details the differing narratives of the 1871 Camp Grant massacre told by the four ethnic groups involved.

27. Elliott and Curtis, "Proceedings," 172–76.

28. Elliott and Curtis, "Proceedings," 177.

29. Foster, "Imperfect Justice," 259–60; Chomsky, "The United States–Dakota War Trials," 52–53.

30. Elliott and Curtis, "Proceedings," 178–81. Curtis used both Jackson's brevet rank of major and his regular-army rank of captain.

31. Curtis to Schofield, June 7, 1873, Fisher Papers, 8:1273. In point of fact, Meacham was no doctor of any kind.

32. Williams to the President, June 7, 1873, U.S. House of Representatives, *Official Copies of Correspondence*, 90.

33. Ray, *Primitive Pragmatists*, 134–45.

34. "The Modocs," *New York Times*, June 18, 1873; quoted in C. James, *Modoc*, 163.

35. Elliott and Curtis, "Proceedings," 181–83.

31. Still Small Voices Swell

1. Curtis to Davis, July 9, 1873, Fisher Papers, 9:1447–48.

2. Davis, July 29, 1873, U.S. House of Representatives, *Official Copies of Correspondence*, 183.

3. "The Modocs—Trial at Fort Klamath," *Sacramento Record*, July 12, 1873.

4. Steele, Morgan, Fairchild, and Atwell to Delano, July 30, 1873, Fisher Papers, 9:1468–69.

5. Atwell to Delano, July 30, 1873, Fisher Papers, 9:1471–72.

6. Luttrell to Delano, June 17, 1873, Fisher Papers, 8:1332–34, italics in original.

7. Luttrell to Elliot, Mendenhall, Hasbrouck, Pollock, Curtis, and Kingsbury, July 1, 1873, Fisher Papers, 9:1437–38.

8. Editorial, *New York Times*, July 12, 1873.

9. Beeson to Grant, July 18, 1873, Fisher Papers, 9:1475–82.

10. "Indian Affairs," *New York Star*, July 23, 1873, in U.S. House of Representatives, *Official Copies of Correspondence*, 317–22, and Fisher Papers, 9:1461–64.

11. T. Townsend, "Lo, the Poor Indian," August 8, 1872, Fisher Papers, 9:1509–16.

12. Bell, *Secretaries of War and Army*.

13. Holt to Belknap, August 12, 1873, U.S. House of Representatives, *Official Copies of Correspondence*, 191–96.

14. U.S. Adjutant General's Office, General Court-Martial Orders No. 32, August 23, 1873, Fisher Papers, 11:1764–70.

15. Love, Mott, Chapman, Child, and Schofield to the President, July 12, 1873, Fisher Papers, 1451–58.

16. John M. Spear to the President, July 30, 1873, Fisher Papers, 9:1492–94.

17. Love to Delano, August 2, 1873, Fisher Papers, 9:1485–86.

18. Wagner, "Untold Story."

19. Cromwell, *Lucretia Mott*, 202–3.

32. Strangled Necks, Severed Heads

1. Curtis to Schofield, September 2, 1873, U.S. House of Representatives, *Official Copies of Correspondence*, 198–99.

2. General Court-Martial Orders No. 34, September 12, 1873, U.S. House of Representatives, *Official Copies of Correspondence*, 203.

3. Townsend to Schofield, September 22, 1873, Fisher Papers, 10:1614.

4. "Retribution! Execution of the Modoc Assassins," *San Francisco Chronicle*, October 4, 1873; Landrum, *Guardhouse*, photo no. 185.

5. "The Modocs," *San Francisco Chronicle*, dispatched October 2, 1873, in Landrum, *Guardhouse*, 64; "Execution of the Modocs," *Daily Alta California*, October 4, 1873.

6. "The Modocs," *Sacramento Record*, October 6, 1873.

7. "The Modocs," in Landrum, *Guardhouse*, 62–70.

8. Case, Diary, entries for September 20–October 1, 1873.

9. "Retribution! Execution of the Modoc Assassins," *San Francisco Chronicle*, October 4, 1873.

10. Significantly, neither Shaw nor Meacham in his later retelling of this incident reported Slolux's accusation of Toby Riddle. It does appear, however, in Case's and Atwell's

accounts. Meacham, as will be seen in the following chapter, invented or omitted details as needed to make Riddle appear both princess and saint. Why Shaw played the same game in this instance is unknown.

11. Wheaton to Assistant Adjutant General, September 30, 1873, Fisher Papers, 10:1621.

12. Case, Diary, October 2, 1873.

13. "Retribution! Execution of the Modoc Assassins," *San Francisco Chronicle*, October 4, 1873; Meacham, *Wigwam and War-path*, 637–45.

14. "The Modocs," *Sacramento Record*, October 6, 1873.

15. Knight, *Following the Indian Wars*, 154–55.

16. "The Modocs," in Landrum, *Guardhouse*, 63.

17. Cothran, "Marketplaces of Remembering," 7.

18. Rao, "Hanging."

19. Haughton, "On Hanging."

20. R. James and Nasmyth-Jones, "The Occurrence of Cervical Fractures."

21. Ray, *Primitive Pragmatists*, 24.

22. Case, Diary, October 3, 1873. However, "The Dead Modocs," *San Francisco Chronicle*, October 5, 1873, reports that Lieutenant Taylor, the officer of the day, through Scarface Charley, told Barncho and Slolux of their reprieve at 1 a.m. It is unclear why the two accounts differ.

23. Case, Diary, October 3, 1873.

24. Case, Diary, October 3, 1873.

25. "The Modocs," in Landrum, *Guardhouse*, 70–74; Landrum's map IV details the arrangement of troops and spectators based on the newspaper account; "The Modocs Executed," *New York Times*, October 3, 1873.

26. Knight, *Following the Indian Wars*, 155; Case, Diary, October 3, 1873.

27. Allen et al., *Without Sanctuary*; Case, Diary, October 3, 1873; "Second Dispatch: After the Hanging," *San Francisco Daily Morning Call*, October 5, 1873; "The Identical Ropes," *Yreka Journal*, January 7, 1874; Dillon, *Burnt-Out Fires*, 333; Cothran, "Marketplaces of Remembering," 11; Meacham, *Wigwam and War-path*, 649.

28. Bieder, *Brief Historical Survey*, 42, 69; C. James, *Modoc*, 257.

33. Exile and Showbiz

1. Grover to Davis, October 4, 1873, Fisher Papers, 1627, italics in original; Wheaton to Davis, October 8, 1873, Fisher Papers, 1660; Davis to Wheaton, October 9, 1873, Fisher Papers, 1662.

2. "The Modocs: They Leave Redding, by Railroad, for Their New Home in Wyoming Territory," *San Francisco Daily Morning Call*, October 24, 1873.

3. Hasbrouck to Breck, November 5, 1873, U.S. House of Representatives, *Official Copies of Correspondence*, 102. This number is two shy of a pre-hanging accounting of Modocs at Fort Klamath that came up with a total of 161 ("List of Modoc Prisoners of War," October 5, 1873, Fisher Papers, 10:1632–39). With four hanged and two sent to Alcatraz, the number of Modocs leaving Fort Klamath should have been 155 if the original count was correct. Apparently it was not.

4. "The Modoc Exiles," *Daily Alta California*, October 26, 1873.

5. Sheridan to Sherman, October 2, 1873, U.S. House of Representatives, *Official Copies of Correspondence*, 100; Hasbrouck to Breck, November 5, 1873, U.S. House of Representatives, *Official Copies of Correspondence*, 102.

6. Martin, "A History of the Modocs Indians," 421–27.

7. "The Modocs," *San Francisco Chronicle*, October 3, 1873.

8. "New Publications," *New York Times*, October 24, 1875.

9. Oregon State University historian John B. Horner said that Jeff Riddle had told him his mother's Modoc name was Dus-wha-re-le and that Meacham was mistaken in choosing "Winema"; Horner to O. Applegate, March 16, 1925, Applegate Papers.

10. Miller, "The Tale of the Tall Alcalde."

11. Meacham, *Wi-ne-ma*, 20–21, 31–37.

12. "The Modocs," *Daily Alta California*, October 3, 1873.

13. H. Wallace Atwell, "The Modoc War," *Sacramento Record*, April 16, 1873.

14. Meacham, *Wigwam and War-path*, 499–500.

15. Meacham, *Wi-ne-ma*, 61–64.

16. "Base Treachery," *Sacramento Record*, April 14, 1873; *New York Herald*, April 13, 1873, Cozzens, *Eyewitnesses*, 234–36. In a longer follow-up story, Fox added the details that Toby scared off Boston Charley by calling out "The soldiers are coming!" and that she accompanied Meacham on a stretcher back to camp crying incessantly and repeating, "Why would they not believe me?" He does not say whether the details came from Meacham or from Riddle. See "The Death of Canby," *New York Herald*, May 5, 1873.

17. M. Fitzgerald, "The Modoc War," 124.

18. Toby apparently was active partner in this fabrication. Her son Jeff's account of Good Friday contains another version of Meacham's invention, likely passed on by his mother; Riddle, *Indian History*, 93–98. In "Marketplaces of Remembering," 128, Cothran writes: "Although the illiterate Toby did not actively collaborate in the writing of the novel [*Wi-ne-ma*], she nonetheless embraced this mythological presentation of her life. . . . [S]he was unconstrained in her subsequent self-representation as a latter-day Pocahontas."

19. "Mr. Meacham and the Modocs," *Sacramento Record*, February 2, 1875. Meacham quoted this review in its entirety in *Wi-ne-ma*, 92–93, but he changed Jeff Riddle's name to Charka and Toby's to Winema. Meacham was market-testing his casting before he used the Indian names, further evidence of how he shaped the facts to his preferred narrative.

20. Meacham, *Wi-ne-ma*, 12–16, 90–102.

21. Bland, *Life of Alfred B. Meacham*, 8–13.

22. Riddle, *Indian History*, 220.

23. Quoted in Cothran, "Marketplaces of Remembering," 99–100.

24. Riddle, *Indian History*, 235.

25. Martin, "A History of the Modoc Indians," 435, 439–40; Hurtado, "The Modocs," 105–6.

26. Curtin, *Myths of the Modocs*, viii.

27. C. James, *Modoc*, 189–92.

28. Hurtado, "The Modocs," 100–101.

34. Requiem

1. Ray, *Primitive Pragmatists*, 25, 70; Dillon, *Burnt-Out Fires*, 338. The story was told by Bap-Pee-Binpatokit, later known as Jennie Clinton, who was a teenager when the war broke out; at her death in 1950 at age ninety-one, Clinton, who had become a Quaker pastor, was the last survivor of the war; C. James, *Modoc*, 60–62, 244–46.

Epilogue

1. University of Oregon Libraries, Biographical Sketch, Frazier A. Boutelle photographs, c. 1860–1924, http://library.uoregon.edu/speccoll/photo/fboutelle.html.

2. Modoc Tribe of Oklahoma, Tribal History & Photos, http://www.modoctribe .net/history.html.

3. Bojorcas, Coiner, and DeGross, "Oregon Termination"; *Klamath Facilities Removal*, 3.12-2–3.12-4.

4. Saxon, "Klamath River Tribes Support Klamath Basin Restoration Agreement," *Indian Country Media Today Network*, June 18, 2014; "Klamath Tribes, Southern Oregon Ranchers Strike Irrigation Deal for the Upper Klamath Basin," *Oregon Live*, March 5, 2014.

5. Trimble, "The Kind of Country They Marched Over," 285.

6. Gates, *Land and Law in California*, 131–32.

7. "Old Land Case Dismissed," *San Francisco Call*, August 6, 1893; "Jesse Carr's Fence to Come Down," *San Francisco Call*, November 16, 1901; "Jesse D. Carr Quietly Passes Away at His Home in Salinas," *San Francisco Call*, December 12, 1903; Johnston, "Two Jesses"; C. James, *Modoc*, 177–80; Bartholomew, "Jesse Carr's Cattle Empire."

8. J. Applegate, "Jesse Applegate to W. H. Rees, December 25, 1874."

9. Quoted in W. H. Brown, *This Was a Man*, 30.

10. S. Applegate, *Skookum*, 319–20.

11. Blake, Blake, and Kittredge, *Balancing Water*, 51–52.

12. Reisner, *Cadillac Desert*, 104–12, 247.

13. Quoted in National Research Council, *Endangered and Threatened Fishes*, 56.

BIBLIOGRAPHY

Unpublished Sources

Applegate, Oliver Cromwell. Papers. Microfilm. Bancroft Library, University of California, Berkeley.

Case, Leonard. Diary. 1873. Manuscript, 0041.2010.040.0001, Klamath County Museum., Klamath Falls, Oregon.

Compton, James. "Kill the Chief: The Skull of Captain Jack." Unpublished manuscript.

Fairchild, Rollin A. "Reminiscences." May 12, 1980. Manuscript. California Miscellany—Additions, Bancroft Library, University of California, Berkeley.

Fisher, Don C. "Ben Wright." Typescript. Lava Beds National Monument, 1940.

——. Papers. Correspondence and related documents from the Modoc War. Donated to the Klamath County (Oregon) Museum in 1967. Accessible in eleven PDF volumes at http://klamathcountymuseum.squarespace.com/fisher-papers/.

Hagen, Olaf T., ed. "Modoc War Official Correspondence and Documents, 1865–1878." Compiled for Lava Beds National Monument, U.S. Department of the Interior, May 1942. Typescript. Bancroft MSS C-A 232, Bancroft Library, University of California, Berkeley.

Hardin, Charles B. Letters to William S. Brown, 1926–1936. Transcribed and copied from originals donated in 1991 by Vernon A. Brown and family of Walnut Creek, California. Lava Beds National Monument Research Library.

Howard, Judson D. Field Notes. Compiled by Gary Hathaway. Typescript. National Park Service, 1988.

"Miscellaneous Ben Wright Information." Undated typescript. Lava Beds National Monument Research Library.

"The Modoc War: The 1864 Treaties." http://modocwar.tripod.com/id14.html.

Parrish, J. L. "Anecdotes of Intercourse with the Indians." Salem, Oregon, 1878. Microfilm manuscript. Bancroft Library, University of California, Berkeley.

Pentz, Charles A. "Modoc War Journal." Undated typescript. Transcribed by Gary Hathaway, National Park Service, from original owned by Austin Meekins. Lava Beds National Monument Research Library.

Powers, Stephen. John Fairchild biographical sketch recorded for H. H. Bancroft. Undated typescript. Bancroft Library, University of California, Berkeley.

Ross, John E. "Narrative of an Indian Fighter. Jacksonville, 1878. Written by HHB between dawn and daylight while the Colonel's horse was standing at the door; the whole night being occupied in the work." Manuscript. H. H. Bancroft Collection, Bancroft Library, University of California, Berkeley.

United States Army Medical Museum, Anatomical Section. "Records Relating to Specimens Transferred to the Smithsonian Institution." http://anthropology.si.edu/naa/guide/_uv.htm#jrg514.

"Verified Statement of W. T. Kershaw," November 21, 1857. *Oregon and Washington Volunteers*, House Miscellaneous Document No. 47, 35th Congress, 2nd session, 41–43. http://en.wikisource.org/wiki/Oregon_and_Washington_Volunteers/23.

Published Sources

Ahearn, Robert G. *William Tecumseh Sherman and the Settlement of the West*. Norman: University of Oklahoma Press, 1956.

Allen, James, Hilton Als, Congressman John Lewis, and Leon F. Litwack. *Without Sanctuary: Lynching Photography in America*. Santa Fe NM: Twin Palms Publishing, 2005.

Annual Report of the Commissioner of Indian Affairs. Washington DC: Government Printing Office, 1863, 1865, 1867, 1868, 1870, 1871, 1872.

Applegate, Ivan D. "The Initial Shot: A Civilian's Description of the First Battle of the Modoc War." *Klamath Falls Express*, January 10, 1895. Reprinted in *Northwestern Fights and Fighters*, ed. Cyrus Townsend Brady, 272–79. New York: McClure, 1907.

Applegate, Jesse. "A Day with the Cow Column." *Quarterly of the Oregon Historical Society* 1, no. 4 (December 1900): 371–83.

———. "Jesse Applegate to W. H. Rees, December 25, 1874." *Quarterly of the Oregon Historical Society* 20, no. 4 (December 1919): 397–99.

Applegate, Lindsay. "Notes and Reminiscences of Laying Out and Establishing the Old Emigrant Road into Southern Oregon in the Year 1846." *Oregon Historical Quarterly* 22, no. 1 (March 1921): 12–45.

Applegate, Shannon. *Skookum: An Oregon Pioneer Family's History and Lore*. 1998. Corvallis: Oregon State University Press, 2005.

Aslan, Reza. *How to Win a Cosmic War: God, Globalization, and the End of the War on Terror*. New York: Random House, 2009.

Baker, Abner S., III. "Experience, Personality and Memory: Jesse Applegate and John Minto Recall Pioneer Days." *Oregon Historical Quarterly* 81, no. 3 (Fall 1980): 228–51, 253–59.

Bancroft, Hubert Hugh. *History of California*. Vol. 7, *1860–1890*. San Francisco: The History Company, 1890.

———. *History of Oregon*. Vol. 2, *1848–1888*. San Francisco: The History Company, 1888.

Bartholomew, Ryan. "Jesse Carr's Cattle Empire." *Journal of the Shaw Historical Library* 25 (2011): 25–33.

Bell, William Gardner. *Secretaries of War and Secretaries of the Army: Portraits and Biographical Sketches*. United States Army Center of Military History Publication 70-12, 1992. http://www.history.army.mil/books/Sw-SA/SWSA-Fm.htm.

Benterou, Mary, Gary Hathaway, Francis Landrum, and Bill Quinn. "The Fields of Battle Tour." *Journal of the Shaw Historical Library* 23–24 (2009–10): 17–39.

Berg, Scott W. *38 Nooses: Lincoln, Little Crow, and the Beginning of the Frontier's End.* New York: Pantheon Books, 2012.

Berkhofer, Robert F., Jr. *The White Man's Indian: Images of the American Indian from Columbus to the Present.* New York: Vintage Books, 1978.

Bieder, Robert E. *A Brief Historical Survey of the Expropriation of American Indian Remains.* Boulder: Native American Rights Fund, 1990.

Bill Dadd the Scribe [H. Wallace Atwell]. *Trans-Continental Railroad Guide.* Chicago: Geo. A. Croffut, 1869.

Blake, Tupper Ansel, Madeleine Graham Blake, and William Kittredge. *Balancing Water: Restoring the Klamath Basin.* Berkeley: University of California Press, 2000.

Bland, T. A. *Life of Alfred B. Meacham.* Washington DC: T. A. & M. C. Bland, 1883.

Bojorcas, Robert, Robert Coiner, and Dennis DeGross. "Oregon Termination: A Study of the Process and Effects of the Federal Government's Policy of Termination on the Lives of Oregon Indians." In *Report on Terminated and Nonfederally Recognized Indians,* ed. Jo Jo Hunt et al., 17–70. Washington DC: Government Printing Office, 1976.

Boutelle, F. A. "The Disaster to Thomas' Command." In *Northwestern Fights and Fighters,* ed. Cyrus Townsend Brady, 305–13. New York: McClure, 1907.

——. "Major Boutelle's Account of His Duel with Scar-face Charley in the First Engagement." In *Northwestern Fights and Fighters,* ed. Cyrus Townsend Brady, 264–71. New York: McClure, 1907.

Boyd, Robert. *The Coming of the Spirit of Pestilence: Introduced Infectious Diseases and Population Decline among Northwest Coast Indians, 1774–1874.* Seattle: University of Washington Press, and Vancouver: University of British Columbia Press, 1999.

Boyle, William Henry. *Personal Observations of the Conduct of the Modoc War.* Ed. Richard Dillon. Los Angeles: Dawson's Book Shop, 1959.

Brady, Cyrus Townsend, ed. *Northwestern Fights and Fighters.* New York: McClure, 1907.

Brown, Wilfred H., ed. *This Was a Man: About the Life and Times of Jesse Applegate.* North Hollywood CA: Camas Press, 1971.

Brown, William S. *California Northeast: The Bloody Ground.* Oakland CA: Biobooks, 1951.

Bunker, William. "In the Lava Beds." *Californian* 1 (January–June 1880): 161–66.

Campbell, John. "The Seminoles, the 'Bloodhound War,' and Abolitionism, 1796–1865." *Journal of Southern History* 72, no. 2 (May 2006): 259–302.

Chomsky, Carol. "The United States–Dakota War Trials: A Study in Military Injustice." *Stanford Law Review* 43, no. 1 (November 1990): 13–98.

Churchill, Edward M. "Betrayal at Ebenezer Creek." *Civil War Times,* October 1998, http://www.historynet.com/betrayal-at-ebenezer-creek.htm, June 12, 2006.

Clark, Keith, and Donna Clark, eds. *Daring Donald McKay, or, The Last War Trail of the Modocs.* Portland: Oregon Historical Society, 1971. Facsimile reproduction of the third edition of 1884 published by The Oregon Indian Medicine Company of Corry, Pennsylvania, owned by Colonel T. A. Edwards.

Clarke, Samuel A. "Klamath Land." *Overland Monthly* 11 (December 1873): 548–54.

Clausewitz, Carl von. *On War*. Trans. Colonel J. J. Graham. London: Kegan Paul, Trench, Trübner, 1911.

Cline, Gloria Griffen. *Peter Skene Ogden and the Hudson's Bay Company*. Norman: University of Oklahoma Press, 1974.

Conrad, Joseph. *Youth, and Two Other Stories*. Garden City NY: Doubleday, Page, 1903.

Cothran, Boyd D. "*Lúgsh* and *Laláki*: Slaves, Chiefs, Medicine Men, and the Indigenous Political Landscape of the Upper Klamath Basin, 1820s–1860s." In *Linking the Histories of Slavery in North America*, ed. James F. Brooks and Bonnie Martin, 97–123. Santa Fe: School for Advanced Research Press, 2016.

———. "Marketplaces of Remembering: Violence, Colonialism, and American Innocence in the Making of the Modoc War." PhD diss., University of Minnesota, 2012.

———. *Remembering the Modoc War: Redemptive Violence and the Making of American Innocence*. Chapel Hill: University of North Carolina Press, 2014.

Coward, John M. *The Newspaper Indian: Native American Identity in the Press, 1820–90*. Urbana: University of Illinois Press, 1999.

Coward, John M., and W. Joseph Campbell, eds. *The Greenwood Library of American War Reporting. Volume 4: The Indian Wars & The Spanish-American War*. Westport CT: Greenwood Press, 2005.

Cozzens, Peter, ed. *Eyewitnesses to the Indian Wars, 1865–1890: The Wars for the Pacific Northwest*. Mechanicsburg PA: Stackpole Books, 2002.

Cromwell, Otelia. *Lucretia Mott*. New York: Russell & Russell, 1958.

Cullum, George W. "Alvan C. Gillem." *Biographical Sketch of the Officers and Graduates of the United States Military Academy at West Point, New York, since its establishment in 1802 to 1890*. Vol. 2. 3rd ed. Boston: Houghton Mifflin, 1891. http://penelope.uchicago.edu/Thayer/E/Gazetteer/Places/America/United_States/Army/USMA/Cullums_Register/1504.htm.

Curry, Andrew. "Pre-Clovis Breakthrough." *Archaeology*, April 3, 2008. http://archive.archaeology.org/online/features/coprolites/.

Curtin, Jeremiah. *Myths of the Modocs*. Boston: Little, Brown, 1912.

Davenport, Frances Gardiner, ed. *European Treaties Bearing on the History of the United States and Its Dependencies to 1648*. Washington DC: Carnegie Institution of Washington, 1917.

David, Robert James. "The Landscape of Klamath Basin Rock Art." PhD diss., University of California, Berkeley, 2012.

Davies, K. G., ed. *Peter Skene Ogden's Snake Country Journal 1826–27*. London: Hudson's Bay Record Society, 1961.

Davis, Jefferson C. "Observations on the Modoc War." In *Eyewitnesses to the Indian Wars, 1865–1890: The Wars for the Pacific Northwest*, ed. Peter Cozzens, 280–82. Mechanicsburg PA: Stackpole Books, 2002. Originally published in the *San Francisco Bulletin*, June 11, 1873, and in *Army and Navy Journal* 10, no. 4 (June 21, 1873): 714.

Deloria, Vine, Jr. *God Is Red*. New York: Grosset & Dunlap, 1973.

De Tocqueville, Alexis. *Democracy in America*. Trans. Arthur Goldhammer. New York: Penguin Putnam/Library of America, 2004.

Deur, Douglas. "'A Caretaker Responsibility': Revisiting Klamath and Modoc Traditions of Plant Community Management." *Journal of Ethnobiology* 29, no. 2 (2009): 296–322.

———. *In the Footprints of Gmukamps: A Traditional Use Study of Crater Lake National Park and Lava Beds National Monument*. National Park Service, Pacific West Region, 2008.

———. "A Most Sacred Place: The Significance of Crater Lake Among the Indians of Southern Oregon." *Oregon Historical Quarterly* 103, no. 1 (Spring 2002): 18–49.

DeVoto, Bernard. *The Year of Decision: 1846*. Boston: Houghton-Mifflin, 1942, 1943.

Dicken, Samuel N., and Emily F. Dicken. *The Legacy of Ancient Lake Modoc: A Historical Geography of the Klamath Lakes Basin, Oregon and California*. Self-published, 1985.

Dillon, Richard. *Burnt-Out Fires*. Englewood Cliffs NJ: Prentice-Hall, 1973.

Donnelly-Nolan, Julie M. "Geology of Medicine Lake Volcano, Northern California Cascade Range." *Geothermal Resources Council Transactions* 14, pt. 2 (August 1990):1395–96.

Drinnon, Richard. *Facing West: The Metaphysics of Indian-Hating and Empire-Building*. Rev. ed. Norman: University of Oklahoma Press, 1997.

Dunbar-Ortiz, Roxanne. *An Indigenous Peoples' History of the United States*. Boston: Beacon Press, 2014.

Eastman, Charles (Ohiyesa). *Indian Heroes and Great Chieftains*. Boston: Little, Brown, 1919.

Echo-Hawk, Walter R. *In the Courts of the Conqueror: The 10 Worst Indian Law Cases Ever Decided*. Golden CO: Fulcrum, 2010.

Engberg, Robert, ed. *John Muir Summering in the Sierra*. Madison: University of Wisconsin Press, 1984.

Etter, Patricia A. "Effect of the California Gold Rush." *The Encyclopedia of Arkansas History & Culture*, http://www.encyclopediaofarkansas.net/encyclopedia/entry-detail .aspx?entryID=4211.

Evans, Elwood. *History of the Pacific Northwest: Oregon and Washington*. Vol. 1. Portland: North Pacific History Company, 1889.

Fagan, David D. *History of Benton County, Oregon*. Portland: A. G. Walling, 1885.

Finneran, Richard J., ed. *W. B. Yeats: The Poems, a New Edition*. New York: Macmillan, 1983.

Fisher, Don C., and John E. Doerr Jr. "Outline of Events in the History of the Modoc War." *Nature Notes from Crater Lake* 10, no. 1 (June 1937), http://www.craterlakeinstitute .com/online-library/nature-notes/vol10no1-modoc-war.htm.

Fitzgerald, Maurice. "The Modoc War." In *Eyewitnesses to the Indian Wars, 1865–1890: The Wars for the Pacific Northwest*, ed. Peter Cozzens, 114–34. Mechanicsburg PA: Stackpole Books, 2002. Originally published in *Americana* 21, no. 4 (October 1927): 498–521.

Fitzgerald, O. P. *California Sketches*. Nashville: Southern Methodist Publishing Company, 1880. http://www.ebooksread.com/authors-eng/o-p-oscar-penn-fitzgerald /california-sketches-zti/page-7-california-sketches-zti.shtml.

Foster, Doug. "Imperfect Justice: The Modoc War Crimes Trial of 1873." *Oregon Historical Quarterly* 100, no. 3 (Fall 1999): 246–87.

Frémont, J. C. *Narrative of the Exploring Expedition to the Rocky Mountains in the Year 1842, and to Oregon and North California in the Years 1843–44*. New York: D. Appleton, 1849.

Fritz, Henry E. "The Making of Grant's 'Peace Policy.'" *Chronicles of Oklahoma* 37 (1959): 411–32.

Gates, Paul Wallace. *Land and Law in California: Essays on Land Policies*. Ames: University of Iowa Press, 1991.

Glazier, David. "Precedents Lost: The Neglected History of the Military Commission." *Virginia Journal of International Law* 46, no. 1 (Fall 2005): 5–81.

Greeley, Horace. *An Overland Journey, from New York to San Francisco, in the Summer of 1859*. New York: C.M. Saxton, Barker & Co., 1860.

Gwynne, S. C. *Empire of the Summer Moon: Quanah Parker and the Rise and Fall of the Comanches, the Most Powerful Indian Tribe in American History*. New York: Scribner, 2010.

Hamont, P. W. "The Modoc Indian War, by One Who Was There." In *Eyewitnesses to the Indian Wars, 1865–1890: The Wars for the Pacific Northwest*, ed. Peter Cozzens, 259–69. Mechanicsburg PA: Stackpole Books, 2002.

Hardin, Charles B. "'Gosh Dash It, Let's Charge': A Story of the Modoc War." In *Eyewitnesses to the Indian Wars, 1865–1890: The Wars for the Pacific Northwest*, ed. Peter Cozzens, 276–79. Mechanicsburg PA: Stackpole Books, 2002. Originally published in *Winners of the West* 10, no. 6 (May 1933): 4.

Harrington, Peter. "The First True War Artist." *MHQ: The Quarterly Journal of Military History* 9, no. 1 (Autumn 1996): 100–109.

Hasbrouck, H. C. "The Last Fight of the Campaign." In *Northwestern Fights and Fighters*, ed. Cyrus Townsend Brady, 320–25. New York: McClure, 1907.

Haughton, Samuel. "On Hanging Considered from a Mechanical and Physiological Point of View." *London, Edinburgh and Dublin Philosophical Magazine and Journal of Science* 32, no. 213 (July 1866): 23–24.

Haynal, Patrick M. "The Influence of Sacred Rock Cairns and Prayer Seats on Modern Klamath and Modoc Religion and World View." *Journal of California and Great Basin Archaeology* 20, no. 2 (2000): 170–85.

Heizer, Robert F., ed. *They Were Only Diggers: A Collection of Articles from California Newspapers, 1851–1866, on Indian and White Relations*. Ramona CA: Ballena Press, 1974.

Herbert, Maeve. "Explaining the Sioux Military Commission of 1862." *Columbia Human Rights Law Review* 40 (2009): 743–98.

Heyman, Max L., Jr. *Prudent Soldier: A Biography of Major General E. R. S. Canby, 1817–1873*. Volume III in the Frontier Military Series. Glendale CA: Arthur H. Clark, 1959.

Hogan, Linda. *The Woman Who Watches Over the World*. New York: Norton, 2001.

Howe, Carrol B. *Ancient Modocs of California and Oregon*. Portland: Binford & Mort, 1979.

Hughes, Nathaniel Cheairs, Jr., and Gordon D. Whitney. *Jefferson Davis in Blue: The Life of Sherman's Relentless Warrior*. Baton Rouge: Louisiana State University Press, 2002.

Hurtado, Albert L. *Indian Survival on the California Frontier*. New Haven: Yale University Press, 1988.

———. "The Modocs and the Jones Family Indian Ring: Quaker Administration of the Quapaw Agency, 1873–1879." In *Oklahoma's Forgotten Indians*, ed. Robert E. Smith, 86–106. Oklahoma City: Oklahoma Historical Society, 1981.

"Indian Perceptions of Crater Lake." Historic Resource Study, Crater Lake National Park, 1984. http://www.craterlakeinstitute.com/online-library/historic-resource -study/4.htm.

Jackson, James A. "The First Blow." In *Northwestern Fights and Fighters*, ed. Cyrus Townsend Brady, 257–63. New York: McClure, 1907.

Jacoby, Karl. *Shadows at Dawn: A Borderlands Massacre and the Violence of History*. New York: Penguin Press, 2008.

James, Cheewa. *Modoc: The Tribe That Wouldn't Die*. Happy Camp CA: Naturegraph, 2008.

James, Ryk, and Rachel Nasmyth-Jones. "The Occurrence of Cervical Fractures in Victims of Judicial Hanging." *Forensic Science International* 54 (1992): 81–91.

Jenkins, Dennis L., Loren G. Davis, Thomas W. Stafford Jr., et al. "Clovis Age Western Stemmed Projectile Points and Human Coprolites at the Paisley Caves." *Science* 337 (July 31, 2012): 223–28.

Johnson, Charles, Jr. "Frazier Augustus Boutelle." In *Dictionary of American Negro Biography*, ed. Rayford W. Logan and Michael R. Winston, 52. New York: Norton, 1982.

Johnson v. M'Intosh, 21 U.S. 543, 5 L. Ed. 681, 8 Wheat. 543 (1823). https://supreme.justia .com/cases/federal/us/21/543/case.html.

Johnston, Robert B. "Two Jesses and the Modoc War." *Journal of the Shaw Historical Library* 5, nos. 1–2 (1991): 1–44.

Juergensmeyer, Mark. "Performance Violence." In *Oxford Handbook of Religion and Violence*, ed. Mark Juergensmeyer, Margo Kitts, and Michael Jerryson, 280–92. Oxford: Oxford University Press, 2012.

———. *Terror in the Mind of God: The Global Rise of Religious Violence*. Berkeley: University of California Press, 2003.

Juzda, Elise. "Skulls, Science, and the Spoils of War: Craniological Studies at the United States Army Medical Museum, 1868–1900." *Studies in History and Philosophy of Biological and Biomedical Sciences* 40 (2009): 156–67.

Kades, Eric. "The Dark Side of Efficiency: Johnson v. M'Intosh and the Expropriation of Amerindian Lands." *University of Pennsylvania Law Review* 148 (2000): 1065–1190. http://scholarship.law.wm.edu/facpubs/198.

Kelman, Ari. *A Misplaced Massacre: Struggling over the Memory of Sand Creek*. Cambridge: Harvard University Press, 2013.

Klamath Facilities Removal Final Environment Impact Statement/Environmental Impact Report. U.S. Department of the Interior and California Department of Fish and Game, December 2012.

Kluger, Richard. *The Bitter Waters of Medicine Creek: A Tragic Clash between White and Native America*. New York: Knopf, 2011.

———. *Seizing Destiny: How America Grew from Sea to Shining Sea*. New York: Knopf, 2007.

Knight, Oliver. *Following the Indian Wars: The Story of the Newspaper Correspondents among the Indian Campaigners*. Norman: University of Oklahoma Press, 1960.

La Barre, Weston. *The Ghost Dance: Origins of Religion*. New York: Dell, 1970.

LaDuke, Winona. *Recovering the Sacred: The Power of Naming and Claiming*. Cambridge MA: South End Press, 2005.

LaLande, Jeff. "'Dixie' of the Pacific Northwest: Southern Oregon's Civil War." *Oregon Historical Quarterly* 100, no. 1 (Spring 1999): 32–81.

——. *First over the Siskiyous: Peter Skene Ogden's 1826–1827 Journey through the Oregon-California Borderlands*. Portland: Oregon Historical Society Press, 1987.

Lamb, D. S. "The Army Medical Museum in American Anthropology." In *Proceedings of the XIX International Congress of Americanists*, 628–32. Washington DC, 1917.

Landrum, Francis S., comp. *Guardhouse, Gallows and Grave: The Trial and Execution of Indian Prisoners of the Modoc Indian War by the U.S. Army, 1873*. Klamath Falls OR: Klamath County Museum, 1988.

Langston, Nancy. *Where Land and Water Meet: A Western Landscape Transformed*. Seattle: University of Washington Press, 2003.

Lansing, Ronald B. *Juggernaut: The Whitman Massacre Trial, 1850*. San Francisco: Ninth Judicial Circuit Historical Society, 1993.

Lemkin, Raphaël. *Axis Rule in Occupied Europe: Laws of Occupation, Analysis of Government, Proposals for Redress*. Washington DC: Carnegie Endowment for International Peace, Division of International Law, 1944. Online at https://babel.hathitrust.org/cgi/pt?id=mdp.39015005077436;view=1up;seq=6.

Limerick, Patricia Nelson. "Haunted America." In Drex Brooks, *Sweet Medicine: Sites of Indian Massacres, Battlefields, and Treaties*, 119–63. Albuquerque: University of New Mexico Press, 1995.

——. *The Legacy of Conquest: The Unbroken Past of the American West*. New York: Norton, 1988.

Lindsay, Brendan C. *Murder State: California's Native American Genocide, 1846–1873*. Lincoln: University of Nebraska Press, 2012.

Lipscomb, Adrian. "William Simpson (1823–1899)—'Prince of Pictorial Correspondents.'" http://www.victorianweb.org/painting/simpson/bio.html.

Lönnberg, Allen. "The Digger Stereotype in California." *Journal of California and Great Basin Anthropology* 3, no. 2 (1981): 215–23.

Madley, Benjamin. *An American Genocide: The United States and the California Indian Catastrophe*. New Haven: Yale University Press, 2016.

——. "California and Oregon's Modoc Indians: How Indigenous Resistance Camouflages Genocide in Colonial Histories." In *Colonial Genocide and Indigenous North America*, ed. Andrew Woolford, Jeff Benvenuto, and Alexander Laban Hinton, 95–130. Durham NC: Duke University Press, 2014.

Martin, Lucile J. "A History of the Modoc Indians: An Acculturation Study." *Chronicles of Oklahoma* 67, no. 4 (Winter 1969–70): 398–446.

McDonnell, Michael A., and A. Dirk Moses. "Raphael Lemkin as Historian of Genocide in the Americas." *Journal of Genocide Research* 7, no. 4 (2007): 501–29.

Meacham, Alfred B. *Wigwam and War-path; Or, The Royal Chief in Chains*. Boston: John P. Dale, 1875.

———. *Wi-ne-ma (the Woman Chief) and Her People*. Hartford CT: American Publishing Company, 1876.

"Medal of Honor to Maj. John O. Skinner," Report No. 1466. *House Reports (Public)*. 63rd Congress, 3rd session, volume 1. Washington DC: Government Printing Office, 1915.

Miller, Joaquin. "The Tale of the Tall Alcalde." In *The Poetical Works of Joaquin Miller*, ed. Stuart P. Sherman, 88–103. New York: Putnam, 1923.

Mooney, James. *The Ghost-Dance Religion and the Sioux Outbreak of 1890*. Fourteenth Annual Report of the Bureau of Ethnology, Part 2. Washington DC: Government Printing Office, 1896.

Muir, John. "Shasta Rambles and Modoc Memories." Chapter 5 in *Steep Trails*, ed. William Frederick Badè. Boston: Houghton Mifflin, 1918. http://www.sierraclub.org /john_muir_exhibit/writings/steep_trails/chapter_5.aspx.

Murray, Keith A. *The Modocs and Their War*. Norman: University of Oklahoma Press, 1959.

Nash, Philleo. "The Place of Religious Revivalism in the Formation of the Intercultural Community of Klamath Reservation." In *Social Anthropology of North American Tribes: Essays in Social Organization, Law, and Religion*, ed. Fred Eggan, 377–442. Chicago: University of Chicago Press, 1937.

National Research Council. *Endangered and Threatened Fishes in the Klamath River Basin: Causes of Decline and Strategies for Recovery*. Washington DC: National Academies Press, 2003.

Newcomb, Stephen T. *Pagans in the Promised Land: Decoding the Doctrine of Christian Discovery*. Golden CO: Fulcrum, 2008.

Nott, Josiah C., and George R. Gliddon. *Types of Mankind: Or, Ethnological Researches*. Philadelphia: J. B. Lippincott, 1857.

O'Connor, Richard. *The Scandalous Mr. Bennett*. Garden City NY: Doubleday & Company, 1962.

Odeneal, T. B. *The Modoc War; Statement of Its Origins and Causes, Containing an Account of the Treaty, Copies of Petitions, and Official Correspondence*. Portland: Bulletin Steam Book and Printing Office, 1873.

Palmquist, Peter. "Imagemakers of the Modoc War: Louis Heller and Eadweard Muybridge." *Journal of California Anthropology* 4, no. 2 (1977): 206–41.

Paullin, Charles Oscar. "A Half Century of Naval Administration in America, 1861–1911." *United States Naval Institute Proceedings* 39 (1913): 1189–1268.

Pettis, George H. "The Confederate Invasion of New Mexico and Arizona." In *Battles and Leaders of the Civil War*, ed. Robert Underwood Johnson and Clarence Clough Buell, 2:103–11. New York: The Century Company, 1887.

Powers, Ramon, and James N. Leiker. "Cholera among the Plains Indians: Perceptions, Causes, Consequences." *Western Historical Quarterly* 29, no. 3 (Fall 1998): 317–43.

Powers, Stephen. *Tribes of California*. Washington D C: Government Printing Office, 1877.

Prucha, Francis Paul. *The Great Father: The United States Government and the American Indians*. 2 vols. Lincoln: University of Nebraska Press, 1984.

Quinn, Arthur. *Hell with the Fire Out*. Boston: Faber and Faber, 1997.

Raines, Rebecca Robbins. *Getting the Message Through: A Branch History of the U.S. Signal Corps*. Washington D C: Center of Military History, 1996.

Rao, D. "Hanging." http://www.forensicpathologyonline.com/e-book/asphyxia/hanging.

Ray, Verne F. *Primitive Pragmatists: The Modoc Indians of Northern California*. Seattle: University of Washington Press, 1963.

Reisner, Marc. *Cadillac Desert: The American West and Its Disappearing Water*. Rev. ed. New York: Penguin Books, 1993.

Report of Governor Grover to General Schofield on the Modoc War, and Reports of Maj. Gen. John F. Miller and John E. Ross to the Governor. Salem O R: Mart V. Brown, State Printer, February 1874.

Report of the Commissioner of Agriculture for the Year 1873. Washington D C: Government Printing Office, 1874.

Report to the President by the Indian Peace Commission. January 7, 1868. House Executive Document no. 97, 40–42, serial 1337. http://history.furman.edu/~benson /docs/peace.htm.

Reséndez, Andrés. *The Other Slavery: The Uncovered Story of Indian Enslavement in California*. Boston: Houghton Mifflin Harcourt, 2016.

Rickey, Don, Jr. *Forty Miles a Day on Beans and Hay: The Enlisted Soldier Fighting the Indian Wars*. Norman: University of Oklahoma Press, 1963.

Riddle, Jeff C. *The Indian History of the Modoc War*. 1914. Eugene: Urion Press, 1974.

Ridge, Martin, ed. *Westward Journeys: Memoirs of Jesse A. Applegate and Lavinia Honeyman Porter Who Traveled the Overland Trail*. Chicago: R. R. Donnelly & Sons, 1989.

Robbins, William G. *Landscapes of Promise: The Oregon Story, 1800–1940*. Seattle: University of Washington Press, 1997.

Robertson, Lindsay G. *Conquest by Law: How the Discovery of America Dispossessed the Indigenous Peoples of Their Lands*. New York: Oxford University Press, 2005.

The Samuel A. Clarke Papers: With an Appendix Compiled from Material in Clarke's Scrapbook. Klamath County Museum Research Papers No. 2. Klamath Falls O R: Guide Printing Co., 1960.

Sides, Hampton. *Blood and Thunder: An Epic of the American West*. New York: Doubleday, 2006.

Simpson, William. *Meeting the Sun: A Journey All Around the World*. London: Longsman, Green, Reader, and Dyer, 1874.

Slotkin, Richard. *Regeneration through Violence: The Mythology of the American Frontier, 1600–1860*. Middletown C T: Wesleyan University Press, 1973.

Smith, Andrea. *Conquest: Sexual Violence and American Indian Genocide*. Cambridge M A: South End Press, 2005.

Solnit, Rebecca. *River of Shadows: Eadweard Muybridge and the Technological Wild West*. New York: Penguin Books, 2003.

Spier, Leslie. *The Prophet Dance of the Northwest and Its Derivatives: The Source of the Ghost Dance*. Menasha WI: George Banta, 1935. Available online at https://catalog .hathitrust.org/Record/001650517.

Standing Bear, Luther. *Land of the Spotted Eagle*. 1933. Lincoln: University of Nebraska Press, 1960.

Stanley, Henry Morton. *How I Found Livingstone*. New York: Scribner, Armstrong, 1872.

The Statutes at Large and Proclamations of the United States of America. Vol. 16, 1869–71.

Thompson, Erwin N. *Modoc War: Its Military History & Topography*. Sacramento CA: Argus Books, 1971.

Thompson, William. *Reminiscences of a Pioneer*. San Francisco: self-published, 1912.

Thoreau, Henry David. *Walking*. Cambridge MA: Riverside Press, 1914.

Thrapp, Dan L. *Dictionary of Frontier Biography*. 3 vols. Glendale CA: Arthur H. Clark, 1988.

"Toby Riddle—Modoc." *Native American Encyclopedia*, http://nativeamericanencyclopedia .com/toby-riddle-modoc/.

Torres, Gerald, and Kathryn Milun. "Translating Yonnondio by Precedent and Evidence." *Duke Law Journal* 39, no. 4 (September 1990): 625–59.

Trimble, J. G. "Carrying a Stretcher in the Lava Beds." In *Northwestern Fights and Fighters*, ed. Cyrus Townsend Brady, 314–19. New York: McClure, 1907.

———. "The Killing of the Commissioners." In *Northwestern Fights and Fighters*, ed. Cyrus Townsend Brady, 286–90. New York: McClure, 1907.

———. "The Kind of Country They Marched Over." In *Northwestern Fights and Fighters*, ed. Cyrus Townsend Brady, 280–83. New York: McClure, 1907.

Turner, Stan. *Years of Harvest: A History of the Tule Lake Basin*. 2nd ed. Eugene: 49th Avenue Press, 1987.

U.S. House of Representatives. *Official Copies of Correspondence Relative to the War with Modoc Indians in 1872–'73*. 43rd Congress, 1st session, Executive Document No. 122, February 1874.

Utley, Robert M. *Frontier Regulars: The United States Army and the Indian, 1866–1891*. Lincoln: University of Nebraska Press, 1973.

Victor, Frances Fuller. "A Knight of the Frontier." *The Californian: A Western Monthly Magazine* 4, no. 20 (August 1881): 152–62.

Wagner, Sally Roesch. "The Untold Story of the Iroquois Influence on Early Feminists." Republished from *On the Issues*, Winter 1996, at http://www.feminist.com/resources /artspeech/genwom/iroquoisinfluence.html.

Waters, Aaron C. "Captain Jack's Stronghold: The Geological Events That Created a Natural Fortress." In *Guides to Some Volcanic Terranes in Washington, Idaho, Oregon, and Northern California*, ed. David A. Johnston and Julie Donnelly-Nolan, 151–61. Washington DC: United States Geological Survey Circular 838, 1981.

Wells, Harry L. *History of Siskiyou County, California*. Oakland CA: D. J. Stewart, 1881.

———. "The Modocs in 1851." *The West Shore* 10, no. 4 (April 1884): 132–34.

Witt, John Fabian. *Lincoln's Code: The Laws of War in American History*. New York: Free Press, 2012.

Woodhead, Daniel, III. *Modoc Vengeance: The 1873 Modoc War in Northern California & Southern Oregon as reported in the newspapers of the day*. Self-published, 2012.

Yeats, William Butler. *Michael Robartes and the Dancers*. Churchtown, Dundrum, Ireland: Chuala Press, 1920.

Zdanowicz, C. M., G. A. Zielinski, and M. S. Germani. "Mount Mazama Eruption: Calendrical Age Verified and Atmospheric Impact Assessed." *Geology* 27, no. 7 (July 1999): 621–24.

INDEX

Page numbers in italics indicate illustrations.

DeWitt, Calvin, 231

"Digger Indians," 23, 24, 65

disease, 34–35, 348, 362n20

Doctor George, 103–4

Dole, W. P., 51

Dooley, Owen, 231, 232

Dorris, Presley, 65, 72, 75, 77, 78, 112; and Kientpoos, 95, 131–32

Doten, Cy and John, 75

Drew, C. S., 46

Drew, Edward, 230

Duffy (Modoc fighter), 156

Dunbar-Ortiz, Roxanne, 181

Dyar, Leroy S., 70, 77, 181, 246, 275–76; and Adams Point killings, 288–89; appointed to Peace Commission, 165; and Modoc assassination threats, 187–88, 195–99; and Peace Tent killing events, 199–200, 206, 208, 227, 299–300, 303, 344; trial testimony by, 301–2

Eastman, Charles, 116

Ebenezer Creek incident (1864), 222–24

Egan, Charles, 230

Ellen's Man, 76, 79, 199; death in battle, 269, 270, 377n12; and Peace Tent killings, 194, 208–9, 301; as war faction advocate, 117, 183

Elliott, Washington L., 296, 299, 306

Enos (Shoshone rebel), 45

Erasmus, C., 13

Evans, John, 87

extermination of Indians, 123, 216–17; and cosmic war, 219–20; genocide as term for, 86; Sherman support for, 171, 219–20, 285, 349

Fagan, David, 45–46

Fairchild, James, 287–88

Fairchild, John, 77–78, 96, 154, 171, 273, 280; biographical background, 74–76; California Volunteers command given to, 96; and First Battle of the Stronghold, 100, 109, 110, 112, 119–20; and Fort Klamath trial, 312, 313; Hot Creek Modocs employed by, 72–73, 75–77; Kientpoos's meetings with, 95, 131–32, 146, 147–48, 149–51, 184, 186; and Kientpoos's surrender, 281, 282; and Peace Tent killing plot, 197, 198; photo of, *fig. 2*; at Second Battle of the Stronghold, 232; on Steele peace mission, 156–57; as supporter of Confederacy, 76

Fay, Jimmy, 64

Field Manual of Courts-Martial, 295–96, 298–99

First Battle of the Stronghold (January 17, 1873): army assessments of, 117–20; army losses in, 239; army movement toward, 96–99; army positions in, 99–101; Modoc battle plan in, 102; Modoc positions in, 107–8; Modoc victory in, 116; Modoc withdrawal from, 120–21; newspaper reports of, 127–28, 136; number of Modoc fighters in, 107; Oregon and California volunteers in, 97, 100, 109, 110, 112, 113–14, 118–19, 149; Second Battle of the Stronghold compared to, 232

Fischer, Adolphus, 269

Fitzgerald, Maurice, 228, 238, 344

Fort Bidwell, 84, 90, 91, 92, 95

Fort Harney, 84, 90, 93

Fort Klamath, 7, 51, 67, 68, 70, 77, 84; hanging of Modoc prisoners at, 330–32; military forces at, 7, 24, 83, 84, 91; Modoc prisoners sent to, 289–91

Fort Klamath military commission trial: American Indian Aid Association attack on, 315; Anderson's and McElderry's testimony at, 303; Atwell on injustices at, 306, 312–13; Boston Charley's testimony at, 309; Bureau of Military Justice review of, 316–18; charges read at, 298–300; composition of military commission at, 296; courtroom scene at, 297–98; Curtis as Judge Advocate at, 297–98, 301, 302, 306–7, 308; Curtis's legal opinion on creation of, 292, 293, 294–95; Davis and, 295–96, 311, 315; defendants held responsible for each other at, 307–8; defense case at, 303–6; defense counsel absence in, 297, 306, 309, 312, 317; determination of procedure for, 292–95; Dyar's testimony at, 301–2; Grant on, 284, 296, 311–12, 317, 318–19; Hooker Jim's testimony at, 302; ignoring of courts-martial rules at, 295–96, 298–99; Kientpoos's testimony at, 303–5; Meacham's testimony at, 302–3; newspaper coverage of, 292, 298, 314; political purpose of, 297, 310; reading of sentences at, 310; rebuttal of defense at, 306–7; Riddles as interpreters at, 298, 299, 300, 312–13, 316, 317; Riddles' testimony at, 300–301; Scarface Charley's testimony at, 303; Schonchin John's testimony at, 305–6; Shacknasty Jim's testimony at, 308; Steele and, 297, 312, 313; Williams and, 292, 293, 294–95, 379n7

Fort McPherson, 339

Fort Russell, 338, 339

Fort Scott, 339

Fort Vancouver, 30, 31, 32, 90, 92, 93, 95, 96, 97, 311

Fort Warner, 83, 84, 85, 90, 122, 265

Fox, Edward, 178–79, 218, 244, 246–47, 264; arrival at war zone by, 133, 135–36; and Kientpoos, 138, 149–51; and Meacham, 138, 142, 143; on Modoc hangings, 328, 332–33; on Modoc War causes, 215–16; national impact of reporting by, 152; on Peace Commission, 139, 216; and Peace Tent killings, 205–7, 214–15, 216, 344, 383n16; and Second Battle of the Stronghold, 229, 230, 236, 237, 238–39; trips to Modoc camp by, 143–51, 178–79

Franklin, Benjamin, 26

Frémont, John C., 33

genocide: term, 35–36, 86; and war, 39, 363n33. *See also* extermination of Indians; massacres of Indians

George III (Britain), 27

Ghost Dance, 102–4, 106–7, 116, 131, 172, 183, 235

Gillem, Alvan C., 122–23, 129, 180, 265; during Civil War, 224–25; military strategy of, 225–27; Modocs' meeting with, 178–79; and Peace Tent killings, 195–96, 204–5; and Sand Butte battle, 249, 253, 255; and Second Battle of the Stronghold, 234, 238, 239–40

Gillem's Camp, 230, 243, 248, 310; battles fought near, 206, 252, 253, 254, 258; corpses brought to, 213–14, 234, 265–66; as "Gillem's Graveyard," 258; hospital tent in, 209–10, 230–32, 237, 255–56, 269; journalists at, 205, 244–45, 246; military forces at, 190, 226, 249–50; peace commissioners at, 186–87, 192, 193, 211; Toby Riddle at, 187, 189, 191

Glen, James T., 84

Gliddon, George R., 81

Goff, David, 33

Good Friday killings. *See* Peace Tent killings

Grant, Ulysses S., 5, 53, 127, 341; and Fort Klamath trial, 284, 296, 311–12, 317, 318–19; and Modoc death sentences, 314, 318, 319–20, 322; and Modoc people, 141, 158, 224; and Peace Commission, 129–30, 159; Peace Policy of, 85, 87–89, 207, 348

Graydon, James "Paddy," 168–69

Greasy Boots (Modoc fighter), 120–21

Greeley, Horace, 134

Green, John, 7, 70–71, 84, 85, 96; and First Battle of the Stronghold, 100, 111–12, 113; and Sand Butte battle, 249, 252, 254–55, 260; and Second Battle of the Stronghold, 226, 229–30, 231

Grover, LaFayette, 69, 84, 161, 214; call for punishment of Modocs by, 96, 138–39; on Modocs as thieves and murderers, 29, 46

Gude, Herrman, 230

Halleck Tustenuggee (Mikasuki chief), 165–66

Hamilton, A., 219

hangings, Modoc: bodies of victims, 333–34; execution depiction, 330–32; family visits prior to, 322–23; Grant's approval of verdict, 318; newspaper reportage of, 327–28, 332–33; public opinion on, 314–16; souvenirs from, 325, 333; spectators at, 333; trial sentences, 310

Hardin, Charles B., 254–55, 263, 268

Harman, Henry C., 232

Harper's Weekly, 216–17, *fig. 5*

Harris, George, 249, 255, 256, 258

Harris, Moses "Black," 32

Harris, Sergeant, 10

Hasbrouck, Henry C., 296; Modocs accompanied into exile by, 335, 337, 339; pursuit of Modoc fighters by, 266, 267, 268, 269–70, 271–73, 280

Haughton, Samuel, 329

Hazelton, J. B., 271

Hearn, F. G., 333

Hermann, Binger, 346–47

Hines, Gustavus, 35, 36

Hogan, Linda, 335

Holt, Joseph, 316–18

Hooker Jim, 77, 114, 156, 182, 312, 325, 335, 338; as army scout, 275–76, 277, 278, 280; death of, 347; and Fox, 145–47; Kientpoos abandoned

Hooker Jim (*continued*)
by, 270; and Lost River battle, 11, 12, 13,
360n22; and Meacham road show, 342; and
Peace Tent killings, 194, 199, 200, 208; photo
of, *fig. 2*; and Second Battle of the Stronghold, 236, 237, 239; surrender of, 274; trial testimony by, 302; and Tule Lake settler killings,
13, 172, 275–76, 279, 284, 287, 305; as war faction advocate, 105–6, 117, 131, 172, 183, 187
Hospital Rock, 99, 101, 183, 195, 203, 204, 248;
and Second Battle of the Stronghold, 226,
231, 236–37, 239
Hot Creek Modocs, 72–73, 283; as army
scouts, 275, 276–77, 278, 280; Fairchild's
employment of, 72–73, 75–77; Kientpoos
abandoned by, 270; Kientpoos's forces joined
by, 77, 78–79; surrender to army by, 273–74;
as war faction advocates, 105–6, 117, 131, 172,
180, 183, 187
Hovey, Eugene, 237–38
Howard, Oliver O., 222
Howe, Albion, 249, 253, 255
Hudson's Bay Company, 30–31, 32
Humboldt River, 34
Humphrey (Modoc prisoner), 335
Humpy Joe, 281, 282
Huntington, J. W. Perit, 49, 52, 53
Huquemborg, Charles, 325, 327, 331
Hyzer, Joseph, 287, 288, 289

Ike (Modoc prisoner), 290–91, 324
Illinois Land Company, 27–28
Indian Removal Act (1830), 73
Indians: Arapahos, 86; assimilationist strategy toward, 28, 56, 87; Cayuse, 23, 63, 292;
Cheyenne, 86; Choctaw, 73; Dakota, 293–
94; deceit and treachery against, 7, 71, 174–
75, 185–86; and disease epidemics, 34–35,
348, 362n20; and Ghost Dance movement,
102–4; Grant Peace Policy toward, 85, 87–
89, 127–28, 207, 214–15, 317, 348; *Johnson v.
M'Intosh* Supreme Court decision on, 27–28,
293; Klamath, 19, 20–21, 23, 31, 50–51, 52–53,
54, 85, 354; massacres of, 33, 38–41, 42–44,
86–87, 175, 309, 315–16, 363n44; Mikasuki,
166, 201; and mythology of white superiority, 23, 24, 35, 91, 94, 97, 118, 227; Navaho, 16,
166–67, 370n9; as "pagans," 25, 26–27, 28, 35,

48, 201, 218; Rogue River, 23–24; Sauk, 55–
56; as "savages," 6, 29, 32, 37, 47–48, 77, 129,
173, 174, 217; Seminole, 165–66, 276; Seneca, 319; Shasta, 50–51; and Trail of Tears, 73;
treaties with, 51–52; Yahooskin Paiute, 52,
103, 354. *See also* Modoc people
Indian scouts: Canby recruitment of, 175–
76; Hot Creek Modocs as, 275, 276–77, 278,
280; from Warm Springs Reservation, 175–
76, 183–84, 226, 248, 249, 269, 281, 282,
378n8
Indian skulls, 242–44, 333–34

Jackson, Andrew, 73
Jackson, James, 67, 77, 148, 226, 266, 268, 272;
Kientpoos on, 150, 304; and Lost River bat-
tle, 1–2, 7–9, 10, 23
Jacksonville OR, 37, 42–43, 84, 93, 328
Jim (Hamburg tribe headman), 50
John (Scott Valley tribe headman), 50
Johnson, Andrew, 224
Johnson, Charles, 232
Johnson v. M'Intosh, 27–28, 293
Jones, Hiram W., 340, 341, 343, 348
Juergensmeyer, Mark, 215

Kelley, Thomas, 268
Kelly, Hugh, 119
Kerr, Charles D., 223
Kershaw, W. T., 42
Kientpoos (Captain Jack): assassination plan
agreed to by, 194; on Canby, 184, 192–93;
Canby's meetings with, 178–79, 181–82, 199–
202; and Council Grove Treaty, 52, 53, 54;
Fairchild's meetings with, 95, 131–32, 146,
147–48, 149–51, 184, 186; and First Battle of
the Stronghold, 114, 128; and Fox, 138, 149–
51; and Green, 70; hanging of, 325–26, 330–
32; Hot Creek fighters' abandonment of,
270; killing of Canby by, 202, 207–8, 209,
246, 305, 308, *fig. 5*; as leader, 183, 194; and
Lost River battle, 95–96, 172–73; on Meacham, 149, 150; Meacham's meetings with,
55–56, 58, 181, 184–86, 199–202; Modoc
removal rejected by, 6–7, 95, 104–5, 159;
multiracial vision of, 105, 172–73; name and
moniker of, 6, 359n3; and Peace Commission
composition, 142, 143; on Peace Commis-

Robeson, George M., 162, 163
Rogue River Indians, 23–24
Rolla, Francis, 254
Rosborough, A. M., 142–43, 148, 151, 153–54, 164
Rosie (daughter of Kientpoos), 282, 323, 337, 347, *fig. 9*
Ross, Jim, 376n27
Ross, John, 42, 47, 90, 114, 315–16

Sacramento CA, 342
Sacramento Record, 137, 298, 328, 344–45
Sand Butte battle (April 26, 1873): army assessments of, 258–60; army casualties in, 258; composition of Thomas-Wright patrol in, 249–50; Green's rescue party in, 254–55; lack of Modoc casualties in, 254, 376n27; location of, 250–51; Modoc motivation and morale in, 248–49, 260; Modoc positioning in, 251–52; Modoc withdrawal from, 271–72, 377n17; newspaper reports of, 263–64; number of Modoc fighters in, 252; retrieving of corpses from, 265–66; tending to wounded in, 255–58
Sand Creek Massacre, 86–87
San Francisco Call-Bulletin, 328
San Francisco Chronicle, 137, 162, 207, 264, 276–77, 328, 332, 341
San Francisco Daily Morning Call, 321, 332
San Francisco Evening Bulletin, 137
Saracen Turks, 24–25
Sargent, Aaron A., 165
Satanta (Kiowa chief), 292
Sauk Indians, 55–56
Scarface Charley, 5–6, 179, 227, 312, 323, 325, 335; Atwell interview with, 337–38; and First Battle of the Stronghold, 112, 114, 128; and Fox, 147, 148–49, 178; and Kientpoos surrender, 279–80, 282; later history of, 347, 353; and Lost River battle, 1–2, 9–10, 13; and Meacham, 57, 345; in meetings with Peace Commission, 132, 158; as peace faction advocate, 105, 117, 131, 172, 187, 279; and Peace Tent killings, 194–95, 209; photo of, *fig. 7*; and Sand Butte battle, 250–51, 259, 260; surrender of, 281; trial testimony by, 303
Schira, Katherine, 12, 283–84, 293
Schira, Nicholas, 12

Schofield, John M., 89, 213, 264, 284, 322; and Fort Klamath trial, 295, 321; strategic assessment by, 90–91
Schonchin, Peter, 12, 324, 377n12
Schonchin John, 52, 114, 171, 178, 227; as Ben Wright Massacre survivor, 44; hanging of, 327, 330–32; in meetings with Peace Commission, 150, 158; and Modoc factions, 106, 117, 172, 180; and Modoc public relations, 148; and Peace Tent killings, 194, 199, 201, 209, 299, 301, 308; photo of, *fig. 10*; as prisoner, 282, 298, 324; sentenced to hang, 310; surrender of, 281; trial testimony about, 300, 301, 302, 303, 308; trial testimony by, 305–6; and Tule Lake settler killings, 12, 306
Schurz, Carl, 346
Scorpion Point, 177–78, 183, 266
Scott, Levi, 32
Searles, William, 232
Second Battle of the Stronghold (April 15–17, 1873): army field hospital in, 209–10, 230–32, 236–37, 255–56, 269; army losses in, 239; army plan of attack in, 225–27; army preparations for, 228; events of, 229–30, 231–35; killing of Indian civilians during, 238–39; Modoc death toll in, 239, 374n18; Modoc morale crisis in, 235–36; Modoc preparations for, 227–28; Modoc withdrawal from, 238; number of combatants in, 245
Semig, Bernard, 209–10, 230–32; and Sand Butte battle, 250, 252, 255, 256, 258
Seminole wars, 165–66, 276
Senecas, 319
settlers, 6; and army deserters, 94; Bloody Point attack on, 36–37, 42, 46, 47, 186; and Carr-Applegate land scheme, 66–68; of Klamath Basin, 7, 12, 31, 153; Lost River claims by, 54–55; Modoc's initial encounters with, 29–30, 31. *See also* California volunteers; Oregon volunteers; Tule Lake settler killings
sexual violence and slavery, 48, 155. *See also* prostitution
Shacknasty Frank, 233–34, 241
Shacknasty Jim, 79, 128, 147, 156, 227, 287, 302, 312, 325; as army scout, 276, 277, 280; as Hot Creek Modoc leader, 77; later life of, 347; and Meacham road show, 342, 345; Modoc

Shacknasty Jim (*continued*)
insurgents abandoned by, 270; moniker of,
75–76; and Peace Tent killings, 194, 199,
208–9, 279, 301, 308; photos of, *figs. 2, 11*;
surrender of, 274; trial testimony by, 308; as
war faction advocate, 117, 131

Shastas, 50–51

Shaw, H. S., 323–25, 328, 333

Shearer, William, 13

Sheepy Ridge, 145, 159, 178, 180, 181, 216, 240,
247, 248, 277; and First Battle of the Stronghold, 98, 99, 100, 113–14, 118; peace negotiations at, 150, 159

Sheridan, Philip H., 214, 339

Sherman, William Tecumseh, 91, 284–85; and
Canby, 129–30, 154, 164, 177, 214; Davis
defended by, 222–23, 224; and Fort Klamath
trial, 317; Modoc extermination supported
by, 171, 219–20, 285, 349

Sherwood, William, 203–4

Shillingbow, Adam, 13

Sibley, Henry Hopkins, 167–70

Signal Rock, 189, 193, 196, 199, 204

Simpson, George, 30

Simpson, William, 244–47, *fig. 5*

Skinner, John, 231, 269

slavery, 31, 48, 64

Slolux, 12, 321–22; and Peace Camp killings,
194–95, 201, 207, 209, 299, 308; as prisoner,
290, 298; prison release and death of, 347;
reprieve from hanging for, 330, 331, 382n22;
sentencing of, 310; sent to Alcatraz, 336, 338–
39; Toby Riddle blamed by, 326, 381n10; trial
testimony about, 300–301, 308

Small, Judson, 110

smallpox, 35, 362n20

Smith, Edward, 211, 341

Smith, Jedediah, 60

Smith, Sidney, 95

Smithsonian Institution, 242, 243

Sorass Lake battle (May 10, 1873), 267–69, 270,
377n11

Spencer, Frank, 103

Spier, Leslie, 103

standard-drop hanging, 329–30

Stanley, Henry Morton, 134, 136, 138

Stanton, Edwin, 223–24

Steamboat Frank, 79, 112, 146, 280, 302, 312,
338; on American mode of warfare, 309; as
army scout, 276, 277; Kientpoos abandoned
by, 270; in later life, 341, 347; and Meacham
road show, 342, 345; moniker of, 76; and
Peace Tent killings, 195, 208, 371n5; photos
of, *figs. 2, 11*; as war faction advocate, 117

Steele, Elijah, 49–50, 51, 137, 148, 151; and
Fort Klamath trial, 297, 312, 313; and Kientpoos, 50, 105, 142, 157–60; as Peace Commission emissary, 154, 156–57, 158, 197; view of
Modocs by, 174

Stevens, Isaac, 292

Stirling, F. S., 231

Stronghold, landscape characteristics, 15–16,
97, 107

Sublette, William, 60

Swamp and Overflow Act of 1850, 66

Tame. *See* Weium

Taylor, R. M., 219

Taylor, Zachary, 276

Tee-He Jack (Modoc prisoner), 287–88

Thomas, E. C., 213

Thomas, Eleazar, 227, 246; appreciations of,
after death, 212–13, 215; and assassination
warnings, 184, 187–88, 189, 190, 195–99,
218–19; and Kientpoos, 181, 184, 199–200;
and Modoc surrender ruse, 192; paternalism of, 218; Peace Camp killing of, 199–201,
206, 208, 216; Peace Commission appointment of, 165

Thomas, Evan, 246, 249, 250, 251, 252, 259

Thompson, William, 46–47, 100

Thoreau, Henry David, 60

Throckmorton, Charles, 309

Tickner, H. C., 237, 250, 252, 258, 267

Tocqueville, Alexis de, 73

Totten, James J., 269

Townsend, Edward D., 322

Trail of Tears, 73

treaties: Council Grove, 52–54, 139, 163, 175,
302; with Steele, 50–52

Trenton Gazette, 152

Trimble, Joel, 93, 94, 226, 354; and Kientpoos's
surrender, 281, 282, 378n9; and Sand Butte
battle, 255, 257–58

Trimble, William Franklin, 110

Tule Lake, 15, 94, 234–35; army camp at, 85, 91, 95, 120, 141, 176, 177–78; and First Battle of the Stronghold, 97, 98, 101, 107–8, 111–12, 113; and hunt for Modoc fighters, 234, 272, 277; and Modoc foundational myths, 16, 184; Modoc villages around, 19, 122, 176; as water source, 255, 270

Tule Lake settler killings, 12–13, 84, 132, 153, 172, 183; Curley Headed Doctor and, 12, 172, 305–6; Hooker Jim and, 13, 172, 275–76, 279, 284, 287, 305; Kientpoos's denial of responsibility for, 95, 173, 307; Modoc justification of, 151; Schonchin John and, 12, 306

Turner, William, 328

Universal Peace Union, 318–19

Valverde, Civil War battle, 168–69

Victor, Frances Fuller, 45

Wa-ga-kanna (Little Canyon), 36–37

Walker, F. A., 6, 69, 70

Wallace, Lew, 214

Walsh, John, 248

Warm Springs scouts, 175–76, 183–84, 226, 239; in battle, 226, 248, 249, 269; and Kientpoos's surrender, 281, 282, 378n8

Washington Territory, 292

Wassanukka (Warm Springs scout), 269

Wasserman, Philip, 214

Watchman (Modoc fighter), 10

water irrigation, 356–57

Watson, 237

Webber, Louis, 250, 258

Weium (Tame), 12, 156, 270, 302, 338; and Fox, 147, 149, 178; Peace Camp killings opposed by, 187, 188, 194; surrender of, 274

We-na-shet (Warm Springs scout), 281

Wheaton, Frank, 92, 132, 335; and First Battle of the Stronghold, 96–99, 113, 115, 117–18; and Modoc hangings, 323, 325–26, 331, 333; overconfidence of, 83–84, 90, 97, 98–99; replaced and restored as commanding officer, 122, 265; strategic plan of, 95, 225–26

Wheeler, Joseph, 223

Whipple, William D., 213

white flag of truce: and Peace Tent killing charge, 299–300, 301–2, 308, 310, 317; Wright ruse using, 43, 44, 174–75, 186

Whitman, Marcus and Narcissa, 292

Whittle, Bob and Matilda, 139, 141–42, 143, 144–45, 147, 148

Wigwam and War-path (Meacham), 341, 343, 344

Wilbur, J. H., 130

Wild Gal, 147, 148, 149, 157, 158, 178, 338

Willamette Valley, 31, 32, 33, 34, 61–62, 63

Williams, George H., 285, 286, 309; and Fort Klamath trial, 292, 293, 294–95, 379n7

Willow Creek, 21, 271, 278–79, 280, 281

Wi-ne-ma (the Woman Chief) and Her People (Meacham), 343, 344

Winema National Forest, 354

Wirz, Henry, 294

Wood, H. Clay, 368n14

Wright, Ben, 48, 186; contemporary assessments of, 45–46; later career of, 44–45; massacre of Modocs by, 39–41, 42–44, 175, 309, 315–16, 363n44

Wright, George, 249, 250

Wright, Thomas, 246, 249, 253

Yahooskin Paiutes, 52, 103, 354

Yainax Butte, 11, 72, 77, 85, 325

Yreka CA, 38–39, 41, 42–44, 49, 86, 96, 212

Yreka Journal, 289, 328

Yreka Mountain Herald, 127

Yreka Union, 328